WIN-WIN CORPORATIONS

ADVANCE PRAISE FOR THE BOOK

'Shashank takes us into the DNA of these successful companies and iconic brands with the ease of a master storyteller. He succinctly presents the history and underlying philosophy that built and holds these companies together. The human interest examples gleaned from the principal actors in each corporation make these nuggets practical and eminently readable and brings life to Win-Win Corporations, whose journey Shashank as a raconteur takes us through as a consummate masterpiece. After a long time we have a business book grounded in reality'—**Ranjit Shahani, vice chairman and managing director, Novartis India Ltd**

'Dr Shah has performed a service in redirecting our attention to the societal role of corporations, especially valuable when managers and entrepreneurs lose their moral compass in the short-term pursuit of untrammelled greed. His text—drawing on original interviews, folksy narrative, management theory, and including a valuable implementation toolkit—is a worthy read indeed'—**Tarun Khanna, director, Harvard University South Asia Institute; Jorge Paulo Lemann professor, Harvard Business School; and author,** *Billions of Entrepreneurs: How India and China Are Reshaping Their Futures – And Yours*

'Dr Shashank Shah's work is a fresh breeze. I have long been associated with the jury for the "Golden Peacock" Awards for corporate excellence. Dr Shah's criteria is a refreshing enrichment of the evaluator repertoire. To me, as chancellor of Sri Sathya Sai University, it is a matter of pride that Dr Shah is one of our alumni'—**Justice M.N. Venkatachaliah, twenty-fifth chief justice of India; and former chairman, National Human Rights Commission**

'*Win-Win Corporations* is a landmark book on how Indian companies from diverse industry and ownership backgrounds keep multiple stakeholders happy while ensuring growth and commercial success. Full of absorbing anecdotes, leadership insights and management lessons, the book is an invaluable read for academics, practitioners and entrepreneurs alike. A stellar debut by a young business author'—**Naina Lal Kidwai, former group general manager and country head, HSBC India; and author,** *30 Women in Power: Their Voices, Their Stories*

'This is an excellent book of case examples of how the stakeholder concept has a long history in the Indian business environment. Executives and students will learn a great deal by paying attention to the lessons here'— **R. Edward Freeman, university professor, Darden School of Business, University of Virginia; and author,** *Stakeholder Theory: The State of the Art*

'A lucid narrative that chronicles how six Indian companies emerged as winning corporations in the eyes of stakeholders. For business executives aiming to win in the marketplace, the book offers salient insights garnered over a decade of personal research by Shashank'—**Nishi Vasudeva, former chairman and managing director, Hindustan Petroleum Corporation Ltd**

'An important contribution to management thinking . . . Shashank has gathered evidence from some of the best regarded corporations in India and demonstrated how their success over the long term has drawn from their significant investments in value creation for all their stakeholders'—**Dr Mukund Rajan, chief sustainability and group ethics officer, Tata Sons**

'An engaging and inspiring read'—**Ravi Venkatesan, chairman, Bank of Baroda; director, Infosys Ltd; and former chairman, Microsoft India**

'Stakeholder integration is one of the four pillars of Conscious Capitalism, and the one that presents the greatest challenge to leaders seeking to implement an approach to business that is rooted in synergistic rather than traditional trade-off thinking. *Win-Win Corporations* illuminates this critical aspect of business in a refreshing and compelling way. Through fascinating case studies of prominent Indian companies, Dr Shashank Shah distils key insights that are highly useful for companies all over the world. My congratulations on a terrific book'—**Raj Sisodia, F.W. Olin distinguished professor of global business, Babson College; co-founder and co-chairman, Conscious Capitalism Inc.; and co-author of *Firms of Endearment* and *Conscious Capitalism***

'In this highly readable book, Shashank deals with the very important and relevant topic of stakeholder management by corporates. Drawing on history, on his insights and on six very powerful cases, he demonstrates how stakeholder management actually creates better shareholder value. I thoroughly enjoyed reading this book and believe it provides learnings and implementable advice to those who want to build better companies through managing their stakeholders better'—**Ajay Srinivasan, CEO, Aditya Birla Financial Services**

'*Win-Win Corporations* by Dr Shashank Shah is a fascinating book on the Indian way of creating successful companies that create shareholder value by focusing on stakeholder satisfaction. It provides new insights into the linkages between real standards of leadership, customer delight, quality, governance, social responsibility, environmental awareness and employee satisfaction—and rounds off with a simple and friendly implementation toolkit. A must-read for all business leaders and entrepreneurs'—**Ashu Suyash, managing director and CEO, CRISIL**

'In an era of increasing obsession with market share and valuations, companies that have balanced their focus on the triple bottom line of people, profits and planet are the only true role models. I am glad to see such companies being celebrated'—**Ganesh Natarajan, chairman, NASSCOM Foundation; and former CEO, Zensar Technologies**

'*Win-Win Corporations* is a refreshing and well-researched account of six well-regarded companies in India to discover the "soul" of a corporation and the "Indian way" that these companies and their leaders follow to create value for their stakeholders and society. At a time when corporations and leaders are viewed with suspicion, the examples in the book demonstrate that it is possible to do well while doing good. The story of the Taj Group of Hotels is a fascinating one and Shashank does a great job of connecting the dots across the different companies that he covers. Everyone who cares about responsible capitalism must read this book'—**Sunil Mithas, professor, Robert H. Smith School of Business, University of Maryland; and author, *Making the Elephant Dance: The Tata Way to Innovate, Transform and Globalize***

'A successful corporation typically defies definition though can broadly be grasped through significant attributes. This book has done a remarkable job in capturing the major attributes of success, most importantly how the company creates sustainable value for each and every stakeholder. In healthcare, it is part of our DNA, where we operate in a society and continuously balance the greater good of our patients with a prudent return on capital'—**Suneeta Reddy, managing director, Apollo Hospitals Group**

'Dr Shah, through his fine empirical and investigative thesis on examples of corporate excellence in India, has amply demonstrated how sustainable stakeholder value has been created in practice by focusing on aggregate stakeholder value. Notably, the examples are an eclectic mix of old economy and liberalization's children. The book vividly illustrates the part of value creation strategy that Professor Michael Sandel would call "*What Money Can't Buy: The Moral Limits of Markets*"'—**M.V. Nair, chairman, Credit Information Bureau of India Limited (CIBIL); and former chairman and managing director, Union Bank of India**

'Shashank Shah's book delves deeply into several leading Indian companies to extract insights into what makes for a Win-Win Corporation that maximizes outcomes towards the needs of stakeholders. Indian corporations are developing their own ethos and this is a timely and insightful work delving into the best practices that resulted in the creation of winners'—**K.R.S. Jamwal, executive director, Tata Industries**

'A wonderfully nuanced insight into the world of corporate India through the lens of culture, governance and values. I was immediately captivated by the name and the topic, as one of the values which our team and I at Multiples emulate is "Win-Win" for every stakeholder. We cannot succeed in our partnership when we don't build outcomes which are aligned. Shashank has captured the stories in an amicable style, which lends to easy reading. The interviews and the journey of the companies play out how leaders set in motion a framework of governance that permeated through to behaviour and practices across the organization, as exemplified by the Taj employees during 26/11. It's a ringside view of how these Indian organizations have evolved over the years to incorporate values, governance and responsibility while facing challenges, without losing sight of the goals and also generating superior financial performance. I congratulate Shashank for these chronicles and hope some of these very real examples will help leaders adopt the guiding principles of "Win-Win" into their success mantras'—**Renuka Ramnath, founder, managing director and CEO, Multiples Alternate Asset Management; and former managing director and CEO, ICICI Ventures**

'The Indian market is perhaps the most difficult market in the world to succeed in. Shashank presents up-close the changing face of India, and the practical strategies adopted by a diverse group of companies for sustainable multi-stakeholder growth. This makes *Win-Win Corporations* essential reading for managers working in India, as well as those looking to understand the dynamics of emerging markets'—**Vijay Singh, CEO, Fox Star Studios**

'Dr Shah has weaved together insights from business, culture, philosophy and social impact in this timely guide for corporate leaders, built on his multidisciplinary research experience. India's demographics, economic growth and rich cultural and spiritual heritage position its business leaders both at an advantage and also challenge them to develop an India-specific corporate strategy. This book shines light on some great examples, home-grown and nurtured uniquely, that can be leveraged for scaling a unique model of doing business in this most interesting and complex country'—**Arunkumar N.T., managing director, UBS India**

'*Win-Win Corporations* is a riveting read full of stimulating stories and inspiring insights. Highly recommend it for budding entrepreneurs, young managers and aspiring management practitioners'—**Indu Shahani, director, Colgate Palmolive (India) Ltd; director, Bajaj Electricals Ltd; former sheriff of Mumbai; and member, University Grants Commission**

'*Win-Win Corporations* is in line with the global philosophy of "inclusive growth" being followed by the Government of India: *Sabka Sath Sabka Vikas*. The six case studies of different industries, covering financial services, manufacturing, distribution, hospitality, etc. are perfect examples of responsible corporate governance. They exemplify sustainability through the EGS ethos: environmental, social, governance. Human capital, customer-centricity and value creation for all stakeholders is central to the culture of a Win-Win Corporation. I recommend that all new-generation CEOs, particularly of start-up companies, adopt it as a handbook for creating their organizations as Win-Win Corporations'—**Mohan Tanksale, chief executive, Indian Banks' Association; and former chairman and managing director, Central Bank of India**

'Shah's *Win-Win Corporations* is a quintessential read for every strategy enthusiast or someone learning the science of strategy in the Indian context. The book beautifully analyses businesses that successfully grew and expanded in India. As you turn the last page of the book, you know you are a better strategist'—**Dr Sanjiv Marwah, director, J.K. Business School**

'Shashank's research is refreshingly grounded in principles that are especially relevant to the Indian context, and written in an easily readable storytelling style. It is a must-read for the Indian manager who wants to do well by doing good'—**Professor V. Kasturi Rangan, Malcolm P. McNair professor of marketing; co-chairman, Social Enterprise Initiative, Harvard Business School; and co-author,** *Business Solutions for the Global Poor: Creating Social and Economic Value*

WIN-WIN
CORPORATIONS

THE INDIAN WAY OF SHAPING
SUCCESSFUL STRATEGIES

SHASHANK SHAH

PORTFOLIO
PENGUIN

PORTFOLIO

USA | Canada | UK | Ireland | Australia
New Zealand | India | South Africa | China

Portfolio is part of the Penguin Random House group of companies
whose addresses can be found at global.penguinrandomhouse.com

Published by Penguin Random House India Pvt. Ltd
7th Floor, Infinity Tower C, DLF Cyber City,
Gurgaon 122 002, Haryana, India

First published in Portfolio by Penguin Random House India 2016

The views and opinions expressed in this book are the author's own and the
facts are as reported by him which have been verified to the extent possible,
and the publishers are not in any way liable for the same.

ISBN 9780670088676

Typeset in Adobe Caslon Pro by Manipal Digital Systems, Manipal
Printed at Replika Press Pvt. Ltd, India

www.penguin.co.in

To
my guru, Sri Sathya Sai;
and
my parents, Shefali and Jagesh

Contents

I.

Introduction

A Millennial's Journey Begins . . .

After 1000 years, the calendar year would now begin with the numeral '2'. It was the turn of the century, and also of the millennium. It was also the time when a new generation was coming of age. Generation Y, also known as the millennials, was crossing the threshold of teenage years. In India, this was the generation that had seen massive transitions in just a dozen years. From primary school to their college years, the world around them changed—almost. The era of postcards was gone, emails were in. Trunk calls and STDs were slowly losing their importance. Cell phones were becoming the order of the day. Computer programmes were no longer subjects to be studied for written exams. Instead, computers had entered every household and were now at par with, if not more important than, the television, which until then had been the prized possession of most Indian homes. The popularity of sitcoms and family dramas on Doordarshan and DD Metro was gradually ebbing away, and Zee TV and Star Plus were taking centre stage. ThumsUp and Limca were now competing with Pepsi and Coca-Cola. Ambassador and Fiat cars were slowly being replaced by Honda and Toyota cars. In just a decade, the life of a typical Indian family, especially in the metros, had changed forever.

As a youngster who had just then entered college, I witnessed all of this up and close. The changes were real and very palpable.

Being a student of commerce, economics and business, I studied the economic history of independent India. While Mahatma Gandhi wanted Indian society to be a Sarvodaya[1] Society, his political successor and the first prime minister of India, Jawaharlal Nehru, took to the path of Scientific Socialism with a strong emphasis on heavy industries. Both Gandhi and Nehru were deeply pained by massive poverty in India and wanted the citizens of a new nation to rise above abject levels of poverty. However, their recipes for achieving this differed. While Gandhi preferred the philosophy of Sarvodaya, Nehru was attracted to the economic policy followed by the Soviet Union of those days. He saw in mighty Russia a concrete example of a society that had rid itself of poverty and had provided all its citizens with food, shelter and employment. He wanted to combine Russia's economic philosophy with democracy. Thus was born 'Nehruvian Socialism'. He passionately believed that science and industry alone could solve the enormous problems of India. Though he died in 1964, his philosophy survived him and guided the Indian economic policy approach up to 1990.[2]

Regrettably, under the Licence Raj,[3] an outcome of the socialist model of development, corporate India faced a difficult period in the second and third decades of the post-Independence era. Nehruvian Socialism considered the public sector as the means by which long-standing challenges of economic development could be addressed by poorer nations. This approach did not give much scope for private enterprises to flourish as there were exceedingly high levels of centralized and restrictive practices which were hostile for businesses to grow and succeed. Up to 1980, government agencies had to be satisfied before private companies could produce something and, if granted permission, the government would regulate production. The government's socialistic approach was characterized by high levels of mistrust and monitoring of businesses, extremely steep taxation policy, and rigid norms and regulations.

My father often shared with me revulsions of the regressive tax system of the 1960s and 1970s, when personal rates of taxation went up from 77 per cent (in 1960–61) to 97.75 per cent (in 1972–73) under Prime Minister Indira Gandhi, and became one of the highest in the world.

After forty-four years of Independence, India finally gave itself a chance to grow, with a difference. In 1991, the then prime minister of India, P.V. Narasimha Rao, and his trusted finance minister, Dr Manmohan Singh, began the long-awaited implementation of liberalization, privatization and globalization of the Indian economy. The decade that followed witnessed a sea change in the way India produced and consumed. New companies sprung up. The HDFC and ICICI banks, with their ATM services, were now as visible as the Bank of Baroda and the State Bank of India branches in Mumbai. New businesses began. The success stories of Infosys and Wipro became drawing room conversations in most families. New infrastructure became visible and accessible. Information and communication technology shifted the access to knowledge from books in libraries to a personal computer in the comfort of a study room at home. The Indian economy had started growing at a rate not seen for over half a century. I still remember watching on television when the Sensex at the Bombay Stock Exchange (BSE) first crossed the 5000 mark. The country was ecstatic. The BSE staff at the Jeejeebhoy Towers (BSE Towers), a stone's throw away from where I lived, celebrated this milestone event by releasing 5000 balloons from the 29th storey of its building.

As I completed my graduation and began my post-graduate studies in business management, I started introspecting on the purpose of business. The text books were filled with examples of profit maximization and growth as the primary objectives of any business. The role of taking care of social well-being was that of the government and other civil society organizations.

However, witnessing the dichotomies of daily life in Mumbai, India's microcosm, I wanted to explore and understand the transformative role that businesses can play in society through an approach that balances economic growth and social good.

For many years, the newspapers and tabloids were filled with success stories emerging from the dot-com boom of Silicon Valley in USA. The likes of Amazon, Yahoo and eBay became dream companies for aspiring talent. Then suddenly, the bubble burst and many super-successful IT companies with unprecedented stock valuations were biting the dust. Between 2000 and 2002, over US$ 5 trillion[4] in paper wealth were washed off at the NASDAQ,[5] the stock market on which the shares of many tech companies were traded. The market value of NASDAQ companies that peaked at US$ 6.7 trillion in March 2000, bottomed out at $1.6 trillion in October 2002.[6] Even before the dust had settled, a new set of stories had started appearing as press headlines.

Success Stories That Turned Sour

In the early 1990s, the US–Congress passed a legislation deregulating the sale of electricity. Some years earlier, it had done the same for natural gas. The changed scenario in energy markets made it possible for companies like Enron to thrive. Founded in 1985, Enron was a US-based energy company headquartered in Houston, Texas. By 1992, it became the largest seller of natural gas in North America. Over a period of time it diversified into a number of businesses, but adopted highly questionable practices for revenue recognition. It 'managed' the Wall Street analysts well and those that were sceptical of its financial statements were verbally attacked.[7] At the heights of its success in 2000–01, it employed over 20,000 people and reported revenues of US$ 111 billion.[8] However, it faced several serious operational challenges, including those in Dabhol in Maharashtra, where it had entered into a contract for a major power plant. By late 2001, a series of revelations emerged. These included irregular accounting procedures bordering on fraud perpetrated throughout the 1990s, and involved its accounting firm, Arthur Andersen.[9] By mid November 2001, the company was on the verge of undergoing the largest bankruptcy in US history. As the scandal was revealed, Enron's shares dropped from over US$ 90 to just pennies within days. Considered blue-chip stock, the Enron debacle was an unprecedented event in the financial world with major investors like the Citibank Group and J.P. Morgan Chase losing huge amounts of money, besides thousands of employees losing jobs.[10] In 2006, Kenneth Lay, the founder and former chairman of the Enron board and Jeffrey Skilling, former CEO and COO, went on trial for their roles in the Enron scandal. The types and details of the charges stated against them formed an encyclopedia of malpractices that can possibly be undertaken by corporations and management executives. The fifty-three-count, sixty-five-page indictment covered a broad range of financial crimes all done with the solo aim of making a quick buck using all means possible and available.

Surprisingly, Enron wasn't alone in its mindless adventurism. A dozen more companies belonged to its ilk, including WorldCom, Arthur Andersen, Martha Stewart, Global Crossing, Qwest Communications, Tyco International, Adelphia Communications, Parmalat and many others. In each of these companies, the boards were found to have consistently ceded power over direction of the company to the CEO (WorldCom); knowingly allowed the company to engage in high-risk accounting practices (Enron); known of violations of law, taken no steps in an effort to prevent or remedy the situation, and failed to act for a long period of time, resulting in corporate losses (Abbott Laboratories); and failed to be sufficiently informed and to act independently of the chairman of the board (Fannie Mae), among others.[11] Within a few years, some of the most admired business leaders had traversed far away from their organization's objectives, only for superlative personal financial gains.

The Enron of India

While India was trying to emulate the developed world, some of its industry captains ventured into replicating the shortcuts to success. The likes of Harshad Mehta and Ketan Parekh had created ripples in the Indian financial world in the 1990s. But the most shocking of all corporate crises that stunned India Inc. was the Satyam Computer Services case, which was eventually referred to as the 'Enron of India'. Satyam's story was similar to that of Enron. A company that received the Golden Peacock Award for Corporate Governance in September 2008, and whose entrepreneurial founder, Ramalinga Raju, was given the Ernst & Young 'Entrepreneur of the Year' Award in 2007, Satyam Computer Services was the fourth-largest software company in India at its peak in 2008.[12] In the previous five years, its total assets had increased over three times. In December 2008, Raju tried to acquire Maytas (the reverse of the word 'Satyam') Properties, a family-owned real estate company, for nearly Rs 7000 crore, through Satyam funds. The institutional shareholders revolted against this move and Raju abandoned the deal within hours of its announcement. This sudden turn of events led to a huge fall in the international stock prices of Satyam. Finally, in January 2009, Raju revealed a major scam behind Satyam's success. He confessed in a letter to the Satyam board that he had fudged the company accounts over many years. The cash balance of Rs 5000 crore on its balance sheet was fictitious, and the actual profit margin was a mere 3 per cent, as compared to the 20 per cent that was repeatedly reported. In his letter, he confessed his wrongdoings and stated that the aborted Maytas deal was the last attempt to fill the fictitious assets with real ones.[13] Ironically, a company whose name meant 'Truth' became the symbol of corporate falsehood.

Satyam and other similar incidents reminded me of a humorous story I often heard as a child. There was a thief skilled in all the stratagems of that 'profession'. There wasn't a single trick he hadn't mastered. One day, after collecting a large number of costly articles and bundling them up, he was moving along a lonely road with the booty on his shoulder. He saw a child standing on the bank of a wayside tank, weeping aloud in great distress. The thief went closer and asked him, 'What has happened to you? Why are you weeping?' The child said, 'I came here for a bath, and my gold chain fell into the waters, right there, where I tried to have a dip. The place is too deep for me.' The thief thought that he could get away with this necklace too, for it was a little child that stood between him and the precious item. So, placing his bundle of booty on the bank, he went down into the waters to retrieve the gold chain. Meanwhile, the smart kid lifted the thief's precious pack and disappeared into the jungle. A couple of minutes later, the thief came out of the waters disappointed, realizing that the chain was but fiction. And what he saw horrified him. He had been robbed of his 'hard-earned wealth' by the shrewd kid who had outwitted him with the story of the illusory chain.[14] The desire to grab as much as possible in as short a time left him with nothing in the end.

While the legal establishment swooped in on Raju and a long-drawn procedure of penalties and punishments began, many questions lingered in my mind. I observed that in all these situations, the victim was the common man, who suffered whether as a small investor (especially pensioners), as a misguided customer, or as an average employee of a company about to close down. In reality, it may not be the absence of rules and regulations, but their actual practice which was the prime problem. Corporate governance[15] depends on all parts of the system—the board, independent directors, auditors and others working together for a larger cause. In Satyam's case, the independent directors failed in their duty, the auditors blundered, all internal checks and balances went haywire, and the regulatory authorities were perhaps lax. All this together contributed to a massive fraud on the trust of corporate India and people at large.[16]

The typical reaction to this situation would be tightening the existing monitoring and control mechanisms at the statutory and governmental levels, and also at the inter- and intra-organizational levels. However, unfortunately every successive scam highlighted that any number of control systems and procedures would be insufficient, till the intentions of corporate executives are upright and honest. Some basic questions about business organizations and the true purpose of their existence arose in my mind:

- Is corporate governance only about the independence of the board and the triune relationship between the board, the management and the shareholders?
- Is it only about the clauses and sections stated in the various corporate governance reports by different committees chaired by eminent experts over varied periods of time?
- Does it serve the interests of the shareholders, investors and the top management of the company alone?
- Does it have a wider role to play in the business as a whole?
- Shouldn't a company also be responsible to other organizational constituencies as well?

Most corporate debacles, including the financial crisis of 2008[17] could be attributed to a skewed focus of corporate management towards a single constituency—the shareholders—who provide funds and financial resources for effective functioning of the organization. The shareholders also help the board of directors to be nominated time and again to positions of eminence at the helm of affairs in the organization and thus, retain their power and control over the organization. It was observed in many organizations that the top leadership neglected the importance of the interests of other organizational constituencies solely in favour of the shareholders.

In Search of a New Paradigm

In this context, I'm often inspired by the example of the human body with its multiple limbs and organs, and the lessons that we can learn from it for our personal and professional lives. It is well known that perfect cooperation and coordination of all the limbs and organs helps in accomplishing the tasks of day-to-day life. How does this happen? Let us take the instance of a tree that bears a large number of fruit. An individual sees these fruit, the eye notices them and the mind desires to have them. However, by mere desire, one does not get the fruit. The legs have to take the individual nearer to the tree. It is not enough if the distance is covered with one's legs. One has to bend down, pick up a stone and aim the stone at the fruit on the tree. When the fruit falls, the fingers collect the fruit and pass it on to the mouth. Then, the mouth has to chew and swallow the fruit. It is only then that the pulp of the fruit reaches the stomach, which produces enzymes to digest it. Upon digestion, the form of the fruit undergoes change. In this whole journey of the fruit from the tree to the stomach, which one limb or organ was responsible? All organs and limbs played a role. They helped in carrying the juice of the fruit to the stomach, the stomach in turn digested it and distributed the energy to all organs through the blood. To ensure that the individual has the necessary energy and strength, all organs have to discharge their respective duties because the body is a combination of multiple limbs and organs. This is the case during a healthy scenario.

Now, let us take another example when an individual is running a fever. To cure this, the doctor gives a bitter medicine. However, does the tongue spit it out? Bitter or not, it swallows the pill so that the body may get better. When the doctor wants to give an injection, does the arm retaliate saying, 'Why should I suffer the prick for the sake of the body?' The brain does not look down upon the kidney for doing excretory work. All limbs and organs of the human body perform their function effectively so that optimal health of the body is maintained. High or low, visible or invisible, work has to progress on a cooperative basis by each limb and organ to ensure a healthy life for every living being. I believe that the principles which apply to the micro-systems of the human body can also apply to the macro-systems of the global body. While there is a difference between the two, one of willing cooperation (by different constituents of a global body) vis-à-vis that of evolutionary development (of individual limbs and organs in a human body), several lessons can be learnt from this analogy.

I still remember the day when my junior colleague Shrikanth, now a senior manager at a leading cement company in Mumbai, spoke to me about a paper on 'stakeholder management' that he had read. With my keen interest in looking for win-win solutions for balancing financial success with the interests of larger corporate constituencies, I too was exploring topics for my doctoral research. The term 'stakeholders' struck a chord somewhere deep within, and there began my journey of exploring this approach to business and its management.

Exploring a Different Approach to Business

According to contemporary management literature, the historical roots of this approach date back to the 1960s, when academicians at the Stanford Research Institute first articulated what was considered at the time to be a controversial proposal and first used the actual word 'stakeholder'.[18] The term 'Stakeholder Management' was chosen as a literary device to call into question the management's sole emphasis on stockholders and instead, suggested that the firm be responsible to a variety of stakeholders, since without their support, the organization would not progress.[19]

In simple terms, stakeholders of a corporation are those constituencies that affect and/or are affected by the organization's decisions and behaviour. Since they have a stake in the organization, they are called so. It is common to refer to a company's employees, customers, owners, suppliers, dealers, local communities and society, natural environment, competitors, financiers and shareholders as major stakeholders. Other stakeholders of an organization might include the media, activist groups and the government and regulatory authorities, which affect the organization but are relatively unaffected by the organization. Stakeholder management refers to an organizational philosophy wherein the company's overriding priority during the organizational decision-making process is to contribute to its stakeholders' welfare in such a manner that essential concerns of fairness and economic viability are in focus.[20]

A major breakthrough in this field of study (in the context of using stakeholder management as a strategic tool) was by Professor Edward Freeman from the University of Virginia's Darden School of Business, through his landmark book *Strategic Management: A Stakeholder Approach*, published way back in 1984.[21] Since then, a number of scholars have considerably contributed to this field of study through various definitions, theories, models, frameworks, principles and propositions.[22] From these studies, it emerges that the stakeholder theory is not opposed to shareholder wealth creation. A major premise of all these studies could be stated as, 'The welfare of stakeholders can contribute to the welfare of shareholders.' Thus, shareholder wealth maximization is not at the cost of, but through stakeholders' welfare optimization.

Historical Roots

The basic concepts and ideals underlying stakeholder management were articulated in different terms in ancient Indian texts. Ancient Indian thought leaders like Satyavrata[23] and Kautilya[24] presented ideas regarding the administration of kingdoms on moral lines leading to the overall promotion of social welfare.[25] The issues of ethical behaviour and social responsibility in administration and management have also been discussed in ancient Greece. Greek philosophers like Socrates,[26] Plato[27] and Aristotle[28] discussed the ethical rules that govern economic principles. These philosophers discussed the laws of 'good life' and postulated that economics should subserve the principles of 'good life' and should help in establishing a peaceful society.[29] They also described that management and administration of the state should aim at promoting the welfare of society.[30] Another study provided interesting insights from world religious scriptures on how businesses can manage diverse stakeholders effectively and ethically. This included a study of texts from five religions: Hinduism, Jainism, Buddhism, Christianity and Islam.[31]

My readings further revealed that stakeholder thinking had deep roots in economic theory, beginning with Adam Smith,[32] known as the father of modern economics, who was trained in the field of moral philosophy and applied his knowledge to explaining a unified system of economic life. Smith argued that societies function best when economic interests and ethical interests coalesce. His argument, eloquently made in the books *The Theory of Moral Sentiments* (1759) and *The Wealth of Nations* (1776), established the notion that economic and ethical interests share a symbiotic relationship. The moral underpinnings of Smith's work are frequently overlooked by many hard-core economists who only tend to refer to the economic theory in *The Wealth of Nations*. However, stakeholder theory embraces both economic and ethical arguments to assist business, governmental and non-governmental organizations (NGO) in recognizing and maximizing the full potential of their symbiotic relationship.[33]

My Research Journey Begins

A detailed study of existing literature revealed that a lot of theoretical grounding had been provided by a number of scholars, researchers and academicians on the need to implement stakeholder management in corporations. However, most examples were of international companies belonging to developed economies. In this, I found an opportunity to study Indian companies and leaders and to understand their perceptions and practices.[34] I was sure I would be able to unravel the Indian way of shaping successful stakeholder strategies.

My research involved two surveys that studied perceptions of managers and seniors leaders from eminent Indian organizations.[35] The first one was an exploratory survey, and the second one was a perception survey. I received a total of 1100 responses in both surveys from nearly 400 companies. With 125 parameters covered in the second survey, I had an insightful set of 50,000 data points. Given that it was a first of its kind study, I had developed a very valuable data set. Besides the administration of surveys, I set out to interview corporate leaders and industry captains across India to understand their philosophy and implementation strategies for successful business management.[36] My study took me to family-owned businesses, public sector enterprises, private companies, multinational corporations and government institutions, among many others. I interacted with chairmen and managing directors,

CEOs and heads of various functions within these organizations. Each of these business leaders had decades of hands-on experience in running successful companies. Their opinions held immense practical relevance and value. Their responses to my semi-structured interview schedule were insightful and revealing of the depth of understanding and clarity of purpose that Indian businesses and their leaders possessed. Let me take you through some of them.

During an interaction at his residence in a Mumbai suburb, G. Narayana, chairman emeritus of Excel Industries Ltd[37] told me, 'The fundamental responsibility of business is not even to make profits, but to generate wealth and share it. Wealth here means money, resources and culture of the organization. But finance is required. Dharma (righteousness) without Artha (wealth) is powerless. The needs of the stakeholders are the seeds for organizational growth. What is good for all stakeholders is good for the leader and the organization.'[38] During our conversation, Mallika Srinivasan, chairperson and CEO of Tractors and Farm Equipment Ltd (TAFE),[39] said, 'Profits are necessary to sustain the health of the individual, society, community and others. But at the same time that alone cannot be the objective of business because it's not sustainable. A business which focuses only on one of the two aspects—profits or welfare—will not last long. There has to be a balance of both these. It can't be others at your cost, it can't be you at others' cost.'[40] I had the opportunity of meeting C.Y. Pal, then chairman of Cadbury India,[41] at his office next to the Mahalakshmi Temple in south Mumbai. During our chat, he emphasized on the top leader's role in ensuring greater stakeholder focus. 'If the top man is sensitive towards getting customer feedback, then automatically in all business thought processes, that sensitivity gets reflected in the decisions,' he said. He shared examples of how Cadbury India handled two critical crisis situations. The first was in 1992–93, when it was rumoured that Cadbury's chocolates contained nickel. The other was in 2005 when TV channels flashed a news items that insects were found in Cadbury's chocolates. Pal shared with me the reorganization of company processes to reassure diverse stakeholders about product safety, which was very insightful.[42]

My interactions with Dr Subir Gokarn, then deputy governor of the Reserve Bank of India, at his office on the 17th floor of the RBI headquarters in Mumbai, confirmed my understanding of Adam Smith's works. He said, 'A lot of prominence has been given to one of his publications, *An Enquiry into the Wealth of Nations*, which characterizes the emergence of a market economy. But perhaps, not the same level of importance has been given to his other publication, *The Theory of Moral Sentiments*. When you look at the original conception of capitalism or market economy, it's really putting these two together that makes it work.' Truly, if the 19th century business leaders would have integrated the ethical and economic ideals of Smith, the world would have been spared the discord and distress that emerged due to competing ideologies. Smith's ethical ideology was conveniently ignored, and capitalism grew with a skewed focus, ignoring the core human elements of business and society.[43]

During our conversation at the ICICI Bank[44] chairman's office in the Bandra–Kurla Complex, Mumbai, K.V. Kamath, now president of the New Development Bank (also known as BRICS Bank), chided companies for their short-term approach to business. He said, 'Executive management are sort of caretakers of an organization. They need to look at the entity with a lens which is reasonably long and cares for the well-being of all constituents of the organization over that period of time. Unfortunately, the quarter-on-quarter syndrome[45] does not allow for that.' He shared with me names of two books that truly inspired him. One was Daniel Kahneman's[46] *Thinking Fast and Slow* and the other was Dan Ariely's[47] book on experiments. The tall industry captain that he is, he humbly submitted, 'If I had read Kahneman's books thirty years back, I would have been a much better manager. But the problem is that he wrote it only a few years ago!'

When I visited the Titan Company's Campus in Bengaluru, Bhaskar Bhatt, the managing director of Titan Company Ltd,[48] (and now chairman of Tata SIA Airlines), had just returned from an official visit abroad. While he was visibly jetlagged, he was equally committed to our conversation. Sharing his perspectives, he underscored organizational culture as the core of successful business management. He said, 'A company can have skills and competencies, but it is the culture of transparency, non-hierarchical consensus-oriented decision-making, inclusive approach, walking the talk, and accessibility of leadership, that are very important. These are not competencies, but behaviours and values. Culture is a strength, not a competency.'

My desire to get an international perspective brought me to USA. I was privileged to meet Professor Edward Freeman, often called the 'Father of Stakeholder Theory'. In a conversation that went on for over two hours at his office in the Darden School of Business in Charlottesville in Virginia, he shared, with great modesty, his four-decade long understanding of business and its management. Contrary to popular belief, he opined that capitalism is the greatest system of social cooperation ever invented. 'Fundamentally, it's about how we cooperate together to produce what no one of us can produce alone. It's about managers and entrepreneurs who put together a deal so that customers, employees, communities and providers of capital, all win at the same time. The purpose of business is to figure out how we cooperate together, how we solve the problem of value creation in a complicated environment. If we figure out how to do that, money follows. Profits are an outcome. To say that profits are the purpose of a business is like saying making red blood cells and breathing are the purpose of life. It's really foolish.'

Differentiating between purpose and profits, Professor Raj Sisodia, co-founder and co-chairman of Conscious Capitalism Inc. (and now professor at Babson College in Greater Boston) told me, 'Profits are necessary and essential for corporations to succeed and grow. But they're not the purpose, profit is the outcome.' During our interaction at Bentley College in Greater Boston, he observed that for a century, the responsibility of companies has been narrowly defined as maximizing shareholders' interests through profit maximization. A very complex human activity has been reduced to a mathematical equation. He elaborated, 'The traditional narrative about business is a narrow instrumental approach which says that all players in that system, from suppliers to employees to community to customers are instruments to be used to make money. In any interconnected system, when you start to systematically trade-off the well-being of various entities for the well-being of one single entity, then you start to harm the health of the system. Eventually, this will weaken and potentially destroy the whole system.'

Professor Sandra Waddock from Boston College is an internationally renowned scholar of corporate responsibility and the chair of strategy at the Carroll School of Management. During our conversation at her office in the aesthetic campus, she lamented that although the financial meltdown of 2008–09 shook people up, it hadn't really awakened them. 'In the last 150 years, this notion of maximizing shareholder wealth has allowed companies to become inordinately powerful with a non-stakeholder non-eco-friendly agenda of maximizing wealth for one group of stakeholders who happen to be the already wealthy.' She shared with me her perspectives on new business models that built a whole new set of relationships with stakeholders. In most of my interactions with international experts, names of many Indian companies that have done well, nationally and globally, would often emerge as examples. Among all of them, the Tata Group was the most popular.

Each interaction built on the previous one, and I was increasingly exposed to hitherto unexplored horizons of the business–human interface. I observed an increasing understanding in business leaders of their responsibilities extending beyond traditional 'shareholder wealth' focus to a larger and all-inclusive 'stakeholder value' focus. Their experiences accentuated that stakeholders' welfare is not necessarily only a means to an economic end. It can be said that the two are, in a long-term perspective, intertwined. In fact, one might go so far as to say that economic well-being is a necessary condition for stakeholder well-being, and stakeholder well-being is a desirable condition for economic well-being.

Over the last decade, my journey of understanding businesses and their management, led me to meet nearly 200 senior executives, heads of companies, industry captains and subject experts across leading national and multinational corporations and industries in India and top academics from USA and Europe[49] to build a veritable knowledge base of insights in the field of stakeholder management and corporate responsibility of a collective experience of 4000 human years. The current book is the first in the series of many more that I envision, to reflect and share ways of perceiving and practising business management in a new and holistic light.

Uniqueness of This Book

This book is an outcome of decade-long, multi-layered research undertaken to study eminent Indian companies and the leaders who manage them. The name 'Win-Win Corporations' (WWC) epitomizes a genre of companies that consistently focus on devising and implementing win-win solutions and mutually beneficial strategies for long-term value creation for the company's shareholders as well as its stakeholders. The book details the philosophy and processes, the means and methods used by WWC to integrate stakeholders' interests into organizational decision-making. Many social, economic and political considerations play a role in this study. Hence, each of them makes for very interesting reading.[50] Every chapter contains interesting narratives and unknown stories about these companies and the approaches they have followed for creating win-win solutions and strategies. The book doesn't just portray facts but also presents background perspectives with which each of those decisions were taken. Along with the 'what, how, when and where' of the initiatives, the book also explores the 'why' behind those decisions and initiatives.

Another unique aspect of the book is that the people who were part of the core decision-making are the main protagonists of each chapter. Hence, the reader can see the situation and the solution from an authentic lens. This would, in turn, help the reader address and tackle similar situations in their personal and professional lives. The most interesting part is that each of the six companies has created win-win strategies in very unique ways. No two companies have followed the same path. Yet, each of them has achieved significant successes. This does not mean that they did not make mistakes or have a flawless record. They did, and I have captured some of those mistakes too. But they were keen to resurface and grow further with greater gusto. The thirty characteristics of WWC as synthesized in the last chapter thus emerge as practical takeaways for organizations of all sizes and types. The implementation toolkits for seven stakeholders provide action items for practising managers of all such firms.

The choice of companies presented in this book is based on a perception study wherein responses from over 700 managers representing 325 companies have been analysed. Each of the respondents was asked to list companies that they believed were well-known for integrating stakeholders' interests with long-term organizational strategy as part of their core philosophy. These six companies were among the top ten that emerged from the data analysis.[51] Accessibility to the senior management was the secondary criterion used in company selection. These companies also represent a diverse set of industries and varied ownership patterns. TVS Motor Company Ltd (automobile industry) is a family-owned organization. Three of the companies are professionally managed organizations with varied shareholding patterns: Hindustan Unilever Ltd (FMCG industry), Larsen & Toubro Ltd (construction industry), and HDFC Bank Ltd (banking industry). Bharat Petroleum Corporation Ltd (oil and gas industry) represents the public sector. The Taj Group of Hotels (hospitality industry) belongs to the Tata Group. The Tatas have a unique ownership structure, and hence cannot be classified as family-owned. The Tata Sons have a controlling stake in all major Tata companies. Two-thirds of the Tata Sons in turn is owned by philanthropic trusts. Thus, majority of the Tata Group's earning ultimately goes towards social welfare and nation building.

A diverse mix of companies provides noteworthy lessons about the Indian way of shaping successful stakeholder strategies. All six companies are industry leaders and have set high standards of all-round performance, including long-term shareholder value creation. In fact, the six Win-Win Corporations included in this book delivered spectacular returns to shareholders, many times more than the general stock market. If you invested 1 lakh rupees divided equally across all six WWC in August 1996, and simultaneously invested 1 lakh rupees in the Sensex,[52] your 1 lakh in the WWC portfolio taken out in 2016 would have multiplied fifty-four times, compared to just an eight-fold increase in the general market.[53]

Figure 1.1: Returns on Investment in Sensex vs Investments in Win-Win Corporations

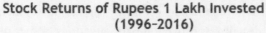

Stock Returns of Rupees 1 Lakh Invested (1996-2016)

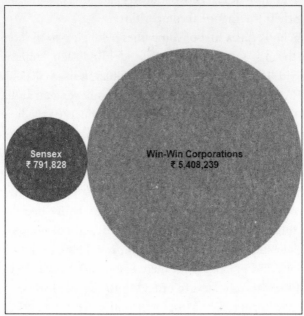

This book is distinctive and the first of its kind in the emerging Indian scenario as compared to studies like *In Search of Excellence*,[54] *Built to Last*[55] and *Good to Great*[56] conducted in USA, where the free enterprise system has stabilized for nearly two centuries. Studying the evolution and stakeholder strategies of visionary companies like those selected in the US-based study by Jim Collins and Jerry Porras would have been an interesting area of work.[57] However, identifying such companies in the transition era of post-Independence India was a difficult task. The protected and controlled structure of the Indian economy between the 1950s and the 1980s impacted many companies in corporate India, some of which do not even exist today. Since the opening up of the Indian economy in 1991, it's been just twenty-five years, and many companies haven't yet established themselves sufficiently well in all aspects. They are gradually yet firmly carving out an identity for themselves in their respective industry categories, sometimes even beating their international competitors.

This book has a mix of companies belonging to different eras. While the Taj Group of Hotels and Hindustan Unilever have grown with India over the twentieth century, Larsen & Toubro and Bharat Petroleum took concrete shape in independent India. TVS Motor Company and HDFC Bank are products of the liberalized Indian economy, though they have been affiliated with institutions that have existed long before. Thus, the six companies present a veritable mix of history, experience, and novelty.[58] I have attempted to study each of them across their entire life span. It is for this reason that many of the interviewees belong to an earlier decade, when certain interesting developments unfolded, and not necessarily the latest leadership spearheading the company. I have also studied the philosophy and practices that these companies have initiated with most of their stakeholders in order to provide a holistic account of their win-win approach. Most other studies tend to focus on select strengths of companies, where they may be doing exceedingly well with a particular stakeholder, such as customers or employees. This tends to give an incomplete picture of the company, as the leadership may be neglecting another stakeholder while benefitting a specific stakeholder. This book thus provides a comprehensive and multidimensional description of each WWC.

The other differentiating feature of this book compared to other landmark studies is that each of those were multi-year projects conducted by a team of many researchers. For example, the *Built to Last* and *Good to Great* research projects had a team size of about twenty-five members. This book is the outcome of a single researcher's decade-long efforts.

Celebrating Seventy Years of a Resurgent India

Writing this book has increasingly convinced me about the depth and distinctiveness of the Indian way of shaping successful stakeholder strategies. What amazed me was the shortest span of time within which India Inc. made a mark for itself, and also created a niche in the international world of business. For nearly 700 years, the Indian subcontinent was under external rule of one kind or another. These included the Mughal and Afghan invasions followed by the European colonial rulers— the Portuguese, the French and the British. Post-Independence, India adopted a democratic system of governance that combined the best of many constitutions, and a mixed economy approach to growth and development that blended the characteristics of socialism and capitalism with a fine balance.[59] Of these seventy years of independence, nearly forty-five years were under the socialistic approach to economic development. It is only in the twenty-five years since the market-based economic reforms have been implemented in 1991 that the Indian economy has truly flourished. In fact, by 2007 itself, Indian foreign investment exceeded the total cumulative foreign investment by Indian companies in the preceding fifty-eight years![60] By the time the country was ready to celebrate the silver jubilee year, India had received a cumulative foreign direct investment (FDI) of US$ 371 billion as compared to negligible investments around 1991. In 2015 alone, India received US$ 63 billion (nearly Rs 4.19 lakh-crore) as FDI, thereby replacing China as the top FDI destination.[61] So it has been a magnificent growth story. In just these twenty-five years, India has risen to become the third largest economy (by purchasing power parity) in the world after USA and China. While USA is the world's oldest democracy, it is also the country where capitalism[62] and free enterprise[63] have been the order of the day for over 200 years. China's exclusive governance structure and control-oriented communist regime makes it a different ball game.

Among these, the story of India Inc. and the rise of its Win-Win Corporations makes interesting reading for managers, entrepreneurs, researchers, practitioners, students and even inquisitive young minds who want to peep into these vast corporations, whose products we use, but don't know what goes into making them; whose buildings we see, but don't know what happens inside them; whose advertisements we enjoy, but don't know what goes into creating them; and whose leaders we admire, but don't know what contributed to their success. I can assure every single reader that there would definitely have been a time when you have used the products or services of at least one of the six companies presented in this book. You could have purchased one among the thirty-five brands of Hindustan Unilever products from any of its 24 lakh retail outlets, or filled fuel in your vehicle at one of Bharat Petroleum's 13,000 pumps. You might have visited one of the many tourist landmarks, stadiums or institutional complexes constructed by Larsen & Toubro, or stayed at a Taj Group hotel. You would have used one of HDFC Bank's 12,000 ATMs in any of the 2505 towns and cities across India where they're located, or accompanied your friend or younger cousin on a trendy TVS bike. Having experienced the product or service, it should simply delight you to now know and understand what went into making these companies and their products and services truly win-win.

II.

HDFC Bank

World-class Services . . . Indian Experience

'If you are to be a good citizen, you cannot work only for a section of people. Good corporate governance has been defined very clearly. Shareholders must get good return for their money. The employee must have a professional environment and a fair compensation. Your suppliers must be paid on time. You must do something for the society you live in. To make 50,000 people follow this, you have to have rules and regulations down the line and have people walk the talk'[1]

—Aditya Puri, managing director, HDFC Bank

On the morning of 18 February 1995, Dr Manmohan Singh, then finance minister of India, landed in Bombay to inaugurate the first branch of a new private sector bank promoted by India's premier housing finance company—Housing Development Finance Corporation (HDFC). After a four-decade long wait, the Government of India had opened up the banking and financial services industry (BFSI) to the private sector. With its experience in financial markets, its reputation, large shareholder base and consumer franchise, HDFC felt that it was ideally positioned to promote a bank in India. So when the Reserve Bank of India (RBI) invited applications for a banking licence, HDFC grabbed the opportunity with both hands with a desire for diversification. Along with ICICI Bank and UTI Bank (now Axis Bank), HDFC

Figure 2.1: Finance Minister Manmohan Singh at the Inauguration of the New HDFC Bank (1995)

Bank was among the first few private sector institutions to receive the banking licence. 'S.S. Marathe, director of RBI at that time, told me that ours was the best application,' recalled Deepak Parekh, chairman, HDFC.[2]

Two decades later, HDFC Bank is the most expensive banking stock in the world. Through its prudent bottom line focus, it superbly rewarded its shareholders with a return on capital employed (ROCE)[3] of 21.28 per cent, the best in the Indian banking industry. Suppose a shareholder invested Rs 1 lakh in HDFC Bank stock in July 1996, his investment would have increased to Rs 1.82 crore by June 2016. In comparison, 1 lakh invested in the Sensex portfolio would have grown to just Rs 7.3 lakh during the same period. Thus, while the Sensex grew seven times, the HDFC Bank stock grew 182 times in twenty years.

Those have been the kind of phenomenal returns it has given its shareholders. The State Bank of India (SBI), India's largest bank, was way behind HDFC Bank with 10.03 per cent ROCE, while ICICI Bank, its closest private sector competitor, had an ROCE of 14.28 per cent. Within a span of twenty years, HDFC Bank achieved what was considered unimaginable—a market capitalization[4] of over Rs 2,75,000 crore that equalled twenty of India's state-run banks put together! The State Bank of India (SBI), India's largest bank, whose balance sheet was three and a half times more than that of HDFC Bank, had a market capitalization of Rs 1,54,000 crore.

Figure 2.2: Financial Snapshot of Leading Indian Banks

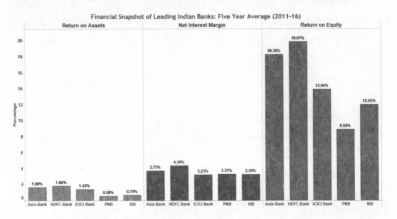

Where the Journey Began . . .

In August 1994, HDFC Bank Limited was incorporated with its registered office in Bombay. It commenced operations as a scheduled commercial bank[5] in January 1995. In the same year, it entered into a strategic alliance with Natwest Markets of the Westminster Banking Group from the United Kingdom and launched its initial public offering (IPO) of Rs 50 crore. Quite unexpectedly for its promoters, it elicited a record fifty-five times oversubscription.[6] In 1996, the National Securities Clearing Corporation Ltd (NSCCL) appointed HDFC Bank as a clearing bank.[7] This marked the beginning of what eventually became a major 'capital markets infrastructure' business.[8] In 1997, the bank declared its maiden dividend on equity shares[9] at 8 per cent. In the same year, it also launched retail investment advisory services. A year later, it launched its first retail lending product—loans against shares. Slow and steady on the path of growth, its branch network touched fifty and returns on equity crossed 20 per cent in the same year. In 1999, the bank launched its first international debit card in India, as also an online real-time net banking system, which was a first in the Indian BFSI.

Entering the new millennium on the wave of information and communication technology, the bank launched mobile banking services, again a first in India. Within half a decade since incorporation, its customer base crossed 10 lakh, branch network crossed 100 and balance sheet size crossed Rs 10,000 crore. The year 2000 was also the year of its first inorganic expansion. HDFC Bank acquired the Bennett, Coleman & Co. promoted Times Bank. This was the first merger of two private banks among the new generation private sector banks. According to the scheme of amalgamation approved by the shareholders of both banks and the RBI, shareholders of Times Bank received 1 share of HDFC Bank for every 5.75 shares of Times Bank.

In 2001, HDFC became the first private sector bank to be authorized to collect income tax for the Government of India. That was also the year when it got its stock listed on the New York Stock Exchange. A decade after its inception, the bank launched its credit card in over 100 cities and within the same year its credit card customer base reached 10 lakh, a proof of its growing popularity among the Indian elite. By 2008, the bank was opening 300,000 accounts a month, and had 40 lakh credit card holders. To consolidate its position in the market, HDFC Bank forayed into the second—and until then the largest—merger in the history of the Indian banking industry. In 2008, the Centurion Bank of Punjab (CBoP) merged with HDFC Bank.

Figure 2.3: HDFC Bank Team at the New York Stock Exchange (2001)

In September 2008, post the crisis on Wall Street, when domestic and international banks were crashing, HDFC Bank was rather anchored. With a balance sheet size of Rs 1,72,000 crore, a 40 per cent rise over the previous year, and a net revenue of Rs 2500 crore, a 50 per cent rise over the previous year,[10] it was poised for greater growth. Not surprisingly, in the subsequent years, the bank grew ten times on most parameters. While net revenues increased from Rs 3854 crore (2006) to Rs 31,392 crore (2015), profits after taxes (PAT) rose from Rs 871 crore (2006) to Rs 10,216 crore (2015). By 2015, it was the most profitable and the seventh largest

bank in India with a market share of about 4.9 per cent of the
Indian banking system's deposits and 5 per cent of its advances.[11]

Figure 2.4: HDFC Bank's Growth Figures

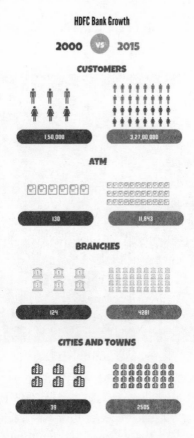

Summing up the core of the bank's growth story, Deepak Parekh
observed, 'Performance at HDFC Bank has been a balance between
growth and enterprise-wide risk. Policies are the same as the
parent institution (HDFC)—follow prudential norms, no overseas
exposure, avoid funding over-leveraged Indian acquisitions overseas,
off balance sheet items and special purpose vehicles.' Over the two

decades since commencement, the bank grew consistently at 30 per cent quarter to quarter, year after year with a 20 to 30 per cent compounded growth in net profits.

Understanding the Industry, Creating an Identity

'The critical success factors for the bank are service, lowest cost, convenience backed by appropriate technology and people. And consistently providing this will make sure that our costs keep coming down and the customers remain loyal to us, which will lead to greater earnings'

—Aditya Puri

In 1994, when the bank got its licence, the banking industry in India consisted of two major players. At one end of the spectrum were the public sector banks (PSBs), and at the other were foreign banks (FBs). At the time, there was a wide gap between them in terms of service standards and products. So the middle and upper-middle classes had to make a very clear choice either to go with the PSBs or FBs. Each had their positives and negatives. So the conversation at the just-born HDFC Bank was around how to combine the positives of the PSBs and FBs, and create an institution where the common Indian is happy and comfortable banking. The positives of a PSB were a friendly, personalized appeal where the manager knew the customers well. Even a person with a low balance could feel comfortable walking in. The other plus point was the wide branch network across the metros and the hinterland. Positives of an FB were technology, better and structured set of products, and a good ambience in terms of the decor and facilities.

The founding team at HDFC Bank decided to position itself in the centre with the positives of both categories. Recollecting the positioning, C.N. Ram, a member of the founding team, told me, 'The competition was from the public sector and the MNC banks. There's a snob value associated with foreign banks, and "affordability" associated with the PSBs. So we had to adapt the affordable propositions of the PSBs but give customers the quality of service they would get from an MNC bank. This means that we had to deal with a fairly low level of average daily balance or average quarterly balance. So we originally pegged it at Rs 5000.' What were the core focus areas of the new bank? 'Right in the beginning, we [the founding team] were all very clear on: high dose of automation, operational efficiency and customer convenience.' So high was the commitment to sustained profitability, a precondition, that within three months of starting, the bank had already made a nominal profit of about Rs 80 lakh!

Figure 2.5: HDFC Bank's Positioning

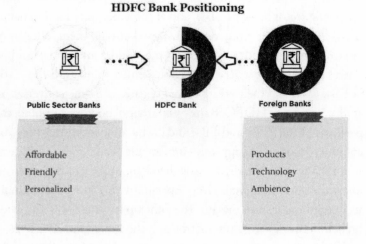

Making the Beginning

In 1995, the PSBs enjoyed near total market share in India. How were the new private sector banks to make inroads? That's where the goodwill of the parent institution HDFC came into play. The parent brand was enormously reputed, well known for governance, integrity and being dependable. It was the kind of institution that people would have dealt with at some point in their lives. There was a very good chance that prospective customers would have had an encouraging experience with HDFC and the halo effect would positively impact the new bank. The belief that if there was a bank promoted by HDFC, it would carry the same kind of value systems, ethics and governance, worked.

The second advantage was the people in the bank itself. Many of them had worked with renowned corporates in the past and had developed a deep personal relationship. In the corporate world, while there is always the bank that stands behind the corporate, the people who are handling that relationship with the client, their responsiveness to and understanding of the client, and the help and support they provided at times when the client needed the most, are factors well remembered. The HDFC Bank founding team had familiar faces from well-known banks including Citibank, Bank of America, SBI and RBI. That helped in getting the first set of customers.

Besides, the products and services were a major attraction. Samir Bhatia, the founding head of corporate banking, recollected, 'Right from the beginning, the bank had decided that whether it is consumer or corporate, it had to invest in technology. So aspects of Internet banking, funds transfer, good tie-ups for cash management, and just the ease of doing service made all the difference. Besides, we had a very good treasury. That's quite a place to open doors in companies. If you have a very good foreign exchange desk and you can provide good advisory services, the customers are happy.' Thus, product, service and technology were initial driving factors. There was also an interest in most corporates to try the offerings by new banks. At that time, there were only two banks that were backed by established private sector institutions—ICICI and HDFC. So they were a natural choice as against a private promoter backed bank. Thus, pedigree became an advantage.

Benchmarking with the Best in Class

'The superior banking experience at HDFC Bank means superior to the class and quality of service customers are used to seeing in the market. It's more against a market benchmark than against our immediate peer'

—Samir Bhatia, founding head of corporate banking,
HDFC Bank

The bank's mission is 'to be a world-class Indian bank,' benchmarking itself against international standards and best practices. The primary objective is to build sound customer franchises[12] across distinct businesses so as to be the preferred provider of banking services for target retail and wholesale customer segments, and to achieve healthy growth in profitability, consistent with the bank's risk appetite. Elaborating on this, Paresh Sukthankar, member of the founding team and deputy managing director at HDFC Bank, shared, 'We have said that we want to be a world-class Indian bank. But we have never looked at this from a short-term quarterly perspective. We have tried to see which benchmarks we would like to focus on in terms of technology, risk management, audit and compliance, or even customer service. In customer service, we focused on turn-around times, error rates, customer feedback, and so on. So we look at providing a range of banking services to a wide range of customers. For this, we figure out the best practices in the various verticals and products that we offer.'

The bank has benchmarked itself against a number of niche and mainstream banking institutions across the globe. For example, Aditya Puri, the founding managing director of the bank, likes Wells Fargo (USA) for its product penetration, cross-selling and virtualized banking; State Street Corporation (USA)[13] for its transactions expertise; Bank Mandiri (Indonesia)[14] for small ticket loans;[15] and the Hang Seng Bank (Hong Kong)[16] for its good returns. 'We aim for global benchmarks and then 20 per cent improvement over that,' stated Aditya.[17] In fact, many analysts observe that HDFC Bank mirrors Wells Fargo in many respects. The San Francisco-based Wells Fargo & Company is the third largest bank in USA. In 2015, it was rated the most valuable bank in the world in terms of market capitalization, far ahead of the Industrial and Commercial Bank of China, and its American competitors, J.P. Morgan Chase and the Citigroup. The bank's secret to success has been its focus on core units like consumer lending, banking services and mortgage origination rather than reliance on subprime loans,[18] complex derivatives[19] or risky trades funded by borrowed money.[20] Just like its role model, HDFC Bank was stable during the global slowdown, is a consistent performer, and the hot favourite of investors. Not surprisingly, in 2015, HDFC Bank had a better return on assets (ROA) at 1.72 per cent, than Hang Seng Bank, the bank Aditya had set as a benchmark.[21]

Mergers, with a Winning Strategy

Effective 26 February 2000, Times Bank Ltd[22] merged with HDFC Bank. The amalgamation added significant value to the bank in terms of increased branch network, expanded geographic reach, enhanced customer base, skilled manpower and the opportunity to cross-sell and leverage alternative delivery channels. At a time when the RBI was rather conservative in permitting new branches, it gained forty ATMs, thirty-eight branches and 170,000 customers through the merger. It got a clear lead of two years compared to its competitors.

While the figures were clearly in HDFC Bank's favour, the industry was looking at the process. Across the world, mergers are rarely a happy process. One of the necessities of making a merger successful is rationalization of people and getting economies of scale on the merged entity. That cannot happen without people being reassigned, released or rationalized—a necessary evil. Yet, what is important is how well this is done. Whenever there is a merger, the promoters who are selling the entity have one thing on their mind: 'I hope my people are well taken care of.' So the real success of a merger is about how fair people think the acquiring entity has been in the process, because that sets the right example, and even allows it to make future acquisitions easily.

Recollecting the post-Times Bank merger days, Samir said, 'Aditya was very fair in terms of evaluating the people that came (from Times Bank). For example, even I was unsure, for at least a month, whether I would continue in my job or would the person coming from the other side get the job. Aditya understood the strengths of people on both sides.' The masterstroke hailed by the industry was making Mandeep Maitra,[23] the HR head of Times Bank, as HR head of HDFC Bank. This gave a lot of comfort to Times Bank employees. It sent a clear signal from Aditya that merit will be given precedence. Mandeep knew the strengths of every person from Times Bank. This made the toughest part rather easy. Industry experts expected that the merger would be a clash of cultures. With every member of the top HDFC team having worked with a foreign bank, it was feared that the incoming Times employees would be treated like mercenaries.[24] However, the bank worked out a win-win strategy.

Mergers take away a lot from the day-to-day running of a business. Managing resources and integration of people, systems and culture is a very difficult and time-consuming task. Many times the acquiring company doesn't know what it's really getting into. So, it has to make tremendous business sense for the acquiring entity. This is one of the primary reasons that acquisitions are fewer in the market, especially in the financial sector. Yet, HDFC sprang another surprise on the market. On 23 May 2008, the RBI formally approved the amalgamation of Centurion Bank of Punjab[25] (CBoP) with HDFC Bank. The acquisition was for Rs 9510 crore, and was the largest merger in the financial sector in India. The buy-out was an all-share deal with every 29 shares of CBoP getting one share of HDFC Bank.

If Times Bank was a big deal, CBoP was a super big deal. CBoP was itself an amalgamation of four banks. The Centurion Bank[26] had acquired the Mumbai office of the Bank of Muscat in 2003, the Bank of Punjab[27] in 2005, and the Lord Krishna Bank[28] in 2006. Implementing the merger was quite a challenge for HDFC Bank because of different computing systems, labour issues and diverse cultures of four banks in one. For instance, the union at Lord Krishna Bank (in Kerala) had opposed its merger with Centurion Bank. There were branches that hadn't serviced a single customer in months.[29] Aditya led from the front and along with Mandeep, personally attended several town hall meetings at the branch offices of the merged banks to allay fears and apprehensions of the staff and communicate the ethos of the HDFC brand.[30] Mandeep used her experience of bringing the two banks together, and did an extensive 'culture audit' post the merger. When it came to appeasing employees in Punjab, she travelled the distance alone.

Narrating the challenges on the operational side, Paresh pondered, 'Literally the day after the merger was approved, all the hoardings had been changed. But at the back end , we had to maintain parallel systems for nine months. We had to do a big-bang conversion and all accounts moved into a particular system. Sounds simple enough, but when you're talking about lakhs of customers, thousands of employees, and ensuring that systems talk to each other at the back end, it's a massive task. But it's not rocket science. It's a question of executing an integration plan with precision.' While the senior team worked hard, the benefits of the merger for the growth of the bank were immense. The merged entity had a strong deposit base of Rs 1,22,000 crore and net advances of around Rs 89,000 crore. Subsequent to the merger, the balance sheet size of the bank increased to Rs 1,72,000 crore, a 40 per cent increase over the previous year, and net revenues touched Rs 2500 crore, a 50 per cent increase over the previous year. The amalgamation added significant value to HDFC Bank in terms of increased branch network, geographic reach, customer base and a bigger pool of skilled manpower. It had been a crucial leap ahead for the bank with a combined branch network of over 1500 branches, compared to 761 before the merger. CBoP had a larger presence in the north (through the Bank of Punjab acquisition) and south (through the Lord Krishna Bank acquisition), and post merger, HDFC Bank benefitted from this. Most of these branches were located in economically developed states like Punjab, Haryana, upper Rajasthan, Maharashtra, Goa, Tamil Nadu and Kerala. Besides, the combined entity became the second largest in Mumbai and Delhi (after SBI).[31] The branches were the key to raising low cost deposits. CBoP's branch geography and infrastructure worked to HDFC Bank's real advantage.

Sharing his understanding of a successful merger, Ram said, 'Mergers cause problems when people are not on board. The top management always has to walk that extra mile during a merger because whatever you plan, you are going to have some kind of issues. Hence, the ability of people to overcome them by showing willingness to walk that extra mile is the core.' Through a well-designed strategy, HDFC Bank succeeded in integrating the customers and employees of five different banks into its own ecosystem, and create the single HDFC identity of customer focus and operational efficiency.

Customers: The Heart of HDFC Bank

'In the financial services industry, we are in the business of acting as a bridge for the people who have the money and want a return, and people who need the money and want to make a profit. We create a bridge and we manage a risk. You deposit with me and you want your money back. When I lend it to somebody, I also want your money back. That is the basic business of banking'

—Aditya Puri

In the two decades since its inception, HDFC Bank has seen a meteoric rise in its customers. At the turn of the millennium, before the merger with Times Bank, HDFC Bank had 150,000 customers.[32] By 2015, this expanded to 3,27,00,000 customers. In 2000, the bank had 130 ATMs. By 2015, this went up to 11,843. Before its merger with Times Bank, HDFC Bank had 124 branches in thirty-nine cities across India. By 2015, its distribution network was 4281 branches across 2505 cities and towns in India, including remote locations such as Kargil and Leh in the north, the interiors of Meghalaya in the northeast, and the Andaman and Nicobar Islands in the southeast. These facts and figures present an exceptional tale of exponential growth. Yet, the interesting piece is that the growth has not just been in urban India.

The bank also focused on semi-urban and under-penetrated rural markets. By 2015, about 55 per cent of its branches were located in these areas. While in 2010, over 80 per cent of its revenues came from the top fifteen cities of India, by 2015, this number changed. Semi-urban and rural areas contributed 15–20 per cent of the total revenue. This was a noteworthy shift in its customer base, both in scale and reach. By 2016, its revenues were generated through three business segments: retail banking (60 per cent), wholesale banking (24 per cent) and treasury services (16 per cent).

Understanding Customers

Customer focus is a critical success factor for any bank. Paresh emphasized that the entire focus of the bank has to be on customers and managing customer relationships. Understanding customers and their needs, structuring products to meet those needs, and having to realistically service different customers through different channels are the critical components. Yet, when a bank is servicing such a diverse set of customers, how does it understand the needs of its customers? During our conversation in his office at the HDFC Bank headquarters in Lower Parel (Mumbai), Aditya summed up the needs of the customers in a simple fashion by giving his own example: 'Let us take me as a customer of the bank. What do I want? I want a proper interest rate, proper service—whatever I have been promised, and I want delivery. Customers don't want too much. And they want right and fair advice. You do that for the customer and they are happy. Our processes have to ensure that we tell our people how to do this much.' In essence, the fundamental requirement of a customer from the bank is to assist them in leading an efficient life. This involves taking care of the smallest of transactions to taking care of some very complex wealth management products.

At a very broad level, there are few basic needs that an average customer has. This includes providing services as promised, maintaining high quality standards, offering customized and cost-effective products and services, convenience, and when the occasion arises having appropriate systems and procedures in place for grievance redressal. Most customers invest their precious savings in a bank so that they can benefit from high rates of interest, leading to an increase in their investments. Besides, all customers want lowest rates of interest while borrowing money. Being a mass scale brand, the bank has been in a position to give such an interest rate. Rohit Mull, then executive vice president and head of marketing at the bank,[33] described these as hygiene factors, which are a must.

Besides, to provide customized solutions and service offerings to different customer segments, the bank attempted to define diverse customer segments, their size, type of products required, credit criteria and credit evaluation parameters.[34] This enabled the bank to know exactly what kind of customers it was acquiring or targeting. 'We knew the wants for the customer segments and made sure the product set was strong enough to service them,' shared Samir Bhatia, who headed corporate banking during the initial dozen years. Moreover, customer service was very important for the bank. If at all there was any customer who was unhappy or who complained, it would be seriously taken into consideration by the top team. Everyone in the bank knew that customer complaints and service were not to be taken lightly.

The bank also aimed at becoming a one-stop shop for the targeted customers' requirements. It was not just about depositing and withdrawing money. It was about managing the customers' lifestyle and giving them a wholesome experience, so that it could manage its customers from whatever stage in life they were starting to whatever they wanted to be. If there were products a customer wanted, and the bank could not provide, it partnered with others who could. 'So you surround the customer with products that he wants and offer it to him at the time he needs it most,' observed Ram. The key was to keep track of a customer's evolving requirements. For a customer who has just started her career, a housing loan would not be an immediate requirement; a car loan or a consumer durable loan would be. These kinds of customer-specific product requirements through constant interaction was the key. Over a period of time, the bank provided a wide range of products required by customers at different life stages, ranging from simple loans to complex wealth management products. (Appendix II.A elaborates on how HDFC Bank developed supply chain financing as a successful business.)

Introducing Core Banking Solutions

'Rather than using technology purely as a means to reduce our costs or get more efficient at the back end, the bank used technology as an enabler to provide something superior or something more convenient to the customer'

—C.N. Ram, founding head of information technology, HDFC Bank

The bank's constant efforts were to enable the customer to do all her work without having to visit the branch, without having to go to another bank. For this, they tried to string together a whole lot of services and also opened a depository and share broking facility. Most of the innovations the bank introduced were kind of latent needs. It was never a question of whether the customer wants it. It was like the 'Steve Jobs approach'. The customer wants it, but doesn't know that such a thing is possible. So, the bank decided to provide many such tech-based solutions to retail and corporate customers. It was the first in the industry to introduce mobile banking wherein transactions could be done through SMS. This was spearheaded in the year 2000 by Neeraj Swaroop,[35] then head of retail banking, through a collaboration with Vodafone. As a result, the customers could send balance-related queries through SMS to a pre-designated number, and the bank would respond in a particular format. This was done using the wireless access protocol (WAP), the early browsers in mobile systems. Eventually, the bank even introduced bill payments through ATMs and mobiles. They were also the first with online real-time banking, which meant that there was no discrepancy between the balance a customer saw when she used telephone banking or the ATM, and what she would get from Internet banking. When this service was introduced by HDFC, many other banks still consolidated the figures from different channels only at the end of the day. HDFC Bank provided the same figures in real-time. For corporate clients, the bank was the first to introduce online corporate banking transaction services. Through this service, corporates could transfer money, pay their vendors and disburse employee salaries through Internet banking. The product was a huge hit among corporates. It provided convenience previously unimaginable. Recalling those days, Ram shared, 'The business team never slackened from dreaming big, because they were assured of a telecom or IT infrastructure that would give them what they wanted. But there always was a business purpose to anything we did. We never did IT for IT's sake.'

In line with this strategy, HDFC Bank was among the first in centralized implementation of core banking solutions. In those days, all other banks in the public and private sectors had branch banking. Each branch was a self-sufficient unit. To understand this, let's take the example of a customer visiting an SBI branch in the 1990s. The branch would process her request, handover a cheque book and pass book, and the account was opened. Everything was done by the branch. However, that was highly inefficient because all the 10,000 branches of SBI did all of this. 'We realized that there was no point in doing all this repeated work with the efficiency that is required at the branch level,' shared Ram. Besides, branch banking also meant that a customer could bank with only that particular branch of the bank where she had an account. It would take a lot of effort for her to deal with another branch of the same bank. Core banking facilitated HDFC Bank customers to go to any of its branches pan-India and expect the same kind and level of service as the original branch. It was said that a customer would receive the same familiar smile from the teller as she would receive from her own branch! The only drawback of this system was that post-submission of the account opening form, it would take a week to receive the cheque book and the ATM card from the bank's central facility. The main advantage was that the customer was no longer a customer of the branch. She became the customer of the bank.

Emphasizing on the larger benefits of this approach, Ram said, 'Customer convenience was the paramount thing. We also wanted to do it in the most efficient and effective manner possible. If you are able to do the same work at half the cost, it goes straight into the bottom line. The shareholders also benefit because there is more of cash to distribute in terms of dividends at the end of the year.' It was a win-win strategy for the industry. For customers it meant convenience, for employees it meant great efficiency, and for shareholders it meant more dividends. Eventually, core banking became the industry standard across the Indian BFSI.

With core banking solutions, every HDFC Bank branch primarily became a sales and service outlet. The focus of the front-end staff was mainly customer service. They did not have to be experts in banking, but rather had to strike the right conversation with customers and understand their needs based on demographics. The focus was to proactively work towards customer delight. During the initial years, the transition from traditional banking to tech-based banking was rather smooth for employees who had joined the bank through lateral entry. Ram shared that most of the front-end staff were people from the hospitality industry, who enjoyed working with customers. 'We just had to teach them a little bit of banking. When compared to corresponding people in the PSBs, they knew less about banking. But the profile was very different. We wanted their ability to service customers. At the supervisory level, we brought in people with a lot of banking knowledge. This was the perfect balance.'

Besides, the bank did a lot of work-flow study in terms of efficiency, and used technology to remove dreariness from the work for all employees. Anything repetitive would make work boring for employees and would often lead to two kinds of problems. One was insufficient verification of documents. As a result, transactions which shouldn't be there in the first place may get processed. The second was that the boredom would prevent employees from thinking innovatively about what they could do for their customers. Emphasizing the core purpose of making the branch a sales and service outlet, Ram said, 'One of the reasons why we felt that this drudgery of taking account opening away from the branch was to be focused on the customer. Ultimately, the employees' brain power should be focused on what else they should do for the customer, which would help both the customer and the bank.' Besides, the bank also made their employees tech-savvy. The operations people went through a lot of training to understand the system in totality so that they could commit to the customers what was possible, and politely refuse what was not possible. Through this approach, the bank empowered employees to use their talents in more strategic and focused ways rather than through monotonous paperwork.

Figure 2.6: Comparing Branch Banking and Core Banking

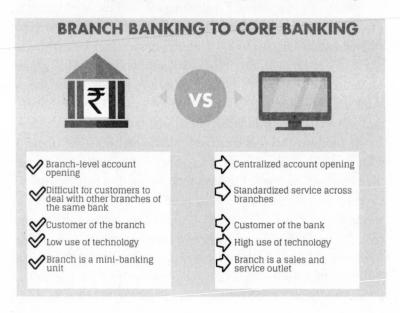

Marrying Technology and Operations

No doubt, HDFC Bank was first in many tech and process innovations introduced in the BSFI. But that also meant that they were the first to face many challenges while achieving their customer promise. One major challenge was the marriage between technology and operations. When the tech team creates something and the operations are not dovetailed to that, there can be a problem of mismatch between customer expectations and delivery. For example, in the same centralized banking process, the branch had to send the account opening documents to the bank's central facility. The operations process involved verification of all documents submitted by the customer. It was necessary for someone to validate the copies submitted with the original documents. In the absence of such verification, the back office would reject the form. Then the form had to travel back to that branch, the branch had to contact the customer, and a lot of time was wasted. More importantly, the bank would lose the customer's confidence. Recollecting some of those exasperating moments in the initial days, Ram said, 'It's very nice to say that technologically we have put a centralized operation somewhere to reduce the bank's cost. But if the operations process does not adhere to the rigour it needs to have, then you've already caused lot of problems. This marriage between technology and operations is the real problem, not only in India, but all over the world.'

If this was the problem they faced when they had about 1 lakh customers, how do they manage with 3 crore and more? The solution was a small process innovation. The bank envisaged imaging as a technique. So instead of physically sending all the forms to the central processing unit, images were captured and sent. What if there is a power failure at the central processing unit in Mumbai, like when there was a major grid failure in all of north India in 2012? In that case, they would send it to another centre, a Disaster Recovery Centre created in Chennai. If Mumbai didn't work, Chennai did! What if both of them faced power failures at the same time? 'While anything is possible in this world, the probability of this eventuality is very less,' quipped Ram. 'At least we can tell our customers that we were proactively prepared, but circumstances were beyond us. As you become more sophisticated in your systems, you also have to assess the risk.' This is critical learning for every company and industry with a heavy tech-enabled operation.

HDFC Bank further used this complex situation as an opportunity to support rural BPOs through image-based data entry. This created jobs for the local educated youth in smaller towns. It provided clear economic and social gains for the families. It also gave a boost to the local economy by countering problems of rural unemployment and distress migration to urban areas. One such example was the bank's collaboration with a BPO unit SAI SEVA (Serve and Inspire Simple Employment for Rural Advancement)[36] in the pilgrim town of Puttaparthi (Anantapur district, Andhra Pradesh). The other examples were of its own rural BPO units in Nellore and Tirupati (also in Andhra Pradesh).

In all of this, the enabler was technology. It provided the ability to transmit images from one location to another, for the image to come up on their screen and to use the screen as the mechanism to look at and do data entry. All it needed was a telecom connection—whether a mobile phone or a leased line. So a lot of disruptive things can be done with little ideation and process innovation. This initiative was a win-win for the bank, its customers and society. Through this rural effort, the bank had the advantage of cheap and committed labour, and didn't suffer from quality issues when compared to Mumbai or Chennai. It made a lot of economic and social sense to outsource to SAI SEVA and other similar rural BPOs.

Over a decade later, the bank used this same process innovation. This time, the semi-urban population was not employees or beneficiaries, but prospective customers. HDFC Bank is one of the largest retail lenders, whether it is car loans, personal loans or credit cards. The typical turnaround time for a car loan through an auto dealership in a metro city is about a day or two. Sales agents of different banks are usually vying with each other to grab a share of the market by providing auto loans to prospective urban customers at the most competitive rates. That has been my experience too. When one of my acquaintances recently bought a car through an established car dealer in south Mumbai, even without reaching out for auto finance, a leading private sector bank called them through the auto dealership, undercutting the rate they were getting from their bank. So the competition is really intense. In a Tier 5 or 6 town[37] of India, that is not the case. First of all, there aren't many potential lenders in those geographies. The typical processing time is a week or more. For a customer belonging to that demography, such a service is quite acceptable because she is used to it. In fact, she might think that it should take a fortnight; and if a bank gets back in a week, it's fabulous! However, HDFC Bank wanted to change this perception and provide semi-urban customers the same experience as metro customers. For this, it used the document image scanning process in a reverse fashion, and reduced the loan processing time to a couple of days. This not only delighted the customers but also raised the bar of their expectations from banks. Sharing his perspective on the benefits of this to the real side of the economy, Paresh said, 'It actually means that by providing such credit access and service, the bank is helping create demand for cars or two wheelers in these areas. Given the traditional hassles involved in getting finances, these are customers who may not have opted for the purchase at all. In 1994, having ATMs, core banking systems and centralized systems was technology. Today, a lot of banks have ATMs and core banking systems. So what matters is how you've leveraged technology to provide the customer greater convenience, quicker turnaround times, lower error rates and smoother service.'

Managing Scale with Evolving Technologies

HDFC Bank brought in a lot of innovation for customer delight. One of their initial services called 'Insta alert', was a great success. With this service, whenever a customer used their debit/credit card at an external outlet or ATM, she would get an SMS within seconds stating that the card had been used at a particular outlet for a specific amount. One humorous outcome of this was that the element of surprise in shopping was lost. Many a time Ram received casual complaints that 'Insta alert' had instantly alerted the wife whenever the husband made a purchase, sometimes a surprise jewellery gift on a wedding anniversary! There were other problems as well. The volume of these transactions became so huge that the infrastructure was not able to keep up with the growth. So the other complaint was that customers were receiving messages at 2 a.m. about a purchase they had made at 6 p.m. Now this led to two complications. One was waking up the customer at an unearthly hour with a beep. Secondly, if the card was lost and had been misused by someone eight hours ago, the distraught customer came to know about it in the wee hours of the morning! So the growth was very good, but managing scale and delivering additional services became a challenge.

Nonetheless, this problem had to be solved. There was no going back on a product because numbers were on the rise and there was immense potential going forward. So the IT team, led by Ram, went back to the drawing board to study the source of this problem. The way this service worked was that the data file was given to an aggregator. The aggregator is the one who actually separated out the customer phone numbers based on service providers such as Vodafone or Airtel or BSNL, and then sent it along the way. So if the aggregator had a constraint, then that would impact the delivery time. Further, at the level of the service provider, i.e. if Vodafone had a problem in terms of the SMS gateway, then that would also impact the delivery of the message to the customer. So the IT team walked the entire process line to figure out the root cause of the problem, and finally realized that in many cases, the delay in generating messages was at the bank's end. While a customer went to the ATM and pulled out money, when did the bank generate the alert message about the transaction? So, a lot of remedial changes were made in the way the system was designed and developed. They also tried to understand a whole lot of infrastructure that helped in delivering the service to the customer.

Sharing the IT team's learning, Ram said, 'Our intentions are very good, but if our actions don't coincide with those intentions, then the effect cannot be as good as you expect it to be. The learning for us was that we never took anything for granted after that.' The bank team ensured that after the data file was released by them, they knew exactly how it was going to get delivered, and made sure that there was feedback about whether or not it was happening on time. So if there was a service level agreement stating that the message will be delivered within two minutes, the team made sure that they were measuring it at their end as well. Two decades later, the 'Insta alert' service is still provided by the bank.[38] The difference is that the two-minute lag time for the transaction information has reduced to two seconds. Having been a customer of HDFC Bank myself, I've seen this change. Now, even before the payment gateway processing is over, I get a message on my cell phone on the Harvard campus in Boston!

Managing scale with nascent technology and an evolving telecom network was a problem faced at the branch level. HDFC Bank was among the first few banks in India where a relationship manager could access all details about the customer on her system. There was no need to ask the customer for any details. With the centralized processing system, even tellers would be interacting with terminals to provide information to customers at their counter. So it was a great experience. However, there was a challenge to this. If the connectivity snapped either due to network issues or volume issues, the teller or relationship manager had no idea of who the customer was. In order to proactively solve the problem and avoid such situations, the bank maintained diverse routings and two different Internet connections in all major branches to ensure seamless connectivity with central servers even if one connection gave way. Ram shared, 'Every year we used to do a test with three times the projected volumes. So if there were infirmities in the system, we could correct those before the volumes were affected. We had a test bed on which we ran simulations. The I-flex[39] guys and our guys constantly worked on scaling the system. We didn't want to lose out. Our reputation was on the line.'

The Continuous Journey of Customer Service

'The winners in the banking industry will be those who establish relationships through actual points of contact and service, what you call as moments of truth. Not through advertising, but through actual contact, and through establishing in the minds of the customer as to this is what these people are'

—Aditya Puri

During the early years of the bank, there was once a demand for a very complex and IT-intensive product by one of their customers. After a lot of discussions with his team, Ram thought that it would not be possible to deliver. He went to Aditya's office and said, 'Aditya, this cannot be done. What they are asking for is too much.' After a momentary pause,

Aditya replied, 'I think the way you should look at this is, if we did this for him, he is my customer for life. Because if you are saying that it is complicated for you, it will be very difficult for somebody else to deliver it. And by providing this solution for the customer, we are creating an entry barrier.' After turning the tables on Ram with a lucid explanation of strategic customer service, he plainly said, 'So Ram, I leave it to you.' Needless to say, they went ahead and did the complex product for the customer. Ram shared, 'At HDFC Bank, the idea is that you don't always look at complexity. What is the business purpose? If it is going to do something of value for the customer and therefore, he perceives value in this relationship, the bank should do it, no matter how complicated it may be.' Through this and many such instances, the bank worked hard to be synonymous with customer service. In the banking world, where product and pricing are largely similar, Aditya always emphasizes that service is the key differentiator.[40]

Customer service is a continuous journey. It gets even more challenging for a bank like HDFC which grows at 25–30 per cent every year. It's quite a challenge to ensure that the 200 new branches added every year, or the existing 3500 branches, are all maintaining the same level of service. Further, the concept of service differs for different segments of customers. A retired person may want to spend ten minutes interacting with people and hence she comes to a branch. For a busy executive, seamless access online or through the smart phone is customer service. To cater to these changing requirements of customers and definitions of customer service, the bank started offering the full scale of net banking on the mobile platform. To capture this ever-changing situation, Aditya humorously observed, 'Customer is like your wife. Her expectations change every day. *'Wife ko naraaz karoge toh khana nahi milega!'* (If you upset your wife, you won't be fed.) So, you better keep adjusting!'[41]

The customer relationship is a natural outflow of the level of service consistently delivered over a period of time. For every new customer who comes in, and for every new transaction for the same customer, the standards have to be met. Over the last two decades, the bank has gone a long way in terms of multiple channels of delivery, 24/7 online real-time connectivity, core banking solutions, offering customer relationship pricing through analytical marketing and much more. 'All of those ultimately boil down to what happens at that moment of truth when the customer actually comes in. It is not static at some point, not something at which you reach and say I have conquered this. Customer service is a journey. And to be brutally honest, we still believe that we have a fair distance to go in this,' shared Paresh candidly.

Challenges with respect to customer service are varied. They could be in terms of how the bank communicates with the customer and creates expectations. There could be gaps between what the bank is providing and what the customer understands. Sometimes there are charges of mis-selling where the customer might believe she did not understand a particular product. There are occasions when a customer doesn't agree with the bank's stand. There are bound to be customer service issues relating to customers who are defaulting. In such cases, even if the bank follows the rule book to try and recover money, there could be differences of opinion. Then there are products such as credit cards—highly transactional products—where there are high chances of vulnerabilities or occasions where there can be a slip up in terms of customer service. The real challenge comes when some customers try to beat the system and figure out ways to put the bank on the back foot.

The solution to this has been two-fold. First is institutionalization of processes and increasing the levels of automation. Secondly, with the ever-increasing number of branches and several thousand new employees added every year, the bank focuses on employee training. The first aspect of this training is to understand the products. However, an equally important aspect is to understand the value of customer service for the bank. This dual approach is important because innovation and customer service need not be about completely new products. In the past, some of the really innovative banking products have caused serious problems for banks globally. So instead, delivering, structuring, repackaging and customization of the service for that particular segment is the key. Aditya accentuated the type of innovation HDFC Bank likes to focus on: 'We may not do what is called "sexy innovation", where we don't understand the risk. But innovation within the market that we want to access and the needs of the customers I think we do very well. And that includes backing it up with exceptional service quality and a low cost.'[42]

Then there are occasions when customer service means none of this. It means being there for the customer when she needs the bank to provide something that was not in the normal course of business. Yet, what mattered was how well the bank helped the customer at that point of time. That defines the strength of the relationship between the two. To elaborate on this, Samir shared the anecdote of the flagship company of a very large business house that posted massive losses in a particular year. HDFC Bank was probably the only bank in that year which went and offered a significantly large line of credit to that company. In the subsequent year, that company turned around really well. In all the years thereafter the customer always remembered that the bank stood by it during its direst hour of need, when virtually everyone else had walked away. 'Now that beats any amount of customer service or product that the bank would ever be able to provide. You can devise a sophisticated product but it will still not match the fact that you were able to stick with the customer when the customer really needed you. So I think those are the things the customers remember really well. That is what really defines the strength of the bank in terms of customer service.'

Managing Risks, Not Taking Them

Paresh has been a part of the bank's risk management team right from the early years. He shared his conviction of the vital importance of risk management: 'If you look at the history of banks who haven't done well, it's not because they had poor customer service or they failed in terms of technology. It is typically because they blew up their portfolio quality. So clearly, one of the critical success factors for any bank is defining the risk parameters appropriate to its own strategy and risk appetite, and then ensuring that it has appropriate risk management practices.' Since the early years, HDFC Bank has built a team of risk management professionals, which assures that loan origination, approval and disbursement processes are separated from each other. Popularly known as the 'three initials system', every loan from HDFC Bank has to be approved by two persons other than the banker who engages with the borrower. Thus, three individuals vested with the credit approving authority verify every loan proposal. 'Since the risk manager has no revenue goals, he can make an independent decision without any conflict of interest, and judge the loan based on its merits,' Paresh shared with me. The bank's seriousness about asset quality can be gauged from the fact that the risk staff don't report to business heads. All information about risk converges at Aditya's level. This process also creates a constructive tension. 'We have a clear system. Any portfolio exhibiting signs of delinquency or delayed payments not in line with the programme is slowed or cut down,' observed Aditya.

For example, the bank made an early exit from small ticket personal loans where the industry suffered huge losses after the 2008 slowdown. It also first started offering credit cards to its existing customers, and that too after a detailed analysis of their creditworthiness. In later years, it had limited exposure to infrastructure loans (about 3–4 per cent when compared to three to four times that as prevalent in the Indian banking industry), a major cause of stress and asset quality in many banks, especially in the public sector. Kaizad Bharucha, executive director at HDFC Bank, reasoned, 'It was difficult to evaluate all the components that go into infrastructure projects.'[43] Among the corporates, the bank sticks to the top tier, which has cushion and experience. Even among these, the caution of the bank is obvious. 'If you have a power project and you have never done a power project in your life, then I don't think my margins provide me sufficient cover to take that kind of risk. Also, if you do not have coal supply, I won't lend to you. Put yourself in my place. If a mithaiwallah (sweet-meat maker) wants to set up a new biscuits factory, are you going to lend?' asserted Aditya.[44]

Samir recalled the kind of leadership and commitment that Aditya provided to the core team to maintain high standards for the fledgling bank: 'My first lesson in the bank came in the early days when there was a gentleman who was a very dear friend of Mr Puri. He was a very wealthy individual and used to come and have tea with him every week.' One day, Samir got a call from the clearing department that this gentleman had issued a cheque, but there was no money in the account. 'Would you like to clear the cheque?' they asked him. This was a standard policy for all corporate customers where the department would call the concerned executive empowered to take such decisions. 'If we were comfortable that the company would fund the money the next day or had the resources, then we would honour the cheque,' shared Samir. This was a kind of customer service. Every day, the bank would get 20–30 cheques of this type. In some cases, cheques would be passed based on clients' credentials. In some cases, the client would be called to confirm the clearance. In the case of this cheque from Aditya's 'friend', Samir thought to himself, 'I know this man comes in fancy cars. He has a lot of money. If I honour it, he will surely repay it.' He thought that if he dishonoured the cheque, Aditya may be unhappy. Besides, it was a matter of customer service, and the client had the capacity to pay. So there wasn't any risk for the bank either. With these thoughts in his mind, he honoured the cheque. Later, when he went to Aditya's office, he explained the situation and said, 'I helped your friend today.' With a plain face Aditya replied, 'I have no friends.' Samir was aghast! He thought he would earn Aditya's appreciation. Instead he learnt a lesson: 'I knew that genuinely when it came to matters of principle and to matters of the bank's interest, there are no friends.' Customer service was never at the cost of the institution's interest. Managing risk was the paramount responsibility.[45]

Empowering 5 Crore Lives in the Indian Hinterland

'If every company would aim at making 10 million families self-sufficient, there would be no poverty. I think that's a major goal of this organization'

—Aditya Puri

The acquisition of the Centurion Bank of Punjab (CBoP) marked the beginning of HDFC Bank's increasing presence and focus on semi-urban and interior areas. The Bank of Punjab had a dominant presence in the hinterland. As shared earlier, Lord Krishna Bank, which merged with CBoP in 2005, had acquired three banks during the 1960s—Kerala Union Bank, Thiyya Bank and Josna Bank. It had a substantial presence in the state of Kerala. Both these banks added about 40 per cent additional branches to the existing network of HDFC Bank, and also gave a product range that was more suitable to semi-urban and rural customers.

Due to a social and regulatory mandate in India, 40 per cent of a domestic bank's loan book is focused on priority sector lending (PSL).[46] PSL is an important role given to banks by the RBI for providing a specified portion of the bank lending to specific sectors like agriculture and allied activities, micro and small enterprises, and specific sections like poor people for housing, students for education and other low income groups. These sectors may not get timely and adequate credit in the absence of such a mandatory arrangement. Almost all banks have a PSL department to achieve annual targets that need to be reported to the RBI and other regulatory authorities. However, from around 2008, HDFC Bank did not have a separate PSL department. Instead, in every single business—corporate, retail, SME or the emerging corporates group—the bank identified businesses, segments and customers that would fall within the priority sector categories. Paresh shared the bank's differentiated approach to PSL: 'We have figured our approach as the only sustainable way of doing PSL. Otherwise you have a focused department, where you go and find out one more opportunity to lend, do it and that's the end of it. Then you are looking for next year's opportunities. The purpose behind the target is lost.' Right from the beginning, HDFC Bank distinguished between financial access and financial inclusion.[47] Aditya often emphasized, 'You give a poor woman a consumption loan. Before, she was a poor woman with no loan. Now (after the loan) she is a poor woman with loan.'[48] While financial access meant opening bank accounts for the rural populace, financial inclusion for the bank meant economic empowerment leading to a life of self-respect and dignity.

In order to achieve the latter, in 2009, the bank launched the Sustainable Livelihood Initiative (SLI). Through this, it reached out to unbanked and under-banked segments of the population with the objective of providing them livelihood finance. Over the last decade and more, increasing levels of literacy, access to information and communication technology, and a number of government programmes at the state and Central levels, have marginally increased the levels of disposable income among the rural and semi-urban masses, thereby improving the demand for basic facilities and products. With a little support, vocational training and financial assistance, a lot could be done to make the rural youth (constituting one-third of the total Indian population) economically self-sufficient. The SLI attempted to do just that. Just like many other banks, it also lent to microfinance institutions (MFIs). Yet, it also lent to self-help groups (SHGs) and joint liability groups (JLGs). Apart from the actual lending activity, SLI contributed towards financing the formation of these groups and their training. An integrated approach of offering capacity building, enhancing occupation skills, providing credit counselling, financial literacy, facilitating sales efforts and market linkages was implemented. The bank believed that a combination of these could make the rural population economically independent and bring them into the banking fold.

According to the Government of India's 2011 census, only 58.7 per cent households utilized formal banking services. According to CRISIL,[49] 37.8 per cent in the southern region and 71.4 per cent in the eastern region had no access to formal banking facilities. For many decades, financial inclusion initiatives aimed at opening banking accounts, especially in the rural areas. In fact, the PSBs received mandates to open accounts in the unbanked and under-banked regions of India. And they did, thousands of them. But there were hardly any transactions. The high-powered Nachiket Mor Committee on Comprehensive Financial Services for Small Businesses and Low-Income Households, set up by the RBI, found that 60 per cent of the rural and urban population in India did not have a functional bank account.[50] The reason being that along with the account opening, it was also essential that the rural customers had a sustainable banking need.

Most often, the loans were not for income-generating activities, but for consumption requirements such as marriage of children. And eventually, due to lack of sustained sources of income, these were written-off, thereby making banking in rural areas a loss-making endeavour. Contrasting with this, the SLI aimed at encouraging the habit of savings through financial literacy. This was in the form of cultivating a habit of saving the money received. Paresh highlighted the virtuous cycle that the SLI approach created: 'An integrated approach helps the individual who is borrowing, because you are also helping her to improve her ability to repay by supporting her earning capacity. This in turn also has a positive impact on her ability to service the loan, and therefore on the bank's asset quality.' The bank envisioned this win-win approach of contributing to society at large by having a well-integrated strategy within the regular course of banking.

Figure 2.7: Differentiating Traditional Banking and Purpose-oriented Banking

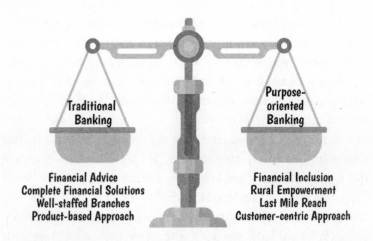

At an operational level, the SLI reached out to 20 lakh households across thousands of villages in twenty-four states pan-India, through 439 rural business hubs attached to the bank's branches. The average ticket size of loans was between Rs 10,000 and Rs 25,000. Interestingly, 100 per cent of SLI customers were women. By 2016, the bank aimed to help

5 crore individuals from 1 crore rural households to rise above the poverty line.[51] Underlining the success of the SLI, the bank reported that through the SLI, rural women availed credit and utilized it for occupations like tailoring, designing jewellery, starting grocery shops and grazing goats. They also sought to take advantage of services such as credit counselling, occupation skills enhancement and connecting with markets. The SLI also linked rural people with mainstream banking facilities and substantively eliminated the role of middlemen and moneylenders who charged usurious rates of interest on small ticket loans to the ill-informed rural folk.[52] Along with the SLI, the bank also planned a conscious spread of its presence in the semi-urban and rural areas. In 2013, 53 per cent of the bank's 3251 branches were in semi-urban and rural areas, up from 34 per cent in 2010. In 2012 alone, 88 per cent of the bank's branches were opened in unbanked markets.[53] 'It may be by 2020, but through this initiative, we would have really altered lives,' affirmed Aditya.[54, 55]

Figure 2.8: A Rural Branch of HDFC Bank

Bank Aapki Mutthi Mein: Embarking on a Digital Strategy

In the decade between 2004 and 2014, there was a sea change in the media through which customers transacted with banks. ATMs that accounted for more than half the total transactions in 2004, were no longer the most preferred medium. Phone and branch banking preferences had also halved in the ten years. With a super tech-savvy generation, Internet and mobile banking accounted for more than half of customers' total transactions with the bank. By November 2015, this increased to 68 per cent.

Figure 2.9: Changing Customer Preferences in a Single Decade

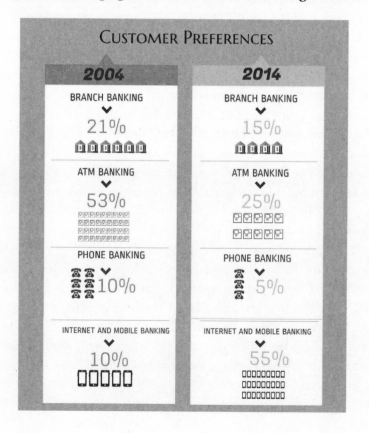

One major reason for exponential growth in ICT-based banking is the quantum leap in access to the Internet and mobile phone pan-India during this decade. India emerged as one of the fastest growing telecom markets in the world, particularly in mobile telephony, with the second largest network in the world after China. The overall tele-density[56] in India increased from 9.08 per cent in 2005 to 73.5 per cent in 2013. The tele-density in urban areas was 145.35 per cent vs 41.9 per cent in rural areas. According to the Telephone Regulatory Authority of India (TRAI), the subscriber base in India almost doubled from 562.16 million in December 2009 to 903.09 million in June 2013. The most astonishing growth was a 40x increase in the number of Internet subscribers, from 5.3 million in March 2005 to 198.39 million by June 2013. The picture continues to be increasingly rosy. According to 2014 estimates, the number of mobile Internet users is expected to rise from about 130 million in 2014 to 900 million by 2025.[57] Given these attractive assessments, it's unsurprising that the prudent bank sensed that the time was ripe to embark on a digital strategy and make the most of this transition.

In November 2014, Aditya visited Silicon Valley, home to the world's largest tech companies like Apple, eBay, Facebook and Google. Since Silicon Valley commentators were predicting digital disruptions in the global banking industry, Aditya was keen to study high-tech innovations and disruptive technologies that could find application in the Indian BFSI. Among many others, he visited MasterCard Innovations, Khosla Ventures, Singtel Technologies and Silicon Valley Bank. In October 2014, Apple launched its mobile payment solution 'Apple Pay' in the US and some other markets. This new product allowed contactless payment through the iPhone 6 in merchant establishments.[58] Aditya also included a visit to Apple Inc. in his itinerary. He observed that the so-called 'digital disruptions' were largely in four broad areas: faster loans (for example, loans.com); convenient payments on e-commerce (for example, Apple Pay); mobile-to-mobile payments substituting cash (for example, AliPay); and remote advisory using analytics. All of these were not creating a bank, but were riding 'over the top' of the banking system. The customer and the payment platform were that of the banks. All they created were applications using networks and information to provide convenience at an attractive price point.[59]

On his return, he discussed with his core team and decided that before these technologies 'disrupt' the bank's business model, the bank would launch a digital strategy. In 2001 itself, when retail banking was at a low, HDFC Bank had set up a data warehouse. The objective was to study consumer behaviour with respect to purchases, frequency, geography and demographics. The idea was to get to know customers better than they know themselves.[60] Fifteen years later, this back-end system acted as its greatest strength. The bank had all the ingredients of success in its digital strategy: 3.27 crore customers, advanced data warehouse technology and analytics for a better understanding of retail consumer behaviour. The only requirement was the creation of 'Apps' to integrate sales, credit and operating processes, for creating a delightfully digital customer experience.[61] 'The network [telecom, social media and digital] has allowed us to change the business model completely by removing the need for physical transfer of documents. It creates information around your customers that, if analysed, can improve customer segmentation and help us deliver more relevant products to customers,' observed Puri.[62] This was the beginning of the bank's transformative journey based on a digital strategy. With an integrated nationwide brand campaign, '*Har zaroorat poori ho chutki mein, bank aapki mutthi mein,*'[63] (Fulfilling all customer needs with the snap of a finger; the bank at your fingertips) it launched a number of innovative digital products over the next one year. Some of these were first in India, probably 'a global first' as well.

Among the digital innovations, 'the ten-second loan' was included. The bank offered a personal loan in ten seconds to existing customers based on a back-end analysis of their creditworthiness. A car loan was processed in thirty minutes. There was also an instant 'top-up' car loan. The bank also set up 'Smartbuy', an online shopping portal connected to its website. Through this portal, HDFC Bank customers could book airline tickets, confirm hotel reservations, and even buy products and services from renowned retail brands through the bank's debit and credit cards or even the direct account payment options. Not only were these products available at a substantial discount to HDFC Bank customers, but buying on Smartbuy gave them an opportunity to earn purchase points and cash-back offers. This was a win-win for the bank because of its inherent advantage in this area, as 50 per cent online payment gateways belonged to HDFC Bank and 37 per cent e-commerce transactions in India were through its debit and credit cards.[64]

In the year 2015, the bank also launched two mobile-based applications: 'Chillr' and 'PayZapp'. Within a year, both of them achieved 1 million downloads each on the Apple App Store and Google Play Store. The Chillr App was developed by a Kochi-based start-up who had approached thirteen other banks in India for selling their product. They were lucky the fourteenth time when the 'much nimbler' HDFC Bank partnered with the app-makers and became the first to provide it to their customers. Though not a virtual wallet, the Chillr App allows customers to instantly send money to anyone by using their mobile phone book. Sharing his vision of the app, Nitin Chugh, head of digital banking at the bank, said, 'Going forward, we see the use of Chillr accelerating, which is in line with the overall trend of the bank leveraging different digital banking platforms to provide access and convenience to customers.'[65] The other super-successful Payzapp, introduced in June 2015, was a complete 'wallet payment' solution for retail products, grocery shopping and flight tickets. Smartbuy was also available on PayZapp. It thus became a one-stop shop on the consumer mobile for purchases across segments. Its USP was the one-click payment solution advantage as compared to a traditional credit card.

Building on its digital focus, the bank hosted a Digital Innovation Summit in March 2016. It invited tech start-ups with a solution catering to the BFSI, to present their solutions to its leadership team, and for exploring exciting partnerships with technologies of the future. Some of the areas included branch automation, payments, customer service and experience, digital and mobile banking, social banking, social platforms, operational efficiency, cyber security, risk, fraud and collections.[66] From the thirty that presented their ideas, the bank selected five fin-tech start-ups to use the bank's platforms and provide their innovative fin-tech solutions to its customers.[67] According to some estimates, the payments market is a \$500 billion (Rs 35 lakh-crore) opportunity if merchant, government and utility payments, and national and international remittances were included. To increase its share in this pie, HDFC Bank is responding slowly and systematically.

Attracting the Right Talent

'While some of us may have been the face of the bank because we have been there for longer, the bank is really all about the 60,000 people that have come along the way'

—Paresh Sukthankar, deputy managing director,
HDFC Bank

Business Today's 9th Best Employer Survey 2011 listed HDFC Bank as India's 10th best company to work for. Its closest competitor, ICICI Bank, was ranked 19th. By 2016, nearly 80,000 young and dynamic bankers worked every single day to accomplish the bank's vision of being a 'world-class Indian bank'. While it had all the best practices that modern MNCs have, including employee development and training, rewards and recognition, and of course, the most attractive of all—ESOPs,[68] what really attracted budding talent from India to join HDFC Bank?

In my interactions with the senior management at the bank, I grasped that the main expectations of employees joining the bank included career and personal growth, rewards and recognition, an exciting work environment, an inspiring mission, and the desire to feel important and part of the organization. Aditya personally emphasized on two: good working conditions and good career. He said, 'If you think only of squeezing them and not looking after their career development and their needs, and giving them a clean and professional environment to work in, you will not be left with the best employees in today's competitive world. And your business will be finished.'

Right from its formative days, the primary people philosophy at the bank has been that if there is an opportunity that is available within the bank, it should be given to somebody from within, rather than give it outside. When the bank spots good talent, even if the employee is inexperienced, he or she would still be given that opportunity, sufficient power to accomplish the work in that profile, and allowed to grow in that job. Aditya emphasized this aspect: 'It has largely been our policy that when we have people from within, we don't go outside. And we take risks on our own people.' HDFC Bank has functional rotation focused on building up people from within.[69] Employee empowerment and giving budding talent the opportunity to grow within the bank are major attractions for being at HDFC. This is one reason why, over the years, people grew very rapidly within the bank—from branch relationship managers to branch managers, to cluster heads and beyond. While the businesses grew, the people associated with them also grew.

Isn't an attractive pay package a reason for being part of the bank? Samir retorted, 'You did not have to pay people more because they knew that if they continued to work here, they were going to grow so rapidly that money would follow. And those who were working for money left, because this wasn't the place for them.' The bank never paid as highly as others did. 'You know, when I joined the bank, it was a flat salary, with no increment, not a penny! Not only that—I was earlier living in Citibank accommodation. I gave that up and relocated to Santacruz to my own house. So I actually gave up much to be a part of the bank. A lot of people who came, came for growth and for the joy of creating something. The moment you join a company for the right reasons, there is no reason why that company should not be successful,' Samir added. Over a period of time, the bank's compensation levels have been appropriately benchmarked with industry standards. Growth opportunities, professional work environment and fair compensation have made it an attractive employment option for budding talent.

Balancing Employee Expectations

'Measurement is integral to HDFC Bank. Nothing goes unmeasured within the organization'
—Philip Mathew, chief people officer, HDFC Bank

While the bank expanded from a few dozen employees in 1995 to over 76,000 in 2015, there have been challenges. Primary among these is expectation management. Since those recruited come from different backgrounds, their expectations from the bank are also varied. Hence, managing these varied expectations is a major challenge. The other is ensuring consistent employee performance—the need to keep doing better and better in the competitive environment of the BFSI. Summing up these two, Philip Mathew, now chief people officer at the bank, said, 'To understand expectations of employees and getting these aligned with the organizational expectations and mission is a major challenge in today's times.'

The other challenge for the highly competitive BFSI is attrition. Gone are the days when a bank job was a dream job that one sought right after graduation and continued to hold till retirement. The post-liberalization generation is not looking for lifetime commitment with a particular company. As a result, a certain level of attrition has become part of any business, more so in the service industry. Indian companies have learnt to live with that. Increasingly they focused on role clarity and detailed job descriptions, fair performance appraisals and attractive compensation packages benchmarked with the best in industry. Besides this, regular opportunity for training and adequate growth prospects if the person performs, can go a long way in ensuring that employees continue in the firm. Despite all of this, high performers and high potential candidates are poached for better opportunities. So how did HDFC Bank deal with this?

I asked Paresh, who represents the HR function on the bank's board. He said, 'I think you can moderate the levels and impact of attrition by making your selection process more thorough in terms of selecting the right people, inducting and training them appropriately, ensuring high comfort levels with the organization and then fair rewards, recognition and career progression. In spite of this, there will be people who will move on, and this creates opportunities for others to grow. Obviously, every time somebody goes, you are losing out in terms of the training that you've invested, or some of the experienced staff that you had. But I think we are a young organization. We have grown by hiring people from different institutions as well. So we cannot grudge having a certain level of attrition.' The bank does take corrective measures whenever there is higher than acceptable levels of attrition in a particular function, geography or level.

Not surprisingly, performance orientation has become the core of HDFC Bank culture. It is ubiquitous across the bank. I was amazed with the variety of processes for almost everything. Right at the beginning of each year, the bank put into place a number of key performance indicators (KPIs) that were number-oriented vital parameters, tracked day after day, month after month, year after year.

About 70–80 per cent of remuneration, transfer and promotion, was based on this transparent system. Didn't this stifle creativity and innovation, I asked. Aditya explained, 'When an organization becomes large and you have decentralized decision-making, then the parameters within which you have to take decisions are specified. And everything has to be a process, whether it is sales, marketing, audit or product development. Otherwise you cannot have a professional assessment of performance. You have to have job descriptions for people, have goals, and give them processes which everybody in the organization understands. The processes don't have to be rigid. They have to be flexible to meet the expectations of customers. Without base processes nothing will work, including corporate governance.'

Figure 2.10: The Culture of Process Orientation at HDFC Bank

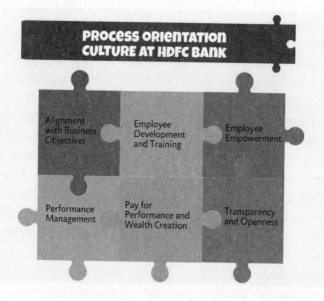

Adding to this, Aditya passionately stressed on the aspect of transparency: 'Every HDFC employee knows that there can't be any pressure on him to do anything wrong, against the regulations and his professional judgement. This is happening daily. Anywhere the customer goes, he will see this. Nobody will think of offering money to anyone in HDFC Bank to get things done because he will probably be thrown out. It's not my statement alone. It has become a part of the bank's DNA.'

A Leadership Machine

'If people are not hiring from you to make them CEOs, you don't have a good management team'

—Aditya Puri

Since the bank started twenty years ago, only two of the founding members are still part of the senior team—Aditya Puri and Paresh Sukthankar—the MD–deputy MD duo. There are some like Vinod Yennemadi, country head (finance and taxation), A. Rajan, country head (operations), Harish Engineer (executive director) and G. Subramanian, head (internal controls and compliance risk), who remained with the bank since inception till their retirement in the last few years. Then there were others who joined the bank's core team, excelled during their years at the bank and then accepted senior positions in other institutions. The HDFC Bank success story attracted the best banking and financial services institutions to look for members from the core HDFC team.

In 2000, Shailendra Bhandari, who built the treasury business for HDFC Bank, left to become CEO and president of ICICI Prudential Life Insurance Company.[70] Luis Miranda, one of the founding members of HDFC Bank, founded IDFC Private Equity in 2002 and served as its MD and CEO. In 2006, Samir Bhatia, head of corporate and SME banking, went on to become managing director, Barclays Global Retail & Commercial Bank (India and Indian Ocean).[71] Other noteworthy exits included Neeraj Swaroop, head of retail and consumer banking at HDFC Bank, who became the CEO of Standard Chartered (India) in 2005.[72] He is credited with developing the bank's network of 475 branches in over 200 cities, employing over 6000 people in a matter of six years. H. Srikrishnan, head of transactional banking and operations from 1997 to 2004, left to become executive director at Yes Bank. In 2012, Pralay Mondal, head of retail business, also left to become senior group president of retail and business banking at Yes Bank.

Each of these bankers got a fine opportunity to contribute to the growth story of HDFC Bank. Their experience and competence was rewarded. In return, the bank's high performance ethos and culture of transparency and ethics complemented their profile as individuals who could lead banking institutions on growth trajectories. In this light, HDFC Bank resembles an HUL in the Indian BFSI. Today, most of the leading private sector banks have senior members of their core teams who have been part of the HDFC story at some point of their career. The bank and its leadership have played a role in developing their potential. As the cone on the top got narrower, they moved on—a win-win for them, for the bank, and for the Indian banking system as a whole.

Figure 2.11: HDFC Bank: A Leadership Machine

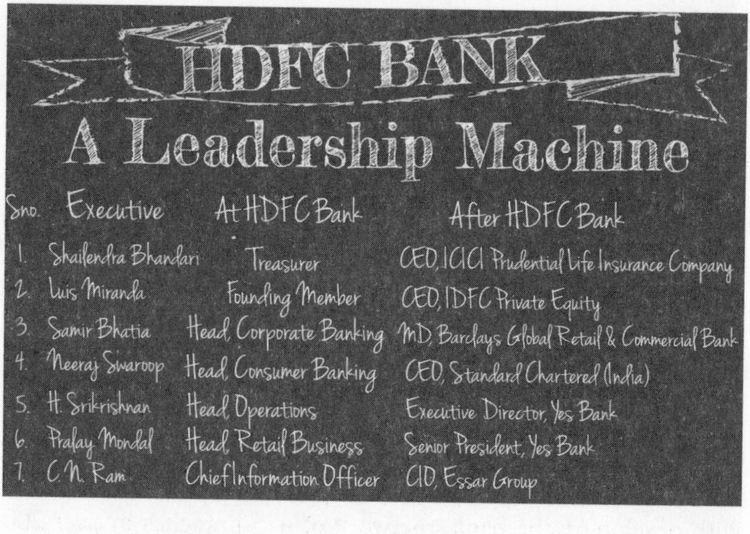

HDFC BANK
A Leadership Machine

Sno.	Executive	At HDFC Bank	After HDFC Bank
1.	Shailendra Bhandari	Treasurer	CEO, ICICI Prudential Life Insurance Company
2.	Luis Miranda	Founding Member	CEO, IDFC Private Equity
3.	Samir Bhatia	Head, Corporate Banking	MD, Barclays Global Retail & Commercial Bank
4.	Neeraj Swaroop	Head, Consumer Banking	CEO, Standard Chartered (India)
5.	H. Srikrishnan	Head, Operations	Executive Director, Yes Bank
6.	Pralay Mondal	Head, Retail Business	Senior President, Yes Bank
7.	C. N. Ram	Chief Information Officer	CIO, Essar Group

Aditya Puri's Leadership Formula

'The leader can be compared to the head, but all other limbs of the body have to function as well'

—Aditya Puri

In my conversation with Aditya, I asked him about the critical success factors for the leader of a bank. He shared three distinct points: 'I should provide the vision, teamwork and walk the talk. I should be a leader and not a dictator. I have to ensure that every person understands the vision and believes in the values that we stand for, and we deliver what we promise. This can only be done by a management structure which is decentralized with clear job descriptions, and the front office being backed by the back office.' These three points form the core of his leadership mantra. And in his four-decade long career in the BFSI, his colleagues and employees have seen these manifest in diverse ways.

'I've known Aditya since he was a corporate relationship manager at Citibank,' shared Samir. 'He would be the only person leaving at 5.30 p.m., when everybody would be working past midnight. I used to see him do his call reports, his credit appraisal memos, annual renewal of facilities for companies. We had to write twenty-page reports on company management, industry outlook, financials, etc. A normal relationship manager would take 3–4 days to actually sit, open various files, refer to them and write. There was no computer in those days. You had to write or type, and it was quite a painstaking process. But Aditya would have his secretary sit before him; he would stand and say, "Type." The entire fifteen-page proposal from start to finish would be dictated in two hours. It was done and he would walk away. His understanding, grasp, recollection and ability to reproduce was so phenomenal that he did not have to sit for longer hours.'

Aditya Puri's corporate journey from his days at the Kandivali office of M&M to the HDFC Bank house office is well known. Yet, the important insight is that his leadership style has been consistent. Even while at Citibank, he used to tell his employees, 'If you're sitting beyond 5.30 p.m. to impress me, then don't, because by then, I'll be gone.'[73] Sharing his approach to work–life balance, Aditya told me, 'If you can't get the balance between work and relaxation, and if you don't understand that without giving you can't have a successful life, then you're in trouble. I am into gardening, golf, trekking, experimenting with furniture, helping children go to school, helping people start their business, and lots more. That is my relaxation and pleasure.'

Aditya has been a hands-on leader. While at a branch, he would personally talk to customers and make sure they were happy. If a customer was loitering around looking lost, he'd call and ask what they wanted. By personal example, he led from the front. Interestingly, he's a managing director who doesn't have a system to touch, but received the award for being the most tech-savvy CEO! It's well known in the industry that he doesn't use a cell phone and doesn't check his emails himself. Even a confirmation and follow-up for my meeting with him on his email was responded to by Goretti, his secretary. So, how does he balance these dichotomies? 'He's like the typical guy who doesn't have to understand anything about a car, but knows how to drive it really well,' said Ram, who executed the bank's IT vision during the first dozen years.

'Aditya was the guy who drove very well. He had the best kind of people assembling things for him. So his job was to make sure that he understood the purpose of technology, and made his team utilize it to the hilt.' He ensured that it was used well for customer service, MIS, risk mitigation, transparency, governance—the list is quite endless. But the underlying focus was always operational efficiency. While he wanted automation to make a difference to customers, he wasn't impractical. When a competing private bank initiated schemes like, 'Before your coffee gets cold, your account gets opened,' Aditya was against over-commitment. Sashi Jagadishan, chief financial officer at the bank, observed that the hallmark of Aditya's management style was his clarity of thought, quick decision-making and his ability to keep things simple. 'He may sound like a tough boss but he has a kind heart if there are no issues related to integrity and attitude at the workplace.'[74]

'Aditya is not a guy who'll control day-to-day stuff. But if necessary, he'll get into depth because he knows exactly how things will work,' recalled Ram. He would often say, 'I'm a very simple guy. I can't understand complicated things. So can you explain to me in one, two, three points?' 'And when you're on the second point you realize that Aditya has a point. Why are we complicating this?' confessed Ram. By the third point, the narrator would have completely catapulted to Aditya's point of view. 'He's a great guy at making you do whatever he wants,' smiled Ram. On the other hand, he has also been an extremely hard taskmaster. He gave opportunities to experiment, and stood by his people even when mistakes were made if he knew that a decision was taken in the right spirit and with the right thought process. 'But if you do not do your job, or wilfully default in doing your duty, then there's no person as difficult as him,' admitted Samir.

During our conversation, Aditya was very emphatic about the need for building the right organization culture and the need for very strong, deterrent action for deviant behaviour. 'There are certain things which employees should not do. If they do any of that, they're removed. No discussion. No apologies. At the initiation stage itself, employees are told that these are things they should not do. You fool around with the customer, you are rude, you share passwords, you don't follow the key processes, and you are out,' he asserted. He was very clear that the bank could not have a hypocritical culture. 'You can't say one thing and do another thing. If you do so, you will be caught in a week. You have to believe in it, you have to follow it through to the last detail and you have to enforce it.' His colleagues shared that Aditya's approach to ethics was very straightforward. He would say, 'You succumb once to unethical behaviour, and they've got you.' So in the nicest possible way, he would avoid people who had such expectations from the bank. Once he knew that the purpose of calling or wanting to see him was for seeking favours, political or otherwise, he'd keep them all at arm's length. He wouldn't take their calls! To get his personal time for a one-on-one meeting was well-nigh impossible. With such an approach, he set the tone at the top. He backed it up by carefully choosing people for the bank who had a similar kind of mentality and value system.

'Only money and only success cannot provide you happiness. What you get by taking and taking is just greed. The day you learn to give is the day when you start learning to be happy,' shared Aditya during our conversation. I realized that at the core of this visionary leader was a good human being. 'If you want to live a happy life, you have to help the downtrodden. You have to understand that you have been given a position which is a confluence of your own capability and the grace of God. You must use that position to exemplify to others what has to be followed.' On being listed among the top ten most powerful CEOs in 2013 by the *Economic Times*,[75] Puri said, 'Power means very little, except for the ability to bring about beneficial change in society. Otherwise, I like to be first among equals.'

The Way Forward

Figure 2.12: The Strategic Evolution at HDFC Bank

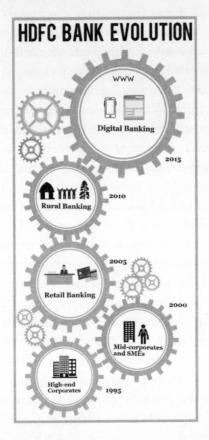

In recent times, start-ups are hailed as the next big success story for India. On reflection I realized that HDFC Bank was also a 'start-up' about two decades ago. A dozen top bankers left their careers with MNC banks to make a difference in India by starting a 'world-class Indian bank'. The secret to its success was evolving with changing times. HDFC Bank consistently and successfully reinvented itself. While the initial years were focused on high-end corporate clients, the turn of the century saw its portfolio expand to include mid-corporate and SME clients. It successfully tapped the challenging retail banking segment. From there, the journey continued through rural banking to the Indian hinterland—attempting to socially and economically empower 5 crore under-banked Indians. When digital banking came knocking on India's doors, the bank was among the first to once again reinvent itself to make the most of the opportunity. While IT remained the undercurrent at every level, it continued to change its operating model, and not just the front-end products, thereby creating win-win solutions in different markets, for diverse segments and through varied platforms.

'The IT part of the bank is only an enabler. Nobody can win an award just because you are IT-savvy. Every other part of the bank, whether it is operations, risk or HR, are all there to help it grow responsibly, quickly and be the trusted lender for the public. The more customers you acquire, the more successful you are. The more your branch network expands, the more people you reach. For all means we have been successful in achieving the vision of being a "world-class Indian bank",' affirmed Ram. While competitors tried to expand at a rapid pace, HDFC Bank took the cautious route, wherein size and market share took a back seat and the bottom line was carefully maintained. Today, the bank is one of the top three in most of the segments it operates in.

The bank's culture for learning, quick absorption of the latest and best technologies and adherence to best practices in governance has been its core strengths. 'The sheer humility of the organizational culture makes it a company that employees and customers love,' shared Samir.

With its remarkable growth trajectory, how would the bank be in the coming decade? Paresh shared HDFC Bank's Vision

2020: 'We'll continue to be in the business of meeting customer expectations, delighting them with better service using people and technology. If customer needs would have evolved, we would also have kept abreast. I think we'd be much bigger, with a larger market share because we're growing faster than the system. And we would continue to create value for our customers, employees, shareholders and the community at large.'

Figure 2.13: Win-Win Learnings from HDFC Bank

LESSONS FROM
HDFC BANK

1. CUSTOMER FOR LIFE

Building and nurturing customer
relationships is a continuous
journey

2. GLOBAL BENCHMARKING

Learning from international best
practices to achieve world-class
service standards

3. CUSTOMER-CENTRIC INNOVATION

Continuous product, process and
service innovation is the key to
customer delight

4. BE AHEAD OF THE CURVE

Evolve strategies with emerging
opportunities in diverse markets,
platforms and products

5. RESPONSIBLE GROWTH

Prudent focus on profits rather
than risky and mindless
expansion

6. PURPOSE-ORIENTED BANKING

Leverage business opportunities
for economic and social
empowerment of urban and
rural communities

III.

Larsen & Toubro Construction

Building India . . . Through Imagineering

'Fifty years ago, when I joined Larsen & Toubro, it was a Rs 5-crore company. Today, it's a Rs 1 lakh-crore complex group. This 2000 times growth has come without deviating from our main theme that we shall work for our nation. In whatever we do, our theme is to build a powerful India'[1]

—Anil Manibhai Naik, chairman, Larsen & Toubro Ltd

In October 2002, Larsen & Toubro (L&T) bagged a Rs 115 crore contract from Lafarge[2] Surma Cement[3] in Bangladesh for the construction of a 17-kilometre long cross-border conveyor belt connecting Lafarge Surma's proposed 12-lakh-tonne cement unit in Chhatak (northeast Bangladesh) with limestone reserves from mines in the East Khasi Hills of Meghalaya (India). L&T's Engineering, Construction and Contracts (ECC) division was to execute this first of its kind project in twenty-four months. Upon completion, the project would serve as a global benchmark in terms of length, location and logistical challenges spanning hills, plains, marshland, rivers, canals and roads.[4] The Lafarge Plant was to manufacture nearly one-tenth of the cement output in Bangladesh, and was an important landmark in the delta country's industrial journey.[5] The work began in all earnestness and was completed in record time. To acknowledge the project's completion, Lafarge organized an onsite meeting for

81

all directors on 9 December 2005. A request was made to Anil
Naik, L&T's chairman and managing director, to participate in
this meeting. L&T's role was doubly associated with the project.
While the ECC division was constructing the conveyor belt, the
engineering division was manufacturing the cement plant. Naik
agreed to participate in this meeting.

During the final test that morning, raw material was
flawlessly carried through the total distance of 17 kilometres from
Meghalaya to the cement plant in Chhatak using the conveyor
belt. In the meeting that followed, Bruno Lafont, chairman of
Lafarge, extolled the work by L&T and described it as 'nothing
short of a miracle'. The senior-most leader from Lafarge was
complementing the topmost leader of L&T in the presence of all
employees associated with the project. It was the best day of their
life. There couldn't have been a better reason to celebrate. Post
the meeting, the team decided to organize a party. They relaxed
in the afternoon and looked forward to the evening party with full
enthusiasm. It was the fructification of their sweat and blood for
twenty-four long months. The party began at 6 p.m. Within an
hour, the telephone at the venue rang. Kumar Vikram, then general
manager of ECC's Bulk Material Handling division, received the
call. He couldn't believe his ears. The person on the other side
blurted, 'Come quickly. The conveyor belt is on fire!' The entire
team left the party and rushed to the site. When they reached the
site, they saw the horrifying scene: the conveyor belt was on fire
like a burning train. Right before their eyes, the result of their
twenty-four-month toil was up in fumes. On detailed inquiry it
emerged that some miscreants had lit the conveyor belt on fire.
The main reason was the non-settlement of some local issues with
Lafarge. They had used this despicable method of arson to teach
the MNC a lesson.

Unable to bear the shock, some of the ECC employees
broke down. They couldn't watch their cherished efforts being

destroyed right before their eyes. Nobody slept that night. The meeting that was held to commend the successful completion of the project became the venue for planning reconstruction. While Lafarge encouraged L&T to claim the damages from insurance, they also requested that the project be redone. Kumar recollected, 'This was a very bad time for us. We thought we had achieved everything. But we had to start all over again. The morale of my colleagues was very low. Everybody felt that it would take at least 8–10 months to get the material.' However, what followed was an exemplary reaction to a Himalayan challenge. The ECC team completed the project within four months and handed it over to Lafarge on 17 April 2006. In appreciation of their remarkable achievement, Lafarge awarded them a bonus of Rs 8 crore. 'This was a great achievement for all of us. Thereafter, our chairman [Naik] mentioned this project with great pride on many national and international fora. The success of this project can be attributed to employee commitment, vendor support and leadership.' In recognition of outstanding design of an industrial structure for this project, the Bangalore-based Association of Consulting Civil Engineers conferred on the ECC the Bhagwati Award in 2007.

India's Largest Engineering and Construction Company

This is one among hundreds of success stories of Larsen & Toubro—India's largest and one among Asia's biggest vertically-integrated engineering and construction companies. With a market capitalization of Rs 159,800 crore and revenues of Rs 92,000 crore,[6] its operations extend across the globe. Acknowledged as India's most admired engineering and construction company, L&T caters to over forty countries. It has manufacturing facilities in India, China and the Gulf, and a supply chain that extends to five continents. Within India, it is said to have a presence in almost every district[7] through a nationwide network of distributors of its products. In 2014, a *Forbes* global study ranked L&T as the world's 58th 'Most Innovative Company'; and *Brand Finance* recognized it as India's eighth most-valued brand at Rs 14,220 crore. It has a remarkable record of achievements including manufacture of the world's largest continuous catalyst regeneration reactor, product splitter and coal gasifier,[8] Asia's highest viaduct[9] (for Konkan Railways), India's first indigenous hydrocracker[10] reactor, and India's biggest marine equipment.

Highlighting his involvement with L&T's significant contribution to nation building, Chairman Naik said, 'In 1965, we were chosen as partners for building nuclear reactors. In 1971, we delivered India's first nuclear reactor and set up nuclear steel generators. BHEL was the only other company selected. In 1972, when India launched its space programme, L&T was invited to participate and we did. I was the one responsible for taking the programme further. I was already in charge of the whole manufacturing and then from SLV (space launch vehicles) to advanced SLV to PSLV (polar satellite launch vehicle) to GSLV (geosynchronous satellite launch vehicle) and now to advanced GSLV. Most of L&T's expertise has been built from scratch.'[11]

Among L&T's recent success stories is the association with India's first nuclear-powered submarine—INS Arihant.[12] Dr Manmohan Singh, then prime minister of India, inaugurated it at Visakhapatnam in July 2009.[13] L&T's Heavy Engineering division built its pressure hull,[14] a critical component. Emphasizing L&T's competencies, Naval Analyst Commodore (Retd) Ranjit Rai observed, 'L&T is India's equivalent of Bechtel[15] and has excellent facilities. It is the only one that had the capability to work with titanium steel and build the nose-cone and stern shafting for the Arihant.'[16] On the morning of 24 September 2014, when Mangalyaan, India's orbiter spacecraft settled in the orbit around Mars, L&T employees and the senior team were jubilant. As the largest private-sector supplier to ISRO's historic Mars Mission, L&T contributed towards the advancement of India's space quest and catapulted it into the exclusive club of nations capable of launching interplanetary space missions. It was even more commendable because this had been achieved on a tiny budget and was a wholly indigenous effort.[17] The very next month, L&T bagged the contract for the design, construction and maintenance of the tallest statue in the world—the Statue of Unity, commemorating Sardar Vallabhbhai Patel, the first deputy prime minister of India.[18] The work on the 182-metre (597 feet) tall statue to be constructed near Vadodara in Gujarat at a cost of Rs 2979 crore commenced on 31 October 2014 and was scheduled for completion in forty-two months. Championed by Prime Minister Narendra Modi during his tenure as Gujarat's chief minister, it is intended to be twice the height of the Statue of Liberty.[19] Included in *Forbes Asia*'s 'Fabulous 50' list five consecutive times, L&T's breadth of expertise is quite amazing—from submarines, to space missions, to constructing the tallest statue in the world—and all of them for national glory!

L&T Construction, formerly known as the Engineering Construction & Contracts (ECC) division of L&T, is India's largest construction organization and the oldest and most well known of L&T businesses. In 2014, it figured among the top fifty international contractors. It ranked 28th among global contractors (revenues outside home country) and 47th among international contractors (revenues from home as well as outside the country).[20] In 2012, the Indian construction industry was the second largest employer with about 3.3 crore people, and contributed Rs 670,778 crore to the GDP. This number is estimated to rise to 8.3 crore people by 2022.[21] L&T Construction plays a pivotal role both in the second most employing industry of India and among all the L&T companies. In spite of having diversified expertise, L&T's revenues are highly concentrated, with the infrastructure and construction segment forming the largest chunk of the company's order book and revenue. In 2015, it contributed 47 per cent of the Rs 92,000 crore revenue and 70 per cent of the Rs 5056 crore profits.[22] Given L&T's super-complex structure, my major focus throughout this chapter is on the legendary ECC (L&T Construction),[23] not only because of its size and contribution to India, but also because of the erstwhile ECC's institutional legacy and distinctiveness.

The L&T Construction Chronicle

'The secret of happiness is not in doing what one likes, but in liking what one has to do. There are two ways of being happy—we either diminish our wants or augment our means'
               —Soren Kristian Toubro, co-founder, Larsen & Toubro

The L&T story goes back to the years before the Second World War. Two Danes who arrived on Indian shores in 1934 started this venture. One of them was Henning Holck-Larsen, a chemical engineer specializing in cement technology. The other was Soren Kristian Toubro, a civil engineer. Soren Toubro arrived in 1934 to erect and commission equipment supplied to Madukkarai Cement Works near Coimbatore, and Rohri Cement Factory in Hyderabad (Sind).[24] A year later, Henning Holck-Larsen arrived in connection with the merger of cement companies that were later grouped into the Associated Cement Companies (ACC).[25] Both represented F.L. Smidth & Co. (FLS) of Copenhagen (Denmark) and had been friends since their college days. When World War II began in 1939, they didn't return home as Denmark was occupied by Nazi Germany. They decided to stay on and with the little money they had, joined Mr Desai from Bombay to start a partnership firm. A table and a chair in a small room—that was L&T's first office. Initially, the firm didn't have much money. So one person would sit in the office to maintain the accounts and make phone calls, while the other went around trying to get new business. This was the beginning of the L&T saga.

To understand what they could contribute to India, Larsen & Toubro explored the country's needs. In the days of war, there was need for ship repairs, besides a runway for planes to land at Santacruz in Bombay. These were among the first projects they took up. Moreover, India needed a lot of European goods to survive. So they became agents for European goods in India. They knew what India needed and how to market it here. That's how their business expanded. After the war ended in 1945, they realized that soon India would become politically independent, and their firm would get a lot of business. So from a partnership firm, L&T became a private limited company with some more shareholders joining them. The new company prudently maintained books of accounts, focused on transparency and worked towards profitability by serving India, mainly Bombay.

In 1944, L&T ventured to become a construction company. Since construction was a risky business, with limited certainty of profits due to long gestation period of projects, Larsen & Toubro felt that the construction business should be run by a subsidiary company which is 100 per cent held by L&T. The principle of this subsidiary company was to take and manage risks. However, in case of an inadvertent outcome, they didn't want the main business to be impacted. But to their advantage, the firm started growing really fast and in 1944, the Engineering Construction Corporation (ECC) was incorporated. It became a private limited company in 1946. Larsen, Toubro, Erick Mogensen (chief of FLS and the Danish Consul in India) and S. Rudinger (FLS nominee employed by India Cements Limited) invested Rs 10,000 each to promote the ECC. The four of them had known each other since their college days and had started their careers together. Western Railway, Bombay Municipal

Corporation and ACC became their first clients. In 1948, the parent firm L&T became a limited company and got listed on the BSE in 1952. It acquired a major shareholding in the ECC. Larsen & Toubro's idea was that the ECC would focus on construction of cement plants, steel plants, power plants and fertilizer plants to support indigenous manufacturing in India and meet the requirements of a nascent nation. L&T would build those factories, import essential technology, and develop a profitable business. They were inspired by the European model of manufacturing and selling heavy machinery and specialized equipment.[26]

The very first bridge built by the ECC was in the mid 1950s. Interestingly, it was for the film *The Bridge on the River Kwai*. It took nearly eight months to build the wooden bridge, and just thirty seconds to blow it up by director David Lean's team. The film was mostly shot in Ceylon (now Sri Lanka), and the bridge built by Mortensen, who was assisting L&T's firm in Sri Lanka, was a carpenter's masterpiece. Very few know that the project was originally budgeted at Rs 8 lakh, but got escalated to Rs 16 lakh. Sam Spiegel, the producer, refused to pay the additional costs. He shouted at Soren Toubro who had arrived in Sri Lanka for a settlement, 'You won't get as much as an extra nickel out of me.' Toubro gently replied, 'Then you won't be able to blow up the bridge for your climax,' and handed over a court order. With superstars waiting to complete the shooting till the dispute was resolved, Siegel reluctantly agreed to a negotiated settlement. The money was paid, and the bridge was blown up in the film's climax. The movie went on to win an Oscar, and the rest is history. Later, Mortensen became the first general manager at the ECC and purchased for a trifle 26 acres of land at Manapakkam on the outskirts of Madras. This made the company permanently headquartered in the city.

Though established in Madras, the ECC did not have much business there till it won the contract to build the Jawahar Wet Docks for the Madras Port Trust in 1958.[27] It was Mortensen who cultivated the culture of quality and timely execution at the ECC in its formative years.

In 1959, the ECC became a wholly-owned subsidiary of L&T. In the same year, a full-fledged design division was established in Madras. By 1963, the division merged with the construction wing helping the ECC bid for turnkey jobs by offering design and construction. Having spent nearly three decades in India, Soren Toubro decided to relinquish executive responsibilities and retired from L&T Management Private Limited, the managing agents of L&T Ltd.[28] He returned to Denmark but continued to serve on the L&T board till 1981. He passed away in 1982.

In 1968, L&T's Engineering Projects division (EPD) in Bombay was taken over by the ECC and transferred to Madras. This enabled it to offer complete construction and engineering services. In 1978, Larsen retired as L&T's chairman after leading the company for four decades. N.M. Desai, son of the founding partner, took over as the chairman. In 1984, the ECC gave up its independent identity as a company and was amalgamated with the parent L&T. It became L&T's ECC—Engineering Construction & Contracts division. C.R. Ramakrishnan, known to all simply as C.R.R., the then managing director of the ECC, became the joint MD of the amalgamated entity. During his tenure, C.R.R. instilled a sense of discipline and a marketing focus at the ECC, and was credited with expanding company operations in north and east India. The famous Baha'i Temple in Delhi, popularly called the Lotus Temple, was constructed under his leadership. By 1994, when the ECC celebrated its golden jubilee, it was the only company in India to offer total turnkey services in civil, mechanical and electrical engineering. To give a greater thrust to design, the Engineering Design and Consultancy Department was established in 1995. Four years later, it became the Engineering Design and Research Centre (EDRC).

In 1991, C.R.R. retired from the ECC after a forty-four-year tenure. Dr Anumolu Ramakrishna (A.R.), another veteran known for his technical excellence, design expertise and innovation, took charge. During the A.R.-decade, the ECC rigorously expanded its international business in all directions. It reached the Middle Eastern countries. L&T Oman became a highly successful venture. It started operations in most South Asian countries, including Sri Lanka, Bangladesh and Nepal; all except Pakistan. In the north, it expanded operations to Russia, Uzbekistan and Kazakhstan; and to Malaysia, Singapore, Thailand and Indonesia in South East Asia. The main concentration was thus on the Indian Ocean-rim countries. During our conversation, A.R. recalled, 'Our objective was to help satisfy the respective country's national plans and at the same time ensure profits for our own company. Profit for the company was next to all other objectives. With a genuine thought of helping, one can even contribute to international relationship-building. That helped us when we went to Ghana and other African countries. They told us that they were fed up of the Western companies, and that we [the ECC] were better suited to their requirements. Thus, we could contribute to their development. I was involved in starting companies in all these countries.'

Under A.R.'s leadership, revenues of the ECC division grew fifteen times from Rs 450 crore in 1992 to over Rs 6500 crore in 2004. Importantly, it was a balanced growth. At one end of the spectrum was the focus on commercial success, like the fastest construction of the Kensington Oval Cricket

Stadium in Barbados (West Indies). At the other end of the spectrum was contribution to social welfare such as construction of 10,000 primary schools post the 2002 earthquake across Gujarat, at the rate of eighty days per school. A.R.'s noteworthy contribution to new design technologies, especially the use of concrete structures (instead of structural steel) was found to be more suitable for building fertilizer plants and bridges in coastal India. This eventually became an industry standard even in Japan.[29] When he retired from service in 2004, he was the senior-most L&T employee, having spent forty-three years in the company.[30] K.V. Rangaswami succeeded him as senior vice president (operations) at the ECC.

In 1999, S.D. Kulkarni had completed his five-year term as L&T's CEO and MD. Naik, then president (engineering) and A.R., then president (construction), were both strong contenders for his role. Finally, the board committee selected Naik as L&T's new CEO and MD.[31] In 2000, A.R. was appointed the deputy MD. By December 2003, Naik was elevated as executive chairman for L&T. The board also approved a five-year extension for him as CMD till 2009.

While L&T was known for its performance and technology focus, it wasn't an attractive stock. Between 1985 and 2000, L&T's share prices hardly went up. In the year 2000, L&T's revenue at Rs 7500 crore was twice the value of its market capitalization at Rs 3700 crore. This was very uncommon. For twenty years since 1983, shareholders hadn't received a single bonus. As the new CMD, this was Naik's first challenge. To change this, he prepared a blueprint with the help of international consultants and embarked on strategic five-year plans he called 'LAKSHYA'.[32] In the first one, beginning 2000, he involved over 7000 employees pan-India to ideate on a vision for greater international presence and shareholder value creation. To ensure greater focus, he reorganized the ECC and other divisions within L&T.[33] The ECC was organized into five business sectors: building and factories, civil and transportation infrastructure, hydel and nuclear power, industrial projects and utilities, and electrical and instrumentation. With a massive increase in scale by 2008, the ECC was further reorganized into four operating companies (among the twelve across L&T): building and factories, industrial projects, heavy, civil and infrastructure, electrical projects and Gulf. At that time, each vertical had target revenues of Rs 4000 crore. From 2011, L&T was restructured into multiple Independent Companies (ICs)[34] within the parent company.[35] This reorganization made it a complex structure of ICs (also known as verticals or operating units) and subsidiaries (depicted in Figure 3.1).

Figure 3.1: L&T Business Structure with Business Verticals and Subsidiary Companies[36]

These verticals and subsidiary companies jointly focused on ten business segments and constituent sub-segments (depicted in Figure 3.2).

Figure 3.2: Segment Composition across L&T Verticals and Subsidiary Companies[37]

Infrastructure	Power	Metallurgical & Material Handling	Heavy Engineering	Electrical & Automation
Building & Factories	EPC - Coal & Gas	Ferrous	Process Plant Equipment	Electrical Standard Products
Transportation Infra	Thermal Power Plant Construction	Non-ferrous	Nuclear Power Plant Equipment	Electrical Systems & Equipment
Heavy Civil Infra				Metering & Protection
Water, Smart World & Communications	Electrostatic Precipitators	Bulk Material Handling	Defence & Aerospace	Control & Automation
Power T&D			Piping Centre	

Hydrocarbon	Developmental Projects	IT & TS	Financial Services	Others
Upstream	Roads	Information Technology	Retail & Corporate	Shipbuilding
Mid & Downstream	Metros		Infrastructure	Realty
Construction & Pipelines	Ports	Technology Services	General Insurance	Construction & Mining Equipment
	Power		Mutual Fund Asset Management	Machinery & Industrial Products

During the annual general meeting (AGM) held in March 2012, the role of L&T's CMD was split. While Naik received a further five-year extension as the executive chairman, K. Venkataramanan was appointed as CEO and MD.[38] By September 2015, Venkataramanan retired, and L&T Construction's S.N. Subrahmanyam was elevated as deputy MD, reporting directly to Naik.[39] In the same year, L&T exceeded Chairman Naik's strategic vision of becoming a Rs 75,000-crore company by over Rs 17,000 crore. Mission LAKSHYA had achieved tremendous success. During the Naik era, L&T's market capitalization grew over forty times, from Rs 3700 crore in 2000 to Rs 160,000 crore by 2015. During the same period, L&T Construction also grew fifteen times, and its profits grew forty-five times. By 2015, its revenue stood at Rs 50,000 crore. Still referred to as the ECC by Naik, he called it a 'jewel in the crown of L&T'.[40]

Figure 3.3: L&T Construction Chronicle

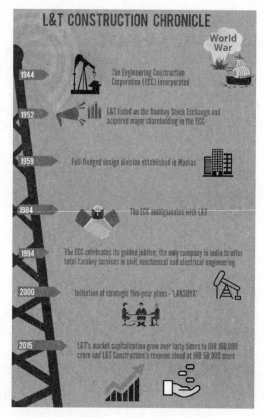

When the Nation Is Your Customer

'The objective of the company is to serve a national purpose of serving the people'
—Dr A. Ramakrishna, former deputy managing director, Larsen & Toubro

I vividly remember my visit to the Manapakkam campus.[41] Every building in the 27-acre campus had a distinctive design. It was as if each of them was curated to showcase the ECC's architectural abilities. Later, I discovered that each of those structures had won awards for excellence in construction. The most interesting part of my visit was the Henning Holck-Larsen Centre (HLC), built in memory of the company's co-founder and chairman emeritus. There is a very interesting incident that happened a decade earlier to the HLC's inauguration. Once, Ramakrishna and Rangaswami were accompanying the nonagenarian Larsen on a tour of the campus. When they passed by the Toubro and Mortensen blocks, they casually mentioned to him that the blocks were named after two people who had shaped the company in its formative decades. Without batting an eyelid, the humorous Larsen said, 'Now I can't wait too long [for a building to be named after him]!'[42] The permanent exhibition at the HLC inaugurated in 2007 (four years after his death) commemorates the ECC's six-decade long journey. It is a tribute to Larsen's inspiring personality and visionary leadership.

During our conversation Rangaswami shared, with a lot of nostalgia, 'We have created all national monuments, which for generations will be attributed as achievements of this company.' On HLC walls were pictures of some of the most well-known landmarks of independent India. It was as if the company had literally partnered with the government to build a new and resurgent country. I feel impelled to share some of the landmarks that we admire, visit and use, but may not know are L&T creations.

Beginning with L&T's spiritual landmarks—the Baha'i House of Worship in New Delhi; and the Virasat-e-Khalsa, Khalsa Heritage Memorial Complex, a grand museum depicting Sikhism at Anandpur Sahib near Chandigarh—are a must-visit for every tourist to north India. The historic Bombay Stock Exchange, and the aesthetically designed Parliament Library in New Delhi are eminent public institutions by L&T. Over fifty-three swanky IT parks where billions are transacted, including TIDEL Park

in Chennai, HITEC City Complex in Hyderabad and Bhavani
Technopark in Thiruvananthapuram, are L&T constructions.
Sports stadiums that echo the cheer of thousands of spectators,
including the Wankhede Stadium in Mumbai, Sree Kanteerava
Indoor Stadium in Bengaluru, and Jawaharlal Nehru Stadium
in Chennai are L&T makings. Iconic institutions of learning
such as the Indian School of Business and the Indian Institute
of Technology in Hyderabad, the Sikkim Manipal Institute
Academy Building and the National Judicial Academy Hostel
Block in Bhopal were built by L&T. L&T has constructed more
than forty-five hospitals in four corners of India, including the Sri
Sathya Sai Institutes of Higher Medical Sciences (providing free
healthcare services) in Puttaparthi and Bengaluru in the south, the
Punjab Institute of Medical Sciences in Jalandhar in the north,
the Central Referral Hospital in Sikkim in the east, and the
earthquake-resistant G.K. General Hospital in Bhuj in the west.
Glitzy, glamorous hotels—ITC's Grand Chola in Chennai and
Grand Maratha in Mumbai were designed and delivered by L&T.
And the most used by frequent flyers of India Inc.—eleven airports,
including the new international airports in New Delhi, Mumbai,
Bengaluru and Hyderabad, that have consistently won international
accolades as among the best in the world, are L&T's contribution to
twenty-first-century India.

It is common for competitors in business to avoid having
the same suppliers or construction contractors. Yet, in the case
of L&T, I observed that in practically all industry categories,
competing companies had massive plants executed by them.
In the auto industry, L&T constructed seventeen automobile
plants including those for Maruti Udyog in Gurgaon, and for
Ford and Hyundai in Chennai. The refineries for Indian Oil in
Barauni, for Reliance in Jamnagar, and for Bharat Petroleum in
Mumbai and Mangalore were all built by L&T. The fertilizer
and chemical plants of Nagarajuna in Kakinada, of Chambal

in Gadepan, of National Fertilizers in Guna and of Tata in Babrala are all L&T projects. Both the internationally acclaimed petrochemical plants of Reliance Industries at Patalganga in Maharashtra and Hazira in Gujarat were built by L&T. Power plants, both atomic and thermal, are the backbone of India's energy security. Most of the vital power plants across India have been constructed by L&T. These include atomic power plants in Kalpakkam, Kudankulam and Karwar; and thermal power plants in Kolkata, Raichur, Bilaspur, Neyveli, Mettur, Haldia, Udupi and Simhadri. If this wasn't impressive enough, L&T has also constructed 400 high-rise towers, twenty-eight cement plants, 13,500 kilometres of highways, 40,000 kilometres of water networks . . . the list is quite incredulous.

Figure 3.4: L&T Construction's Product Portfolio

Interestingly, the company has been proactive in capturing emerging opportunities as well. To capitalize on the Government of India's 'Smart City' thrust, L&T Construction formed a 'Smart World and Communication' Business Unit to collaborate with L&T Infotech, L&T Electrical & Automation and L&T Technology

Services and provide end-to-end solutions to customers in smart security solutions, smart communication networks and telecom infrastructure and smart infrastructure.[43] Across all its projects, L&T's unique capabilities in disciplines of construction—civil, mechanical, electrical and instrumentation—and the expertise and experience to undertake engineering, procurement and construction jobs, and lump sum turnkey (LSTK) contracts with single-source capability have been its greatest strength.

As I concluded my HLC visit, I couldn't help but feel overwhelmed by the quantum of work a single company had done in just seventy years. Each of these were long-gestation and mission-critical projects. Also, the five decades post Independence were not the years when latest technology was available in India. Yet, the commitment of the Danish founders to contribute to nation building in India made all the difference. I reflected; their tagline, 'Builders to Nations', wasn't an exaggeration. Talking about taglines, G.D. Sharma, former vice president and head of human resources, shared with me that when he joined the company, he was handed 2890 taglines as part of an internal competition. The one finally selected was: 'L&T: It's all about Imagination and Engineering'. This eventually became what it is today—'It's all about Imagineering'.

The Seventy-seven Day Wonder

'On the morning of 7 November 1999, the chief minister of Andhra Pradesh, Chandrababu Naidu, telephoned me and said that the Tirumala Hills have a water supply that will last only for two months. All pilgrims will get affected (if there isn't water atop the hill shrine). You must immediately help,' recalled A.R. during our conversation. The Tirumala Hills in the Chittoor district of Andhra Pradesh is the abode of Lord Venkateshwara. It is among the holiest Hindu shrines in the world and is visited by 1 lakh pilgrims every day. On special occasions like the annual Brahmotsavam, the number of pilgrims shoots up to 5 lakh. The annual pilgrim estimates range from 5 to 20 crore, making it one among the most-visited holy places in the world. In the past, L&T had constructed many structures for the benefit of pilgrims, including the famous 'Q' complexes, the Asthana Mandapam and the administrative office building complex for Tirumala Tirupati Devasthanam (TTD).[44] However, a water supply project for Tirumala Hills, which are 3200 feet above sea level, and about 10.33 square miles in area, would take at least a year for completion.

It was Deepavali Day. A.R. called K.G. Hariharan (K.G.H.), executive vice president and head of industrial projects and utilities at the ECC, requesting him to go to Hyderabad and meet the Andhra Pradesh chief minister the very next day. K.G.H. was not prepared to face the CM without extensive knowledge about the problem. But A.R.'s persuasive skills made all the difference. The very next morning, K.G.H. reached Hyderabad with his colleagues, Subbiah and Jagannathan. At 7 p.m., they had a meeting with some of the senior-most state secretaries headed by Rambabu, additional chief secretary, AP Secretariat. They explained to K.G.H. that the goal was to transport water from Tirupati, the foothills of the holy shrine, to the Tirumala Hills, where the temple complex was located.

The project involved the transportation of water over a height of around 800 metres, construction of ground-level service reservoirs, electrical substation, piping mains and accessories. It also called for design, supply, installation, testing and commissioning of pipelines, erection of pumps with motors and surge protection equipment. It was a comprehensive engineering, procurement and construction (EPC) project, a concept that the ECC had successfully pioneered in India. EPC was known for good quality and economic construction. Regrettably, most government contracts are item rate contracts as opposed to lump sum EPC contracts. This led to variability in designs and a consequent rise in the frictional cost of interaction between the nodal agency and the construction contractor.

The secretaries wanted the project cost estimates within twenty-four hours. This was the first challenge for the team since they didn't have complete technical data. However, they managed to prepare a rough estimate overnight. The next evening, the CM met them and expressed immense confidence in L&T's ability to achieve the steep targets. He wanted the project to be completed within sixty days. This was impossible. With great hesitation, K.G.H. committed to complete the project within ninety days. Though the team made the commitment, they realized that the stakes were extremely high. Failure to meet the deadline would not only affect the team, but A.R. and L&T as a whole. Given the dire need for water, the CM had not even called for an open tender to save time that would be lost in a tendering process. He had reposed his faith on L&T's ability to deliver. Non-accomplishment would impact his political reputation as well; and as always, the opposition parties were likely to allege collusion.

Leaving behind all pessimism, K.G.H. and team got into action. One of the first challenges was to gather the required workforce. K.G.H. immediately shot a telegram to his trusted worker Abu from Kerala, to arrive in Madras (now Chennai) within thirty-six hours. Not surprisingly, when K.G.H. returned to Madras, Abu was waiting for him at the entrance of his office. He told Abu, 'Go back home and collect 150 workers and reach Tirupati in three days.' Without question, Abu said, '*Seri*, Sir.' (Yes, Sir.)

On 18 November—the day of the Bhumi Puja (ground-breaking ceremony)—the countdown began. Through hectic consultations within the team, the design concepts and engineering plans were finalized by 30 November. The major requirements for the project included: four units of 640 KW pumps and motors, connected fitments in the pump house, and 2000–3000 workers to carry out civil jobs, including the entire electrification and automation. The first stumbling block was the 640 KW pumps and motors. It was nearly impossible to procure them in less than 120 days. So the first call K.G.H. made was to a very senior executive of Kirloskar Pumps & Motors,[45] 'I need four 640 KW pumps and motors. How fast can you deliver them?' 'Minimum six months,' was the answer. 'I'm talking about six days, and you're talking about six months,' retorted K.G.H. 'You keep expressing your love and admiration whenever we interact. However, when I genuinely need your help, you're not with me. If you really mean what you say, I want these pumps to reach us in the shortest time.' His answer was, 'I can, perhaps, give it in four months.' Then K.G.H. said, 'This is for Tirupati.' The name of the Divine seemed to help. The response from the other side was, 'I will make it in sixty days.' After a lot of back and forth, they mutually agreed to forty-five days. 'In the history of this industry, such heavy-duty pumps had never been supplied in less than six months,' observed K.G.H.

The team moved to the third challenge—steel procurement. The project required 450 tonnes of steel plates of a particular width that no steel manufacturer in India rolled. Again, K.G.H. called a senior executive of a renowned steel plant: 'I need these plates.' The answer was, 'Hariharan Saab [sir], we do not roll steel plates of this width.' K.G.H. shot back, 'Don't tell me what width you roll. I know that perfectly, since I was the one who built this plant for you . . . I want these plates in three days.' K.G.H.'s colleagues were stunned to see his tenor. However, the passion to achieve the impossible had got the better of him. He told the steel plant executive, 'I will send a team of people. You start rolling plates of 1.5 m width, I will arrange laser-cutting to the width of 1.25 m. I know you'll incur a loss of more than 20 per cent, but remember you are doing this for Lord Balaji!' He continued in a humorous vein, 'In doing so, you would have washed your sins to a certain extent. Don't you think it is a good opportunity?' From the other end he heard peals of laughter. Finally, they confirmed, 'I'll do it Saab.'

Now, they tackled the fourth challenge. The list of problems seemed endless. They needed around 450 tonnes of steel that no major steel company was willing to provide at such short notice. With a lot of research they came across a company, which hitherto was never known to make steel in plate form. Astonishingly, this company agreed to manufacture and transport the steel from Delhi to remote Madurantakam in Tamil Nadu in just three days. Challenge number five was that these steel plates had to be rolled into pipes, each about 12 metres in length within seventy-two hours! What appeared as a 'divine intervention': the only spiral building company in south India, PSL Holdings, enthusiastically came forward to execute this task. During normal course, manufacturing these pipes would take at least a month. Instead, the rolled pipes reached Tirupati from Chennai within seven days. K.G.H. termed this project a 'seventy-seven-day wonder', because the team had set seventy-seven days for completion as the target timeline.

The sixth challenge was the transportation of these pipes through steep slopes to the desired spots. K.G.H. discussed with Abu and they jointly inspected the topography. An idea flashed. They decided to launch the pipes using the tall trees of the terrain. Interestingly, the first challenge related to manpower had brought in a multiplied solution. Within seven days, the ECC mobilized 2500 workers from across India. A human chain was used to transport the material for concreting up the treacherous terrain. To ensure high levels of workers' enthusiasm, A.R. visited the project site in December 1999. As the work was in progress, he walked down the hills and met all the workers and staff. This was a great morale booster. A unique aspect of workers' commitment that stood out was the oath taken by Abu and his predominantly Muslim labour force. They vowed to stay off liquor, smoking and non-vegetarian food for the entire duration of the work.[46] The workers epitomized genuine secularism in action.

The testing and commissioning of the pipeline was scheduled for 1 February. K.G.H. called his colleague onsite—Jagannathan—and inquired about the pressure. Jagannathan joked, 'Which pressure Sir, mine or the line pressure?' With exhilaration, he almost shouted, 'Water has reached Tirumala, sir!' At the other end, K.G.H. shed tears of joy and relief.[47] Mission Seventy-seven had been accomplished. It was the most challenging project in his quarter-century-long career. It was a project where passion worked for reasons that went far beyond money and status. On 2 February, the water supply began to the Tirumala Hills, twelve days before the ninety-day commitment made to the CM. 'Prime Minister Atal Bihari Vajpayee came to Tirumala and appreciated how well this project was done. And we attributed that if this could be achieved, it is God's grace and not just our efforts. Many times it appears that things are happening on their own, but God's grace is always needed for accomplishing any task,' observed A.R. with a sense of humility.

Customers: The Core of Larsen & Toubro

'L&T exists because of its customers and well-wishers'
—A.M. Naik

The Tirumala Water Project is both an exception and an example—an exception because of the devotional fervour associated with it, an example because it implemented all customer-related best practices L&T is known for. During our conversation, A.R. crisply summed up customer expectations: 'Customers want their projects done economically, very fast, and in good quality so that they are durable and safe. We provide all this, and the customer is happy. For this quality, the customer has to pay us a little more than they would pay other contractors. They are willing to pay this premium because if the work is completed ahead of schedule, they will benefit as the interest during construction (IDC) would be lower for them, and profitability would be higher. So customer satisfaction comes from timely completion, quality and economy.'

It was Soren Toubro's philosophy that no effort is too great to ensure customer satisfaction; that there must be attention to detail in the quest for perfection; and there must be pride in whatever is being done. In the 1990s, under the leadership of S.D. Kulkarni, the TQM philosophy received great emphasis at L&T. Highlighting the transition A.R. said, 'Earlier, the orientation was towards marketing rather than on quality goods, on-time delivery and customer relationships. TQM changed all that and made L&T a learning organization.'[48, 49] Two decades later, most projects of national importance are still bagged by them. The premium that customers, including government agencies, are willing to pay, is for the timely delivery of high quality output. To ensure this, the company put into place strong processes at all levels.[50]

Like a consumer durable company, L&T also has an extensive after-sales service set-up. Company personnel periodically visit customers to solve any major problems with equipment and systems. Kumar Vikram shared the purpose of such customer visits: 'This is to ensure customers that we haven't forgotten them. We still go and examine periodically the working of the first machine we commissioned in 1993. We are in touch with the customer and have contacts of those running our machines so that we can interact with them on the phone as well.' Rangaswami emphasized that full importance must be given to customer needs. This could be done through proper networking and regular interactions. The annual customers' meet served as a platform for top management to learn directly from customers about their expectations and also get feedback. Unlike FMCG companies, most of the ECC's final products were not for direct consumption but were infrastructure or inputs for a final product or service. Hence, it had to ensure that customers were also profitable. A.R. told me, 'We are able to satisfy customers with good ideas and fast construction so that they're able to earn returns on their investment. So it is not as though only we are making profits. We help our customers make profits. If customers are happy, they will give more business.' This was L&T's win-win approach to customer delight.

Growing Green

While one side of the coin is customer profitability, the other side is environment sustainability. To better understand the importance of this, it is interesting to note that in the decade between 2005 and 2015, in Delhi NCR (the national capital region) alone, over 1 lakh hectares of area was constructed. Roughly this amounted to constructing 134,000 football fields.[51] According to a World Health Organization report in 2016 that studied pollution in 1600 cities worldwide, ten of the twenty most polluted cities were in India.[52] Increasing focus on infrastructure made construction projects across India a big contributor to all forms of pollution—air, water, soil and noise.

During our conversation, Rangaswami shared the five cardinal principles for the construction industry that would help maintain this balance. 'I always used to advocate three cardinal principles to any project manager: contain costs, focus on quality and finish the job on time. Then we added the fourth dimension—safety.' In the formative decades post Independence, timelines for construction projects were measured in years. With the availability of sophisticated technology, timelines shrunk. Years became months and weeks. As we saw in case of the Tirumala Project, it was days. However, the perils of onsite construction were on the rise. In 2010, the US Bureau of Labor Statistics noted that construction accounted for more fatal work injuries than any other industry.[53] Reportable accidents were increasing in number and sometimes they were fatal. Thus, safety became a sine qua non at L&T. Rangaswami continued, 'In this decade, the fifth cardinal principle is sustainability and environmental protection. In the construction industry, we use a lot of natural materials like river sand and stone that are fast depleting. While we should meet our present requirement, we shouldn't endanger requirements of future generations.'

L&T Construction provided solutions at multiple levels. One of them was the use of alternate materials for construction. A.R. shared with me his concern: 'If we make all structures in India with bricks, then we would have to remove 1 metre of soil across the country. This process isn't sustainable. A combination of products is required, thereby reducing the use of soil to a certain limit.' L&T was one of the pioneers in testing and putting to use fly ash, and other alternate materials.[54] One of the products L&T promoted with most industries and clients was ready-mix concrete instead of sand quarrying. By replacing the admixture used onsite at the Chennai Metro Rail Project in 2015, more than 10 lakh litres of water (30 per cent of total consumption) was saved. Thus, the company consistently innovated and encouraged the use of alternative materials for natural resource conservation.

Since more than a decade, the company has also been increasingly focused on green building concepts.[55] These help customers reduce energy and water consumption, utilize recycled material and locally source most construction material. By 2015, L&T's green products and services portfolio increased to Rs 10,767 crore and contributed to 18.16 per cent of overall sales. The company has built over 4.6 crore square feet of green buildings. A.R. gave the example of this approach used at the Bangalore International Airport (BIAL) in Devanahalli. In the design concept itself, L&T included north-light roofing that provided natural light and reduced dependence on artificial lighting. Reduction in the use of air conditioning ducts was made possible by using the space within columns such that separate ducts were not required. The general level of air conditioning was less and power consumption was also less. Materials like granite were used in a way that there wasn't much dust generation. Consequently, maintenance became easier and inexpensive. All these facilitated reduction in overall energy consumption and wastage of materials.[56] Not surprisingly, for over a decade, BIAL continued to be a benchmark in green practices among airports.[57]

In spite of all these efforts, L&T is just one among 200 contractors in the organized sector, besides 35,000 contractors in the unorganized sector of the Indian construction industry. V.S. Ramana, now head and general manager of CSR at L&T Construction, stressed on the gravity of the situation: 'This industry needs to become a lot more sensitive and sophisticated. It has been an ignored industry. Even the film industry was given industry status before the construction industry. The planners, policymakers and the government have focused so little on this industry. We still operate in a PWD environment. So the lowest tender gets the award.[58] At the end of the day, the quality of roads speaks volumes.' While companies like L&T have provided leadership in growing responsibly, the entire industry needs to be more responsive, responsible, quality-driven, safety-driven, and socially relevant to have real impact. Hopefully, L&T's example will inspire others.

Figure 3.5: Five Cardinal Principles in the Construction Industry

Harmonizing Supplier Demands with Tight Project Deadlines

'Materials management of the company should be such that you are fair to your vendors, suppliers and subcontractors. This benefits the company in the long run because they are not dependent on you as you think. You are also dependent on them'

—T.S. Sundaresan, former vice president and head, supply chain management, L&T Construction

Materials management, the most important link in supply chain management, supports the global operations of L&T Construction by catering to the needs of all offices, factories and projects in India and abroad. This function includes procurement from indigenous and overseas sources, logistics management, inventory management at regional stores and disposal of obsolete/unserviceable items. Given the company's commitment to quality, the Materials Management Department received ISO 9001 certification through BVQI.[59] The 3R approach (Reduce, Recycle and Recover) formed the core of its sustainable sourcing approach. By 2015, there was more than 92 per cent increase in the use of recycled steel in all its projects.

When the average requirement of steel per project is about 1000 tonnes, the annual requirement across projects would run into lakhs of tonnes of steel, cement, sand and other construction materials. In such a scenario, how does a material management and supply chain process work? The typical chronology at L&T starts with the 'project kick-off' meeting. This multifunction meeting is held when business units get an order from the client. One of the functions is materials and procurement. During the meeting, the major materials required are listed. The tentative time by which these are required and whether local or imported, all details are shared by the project team. These are then entered into the system, only after which orders can be placed.

Sundaresan elaborated, 'Suppose there is a massive water project and the project team needs 40,000 tonnes of steel. No single supplier would be able to provide that much quantity. So we inquire from the team whether they want imported or local material. After getting the information and the client's approval, we call domestic suppliers such as SAIL and Tata Steel and find out whether they can supply and at what special price. These are preliminary discussions. Later, when engineering drawings are ready, we place orders for the exact quantity.' This is followed by a monthly meeting to know site-wise requirements of raw materials, and tentative requirement for the subsequent month. This enables the company to place orders for the total quantity from various suppliers. In case of lorry strikes, alternative arrangements can also be planned for.

L&T also followed an elaborate and computerized vendor registration system, which monitors material delivery and timely payments to thousands of vendors pan-India. The company ranked vendors based on their performance. This helped in identifying the best suppliers. The headquarters in Chennai and all regional offices were linked with this in-house system called the Enterprise Information Portal (EIP). To ensure optimal transparency of processes, all functions, including disposals, e-auctions and executive reports, were managed by the EIP. Through the annual rate contract system, L&T settled on a rate with its suppliers such that the material was available at a rate cheaper than what other contractors could buy. This enabled it to remain competitive in the market.

During A.R.'s tenure, L&T started the annual suppliers' meet, a new practice in the Indian construction industry to ensure a two-way communication process. Held in every region, L&T invited its top management, directors and heads from other businesses to participate. In this open forum, suppliers are free to talk, share their views, and state any complaints they had. This provided them an opportunity to voice their concerns with the top management, which is usually difficult for small suppliers to a complex, multilocation company. Suppliers were also encouraged to share solutions. A.R. shared his vision behind starting this initiative: 'My intention was to see that there is no corruption. In spite of so many rules for procurement, there is much corruption in the government. So I wanted a common platform to openly tell all suppliers that they should pay nothing beyond what is official to any of our employees. We also wanted to reassure them that we are partners in business and we understand their problems when there are delays, but we want quality raw material. This approach is one of the important aspects leading to our satisfying relationships with suppliers and subcontractors.'[60]

Given the nature of projects executed by L&T, a lot of big ticket purchases were made. For this scale, suppliers across India were really keen to partner with them. This gave them an upper hand to choose and dictate terms. Instead, they indulged in interactive conversations with suppliers as equal partners. As a matter of policy across all group companies, L&T encourages local sourcing of raw materials.[61] Typically, diverse vendors offering capital equipment were called for discussions with the plant and machinery team. Each of them highlighted their features and submitted their best price. Sundaresan shared that the purchase decision was made keeping in mind the price and past experience. 'But once the order is given to a particular supplier, the others feel that in spite of their visits to the office from outstation, and time spent on discussions, they couldn't get a favourable response from us. In such a scenario, I explain to them the reasons for which the order wasn't given to them, and also assure them that the next time if they better their price, they'll surely get the order. By and large, they are convinced through this interaction.' L&T's experience has been that good relationships through a humane approach with suppliers, beyond pure financial and legal considerations, plays a major role in difficult times.

In some gigantic projects, certain portions of work have to be finished in 12–18 months. Yet, the equipment delivery for items like cranes itself takes 18–24 months. Given that these are very expensive, they cannot be purchased till the contract is legally confirmed. So it's a complex situation. Many a time, second-hand equipment is purchased because leasing is exorbitant.[62] At such times, the rapport with suppliers plays a key role.

In December 2006, L&T bagged a Rs 5400-crore contract to build a new passenger terminal with international, state-of-the-art specialist airport systems, and a 4.43-kilometre runway for Delhi International Airport. One of the longest in Asia, the runway was to be ready within eighteen months, and the terminal that would annually handle 3.7 crore passengers (almost thrice the existing capacity), would be completed within forty months, well in time for the Commonwealth Games in Delhi in 2010.[63] The project involved concept enhancement, design, procurement and construction. Sundaresan shared that during this construction project, one supplier of crushers helped enormously. Typically, if suppliers had an order for five crushers with some other customer for the next month, they convinced them to accept three and diverted the other two to L&T so that their work could start. This was done because of the good relationship that the company shared with them. This collaborative approach facilitated quick mobilization of all equipment on time and enabled on-time completion.

Summing up the L&T approach, Sundaresan said, 'Whatever policy you have, if you cultivate a genuine relationship with suppliers, based on mutual trust and faith, they will reciprocate. The capacity to negotiate and get the best deals is not the only factor. This has to be balanced with payment of a reasonable price because they are also a company like yours; they must have a reasonable return on their capital, and be happy for what they're doing for you. The relationship should be that of partnership.' A decade later, the T3 terminal at New Delhi's Indira Gandhi International Airport was ranked the fourth best airport in the world.

Meeting Employee Expectations

'In any business you can have land, money and equipment, and make buildings; but all this is nothing compared to your people. Unless your people are happy, you cannot do anything'
—Henning Holck-Larsen, co-founder, Larsen & Toubro

With his four-decade experience, A.R. captured the essence of employee needs: 'Employees can be satisfied if they have a proper salary, they are able to lead a good life, continuously learn and equip themselves in such a way that they are beneficial to the growth of the company and serve the needs of the nation. Employees are happy to do what they are good at. Job satisfaction is more important than money. Family life is also very important, as in our construction business, the employees need to travel a lot.' These needs were not very different from those identified in the 2016 *Business Today-PeopleStrong* survey. Compensation and benefits, higher job role and responsibility and work environment and culture ranked as the top three aspects that made a job attractive.[64]

In 2015, the total number of permanent employees across L&T companies (except L&T Infotech) was 44,081, and that of contract workmen was 411,604. Historically, almost 80 per cent of L&T Construction staff resided at project sites in distant parts of India and overseas. The remaining 20 per cent were in technical, support, design and administrative roles. The company nurtured both these categories of employees in distinct ways. For those working in the techno-admin roles, short-term rewards and recognition acted as a means for continuous motivation to give their best to their team, department and the company at large. Within a period of 3–5 years after joining, this category of employees expected exposure within diverse functional areas and verticals to get a well-rounded perspective of business and the organization's functioning. Such grooming helped them command leadership roles going forward. The employees expected that the company facilitate the process of their long-term career growth. A consistent feature observed across companies was the importance given to the immediate boss. For those working in techno-admin roles, the immediate boss represented the company. Hence, the superiors needed to coach their juniors by sharing whatever knowledge and experience they had.

Attractive compensation was also important for employees in this industry. At the entry level, pay packages played an important role in job selection. However, construction being at the lower end of the value chain, it became increasingly difficult to attract younger talent. As L&T scaled up the technology chain providing high-end engineering solutions, hiring talented and qualified human resources was a continuous challenge.[65] Retention was another challenge. Traditionally, companies like L&T were known for lifetime employment cultures. Most leaders within the company grew up the ladder and occupied top positions. C.R.R., A.R. and Rangaswami had all served the ECC for forty years before retiring from the senior-most position.[66] Even Naik joined L&T in 1965 as a junior engineer and fifty years later, continued to lead the group as executive chairman. However, the entire concept of loyalty and continuity changed post liberalization. Increasing competition from IT, finance and other service companies made it difficult for construction companies to retain top talent. They weren't able to match pay packages with the service industry. Naik emphasized that it was not possible for a construction company like L&T to pay more as they worked on a 10 per cent margin, compared to 30 per cent margins in IT companies. He reminisced how his generation of employees at L&T suffered frozen salaries during the super-socialistic decade of the late 1960s. When the economy opened up, the next generation earned many times over from the IT industry.[67]

To ensure a balance between an ability to pay and retaining top talent, the company began to change its established stance. Why pay everyone the same? Pay a little more to better performers, and pay an amount acceptable to others.[68] With a large spread across industries, L&T found it difficult to align rewards and expectations across various divisions. The top management wanted to ensure that there wasn't too much variation within its various divisions. Sharma shared his compulsion when this approach was first implemented: 'I have to necessarily distinguish between two individuals, wherein I tell one of them that you're performing well, but the other person is performing extremely well, so his rewards will be twice yours. We have to force the concept of differentiation and look at performance with a magnifying glass, which we never did earlier. So a little harder look at performance, capability and competence was needed.'

The historical context played a major role in creating some HR challenges. Since 1974, there was a culture shift in L&T due to a change in management. As expatriate managers left the company, senior Indian managers became directors. A public sector mentality set in and seniority became the criterion of assessing performance.[69] 'We had several bright people working much below their real potential. Because of the move away from merit-based promotions, their urge to leave was high and we could not stem the attrition,'[70] observed Naik. In April 1999, when he became CEO, he realized that it would be impossible to attract talent unless L&T changed its appraisal and reward approaches. He brought back the merit-based system. It was quite a task to convince senior managers who argued that when the company had succeeded all these years, where was the need for change? Yet, as L&T was increasingly engaged in global projects, the top management understood the changing environment. 'To tackle the ever-changing dynamics of the business world, it's very important to continuously develop our human capital, and make them ready to face challenging situations. Our learning and development initiatives are designed keeping in mind the overall business strategy and organizational requirements,' shared Naik.[71] 'My single biggest challenge is that I don't know how to make the younger generation feel for L&T as we feel for the company,' he often lamented.

The company[72] followed a 5R approach to ensure greater recruitment and higher retention of talent: Recruitment, Remuneration, Recognition, Retention and Recreation. Trainees formed the core of recruitment at L&T Construction. An extensive recruitment process ensured quality induction.[73] Unlike the previous generation, where it could take about forty years to head the company, L&T provided accelerated promotion possibilities for employees with consistently high performance to set an example for the others. Leadership potential at various levels was identified and selected employees were given special training. Naik maintained, 'If you have leaders who are entrepreneurial, and at the same time inspire professionals to perform at their very best, you can multiply value manifold.'[74] He emphasized the need to marry professionalism with entrepreneurship as sine qua non for value creation.[75]

Empowering Employees for Empowering the Company

Between 1987 and 2004, there were three attempts to acquire L&T. In 1987, Dubai-based businessman Manohar (aka Manu) Chhabria emerged victorious in a protracted battle to control Shaw Wallace. Next, he turned his attention to L&T. The company lacked identifiable promoters, and hence was an attractive target for a takeover. Manu started picking up L&T shares from the market, and by July 1988, his stake grew to 1.5 per cent of L&T's equity. This led to speculation in the markets that India's largest engineering firm was about to be taken over.[76] It is believed that L&T Chairman N.M. Desai sought the help of Dhirubhai Ambani, chairman of Reliance Industries Ltd (RIL), to prevent a takeover. Dhirubhai agreed to help and between 1988 and 1989, picked up almost 18.5 per cent shares of L&T from the open market at a cost of Rs 190 crore. Given the stake, he sought and was granted chairmanship of the L&T board. His sons, Mukesh and Anil, also joined the board.[77] At that time, L&T was building a 30-million-tonne naphtha-cracker refinery complex of Reliance Petrochemicals in Hazira. It is understood that Dhirubhai had plans of a full technology transfer to L&T after completion of the Hazira Project. The technology, which was the expertise of a few multinationals, would help L&T to independently bid for petrochemical project contracts anywhere in the world. However, between 1989 and 1991, there were four changes in India's Central government. The Rajiv Gandhi government completed its term in 1989. In that year's general elections, V.P. Singh came to power as prime minister. However, his government fell within eleven months and Chandra Shekhar became the prime minister in 1990. His government was also short-lived, and in the elections that ensued, the Congress Party came to power with P.V. Narasimha Rao as the prime minister. Given that the Government of India had nearly one-third stake in L&T through leading financial institutions such as GIC, UTI and LIC,[78] and due to pressure from opposition parties, there was an increasing demand that L&T should remain an independent and professionally managed company. Its management control shouldn't be taken over by another family-owned group. Dhirubhai yielded, but continued as a passive investor with ownership of nearly 10 per cent of L&T stock.

After the 1990s, L&T management was united and employees stood by it to keep the professionally managed character of the company intact. 'We never realized that we were not owners, till we were taken over. This was uppermost in my mind when, in 1999, I decided to bring in employee ownership. After all, Mr Larsen and Mr Toubro were basically employees; they were not businessmen,' reminisced Naik.[79] Interestingly, from March 1989, when N.M. Desai retired as chairman, the L&T board had no whole-time executive chairman. After Dhirubhai Ambani stepped down, S.S. Marathe served as non-executive chairman. During the AGM in July 2003, shareholders demanded that a company of L&T's size should have a full-time executive chairman. In December 2003, Naik got the coveted job to lead his dream company. He was the first chairman of L&T who had risen from the ranks to lead the company.[80] He joined as assistant engineer in November 1964, and rose to the top position in four decades.

Around January 2000, the Boston Consulting Group[81] recommended that L&T should exit all non-core areas of business.[82] It suggested a spin-off of its cement division into a separate entity. The low return on capital employed was the primary reason for its recommended divestment. Notably, L&T's cement business had the least symbiotic relationship with the rest of its businesses. While the product was satisfactory and the production facility was world class, the cement manufacturing location was the biggest limitation. It had set up a gigantic 4-million-tonne facility in Hazira with a modern dock to facilitate exports. Regrettably, the Asian Crisis of 1997 badly affected its expectations in the international markets. Its geography made domestic transportation of bulky cement prohibitively expensive.[83] By June 2000, L&T announced that its cement business would be demerged from its core activities, and an investment banker would have the mandate of looking for a suitable partner for it.[84]

By November 2001, the Ambanis sold their 10 per cent stake in L&T to Grasim Industries, owned by the Rs 27,000-crore Aditya Vikram Birla Group. A direct competitor in the cement industry, Grasim was interested in acquiring L&T. In February 2002, Kumar Mangalam Birla, MD of Grasim Industries, made an open offer at Rs 190 per share for L&T, including its cement division. However, Naik, was keen that L&T should retain its diverse ownership and professional management, and not be taken over by another family-owned group. After a lot of back and forth with the government, financial institutions, the Securities and Exchange Board of India (SEBI) and the Birla Group, Birla exited by selling its stake (acquired from RIL) to the L&T Employees' Trust in June 2003. By July 2004, a majority stake in the demerged L&T Cement division was acquired by the A.V. Birla Group at Rs 2200 crore.[85] This deal was a master stroke hailed by national and international experts as a win-win strategy that prevented a takeover, divested a non-core business, and strengthened employee commitment through the creation of a special fund. This arrangement also ring-fenced L&T against future takeover bids.

Within the first ninety days of the formation of the Employees' Trust, a stock option scheme was launched by L&T. This created a lot of value for the top management of the company. 'Otherwise, I would have lost all my senior managers. Stock options are the reason we have a fairly stable top management,' affirmed Naik. Since 2006, the management staff (numbering a few thousands) was also extended ESOPs. At that time, of the 27,000 L&T employees, the ECC alone had 13,500 staff. L&T was said to be the first non-IT/non-finance company in India to award ESOPs. From then on, Naik provided a futuristic orientation and motivated L&T employees with the question of whether they wanted to remain independent or be taken over. The employees wanted to remain independent. 'If you want an independent, professional company, you have to make it so expensive that people stay away from you,' he would tell them. He visited thirty-eight company locations during his initial years as the CEO, and made presentations to convince employees to focus on value creation, thereby reducing the vulnerability of a takeover and increasing the likelihood of remaining independent. Gradually, attitudes began to change. 'Today, my junior manager looks up L&T's share price on the Internet since he has 500 shares. This is how shareholder value begins to get created in the minds of employees,' explained Naik.[86]

Between June 2003, when L&T was valued at Rs 6000 crore, and March 2015, when its market cap was Rs 159,800 crore, the value amplified twenty-five times. A four-layered risk management process strengthened L&T's resolve to value creation. Naik himself sat on committees that evaluated projects beyond Rs 1000 crore. Almost 50 per cent of projects were of that size.[87] Thus, his personal commitment institutionalized the process, which was an international best practice in the infrastructure industry.

Given his active involvement with L&T's engineering business in Mumbai, Naik's involvement with its construction business headquartered in Chennai was limited. However, after taking charge as CMD, during one of the site visits to IIT Chennai, he discovered that projects below Rs 25 crore were making losses. He informed Rangaswami that the ECC should not accept any projects below Rs 25 crore. In the subsequent two years, he raised the bar to Rs 100 crore. A decade later, the ECC took no project below Rs 250 crore. Thus, Naik continued to focus on the macro picture for sustained shareholder value creation.[88] L&T-ites often remarked that after Naik became CMD, engineers began to speak the language of finance and economics![89]

As on December 2015, 12 per cent of L&T was still owned by the Employee Welfare Foundation.[90] Needless to say, when employees become shareholders, a natural win-win emerges as the company's financial success benefits them, tangibly and intangibly. This leads to a virtuous cycle of efficiency and enthusiasm to achieve higher growth. The interests of shareholders and managers get aligned. In his own tenure as chairman, Naik's vision of enabling L&T and its employees to carve their own future came true.

Along with the emphasis on employee empowerment, L&T Construction's work culture laid emphasis on the freedom to experiment, continuous learning and training, transparency, quality in all aspects of work and rewards based on performance and potential. The undercurrent to all of these is the culture of empathy and concern for employees. A notable example of this was when an employee's mother had a heart attack and he wasn't able to get an air ticket to visit her in Jaipur. Naik reassured him, 'Don't worry; if you are unable to get a commercial flight, we will keep the company aircraft ready for you.'[91] Instances like these are the 'proof of the pudding'.[92] By 2013, the *Business Today–PeopleStrong* survey ranked L&T among the 'Top 5 companies to work for', and the first in the engineering and automotive sector.[93] It also received Ma Foi Randstad's 'Most Attractive Employer Award' for many years. By 2015, L&T's attrition rate was 13.9 per cent, with maximum attrition in the age group below thirty years. This was marginally lower than the average of 14 per cent attrition across Indian companies and slightly higher than 13.81 per cent attrition in APAC countries.[94]

The Real Strength of a Construction Company

In 2015, L&T employed nearly ten times its number of permanent employees as contract workers. This included temporary labour working at grass-root levels across national and international sites. They formed the company's foot soldiers, whose strength and labour enabled it to deliver mammoth projects within identified timelines. However, this category of employees had unique expectations.

Given that they stayed onsite for months, and sometimes years, they wanted facilities for the physical comfort of their families, a conducive atmosphere at project sites, decent accommodation, transportation, schooling and other social requirements for themselves and family members. They also expected that the organization take sufficient precautions for their health and safety.

While these demands appear basic, there were challenges of demography, diversity, scale and implementation on a regular basis. On any given day, the ECC employed 150,000 unskilled workers at its project sites. Nearly 85 per cent of these workers were without any formal vocational education. So, a major challenge for the company was the non-availability of effective trainers at all projects sites that could communicate with onsite workers in their native language. Besides, given the lack of formal education, the workers found it difficult to appreciate traditional training methodology such as a classroom lecture to explain issues of efficiency and effective work methods. Their attention spans were limited, and so were their priorities and commitment towards safety and quality, besides the discipline required to achieve both. Moreover, given its numerous international projects, the challenge for the HR function was to evolve fair and transparent policies that ensured a harmonious blend of diverse cultures and yet retained the company's distinct character as a company of Indian origin. The need to standardize its HR processes across locations, and to improve its cycle times and role-based access to information, was urgent.

Equalizing Efficiency with Empathy

L&T used IT and visual media to innovatively communicate with workers. To address the challenge of the construction workforce understanding instructions only in their native language, and the non-availability of effective trainers at all sites, it designed an e-learning module in nine Indian languages to impart training to workmen. This consisted of a cartoon film of 30–45 minutes that explained with great colour and variety the various hazards and risks at construction sites and the precautionary measures to be taken. The interesting visual interface was very well received by workers. Given the mandatory nature of HSE (Health-Safety-Environment) induction training to all workmen at all project sites before deployment, more than a million workers were trained through these modules since introduction. Rangaswami underscored the increasing importance given to safety. While in earlier times projects were done in four to five years, the use of modern equipment necessitated completion in half the time. Consequently, the perils of construction at site increased. 'Therefore, we started a safety department and ensured that there would be zero accidents. Though this involved a lot of investment, we were committed to teaching the workmen what to do, what is safe practice, and ensure there are no accidents at all.' Noticeably, between 2012 and 2015, the number of fatalities per lakh workforce reduced from 11.09 to 8.98.[95]

An interesting anecdote depicts L&T's commitment towards employee safety. Sometime after 2006, Naik visited two hydropower plants in Kullu-Manali. One was a Rs 210-crore project and the other, Rs 115 crore. L&T Construction had already been working on them for five years. On the way up the hill to the project site, he found that there were no railings on the road. He thought this to be very dangerous because the road remained muddy for six months in the year. Thereafter he made a rule that the company would not accept any hydropower project less than Rs 750 crore so that it could provide safety measures to the employees by making necessary arrangements. A decade later, L&T stopped bidding for projects less than Rs 1000 crore.[96]

For comfortable onsite accommodation for workers, L&T constructed labour colonies with essential amenities in all major projects. For example, during the Delhi International Airport (DIAL) Project, over 1 lakh workers were employed and 30,000 were provided comfortable housing. The housing colony also included facilities such as a medical centre, drinking water, canteen, general stores, sanitation facilities, solid waste disposal, safety, security, environment quality and waste-water treatment.[97] Further, it consistently strived to ensure that for remote projects, such as its hydel power project in Arunachal Pradesh, accommodation, transportation, schooling and other social requirements were constantly reviewed, upgraded and changed. Rangaswami shared L&T's commitment to workmen's children's education: 'If our job site is sufficiently big, we open a school, or else assist in opening a school by supporting a bigger chain of schools [such as Delhi Public School or Kendriya Vidyalaya] existing in that area. We provide them the infrastructure and they run the school. So not only our children but children from surrounding areas also come and attend.' It was one such onsite L&T workers' residential complex in Riyadh (Saudi Arabia) that Prime Minister Narendra Modi visited on 2 April 2016. L&T was part of a consortium building a section of the Riyadh Metro. To a gathering of over 1000 L&T workers and staff, Modi said that the work being done by Indian workers abroad not only earned money, but also raised the stature of India. Subsequently, he had dinner with the workers.[98] This was one among dozens of landmark projects for government and private agencies that L&T did in the Middle Eastern cities of Riyadh, Dubai, Kuwait, Doha, Oman and Abu Dhabi.

Challenges are many, and newer ones emerge as the Indian construction industry dares to take on audacious projects in competition with international players. Companies like L&T have endeavoured to retain their 'Indian-ness' by finely balancing financial prudence and social welfare. Their skill-building initiatives for the construction sector are another first in the country. In my research of over 100 corporations across multiple industries, there isn't another example of an industry-specific skill-building institution like the one led by L&T through collaboration with industry peers and government agencies, such that the benefits accrue to the industry and the economy. Such an institution is a win-win for all participants. (Appendix III.A elaborates L&T's visionary steps in skill building. L&T also collaborated with other social welfare institutions for executing massive developmental projects. Appendix III.B details a series of such projects undertaken in the area of drinking water supply between 1994 and 2006 that benefitted over 1.2 crore people across three states of south India.)

Leadership Perspectives

'In a construction company, you have to take care of and deal with so many outsiders who are your stakeholders. Your success is not complete unless all of them are satisfied'

—Dr A. Ramakrishna

During our conversation, Rangaswami emphasized on the five 'M's that are critical success factors in the construction industry. The first being 'material', which should be of good quality and procured in time. Zero-wastage was vital. The second is 'men' (meaning human capital). Getting the right number of workmen and administration staff was crucial for high productivity. The third is 'machinery'. Optimum productivity is possible with the perfect blend of men and machinery. Hence, getting the right equipment for the right job is very important. 'Money', the fourth 'M', is to be productively utilized. An adequate return on capital employed (ROCE) was the measure of its optimality. Finally, 'management', (meaning effective and efficient systems and procedures), is the path to get the best out of the other four 'M's. He summed it up in a nutshell: 'Doing the job in time, with the right quality, and getting profit without exploiting anyone, without any accident or damage to the environment, is the nutshell of the construction industry. This is done through the management of the five "M"s.'

'What is excellence?' A.R. asked me. 'There are similar organizations and if you are just like the others, you will not achieve superior performance. Stakeholder focus is necessary because it helps people get a certain amount of satisfaction that your organization is helpful to people around you. That will get a positive response from others and they'll continuously support you for your success.' He emphasized this to be an absolute essential for success. Success didn't only mean results in financial terms. It also meant all-round happiness and satisfaction of a country's requirements. Without this holistic approach, a company cannot be successful. He asserted, 'Even if successful, that success will not be durable. If you want the organization to succeed generation after generation, the stakeholder focus helps because the stakeholder requirements are also changing and you have to change your strategies for that.' Visibly, L&T's stakeholder strategies have been shaped with changing times, while retaining their Indian roots.

Widely recognized as an authority on construction, A.R.'s win-win approach to business was groomed in the company he worked for all his life—L&T. He believed that business leaders need to face challenges and for that, understanding human relationships and trying to think from the other person's viewpoint would give good results. 'How can you help solve the other person's problem while solving yours? With this balanced approach, most problems can be solved.' In his experience, even the government's approach can be changed if they are convinced that the company's intentions and actions are in the larger interest. Even opposition parties who criticize the ruling party's policies get convinced through dialogue. 'I have experienced in so many projects where both the ruling party and opposition parties supported us because they perceived us as doing good work, which is beneficial to society and beneficial to them for future elections. If you work for serving the people, you are automatically serving God, and it will give good results.'[99] These words were loaded with the experience of fifty long years in the construction industry, working with private, public, social, government and international agencies. I was impressed to note that such evolved leadership perspectives do exist in India Inc.

Where Does L&T Go from Where It Has Reached Now?

In 1994, after L&T successfully thwarted takeover bids, an article in *Economic and Political Weekly* posed the aforementioned question. In response, the new CEO and MD of the company S.D. Kulkarni promised that by the turn of the century, L&T would reach its target of being a 10,000-crore company. It almost achieved its financial targets within that decade. More importantly, it was recognized for being one of the best managed companies in Asia, and a leader in corporate governance with a noteworthy track record of transparency.[100] When Naik donned the CMD's mantle, similar questions were asked. He shared L&T's strategic vision of becoming a 75,000-crore company by 2015. That mark was crossed much earlier than the stipulated date. In the final year of Naik's leadership, the company is on the verge of becoming a 1 lakh-crore company. Yet, L&T hasn't been just about reaching financial objectives. Interestingly, all technical recommendations for accelerating quality infrastructure growth in India, as made in a 2009 McKinsey Report,[101] were already in action as best practices at L&T. This included upgrading design and engineering capabilities, building long-term supplier relationships, adopting lean construction principles, institutionalizing risk management, and providing lump sum EPC contracts. L&T continued to be ahead of the curve in proactively shaping successful multi-stakeholder strategies.

Often, parallels are drawn between L&T and two MNCs, primarily because of their size and type of businesses—General Electric,[102] that grew on the back of the American dream, and Siemens,[103] that became a giant behemoth during the era of rapid industrialization in Europe. Naik visualized L&T as the Indian equivalent of Mitsubishi Heavy Industries,[104] which can take on any global competitor in advanced technological missions, be it nuclear energy, aerospace, defence or infrastructure.[105] As the Naik era is concluding, the murmur on L&T's succession plan and future direction has become audible. To this, A.R.[106] remarked, 'One day L&T will have so many companies, it will have a centre like Tata Sons. Like the Tatas, L&T doesn't have family control. However, it has to develop its own style of retaining talent and keep growing.' Naik's superhuman commitment to work is legendary. In a career spanning fifty years, he has actually worked the equivalent of eighty years, being the first one to reach the office at 7.45 a.m. and being the last to leave at 10.45 p.m., every single day. Identifying a substitute for Naik may be well-nigh impossible. However, identifying a core team for the next decade is vital. Nonetheless, the real focus of this new team shouldn't just be announcing a growth figure for 2025. Rather, it would need to concentrate on sustaining the core of a conglomerate that is neither public nor private. Its founders envisioned it as a national organization contributing to nation building. In the last seven decades, its roots have gone deep enough and shoots have spread far enough. The future necessitates that the roots be consistently nurtured with the commitment to its essential purpose, so that the shoots can spread farther to achieve its vision of sustained and balanced value creation.

Figure 3.6: Win-Win Learnings from Larsen & Toubro Construction

LESSONS FROM LARSEN & TOUBRO CONSTRUCTION

1. ON TIME EVERY TIME

Timely completion of projects
gives an edge over competition in
the construction industry

2. A LEARNING ORGANIZATION

Employee training and
development are imperative for
efficiency, effectiveness and
safety

3. GO GREEN

Environmental prudence reduces
resource consumption, increases
project sustainability and
enhances goodwill

4. TRUST AND TRANSPARENCY

Fair dealing with all stakeholders
is the key to long-term, mutually
beneficial relationships

5. SKILL INDIA

Use of technical expertise for
skill development can benefit the
company, industry and country

6. BUILDING THE NATION

Core competence can be used for
nation building by integrating
profit with purpose

IV.

The Taj Group of Hotels

Atithi Devo Bhava . . . Ambassadors of Indian Hospitality

'I built the Taj Mahal Hotel to attract people to India. I have no desire to own the place'[1]

—Jamsetji Nusserwanji Tata, founder, Tata Group

One fine evening in the late 1890s, Jamsetji Tata, founder of the Tata Group, and a doyen of Indian industry, accompanied a foreign guest to a hotel in south Bombay. He was told at the entrance that while his guest was permitted, he could not enter the hotel. He was shown a board which read, 'Dogs and Indians not allowed.' Enraged, he vowed to build his own hotel, so luxurious and superlative in standards that others would pale into insignificance. To match international standards, he hired a European architect, someone from France or Italy. After a lot of effort, the architect started the project. A few months into the construction, he went back to his continent for an extended leave. Upon his return, he was aghast to see the hotel building constructed in the wrong direction. The front entrance was on Merry Weather Road near Colaba Causeway, and the rear faced the majestic Arabian Sea. His most precious project was ruined and he did not have the courage to show his face to the patron, Jamsetji. So heartbroken was he that he went to the top floor of the hotel building still under construction, and jumped to his death!

When I grew up in Bombay, these were the kinds of stories that we were regaled with every time we passed by the grand Taj Mahal Palace Hotel at Apollo Bunder. These stories sounded so larger than life that they fascinated my childlike mind. Alas, these are only legends with no truth in them! Over the last 115 years of its existence, the Taj story has been captured in over ninety national and international travelogues and bestsellers. Dozens of researchers have studied its history, architecture and evolution. Most of them have documented the real stories behind the ideation, construction and existence of one of Mumbai's finest landmarks. Let's take a look at the real stories of why Jamsetji initiated the construction of the hotel. One reason was that in spite of being one of the most important trade destinations, even in British India, Bombay did not have any hotels of an international standard. So, when repeated comments were made about this evident insufficiency, Jamsetji said, 'I will build one.' He had intense pride and affection for Bombay, and wanted to give back something that would be cherished forever by its citizens. In fact, so great was his passion that the money spent for the construction of the Taj (over Rs 20 lakh) was not from Tata & Sons, but from his personal funds.

On 1 November 1889, he bought the lease of two and half acres of reclaimed land near the harbour. The construction began in 1900.[2] The mythical story of the European architect who committed suicide has also been disproved by the original drawings of the Taj found in the Bombay University library. They were signed by Raosaheb Sitaram Khaderao Vaidya, a Hindu engineer, and his assistant, D.N. Mirza, a Parsi.[3] After Vaidya's death in 1900, W.A. Chambers completed the project. All of them had worked with Frederick William Stevens, an English architectural engineer who was the mastermind behind the designs of the Victoria Terminus and the Municipal Corporation Building, landmark locations in Bombay's multi-century heritage.

Now, for the story about the entrance of the hotel. It was meant to be on the Colaba Causeway side for three reasons. First, the carriages bringing elite guests to the hotel would have an easy entrance because the parking space was closer to the western side of the hotel. Secondly, the U-shaped wings of the hotel aimed at capturing the afternoon breeze that blew in from the backbay rather than the harbour side. Lastly, Jamsetji wanted the majority of the guests to have rooms overlooking the sea. So visionary were his plans that he even purchased two islands near Uran so that guests at the Taj could use them for picnics![4]

The Taj's greatest memory lies in the fact that it was inaugurated in the lifetime of its founder. On 16 December 1903, an ailing Jamsetji presided over its inauguration. The construction was still in progress. However, the first wing with two complete floors welcomed seventeen guests that day. It was a culmination of his two-year long efforts, when he went all over the world to shop for his dream hotel—electrical machinery from Dusseldorf, chandeliers from Berlin, fans from USA, and the first-spun steel pillars from the Paris Exhibition, where the Eiffel Tower had been constructed only in the previous decade. The architecture was a blend of Moorish domes, Florentine Renaissance, and Oriental and Rajput styles. The hotel boasted of its own power plant with electricity and a carbon-dioxide gas ice machine plant that provided refrigeration and helped cool the suites. These were among the very first anywhere in India.[5] When Jamsetji breathed his last the subsequent year in Europe, the Taj, literally meaning 'crown', had begun its journey of shining as a jewel in Bombay's firmament.

The Journey from the Taj Hotel to the Taj Brand

Why do I write so much about just one of the 100 hotels belonging to the Indian Hotels Company Limited (IHCL)[6] across sixty-three locations in India, North America, the United Kingdom, Africa, the Middle East, Malaysia, Sri Lanka, the Maldives, Bhutan and Nepal? It's because of the historic role it played. For seventy of the 115 years of its existence, the Taj Bombay was the only property of IHCL. During these seven decades, it witnessed many a milestone. While it became the first choice of maharajas across India and royalty and heads of state from across the world whenever they visited Bombay, it also got converted into a 600-bed 'hospital' during the First World War.[7] In November 1933, the Harbour Bar at the Taj was India's first air-conditioned bar. Interestingly, it was the first bar in Bombay and had Licence No. 1. When the government first imposed alcohol prohibition in 1939, the Taj slipped into losses for the first time. It soon recovered as army men packed its rooms during the Second World War. Sometime in the early 1960s, J.R.D. Tata, then chairman of Tata Sons, briefly flirted with the idea of selling the hotel as it wasn't doing well enough. However, he soon changed his mind. One of the reasons was the advent of jumbo jets which convinced him of the tremendous potential the hotel held for the future of tourism in Bombay. The other reason was Colonel Leslie Sawheny, Dorabji Tata's brother-in-law, who took charge of the hotel and literally turned it around in a decade, physically[8] and financially. Among his trusted aides was Ajit Baburao Kerkar, recruited in London as assistant catering manager in 1962.[9] By 1970, J.R.D. made Kerkar the managing director of Indian Hotels. He shared J.R.D.'s vision and was given immense freedom to achieve it. Over the next two decades, with abundant autonomy and authority, Kerkar expanded IHCL's footprint from a single hotel to many dozens across India. The first addition was the Taj Mahal Tower, constructed just next to the main hotel in 1972. In the same year, the Oberoi Towers inaugurated their property at Nariman Point, just 2 kilometres away. Such was the bonhomie displayed by the Taj that it published print ads which read, 'Taj welcomes its friend to share the fortunes of this great city.'[10]

Figure 4.1: The Taj Mahal Palace Hotel and Tower, Mumbai

Between 1973 and 1987, five new Taj properties were constructed every two years. Some of these were green-field projects like the Taj Mahal in Delhi, the Taj Bengal in Calcutta and the Taj Coromandel in Madras. Many others were acquired, including the grandiose palaces of the erstwhile maharajas of Jaipur, Jodhpur and Udaipur. IHCL renovated them to make them shine in all their magnificence. Then there were tourist destinations in whose growth and development the Taj played an important role. In the early 1970s, Goa was a place accessible only by road (almost a twenty-four hour bus journey) or by a daily costal ship, again a twenty-four hour sail. There was a single flight daily, possibly a small forty-seater turbo prop aircraft. No one used the train, as it meant having to change trains to reach Goa. With this scenario, Kerkar accepted an invitation from the then chief minister of Goa to visit and select a suitable site for a hotel. After an arial survey, he selected the Aguada site. Shirin Batliwala, former vice president of food and beverage at IHCL, shared with me how against much opposition, he went ahead with the construction of the Fort Aguada Beach Resort, later called the Taj Holiday Village in Goa. By 1983, the Aguada Hermitage was ready as a retreat for all commonwealth heads of government including the then prime minister Indira Gandhi and the British prime minister Margaret Thatcher.[11] Camellia Panjabi, a TAS officer and then executive director of sales and marketing at IHCL, played a vital role in putting Goa on the tourist map of India. She also led the efforts in 1987, when the Taj Malabar in Cochin was built to usher in Kerala as an attractive tourist destination (in collaboration with the Kerala Tourism Development Corporation). Even before the term 'God's own country' was popularized by Amitabh Kant, then Kerala tourism secretary, putting Kerala on the global tourist map is considered to be a Taj initiative. In the 1980s, IHCL also went international with hotels in Zambia, Yemen and London.

Kerkar's eye for detail ensured the best architecture designs and authentic regional cuisines in all Taj Hotels, whether Calcutta, Madras or Bangalore. Similar was the focus on introducing authentic international cuisines in India. Shirin explained to me that till the early 1970s, Chinese food in India was mostly a version of Hakka and Cantonese. With the opening of the Golden Dragon at the Taj Mahal Palace Mumbai, India was introduced to authentic Sichuan food. The Trattoria, the first Italian restaurant, opened in 1981 at the President (Cuffe Parade, Bombay). Thai, Mexican, Middle Eastern and modern Japanese food were all introduced by the Taj. Kerkar also believed that every Taj hotel should have the best address in the city. So superlative was his passion in this matter that when the government introduced the system of PIN codes for postal services, the Taj Mahal Palace Mumbai fell under the PIN code 400039. Kerkar could not accept that the Taj address was Bombay 39. So he moved the relevant ministry and had the Taj's PIN code changed to Bombay 400001! Unsurprisingly, even five decades later, IHCL's greatest assets are its landmark locations in every city. Of the Kerkar years, J.R.D. had once remarked, 'IHCL not only expanded, it exploded!'

However, with the focus on opportunistic growth and expansion, a relative fall in quality set in. That's when a lot of competition started coming in. The Oberoi and ITC were two major hospitality chains that emerged in a big way in the 1980s and the 1990s. The three together controlled 65 per cent of market share in the Indian hospitality industry, with IHCL holding 35 per cent.[12] With a need for greater consolidation and systematization, Ratan Tata, chairman of Tata Sons, brought in R.K. Krishna Kumar, to lead IHCL in 1997. A Tata veteran of three decades and former managing director of Tata Tea, Krishna Kumar had enormous experience in sales, marketing and people development. He brought immense professionalism into the company and introduced a number of innovative practices. Among other important initiatives, he undertook the rationalization of select Taj properties, market-level remuneration across hierarchy,[13] and the introduction of a new performance management system called 'Taj People Philosophy'. He also introduced a new management structure that replaced segmentation by region with segmentation by product.[14]

Given the price range, over two-third of customers for Indian luxury hotels were from outside the country. They typically accounted for half the revenue and three-fourths of profits. The liberalization of Indian markets in 1991 brought in a sea change in people's economic and demographic status. International hospitality brands had begun to realize the immense potential in Indian markets. Just to give a brief comparison, around the year 2000, there were about 60,000 hotel rooms across India. Compare this with 1.1 lakh rooms in Manhattan (New York), and 50,000 rooms in Orlando (near the Walt Disney World Resort).[15] Around the same time, the number of tourists visiting India annually was 26.5 lakh, compared to 2.3 crore to the UK, 3.1 crore to China, and 5.1 crore to USA.[16] Predictably, the best of international brands made their way to India. To retain its historic advantage, IHCL had to match international standards. For this, it needed to groom employees who could bring international standards into guest service and hospitality. At such a time, in IHCL's centenary year, Ratan Tata brought in Raymond Bickson as managing director of IHCL. He was the first expatriate to lead a Tata company in India in a century. Hailing from the Pacific Islands of Hawaii, he had over three decades of hospitality experience with the best international brands. However, it was important for him to balance the internationalization of IHCL's services, and at the same time retain its unique Indian heritage and flavour. Krishna Kumar became IHCL's vice chairman and provided guidance to maintain this fine balance. The journey to the next 100 years had just begun.

Understanding Indian Hospitality, Understanding 'Taj-ness'

'Culture eats strategy for breakfast'
            —Karambir Kang, area director, North America, IHCL

If you were to visit a village in India, even as a stranger, you would be welcome in most homes. In the simplest of dwellings, the host would welcome you with a namaste, spread a mat on the mud floor and offer a glass of cool water and a snack. This shelter and warmth is the projection of what hospitality is also about. In India, one of the things that really typifies that spirit is *Atithi Devo Bhava* or the guest is God. In this verse from the *Shikshavalli* of the *Taittiriya Upanishad*, at the time of graduation, students are instructed to unfailingly respect parents, teachers and guests as God. Connecting with that theme, Bickson observed that at the Taj Hotels, whether guests come from near or afar, the philosophy is to serve them, make sure they feel welcome, protected and safe, and their welfare is taken care of.[17] His dozen years' association with the Taj and its people helped him understand the Indian ethos and appreciate the civilizational values that evolved into virtues of tolerance, understanding and respect. These were visible in the working of the Taj and Tata leadership. 'Working with a brand that has been so well known in this emerging market is a privilege,' he admitted.

While Taj Hotels have received many minor and major facelifts, the face of the Taj and perceptions about it have remained quite the same through a dozen decades. A term often used to describe this unquantifiable aspect of the Taj culture is 'Taj-ness'. 'So what does Taj-ness really mean?' I asked Karambir. 'It's an overall feeling that you get when you're in a Taj property, just by looking at it and by being there. It's something more sensory than tangible.' Two important aspects emerged in our conversation. Firstly, the emotion of genuine warmth that the Taj represents. 'About twenty years ago, our highly respected competitors like the Oberoi, were known to be cold and efficient, while we were known for warmth and emotional connect in our approach. Now, the international companies mostly have a transactional, cookie-cutter approach to service. But the Taj has mastered the art of an emotional connect and hospitality,' he shared.

Secondly, the approach of service to the guest is displayed by all Taj employees. 'Something that is common among all our employees is that they interact with you at a deeper level. We highly encourage that. We hire for attitude, and accept people who have that intense desire to serve. That is the differentiation for the Taj,' he emphasized. I realized that this Taj-ness was the company culture, built over many decades. In essence, it means that the guest is the reason for the Taj's existence, and everything it does has to be around the guest. The moment the hotel staff welcomes a guest with a namaste at the entrance of the hotel, the guest becomes the responsibility of the Taj—that is Taj-ness in action.[18]

What is so unique about the Taj brand? The first aspect is its importance within the group and its senior-most leaders. Until the acquisition of the Jaguar Land Rover in 2008, the Taj was among the most high-profile brands of the Tata group. The hotels were extremely important for both the former chairmen—J.R.D. and Ratan Tata—who were at the helm for seventy-five years. Especially the Taj Mumbai, which was the focal point and centre of meeting, a venue for welcoming company guests, celebrating social and private occasions, and a lot more. The connection continued with the next chairman, Cyrus Mistry, whose father, Pallonji Mistry built the Taj Mahal Palace and Tower.[19] The second aspect about the brand is its perception in the eyes of the common man in India. For over a century, the Taj has dominated the psyche of the Mumbai elite as being the epitome of luxury and fine service. Its top brand status is indicative from its valuation in excess of Rs 4000 crore.[20] This impression is reflected in many Bollywood movies, especially in the 1960s and the 1970s, where the hero would say, *'Chal, Taj mein coffee peete hain.'* (Let's have coffee at the Taj.) While this may not be with special reference to the Taj Mumbai, 'Taj' had become increasingly synonymous with five-star hotels, almost as a generic term.

Redesigning the Taj Brand, Redefining the Taj Experience

By the mid 2000s, specific feedback repeatedly poured in. This can be explained through an example.[21] A guest from London wanted to tour India. A senior executive at the Taj recommended a fortnight for travelling to north and west India, and suggested a number of places for sightseeing, including Delhi, Agra, Jaipur,

Jodhpur, Udaipur, Khajuraho and Varanasi. The guest liked the itinerary and enjoyed the hospitality at the Taj Hotels across these places. At the end of the fortnight, he came to Mumbai to meet the executive and discuss his memorable visits. He expressed his desire to come back to see Goa, Kerala and the Himalayas and of course, the Buddhist tourist circuit. He had some specific feedback for the senior management. While he enjoyed his stay at the Taj Mahal Hotel in Delhi and the Taj Rambagh Palace in Jaipur, he did not quite enjoy the quality of infrastructure at the Taj Agra. The guest was given the reason that the Taj Agra property was formerly a Holiday Inn and hence, not designed to offer the luxurious experience which the Taj was known for. This meant little to the guest who insisted that the Taj should ensure consistency of experience across all properties.

One of the challenges IHCL faced was that a number of its hotels were acquired properties, and hence not up to 'Taj' standards. Inopportunely, the company had continued to refer to all its hotels with the Taj brand. So, many guests increasingly expressed dissatisfaction over properties that had the Taj name, but not the Taj experience. During our conversation, Deepa Misra Harris, then senior vice president of sales and marketing at IHCL, shared that by the early 2000s, studies showed that the Taj brand was under some stress. She explained that the four pillars a brand needs to drive it forward are relevance, esteem, differentiation and knowledge. If a brand drives knowledge, i.e. how well the brand is known, along with relevance, the pitfall could be commoditization.[22] The Taj needed to work on differentiation and maintenance of its historical esteem. IHCL decided to ensure the highest levels of brand differentiation and embarked upon a rebranding exercise.

In the international hospitality market, different brands even within one company are significantly differentiated based on diverse products and service levels available at varied price points. The typical segmentation consists of five distinct categories: five-star (called luxury hotels), four-star (called upper upscale hotels), three-star (called upscale hotels), two-star (called mid-scale hotels) and one-star (called budget hotels). The changing demographics in India and the rising middle-class brought IHCL to an interesting inflexion point.

A remarkable change was in the offing over the next quarter century. The number of outbound Indian tourists was expected to grow from around 40 lakh in the early 2000s to 2 crore by 2015, and touch 5 crore by 2020.[23, 24] The number of inbound international tourists to India was estimated to reach 1 crore by 2020.[25] India accounted for only about 0.6 per cent of the global tourist arrivals, indicating a huge area of untapped opportunities in travel.[26] Moreover, between 2005 and 2025, the Indian middle-class population was expected to rise phenomenally from 5 crore to 60 crore.[27] Over 2.3 crore Indians (more than Australia's current population), would be among India's wealthiest citizens, able to regularly access luxury hotels.[28] IHCL realized that with increased earnings and rising disposable incomes, aspirations would be on the rise.[29] To capitalize on this, the best of international hospitality companies, including Hyatt, Starwood and Marriott were establishing base in India with dozens of sub-brands catering to specific segments. Krishna Kumar, then vice chairman at IHCL, believed that it was the right time for the company to take the plunge.

IHCL hired Landor,[30] a global brand consulting firm to research across markets in India and South Asia. Thereafter, the operations and marketing groups of IHCL and consultants from Landor worked together to map its typical customer. Based on research and consumer insights, the Taj decided to go for the 'sun and planets model'.[31] According to this model, the Taj would be the central luxury brand (five-star category) consisting of its palaces and super-luxury hotels.[32] By 2016, thirty hotels with 5264 rooms were operated under the Taj luxury brand. IHCL then launched an upper upscale brand called 'Vivanta by Taj' (four-star category). This one was an endorsed brand because it shared some values with the mother brand 'Taj'.[33] The term 'Vivanta' comes from 'bon vivant', meaning a person who enjoys a sociable and luxurious lifestyle. So everything in Vivanta was about the beauty of life. It was designed for the work hard, play hard traveller, looking for a contemporary and imaginative take on hospitality.[34] With its launch in 2010, the Taj rolled over nineteen of its hotels and resorts to Vivanta. The brand positioning was so well-received by target customers that in 2014, *Condé Nast Traveller* named 'Vivanta by Taj' the third best hotel brand in the world. By 2016, forty hotels with 5521 rooms were operated under the Vivanta by Taj brand.

The third IHCL brand was 'Gateway', the upscale (three-star) category.[35] It was to be a standalone brand not umbilically linked to the mother brand 'Taj'. IHCL already had a Gateway hotel in Bangalore. So, the company decided to use that brand name for its upscale category of hotels pan-India symbolizing its presence in all 'gateway' cities of the country. The Gateway brand aimed at offering consistent, quick and crisp service to business and leisure travellers by satisfying their needs for comfort, familiarity and flexibility. These services were offered across eight zones: enter, stay, hang out, meet, work, work out, unwind and explore.[36] Within a year of its launch, Gateway was the third strongest brand in India according to Nielsen research. By 2016, there were thirty-two Gateway Hotels and Resorts across India with 2804 rooms.

The last was the budget brand, 'Ginger'. Formerly planned as IndiOne, the name Ginger was selected by Ratan Tata who wanted a very fresh and out-of-the-box name for this category. Launched under a new company called Roots Corporations, an IHCL subsidiary, Ginger Hotels had no direct connection with the 'Taj' brand. It was promoted as a Tata Enterprise. Inspired by Professor C.K. Prahlad's concept of the bottom of the pyramid, it catered to a new concept of 'smart business hotels' without frills

and fuss.[37] The Ginger chain of hotels aimed at providing state-of-
the-art facilities at one-third the tariff of similar offerings in high-
end hotels. With the first hotel in Whitefield, near the upcoming
IT hub in Bangalore, all Ginger hotels were strategically located
close to central business districts.[38] Within just five years of its
launch, the South Asian Travel Tourism Expo named Ginger the
'best budget hotel chain' in India.[39] Within a decade of its launch,
Ginger became the largest pan-India budget brand hotel with
over thirty-four properties and 3170 rooms. Its direct competition
being the unbranded mom-and-pop kind of hotels, Ginger scored
on three critical factors: trust, security and consistent service.

Through the rebranding exercise, IHCL came up with a SORD
(Statement of Relevant Differentiation). The SORD listed what
each brand would deliver and the values it would personify. The
company did a full engagement with employees and customers to
create the brand's persona and the guest experiences around it.[40]
This could be explained through a simile of the car industry and
the example of Tata Motors. A twenty-year-old youth just out of
college buys a first car—Nano. In the next decade, he graduates to an
Indigo. In his fourth decade, with a family and grown-up children,
he may want a Safari. And by the time he is in his fifties or sixties,
and has reached the prime of his career, he may want to experience
luxury and go for a Jaguar or Land Rover. Similarly, based on the
age and stage, purchasing power and disposable income of different
categories of guests, each of these brands would provide the right
match to their anticipations. Ginger would be suited for fresh
recruits, Gateway for middle management, Vivanta by Taj for senior
management, and the Taj luxury hotels for chairmen and CEOs.[41]
IHCL wanted lifetime clients from the 'growing India' brand.

The new brand architecture was among the biggest win-win
strategies for IHCL. On the one hand it created a much larger
customer base for itself across segments, thereby increasing
opportunities for greater sales and occupancy. On the other hand,

for the first time in India, a single hospitality company provided options to customers to choose from hotels belonging to different price points and catered to specific service requirements at that price. The main objective of this entire exercise in the centenary decade of the Taj was to further enhance its brand value and perception, which would, in turn, spillover to its proud ownership, the Tata Group. In 2010, the Credit Suisse Research Institute ranked the Taj Hotels, Resorts and Palaces among the top twenty-seven global great brands of tomorrow, and cited its rebranded architecture as one of the key enablers for the Taj's transformation and proliferation across segments.[42] Five years into the implementation of the rebranded architecture, at the 2014 annual brand study[43] by Young & Rubicam's[44] Brand Asset Valuator (BAV), the Taj emerged as the number one breakaway brand[45] in India on seventy different parameters.[46] Redefining the Taj experience and redesigning its brand architecture had started showing tangible results.

Figure 4.2: The Taj Brand Architecture

TAJ BRAND ARCHITECTURE

	Luxury	Upper Upscale	Upscale	Economy
Brand Identity	Taj	Vivanta by Taj	Gateway	Ginger
Relationship with the Taj Brand	Core Taj	Endorsed by Taj	Not Linked to Taj	Not Linked to Taj
Verbal Brand Drivers	Reinventing Tradition	Stylishly Spirited	Welcoming Perfection	Smart Basics
Brand Beliefs	Charming, Passionate, Progressive, Attentive, Responsive	Contemporary, Radiant, Agile, Creative	Crisp, Courteous, Consistent	Smart, Informal, Fresh

Globally Reputed, Globally Present

The Bickson decade also saw a lot of international expansion. The rising income levels had led to Indians travelling all over the world. Bickson shared one of his experiences while attending a board meeting in one of the most expensive hotels in Italy on Lake Como. He was having dinner with the owner and fourteen international guests. There was lot of noise outside and so one of the guests remarked in jest, 'What kind of a noisy hotel do you run here?' The owner replied, 'Don't blame us. Blame Raymond!' Bickson gave him a confused look. 'How am I responsible for the noise in your hotel?' The owner laughed, 'Raymond, it's an Indian wedding. They've rented the entire hotel!' There was mirth across the dining table. The message was loud and clear. Indian guests had come of age to use the best hospitality facilities anywhere in the world. To tap these growing numbers who wanted Indian menus and experiences, IHCL started to collaborate with leading hospitality chains in markets where it had no properties. In 2006, it entered into a strategic alliance with South Korea's Shilla Hotels and Resorts,[47] and inked a marketing alliance with Japan's Okura Hotels and Resorts in 2007.[48] Hearing about these international collaborations, the chairman of Manny Berbere, owner of four palace hotels in Switzerland, called Bickson and expressed an interest to form an alliance with IHCL. 'Manny, why do you want to collaborate with the Taj?' he asked. The response helped him realize the potential of Indian tourists at world-class destinations. 'In the summertime, there are so many Bollywood movies made in Switzerland. My palace hotels are filled with Indians who want to see where these movies are made. So, I have Indian chefs to cater to a large number of Indians coming to Switzerland. It's a market that I want to tap further with the Taj.'

Given this immense potential, IHCL made landmark acquisitions across important source markets.[49] In 2005, it acquired the W Hotel in Sydney and the famous Pierre Hotel in New York on a thirty-year lease.[50] It expanded its presence in USA, a vital source market, through two more acquisitions—the Ritz-Carlton in Boston and Campton Place in San Francisco. Deepa explained the logic: 'If we have a presence in source markets, the guests there will know and experience our brand. So when they come to India, they would prefer the Taj. The more you grow in your source markets, the easier it will be to retain market share in India.' This was a major concern as competition in India had reduced the company's market share to 12 per cent.[51] So, it embarked on a massive expansion drive. From sixty-two hotels and 7900 rooms when Bickson took over, IHCL expanded to 15,000 rooms and 120 hotels in a single decade. At the same time, the Indian market had grown from 62,000 rooms to 210,000 rooms.[52]

Then came another setback. The hospitality industry was acutely affected by the 2008 financial crisis and subsequent downturn in world economies. IHCL had acquired most of its properties at the peak of its prosperity and paid exorbitant prices for some investments. Post crisis and the Mumbai terror attacks, the valuation of properties and room rents dipped. Consequently, many expansionary decisions were slowed down to ensure consistent financial viability. To set off losses, especially in foreign markets, the 100-room W Hotel in Sydney was sold in 2014 for Rs 180 crore, and the Taj Boston was sold in 2016 for Rs 815 crore. The primary objective now was to strengthen properties in India and South Asia, the Taj's core markets. Most new developments were planned through the asset-light management contract route, where new properties would be managed by the Taj under its brand. In exchange, IHCL would receive a commission of 10–15 per cent on revenue generated. In spite of the international uncertainties, IHCL's international strategy did have a positive impact on the Taj's revenue. Revenue contribution from outside India increased seven times from 5 to 35 per cent between 1991 and 2014.[53] The company moved many notches higher even in its quality standards. At the 2012 Tata Business Excellence Convention,[54] IHCL topped the honours list and was declared the winner of the prestigious JRD QV Award 2012.[55]

Figure 4.3: Sales of Leading Indian Hospitality Companies

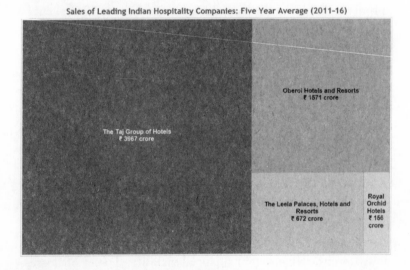

Sales of Leading Indian Hospitality Companies: Five Year Average (2011–16)

The Taj Group of Hotels ₹ 3987 crore

Oberoi Hotels and Resorts ₹ 1571 crore

The Leela Palaces, Hotels and Resorts ₹ 672 crore

Royal Orchid Hotels ₹ 156 crore

In September 2014, Rakesh Sarna, a three-decade hospitality veteran with Hyatt Hotels, took over from Bickson as the new managing director. He brought back greater autonomy for general managers as under the Kerkar era. He also modified the strategic structure from a strong verticals and brand focus under Krishna Kumar and Bickson to a strong geography focus. Accordingly, each property head would report to area general managers or directors, who would report to region heads, who in turn would report to Sarna.[56] In 2015, the shifting of IHCL top brass from the Oxford House Office in Colaba to the top floors of Express Towers at Nariman Point was a symbolic change in company strategy and the way forward. With seventeen hotels in the pipeline, Sarna had a growth plan in mind for Indian markets that were heading for their heydays.

Underscoring the immense potential of the industry in India, the World Travel and Tourism Council Report 2016 on India reported that leisure travel spending in India was expected to grow from Rs 6.29 lakh-crore in 2016 to Rs 13.32 lakh-crore by 2026; and business travel spending from Rs 1.3 lakh-crore in 2016 to 2.6 lakh-crore by 2026. Noticeably, domestic travel spending generated 82.5 per cent of direct travel and tourism contribution to India's GDP in 2015. In monetary terms, this was expected to rise from Rs 6.28 lakh-crore in 2016 to Rs 13.3 lakh-crore by 2026.[57] It increasingly emerged as the primary driver of the sector's growth.[58] Sharing his vision going forward, Sarna said, 'Our strategy will not be asset-light or asset-heavy, but asset-right. The aim is to be globally reputable, not globally present.[59] The Taj is the rightful custodian of Indian hospitality, and it should be proud to be Indian.'[60] Rightly so, the potential of the domestic travel industry was immense, and IHCL would do very well by firmly establishing itself as the leader across categories and price points and capture a huge chunk of 'wallet-share' over the next decade. In order to be successful with competition, the company identified critical factors for consistent performance. These included: quality of accommodation, brand recognition, service levels, convenience of location, and quality and scope of other amenities, including food and beverage facilities.

In August 2016, Sarna launched a global initiative called Taj-ness, symbolizing the celebration of all that is good within the Taj Group of Hotels. It aimed at paying homage to Jamsetji

Tata's vision of sincere care as the core of Taj hospitality. This Taj-ness would come to life for the guests in the hotels, not only reflecting the heritage but also honouring the local culture through a set of rituals unique to every hotel, and rooms that provide the utmost in contemporary comfort. This vision of Taj-ness was to be tangibly rolled out across all 100 Taj Hotels in India and internationally by the end of 2017. Extending the concept of Taj-ness to financial prudence and multi-stakeholder responsibility, Sarna emphasized, 'Tajness is also a commitment to our shareholders and partners through the delivery of consistent growth, to our environment and communities by being a responsible corporate citizen and for the members of the Taj family in the pride they feel when they deliver excellence.'[61] In 2015, the Taj Hotels, Resorts and Palaces featured on the *Forbes* list of Ten of the World's Best Luxury Hotel Brands. It was considered to be the largest company of its kind in South Asia.

A dozen decades, five visionary leaders, and the Taj's journey of excellence continued. By 2016, IHCL had 120 hotels in India, sixteen hotels abroad, and a total room inventory of 16,759 managed by nearly 20,000 employees.[62] Some of these were owned, some leased/licensed and some others under management contracts. Even 100 years later, its hotels continued to be the preferred choice of royalty and heads of state, whether it was the emperor of Japan or the king of Spain, the President of France, China or USA; the prime minister of Australia, the UK or Bahrain. Over these decades, the undercurrent of the Tata philosophy and the culture of Taj-ness continued as the foundation of its existence. As someone who had the opportunity of working with Kerkar, Krishna Kumar, Bickson and Sarna, Karambir observed, 'IHCL as a company, and the Taj as a hotel, are distinct from others. The Taj is a company with a soul, which you can feel.'

Figure 4.4: The Taj Century

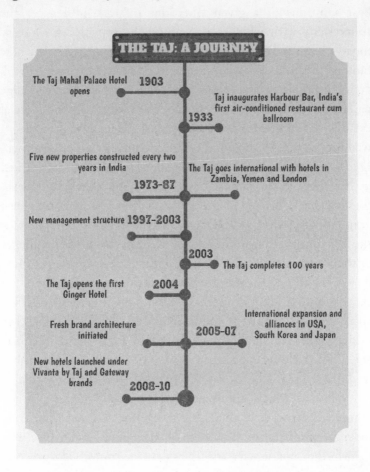

Delighting Customers: The Raison d'Être of Existence

'We must differentiate ourselves from our competitors through a greater understanding of customer needs and a culture built around customer-centricity, innovation and a focus on profitable growth'
—Cyrus Mistry, former chairman, Tata Sons

Customer-centricity is not based on a guide book about best solutions in a given situation. Instead, it denotes the spontaneity with which solutions can be provided for guests' most pressing requirements. On 15 April 2013, the now famous Boston Marathon suffered casualties from a bomb attack. In the subsequent hunt for two identified suspects, huge parts of Boston city were under lockdown, and all commercial establishments were closed. On one of those days, there was a wedding at the Taj Boston, in the heart of the city downtown. Due to the events of the preceding days, the bride hadn't picked up her gown. It was almost impossible to get it that day as well. She was heart-broken at the prospect of a marriage without a grand wedding dress. While it wasn't the hotel's problem, given the Taj culture, they wanted to help. From the general manager of the Taj Boston, to the ground staff, all were thinking, 'How do we do it?', when one employee recollected that the hotel shop had a wedding dress that would befit the occasion. They volunteered to modify it and make it available by evening. The bride, a guest at the Taj Boston, was delighted at the efforts the hotel made for a personal requirement connected with her wedding.

Ways in which guests are engaged with at the Taj are numerous. Another common example is when hotel staff come to know through any indication in the guests' room that it is their birthday or anniversary. They alert the concerned team, and soon a group of staff members walk into the guest's room with a personalized cake to celebrate the occasion.

'So for us, guest engagement is catching those little cues regarding guests' requirements and then acting on them to go one step beyond that,' shared Karambir. Bickson underscored the need for developing a global mindset among employees even while working in Indian properties so that they are able to understand guests' special needs and fulfil them. For example, the Taj Boston's menu exclusively provided all specialties of New England,[63] because that's what guests would expect. In addition, the Indian chef also prepared special Indian delicacies. Back home, employees at the Taj Goa needed to understand the requirements of Russian guests who constituted a large proportion of visitors. 'If you don't understand what the Russian market wants, they will not come to your hotel and spend the type of money they do. So we need to be not just India-centric in our approach, but also very global-minded,' observed Bickson. Not surprisingly, Rohit Khosla, former general manager (GM) of the Taj Samudra (Sri Lanka), hired Chinese staff members to ensure increasing comfort of interaction for the large proportion of Chinese guests visiting Taj properties in Sri Lanka. In the hospitality business, a certain degree of customization is necessary within a broad standardization, unlike a mass-manufacturing unit where each product has to be identical. For this, innovation is the key. In the years ahead, technology-based innovation would play a vibrant role in ensuring greater customer delight and engagement.[64]

What about those decades when computers and technology had not become mainstream in India? How were customer service and hospitality management standards maintained at the Taj? Shirin shared with me her experience as the first woman general manager of the Taj Bengal in Kolkata: 'At a time when computers had not yet entered the country, GMs were expected to devise their own system of keeping track of guest history, financial indices and market information. At any time, a GM would receive a call from Mr Kerkar, asking for the name of the VIP guests and their suite numbers, the price that the hotel was paying for potatoes or high-speed diesel, or the name of the company who gave the highest room nights last month!'

Meeting Expectations of NextGen Customers

In the last decade, India has witnessed a paradigm shift in consumption due to changing lifestyles. In earlier years, customers would go to luxury hotels to enjoy services and facilities that were much better than what they used at home. With changing technology, even car stereo systems are better than the music systems provided in mid-segment hotels. Most middle and high income homes in India today own a plasma screen or high-definition TV, which is much better than what is available in most hotels.

Furthermore, with changing demographics, a large chunk of guests now belong to Generation Y, also called the millennials. Born between the early 1980s and the late 1990s, their requirements are very different from Generation X, also called Baby Boomers (born post World War II). At present, most hotel infrastructure is designed around tastes and preferences of Gen X, the most affluent group of people in the world. However, Gen Y's style of working is very different.

While Gen X uses a study table, Gen Y works everywhere else but a study table. They would want to work in a lounge or in coffee shops. Gen X primarily depended on the phone. Gen Y survives on the Internet. Hence, Wi-Fi has become a necessity. A survey finding revealed that on average, a Gen Y guest used at least three devices. So the hotel and room design needed to be modified to accommodate these changing requirements. Karambir shared how the Taj Mumbai was among the first to invest in the newest technology in its entertainment system—the first to bring in flat-screen televisions, the first to enable on-demand channels in India, and access to the Internet on the television.

It doesn't end with gadgets. Even bathing preferences have changed. The earlier generation enjoyed bathtubs. How many actually use bathtubs now? The current generation needs experiential showers available in upmarket spas such as Brazilian rainforest mist and thunderstorm showers. They prefer different kinds of mood lighting at various times of the day and night. So, a lot of product and service innovation is essentially possible through technology. That's the transition Taj properties are attempting to make to conform to the imperatives of changing product and service design for Gen Y.

Recreating the Maharaja Lifestyle: A Taj Innovation

IHCL's greatest advantage is the wide variety of experiences that it can offer to its guests: from tech-based innovation for its savvy millennial customers to the traditions and luxuries enjoyed by the maharajas of pre-Independence India. The word 'palaces' in the name Taj Hotels, Resorts and Palaces are real palaces in which many of the royal families still live. These palaces have a dual advantage. On the one hand they provide a chance to the guests to indulge in royal opulence while on the other, they help in conserving India's legacy.

'I've spent my whole career in luxury chains. I thought I had seen luxury before. But the royal lifestyle and protocol are something I've come to fully respect and appreciate. We are the only company in the world that has fourteen real small and big palaces. Not the Disneyland Palace or the Trump Taj Mahal in a casino!' remarked Bickson. Undoubtedly, the Lake Palace[65] Udaipur, the Rambagh Palace[66] Jaipur, the Umaid Bhavan Palace[67] Jodhpur and the Falaknuma Palace[68] Hyderabad, are the four major palaces with the Taj. He confessed that creating a guest experience around the royal services in a palace was an eye-opener for him and could be a lesson in hospitality for every international chain. Interestingly, all the palaces have been carefully renovated to ensure that the original architectural heritage is retained.[69]

The customer experience around each palace was uniquely designed to provide an authentic experience to guests. For example, when a guest books a room in the palace, an option of being picked up by a regular car or a vintage car is provided. The whole experience of being driven in a vintage car is a rarity. The most important thing in the erstwhile palaces was the grand welcome for kings; so the arrival experience had to be spectacular. For this, IHCL did a lot of research and created a unique arrival experience for each of the palaces. So, at the Umaid Bhavan Palace, they have the sword salute. The innovation to that was a sword salute with a canopy. It is done every time any guest enters the palace. At Lake Palace, the arrival is heralded by showering petals on guests. At Falaknuma, the team decided that the guests' car would be stopped at a certain point, and they would be ushered into a horse-drawn carriage for the short ride uphill to the main entrance.[70] The other exotic experience was dining. The Taj created bespoke experiences to provide the majesty of royal dining. The guests could dine in a tower, in a turret, in a pontoon, or anywhere they wanted.

The Taj wanted to deliver on the primary pillars of heritage and authenticity on every aspect of the erstwhile royal life. So, the bathing experience was another specialty. At these palaces, the Jiva Spa[71] experiences were run on signature themes like the coronation bath ceremony, which was a special occasion for a young prince on the morning of his coronation. A two-hour coronation bath ceremony at the Jiva Spa within the palace is typically accompanied by live musicians in the background to recreate the moments of a bygone era. At the Nadesar Palace, Varanasi, this bathing experience consisted of a royal Abhishekam (ceremonial bath) with waters of the River Ganga. Each of these featured palace experiences were beautifully mapped out. The moment these were created and delivered onsite, company revenues increased.[72] Thus, innovation was happening at every level—in rooms, in entertainment, in food and beverage, in culinary items and many more areas. Deepa summarized the roadmap of the Taj's innovation journey: 'Look at insight, deliver on it, innovate on it and continuously keep innovating.'[73]

Collaborating with Competitors: Customer-centricity at Its Zenith

Karambir shared a very unusual instance, perhaps the only one of its kind, in the history of the Taj. Some time in 2009, the renovated Taj Mumbai had just been reopened to the public. However, some work was still in progress in parts of the hotel. So half the hotel wasn't functional. On one particular evening, a large wedding of a very prominent businessman's daughter was scheduled. On the morning of the day when the reception and dinner were scheduled, there was a short circuit that caused a resultant fire in the basement of the hotel. The matter was quite serious and the hotel was practically required to be shut down for a couple of days for safety reasons. In the preceding months, there was already a lot of damage due to the terror attacks, and a cumulative effect of those fires was one among many things the management was grappling with. On the other hand, this business tycoon had invited 400 guests that evening. It was just impossible to conduct the event at the Taj or even relocate to Lands End, a long distance from Colaba. Karambir, then GM of the Taj Mahal Mumbai, and his entire team were in a situation of flux. They just didn't know what to do. They naturally couldn't tell the guest to cancel his only daughter's wedding reception. The tension in his office was palpable.

At that time, the team led by Hemant Oberoi, then grand executive chef for Taj Luxury Hotels, finally decided

to do something unprecedented just to ensure that the
guest's function was successfully celebrated. Probably, for
the first time in the history of the hospitality industry, the
Taj called their competitor, the Oberoi Hotel. For those who
aren't aware of Mumbai's geography, the Taj Mahal Hotel
is located in Colaba, and the Oberoi–Trident at Nariman
Point. They're on either side of the peninsula jutting into the
Arabian Sea, at a distance of about 2 kilometres. While they
had been competitors for over thirty years, they had also been
joint victims of the 26/11 terror attack. So, mutual empathies
were high. Karambir picked up the phone and called the
GM of the Oberoi–Trident. He explained the situation and
said, 'I know you have a hall which is available; our food is
already cooked. Will it be okay if we shift the wedding there?'
Imagine, food from the Taj served in the Oberoi; the Taj
guests, served by the Oberoi staff! For those who understand
the intense competition in this sector, this is an unbelievable
situation. Yet, at such a time, the century-long goodwill of the
Taj came to the fore. The Oberoi willingly agreed to oblige
in this hour of dire need. Karambir told me, 'I think that
kind of brotherhood among us developed because we all went
through that terrible time together. They instantly said "yes"
without even thinking.' So it was perhaps for the first time
in history that two competitors worked together. He called
it a truly win-win situation—victory for the Taj because the
guest's function was honoured, victory for the Oberoi because
it had played the Good Samaritan[74] to its elder competitor and
emerged in very positive light. Most vitally, it was a victory for
the guest. 'I think that's something which is clearly an example
of Indian hospitality. You wouldn't see such a thing happening
anywhere else in the world! Most importantly, the guest had a
memorable wedding for his daughter.'

Figure 4.5: The Taj Way of Delighting Customers

Employees: The Engine of the Company

'The bellman, laundry attendant and others who interact with our guests are our true brand custodians, because they make all the difference when they take care of our guests with sincerity'
—Rakesh Sarna, managing director and CEO, IHCL

H.N. Shrinivas, then senior vice president of human resources at IHCL, categorized employee needs into three broad buckets. The first is the psychological need of pride and belongingness with the organization. Somewhere deep in their psyche, it should convince employees that they are working for a reputed, stable, secure and respected organization. The second is an aspirational need to learn, grow and achieve. The third is obviously financial needs. Employees look for attractive remuneration such that they can achieve a certain lifestyle and look after their children and family. They would expect the company to have welfare programmes and policies to support the medical and social needs of their families.

To emphasize on the uniqueness of multilocation hospitality chains, Shrinivas shared the example of Nagender Singh, the GM of the Vivanta by Taj Hotel–Sawai Madhopur Lodge near Ranthambore National Park (Rajasthan), who led a team of fifty employees. 'He lives with them, he's the boss, and the decision-making authority for their lives, careers, and whatever else they're aspiring for from the Taj. He represents the Taj for them.' So, the biggest people challenge and opportunity in a hospitality group like the Taj is decentralized decision-making. With properties in eighty locations across India and overseas, direct, face-to-face communication with managers and employees is well-nigh impossible. Most employee-related decisions are driven by the local hotel manager's leadership style. Thus, with eighty locations, there are eighty different styles of implementation. Hence, ensuring the implementation of a uniform service culture and people philosophy on the ground is a major challenge.

The other challenge is the financial stress that the hospitality industry has been going through since 2008. In such situations, business results can be delivered primarily by managing productivity and efficiency with a huge thrust on cost management. This balance between cost management and people welfare emerges as a challenge for a company which espouses the Tata ethos. The third set of challenges could revolve around consistently delivering a high-quality consumer experience in luxury hotels, including talent spotting, training and talent management. Differentiating the brand based on this unique consumer experience is the core. The Taj, being the market leader, is benchmarked nationally and also internationally. So it has to work harder to stay ahead of the rest to command a premium, drive loyalty and be the preferred choice at a time of surplus supply and limited demand.

Shrinivas drew a parallel between engaged, committed and passionate employees and a car's engine. The responsibility of the management that plays the driver's role is to steer the car (company) in the direction of customer engagement. If this is done, the destination of financial results can be achieved. If the engine is powerful, the speed will be higher and the car is likely to outperform others (competitors) in the race. The management, at the steering wheel, has to intelligently manage sharp twists and turns and ensure that the engine power is consistently used towards customer engagement alone. The Taj's methodology of ensuring that the engine consistently operates at optimal strength and power was shared by Bickson.

During our conversation in his office on the first floor of the iconic Taj Mahal Palace Hotel, Bickson elaborated on the flagship hotel of the company. For over 113 years, it had incessantly worked 24/7, 365 days, with 680 staff per shift. Among the staff, one would find third and fourth generation employees working as front-office managers, whose fathers would have worked at the Taj. He shared the example of the restaurant manager of Shamiana, whose daughter Parvathy Omanakuttan won the Miss India 2008 beauty pageant and was adjudged first runner-up at the Miss World beauty pageant. The daughter of Mona Chawla, the director of housekeeping, is the famous Bollywood star Juhi Chawla. For all of these multi-generation employees, the hotel was much more than just a place of work. He believed that they were proud of their association with the Taj because it helped them and their families to build careers, improve their social status and provide stability in life. Shrinivas gave full credit to the efforts of Jamsetji and J.R.D. Tata in demonstrating finer human values in action. These inspired subsequent generations of Tata employees to practise excellence in normalcy and in adversity.

Within the 'Bickson-Decade', the number of IHCL employees doubled to 26,000. His concern was that going forward, as the company expands its footprint, the greatest challenge would be to groom employees within a few months and make them capable enough to represent the company at any of its national and international properties. He reflected that the hospitality industry could do well by learning from other service sector peers.[75] He believed that e-learning and technology could play a major role in preparing a 'Taj' cadre of people. This would enable them to stand before guests as a Taj employee and deliver to their expectations.[76] Rakesh Sarna, the new managing director, extended this to the next level: 'You need to build organizational capability for the present and future. This can be done only by grooming potential leaders, people who can take over, who cannot just carry on the legacy but do a better job with it.'[77] Bickson shared the findings of an internal survey that found 50 per cent of IHCL staff belonged to Generation Y. He emphasized the continued necessity for innovative people practices that attract the Indian millennials to work for the Taj and make a career with the company. 'You have to change your business model for your external and internal clients.'

Employee Training, with a Difference

'In the hospitality business where one has to deal with people, one can be the best waiter, but if one doesn't know how to do it with a certain style, elegance and dignity, you've diminished your company's value,' observed Bickson. He believed goodness is inherent and cannot be taught. Instead, the company has to look for nice people, and the selection process plays a vital role. I guess for this reason, the Taj tended to recruit most of its front-line and junior staff from interior towns, where traditional Indian values of respect for elders and teachers, humility, empathy, discipline, honesty, kindness to children and support to senior citizens are still visible. Added to the advantage of larger labour pools and lower remuneration, the advantage of recruiting from smaller towns helped in accessing manpower with 'inherent goodness', a virtue apparently evaporating from cities where the glamour of success could entice youth to compromise the means for the end. For the next level of recruitment—supervisors and junior managers—the Taj reached out to the top 100 hotel management and catering institutes across India. Along with testing domain knowledge and personality through the use of psychometric tools,[78] the company also looked at the candidates' sense of values and desire to contribute to the organization. For topmost positions, the Taj preferred candidates from second-and third-tier Indian business schools.[79] This was based on the company's experience that candidates from lower-tier business schools adjusted well in a customer-centric culture and weren't driven solely by monetary considerations. Karambir shared that when he was the GM at the Taj Mahal Palace Hotel Mumbai, the final interview of every candidate would be with him. Most GMs across the company followed this practice, primarily because a direct interaction with prospective employees would enable an understanding of whether the candidate would fit into the Taj culture. This approach of hiring from smaller towns was inductive, and based on experience gained over many years—that individuals with specific backgrounds demonstrated certain virtues that were vital to the Taj ethos, and hence, they were preferred over others. Issues of gender diversity and affirmative action also emerged as focus areas in the company's recruitment system.

The next step was training new employees by giving them tools, and exposure to experiences that made them efficient and inspired them to work with flair and sincerity. The TMTP (Taj Management Training Programme) and HOMT (Hotel Operations Management Trainee Programme) were two major programmes at IHCL. The former, a quasi-MBA, focused on managerial recruits; the latter, trained supervisors and junior managers. Both had a blend of technical and soft skills coupled with hands-on experience at various Taj properties. While most hotel chains trained front-line employees for a year, IHCL insisted on an eighteen-month programme even for its managers.[80] The company believed that a future general manager should have cross-functional exposure in all hospitality areas, including sales and marketing, finance, front office, food and beverage and human resource management. In select areas, the trainees underwent a two-year programme. A combination of theory and practice helped trainees imbibe lessons in classrooms and practise them in real situations.[81]

Most training was provided by heads of departments from various Taj Hotels. This brought authenticity in the process of transmitting company values and culture, rather than mere theoretical concepts by external consultants. The Certified Taj Departmental Trainers (CTDTs) formed the backbone of the company's learning and development initiatives that delivered nearly 25 lakh person-hours of training. Nearly 60 per cent of Taj executives were CTDTs. After a certain quantum of training, trainees were encouraged to take independent decisions while serving guests to enable them to get real experience. Shrinivas believed that the values taught in homes and schools to recruits from smaller towns, coupled with the Taj training, got translated into service values while dealing with guests. The Special Programme for Employee Education and Development Plus (SPEED+) aimed at meeting the career aspirations of associates at the staff and contract level after the initial training. Advanced management programmes were also conducted for employees across levels, including executive MBAs, through tie-ups with leading management institutes. For this, leadership competencies and individual development needs were assessed through an institutionalized talent management programme called 'Emerging Leaders' that comprised a series of diagnostic studies.[82]

Employees: Ambassadors of Customers

The Taj philosophy is to make its employees the ambassadors of customers. All through the training, they are groomed to approach every problem and tackle every situation from the customers' perspective. To empower them in this decision-making process, they are assured that for any decision taken by them to delight Taj guests, everyone, right up to the CEO, would stand by them. This emboldened employees to think while keeping in mind customers' interests.[83] The strategic rationale behind this approach was that employees should understand and meet customers' needs in such a way that the delighted guests have a compelling reason to do business only with the Taj Hotels. 'We want our guests to consciously reject the competition's offerings in every location, regardless of price,'[84] emphasized Shrinivas.

Figure 4.6: The Forty-one Opportunities to Delight Guests

An in-house study at the Taj found that on an average, a guest comes in contact with an employee forty-one times every day. This could be in the form of a wake-up call in the morning, passing by the guest in the corridor, opening the car's door, serving at the restaurant, connecting a telephone call, interactions with the concierge and bellman, and many others. The pessimistic way of looking at this could be that there are forty-one opportunities when employees can blow up the hotel's reputation. However, the Taj looked at these as forty-one opportunities to consistently deliver the Taj service levels and communicate the message of its brand to its guests. The company made all efforts to ensure appropriate processes and mechanisms to capture these forty-one 'moments of truth', and reward those employees who deliver the Taj-ness. Deepa shared how IHCL was the only hospitality company that actually measured employees on account servicing. Clients are asked about their opinion on employees' performance. Thus, the customer ends up appraising employees and not just the supervisor. That score plays a significant role in overall employee performance assessment. This seemed insightful, and a fair way of scoring employee performance.[85]

Innovatively Engaging NextGen Employees

Karambir was GM at two important Taj properties in Mumbai: Taj Lands End in Bandra and the flagship Taj Mahal Palace and Tower in Colaba. Both these properties had very distinct employee demographics. 'When I was the GM of Taj Lands End, the average age of my employees was twenty-four years. When I came to the Taj Mahal Palace, it was forty-four years. Consequently, the attrition rate at Lands End when I took over was almost 40–45 per cent. At the Taj Mahal Palace, it was in the teens.' Not surprisingly, even as Bickson had told me, a lot needed to be done differently in order to attract and retain millennial employees. This is true across industry categories,

especially in the service sector, as high levels of motivation
are critical in people-oriented, front-facing businesses. 'The
millennials want everything immediately. They're well-
connected and want to become GMs in two years!' wisecracked
Karambir. 'They think they know everything, which is fine.
You have to deal with those expectations as well, and also
give them a reality check.' He shared the interventions at
Lands End which aimed at improving employee engagement
levels for millennials. It started with efforts in the cafeteria—
improving the variety of food, placing multiple televisions,
organizing inter-departmental games every month and having
some kind of competition. To bring that kind of involvement,
for the first time, an annual day was organized where the
staff displayed their talents, and they surely had a lot of it!
Then there was a family day, when the staff brought their
family members to the hotel. 'I think when you start involving
families with the place of work, it forms that bond with the
organization,' he observed. Also, mentoring them to pick the
best management training programmes at the Taj and giving
them challenging assignments worked really well. Karambir
would throw a challenge at them: 'We want to open a new
restaurant. These are the guidelines. Work on them and let me
know what would you do?' Such new concepts excited them
and a lot of them would get together and be involved in the
planning and the execution. Thus, a vibrant environment, team-
building efforts, involving family, mentorship and executing
challenging assignments were initiatives that worked really
well in creating greater engagement with Gen Y employees.
Not surprisingly, IHCL had the highest employee engagement
scores in the global hospitality industry,[86] and was the only
hospitality company in the world to be a five-time successive
winner of the Gallup Global Great Workplace Award between
2010 and 2014.[87]

Figure 4.7: The Employee Strategy at the Taj

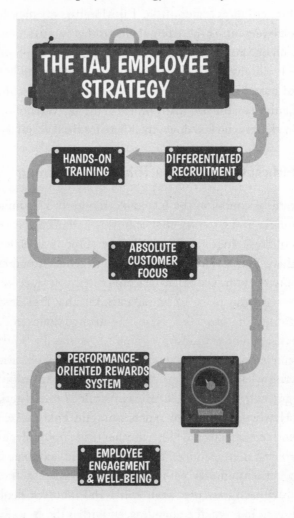

Unlike most companies, the Tata approach is not purely transactional. Owing to Taj the Mumbai's healthy relationship with its independent union, its employees chose to maintain a distinct identity rather than merge with other large unions affiliated with major political parties. That could have generated considerably more strife for the Taj management. Yet, it was not to be. In fact, a former union leader of the Taj Mumbai was stabbed by an extremist representing the external unions that wanted to penetrate the Taj union. Post the incident he had said, 'The Taj hotel is my temple. I will give my blood for it. It is everything [to me].'[88] As it turned out, the union leader was not alone in his desire to give blood for the Taj. He had many others of his ilk, who not only gave their blood, but even laid down their lives for the Taj and its guests.

The Darkest Cloud, with a Thick, Silver Lining

'Mumbai is a symbol of the incredible energy and optimism that defines India in the twenty-first century . . . The Taj has been the symbol of the strength and the resilience of the Indian people . . . The resolve and resilience of the Indian people stood in stark contrast to the savagery of the terrorists'[89]

—Barack Obama, President of the
United States of America

Articles, reports, books, documentaries and films have been made elaborating what happened during those fateful sixty-eight hours that began at 8.30 p.m. on 26 November 2008 (often referred to as 26/11), when ten terrorists representing the Pakistani extremist outfit Lashkar-e-Taiba (LeT),[90] travelled over 500 miles through the Arabian Sea from Karachi to Mumbai, and laid siege in parts of India's 'maximum city' with nearly 2 crore residents. The attack, planned with military precision, killed 166 innocent people and injured over 300. Amid resounding gunfire in the heart of south Mumbai, Operation Black Tornado, led by the National Security Guards (NSG) of the Government of India, neutralized the terrorists. Nine of the terrorists were killed, and one, Mohammed Ajmal Kasab, was caught alive in a Skoda car near Chowpatty Beach while trying to escape.

On most days, the Udyan Express from Bengaluru is delayed and arrives late at platform number 15 at the Chhatrapati Shivaji Terminus (CST) Station at 9.30 p.m. If it had arrived at the same time on 26 November 2008, I would have probably lost my dearest mother, returning from a pilgrimage. Fortunately, the train was on time, and she was out of the station only thirty minutes before Ajmal Kasab and his fellow terrorist Ismail Khan mercilessly sprayed bullets at hundreds of commuters on the CST platform—men, women and children. They killed fifty-eight people. Around the same time, in another part of the city, our five-decade old neighbours, Sevantilal and Sarla Parekh's only son, Sunil, and his wife, Reshma, had just entered the restaurant Tiffin of the Oberoi–Trident Hotel for a dinner meeting. Over thirty-six hours later, we received the tragic news that they were among the nine guests who were cruelly shot dead by two terrorists at the Trident. Their daughters, Anandita and Arundhati, were aged just twelve and eight then.

Of all the places targeted in Mumbai, the one where the fight with the terrorists lasted the longest was at the Taj Mahal Palace Hotel. Like the Opera House to Sydney and the Eiffel Tower to Paris, for over 115 years the Taj has been a prominent symbol of Mumbai. Even before the Gateway of India[91] was built in 1924, the hotel was the most outstanding structure on the Bombay coastline. In attacking the Taj and trying to destroy its century-old heritage wing, especially the historic dome, LeT wanted to leave a visible scar on the success story of India Inc. that was epitomized by one of the oldest institutions synonymous with Mumbai and its history. Over 1200 guests and 600 employees were inside the hotel for functions as diverse as a high-profile wedding reception, a Bohra Muslim wedding, Unilever CEOs Global Meet with thirty senior leaders from Unilever worldwide, and two other corporate meetings. The

Indian, Chinese, Japanese—indeed all restaurants—were full that Wednesday evening, when the first gun shots were heard.

The natural question then is how did the final number of casualties (guests and employees included) remain as low as thirty-one? With 1800 vulnerable people, and four terrorists loaded with latest ammunition, the fatalities could have been ten to twenty times that number! The primary reason for this was the employees of the Taj, who went way beyond the call of duty to save as many guests as possible. Krishna Kumar remarked that all employees knew the exit routes. However, it was beyond his comprehension that in spite of that, not a single employee gave in to the natural survival instinct and left the premises. Karambir called them the real heroes of the Taj. Even before the NSG commandos could formulate a strategy to safely evacuate the guests from the premises, the employees had used their prudence and ensured that they were in safe areas, until help arrived.

Chef Hemant Oberoi's valiant team formed a human chain to protect 60–70 guests while escorting them from Wasabi, the Japanese restaurant, down the spiral steps into the kitchen, and out. Thomas Varghese (head waiter), Vijay Banja (executive chef), Hemant Talim, Kaizad Kamdin and Zaheen Mateen (chefs) and Rajan Kamble (engineer), employees serving the hotel in different capacities for many decades, voluntarily faced the line of fire while evacuating guests through the exit routes of the labyrinthine Taj. They laid down their lives by blocking the gunmen's path, and were spewed with bullets from those vengeful weapons. Mallika Jagad, the twenty-four-year-old banquet manager for the Unilever event, and her team, used their extraordinary presence of mind, switched-off the lights and bolted the doors of the banquet room on the second floor of the hotel where the event was on. For over a dozen hours, she and her team took care of the guests who were ducking and squatting below the tables. Her team provided water and napkins from time to time for over ten hours. Finally, in the early hours of the morning, they were rescued by the fire crew through the windows. Amit Peshave, the twenty-seven-year-old manager of Aquarius, the Taj's 24/7 poolside cafe, had by instinct found his way out of the hotel's transformer room, from where another door opened out into Merry Weather Road, to the street on Colaba. However, his conscience tugged at him, and he came back to save thirty-one diners at the Shamiana restaurant. He was miraculously saved even though a grenade exploded close to him.[92] The telephone operators risked their lives but continued to hold fort in the control room to ensure that the guests in various rooms within the hotel received information and instructions in real time.

Who can forget Karambir Kang, the forty-year-old GM of the Taj? His heroic leadership of the hotel not only got it the Best Overseas Business Hotel Award,[93] but also universal appreciation for making the best possible efforts to save the lives of thousands of guests, even when his own family, wife Neeti and sons Uday and Samar, were getting asphyxiated on the sixth floor of the Taj. In our conversation he recalled, 'You know, at that time, we didn't know the magnitude of the attack, and the number of gunmen. Were they four or ten? But in spite of that, in the given circumstances, we just took the right decisions with whatever knowledge we had. We all felt responsible for each other and for our guests. It's not that somebody was telling them to do whatever they did. But, independently, in different pockets of the hotel, they all acted the same way. It was remarkable.' He believed that what happened that day was a tangible expression of the employees' belief that the Taj was their family. The place had given them livelihood, made their lives, educated their kids, and enabled them to build their homes. 'The Taj is like a temple. It's revered by the staff,' he told me. Even in adversity, the employees stood by the company ideals and ethos.

Given the details already in the public domain, there is little scope for further elaboration on what happened during those three days inside and outside the Taj. The important questions from an organizational perspective are: What did the Taj do after the massacre? What were the reasons for which Taj employees behaved the way they did during those horrific hours, even risking their lives? What are the lessons that other corporations can learn from the events that unfolded on 26/11? I asked Bickson, who was himself stuck inside his office for nearly sixteen hours, 'What was the reason for the Taj employees' behaviour that day?'

'The reason my people created those human chains and essentially put themselves in between the terrorists and the guests was that they considered this hotel as their home. You cannot come to my house and you cannot harm my guests because they are my family. It was a direct manifestation of the Indian philosophy that the guest is God,' he said.

Shrinivas described the hapless scene outside the Taj. The terrorists were inside the hotel, the higher floors of the heritage wing were ablaze, and constant gunshots were being heard. Ratan Tata, Krishna Kumar, and all senior people from the company were standing helplessly on the pavements outside, not knowing what was going on inside or how many people had been killed. It was a horrendous feeling. Hundreds of employees from other shifts had flocked to the venue and were squatting on nearby roads. The police had laid siege around the hotel. In such a scenario, instead of lamenting the loss, his team took the traumatized employees sitting expressionless on the pavements to the nearby Holy Name High School, and requested the priest to permit them to use the hall, to which he kindly consented. Batch by batch, morning, afternoon, night, next-day morning, afternoon and night, his team continued to interact with employees and console them. Within a few days, employee assistance centres were set up in ten locations across Mumbai, each with two post-trauma counsellors, a medical doctor, a car, a van and two drivers. Details of Taj employees in each of those areas were prepared and they were brought to those centres along with family members. Shrinivas and his team explained to them what had happened, encouraged them that the Taj would once again bounce back from this rare tragedy, assured them that their jobs were not lost, and that they should unitedly fight the situation. 'All this spontaneously happened in the first fortnight. In those days, we hardly slept,' he recalled.

At another venue, Deepa was sitting in a 'war-room', a crisis and emergency microsite that was put together for handling everything from lost baggage to finding people, and providing minute-to-minute updates on what was happening. 'It was a best practice in terms of how a microsite could have been used,' she said. At that time, a lot of requests for help were coming in from people in hospitals, whom the Taj was paying for. There were some people who had nobody to pay their bills. There was this dilemma as to whether the patient was connected to the tragedy at the Taj in any way. At that time, Krishna Kumar walked in with a message from Ratan Tata that the Taj should not distinguish while helping people, whether security forces, police, fire service, hotel employees, guests of the Taj or general public, whether killed or wounded. Tata had decided to form a trust which would pay for everybody injured anywhere in the city during 26/11.

Not only then but in the future too, for those affected by natural or man-made calamities, the Taj Public Service Welfare Trust was announced on 15 December 2008, only seventeen days after the disaster. Besides IHCL, Sir Dorabji Tata Trust[94] and Sir Ratan Tata Trust[95] committed a significant initial contribution to the newly formed trust. Ratan Tata himself was a part of the board of trustees that included Krishna Kumar and Raymond Bickson, among others.[96] Tata instructed the team to go to every hospital where the injured were being treated. If the hospital hadn't taken care of the bills, the Taj would do the needful, irrespective of whether the person was injured at CST or the Trident–Oberoi. Even hawkers and street vendors, who were injured during the attack, were taken care of.[97] Deepa emphasized that it was a part of the Tata culture to go beyond the ordinary and contribute. The staff witnessed the company's reaction being in total alignment with their sacrifice in the larger cause of human welfare.

Besides a number of other relief measures, the company decided that families of Taj employees who died during the attack would be paid their deceased members' salaries for the rest of their lives, as well as all medical benefits and education for dependents up to the age of twenty-four. Within a week of the attack, Ratan Tata wanted to meet the family members of all deceased and injured employees. They were flown into Mumbai for the meeting.[98] During the gathering, the wife of Thomas Varghese, a forty-nine-year-old waiter at the Taj, who came in between the terrorists and guests and took the bullets on himself, spoke to Tata. She said, 'My husband died for a cause and will always remain a role model for me and my children. I never knew I was living with such a great man for the past twenty years. All I want from my children is that they too should practise these values, stand tall in their lives and acquit themselves creditably before God Almighty. Practising those values is far more important than whatever money you are planning to give as a settlement.' For the first time, in decades, in full public view, Ratan Tata's eyes welled up. Recalling those moments, Shirinivas said, 'Interacting with the families, we realized that designations mean nothing. There are such great people in such simple positions. It is because of them that there is goodness in society.'

Figure 4.8: The Media Communication Released by the Taj on the Day after the Terror Attack

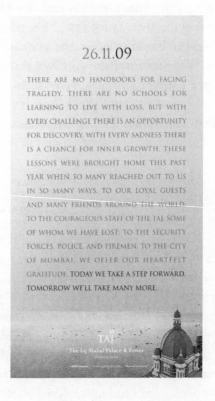

'We may have been knocked down, but not out,' Ratan Tata avowed. To communicate a message resonating this spirit, the Taj ran a three-part communication campaign 'Taj Forever', which aimed at healing, moving forward and communicating to the world that 'Taj is forever'. The first part emphasized defiance. 'It really hurt us that our flagship hotel was targeted. We were so emotional about it, and that was the message we tried to communicate by publishing defiant messages,' Deepa shared. The second part of the campaign contained healing messages to people who were injured and affected through this tragedy. The final part of the campaign emphasized that the hotel was renovated and the Taj was once again ready to welcome its guests.

It was a common resolve that the Tower wing should be opened in record time. Within just three weeks of the attacks, it did reopen. It even went ahead with other planned events for December 2008 including launching the Vivanta by Taj in Bangalore, the Pashan Garh Lodge Resort in Panna (Madhya Pradesh) and the Taj Club House Chennai.[99] The message to the world was that the Taj was not going to be bogged down by such acts of cowardice.

Figure 4.9: The Taj Mahal Palace Mumbai Announces Its Reopening

The weekend before the Taj was reopened, a staff-only programme was organized where spiritual leaders from all major faiths conducted prayers and healing rituals. For forty-five minutes, the names of all 1700 employees of the Taj Mumbai were read out to appreciate the unity with which they stood behind the company. 'Just to hear all our names echo in that hall was so reaffirming. It united us in a way that went deeper than the usual team-building programmes,' reminisced Bickson. The next day, 1000 people, including guests, friends and family, applauded continuously for fifteen minutes, tears streaming down many faces, as the 540 Taj employees who were on duty on the night of 26/11 strode proudly through the lobby on a red carpet.[100] They were the real heroes of a real adventure—the game called life. To share their solidarity with the families of those who had lost their loved ones, the Taj placed a memorial in the lobby, with the names of all thirty-one victims. It was a humble tribute to their bravery and sacrifice in the darkest hour of the hotel's history. It was a memorial for the future generations to commemorate the ideals the departed employees had placed before the company and its guests. In the months following the attack, the employees at the Taj Hotels were trained in advanced security, safety and disaster management in collaboration with a specialized Israeli company.[101] Traditionally, hospitality and security don't go hand in hand. Yet, what 9/11 did to the American airline industry, 26/11 did to the Indian hospitality industry. The fun and freedom of going to a five-star hotel and relaxing in a cocoon was lost in large measure for good.

On reflection, there are three lessons that companies and institutions can learn from the Taj in light of their response to the terror attack. Firstly, the way in which Ratan Tata and the entire management of the Taj handled the aftermath. It was the most mature response to an event of that magnitude. What left most people spellbound was that within three weeks of the

Figure 4.10: Ratan Tata and the Taj Senior Leadership Celebrating the Reopening of the Taj Mahal Palace Mumbai

attack, the Taj once again opened its doors to welcome guests. It was symbolic of defiance coupled with courage. Secondly, the response towards their employees. Typically, when two-thirds of a hotel is closed down, any organization would retrench some part of its employee base, as large as 1800 people. However, the Taj didn't. Not a single person was retrenched. Instead, the period was used to further train the employees and raise service levels. Many were transferred to other Taj properties so that they could continue their good work. Lastly, the manner in which the Tatas decided to take care of the families of the deceased, not only the employees but also from the public at large, was beyond normal expectations. These lessons go far beyond a win-win solution or strategy. They were far beyond any economic or even ethical considerations. They were in the realm of morality and bordered upon spirituality. An acknowledgement to this came from a person no less than the President of USA. In 2010, during his historic ten-day visit to India, President Barack Obama chose the Taj as his residence in Mumbai to show his solidarity with the victims of 26/11. During the visit, he said, 'To those who have asked whether this is intended to send a message, my answer is simply, absolutely!'[102]

Figure 4.11: Three Lessons from the Taj after the Terror Attack

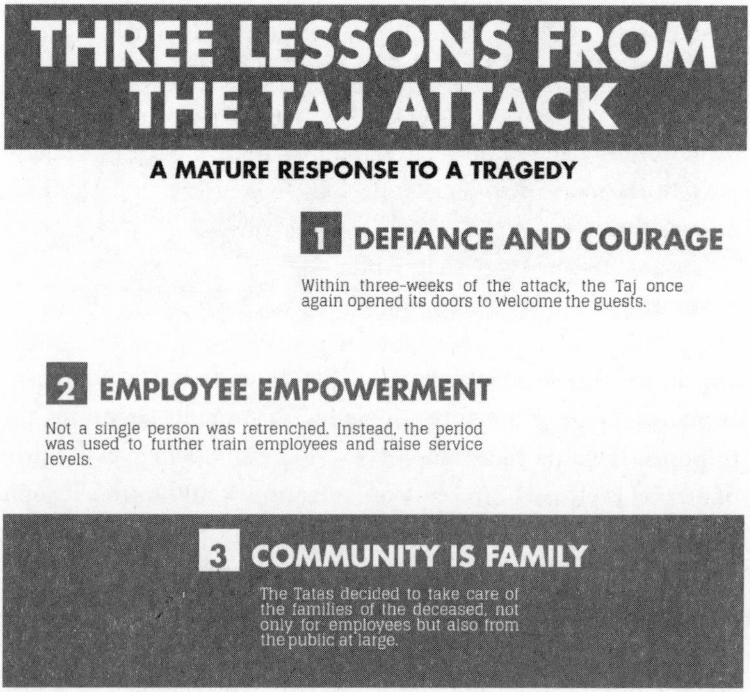

THREE LESSONS FROM THE TAJ ATTACK

A MATURE RESPONSE TO A TRAGEDY

1 DEFIANCE AND COURAGE

Within three-weeks of the attack, the Taj once again opened its doors to welcome the guests.

2 EMPLOYEE EMPOWERMENT

Not a single person was retrenched. Instead, the period was used to further train employees and raise service levels.

3 COMMUNITY IS FAMILY

The Tatas decided to take care of the families of the deceased, not only for employees but also from the public at large.

Legendary Hospitality Integrated with Social Responsibility

'The future of the hotel industry will see two major trends surfacing: a more responsible industry with regard to conservation and the environment, and a more socially-conscious traveller'

—Raymond Bickson

In our conversation, Vasant Ayyappan, then associate vice president of corporate sustainability at IHCL, took me back in time, and made me imagine India in the late 1800s. The British ruled India. Mughals were ousted from power from the Delhi Durbar. Rajas ruled their small kingdoms. The rich were really rich. Yet, by and large, there was abject poverty across the country due to the colonial rulers who had oppressed and plundered India for over five centuries. In that kind of atmosphere, there was one businessman who believed that the real purpose of business should not be to just make money. It should be to give back to society many times more than what one has taken from it. That was Jamsetji Tata.

Vasant emphasized that while such an approach seemed so daunting in today's scenario, that somebody could think of it over 100 years ago was really visionary. The same historical context was referred to by R. Gopalakrishnan, then director of Tata Sons. During our conversation, he narrated how the vision of Jamsetji Tata in the 1890s was repeated by J.R.D. Tata in the 1960s and by Ratan Tata in the early 2000s. While the words were different, there was a consistency in the message about the group's core purpose that if we make profits, we've earned it from the community, so we have to give it back to the community in some form. The whole recycling of wealth and prosperity between the firm earning the profit and the people who gave it formed the core of the Tata Group's philosophy of business. He compared it to the dependability of Arundhati (Star Alcor) that forms a double star with Mizar (considered Maharishi Vashishtha) in the Ursa Major constellation (considered as the Sapta Rishis or seven sages). Just as Arundhati is always seen with Vashishtha, community and societal welfare activities are always seen as an integral part of the Tata Group's presence across businesses.

Contributing to a Dignified Demographic Dividend

Given that they are in the food business, the initial approach of corporate responsibility at the Taj was in the form of distributing excess food to old age homes and orphanages. Vasant recalled the transition from this approach: 'We could have sat back relaxed thinking that we've done our bit towards poverty eradication by feeding the poor. But very quickly we realized that the people to whom we were giving food were becoming dependent on us. So it wasn't really a nation-building activity. We needed to teach people how to fish.' The corporate sustainability (CS) team at the Taj reflected on how they could contribute to nation building. While the list of issues was endless, they wanted to use their core competence to make a difference. They mapped the Tata ethos, the Millennium Development Goals,[103] the Prime Minister's Ten Point Social Charter[104] and their core competence and decided that given their expertise in hospitality, they would focus on 'building sustainable livelihoods' in areas connected with the industry. Their belief was that by economically empowering the youth, the company was actually empowering the entire family, and thus, contributing to a stronger India. In 2015, the travel and tourism industry contributed to 3.7 crore jobs (8.7 per cent of total employment) in India, and was expected to rise to 4.6 crore jobs (9 per cent of total employment) by 2026.[105] Hence, the opportunity to make a difference was enormous. An easy approach would have been to bring the youth below poverty line to the company centres, train them, make them employable, and send them back. However, the CS team decided to follow the difficult path of going into the community and establishing centres in very backward and rural areas. The focus was on the youth who did not have the opportunity or money to come to urban centres.

An initial survey revealed that the average monthly salary of a family of five in rural India was Rs 1700. That meant just Rs 11 per person per day. So, by the time the male child was fourteen and the girl child was thirteen, there was huge pressure on them to move out of the home and start earning. Typically, the boy moves into the nearest town and works at a bicycle shop or a dhaba. The monthly salary of Rs 2000 makes him happy and he sends Rs 500 home. Yet, very quickly, he realizes that he isn't able to live within Rs 1500. So he moves out from wherever he is living, and starts staying in the motor mechanic's place. To save even more money, he starts skipping a meal every day. Five months down the line, he's disillusioned as the life before him isn't rosy. This is the time that somebody approaches him and says, 'I'll teach you how to make a quick buck.' This quick money could be through facilitating prostitution or petty thievery or drug peddling. With this, his income increases five times, and his parents are delighted to receive a few thousand rupees from him every month. They bless him immensely for his contribution to the family. This goes on for six months, until one fine morning, a police van turns up before his house . . . Once they get into jail, they're finished for life. First, they get a police record. Secondly, they meet with hardened criminals. Finally, even if they're out of jail, society does not accept them or reinstate them without prejudice. India's future can be saved and demographic dividend truly reaped when corporations can help by preventing these able-bodied youth from getting into anti-social activities, and by giving them vocational training to become self-sufficient.

The Taj started its skill-building journey in the tribal belts of India with the largest amount of poverty and backwardness, including the northeast, Jammu and Kashmir. These centres were started in collaboration with NGOs. The Taj trained the trainers, provided a curriculum and vital resource material on areas such as housekeeping, food and beverage, bakery services and more. It was estimated that by 2012, the industry would need an estimated 3,00,000 spa therapists. To contribute to this, the Taj Jiva Spa offered a three-month training course in spa services at the training centre set-up in Dimapur in Nagaland.[106] Besides the inputs from Taj experts, trainees would get an opportunity to briefly work hands-on at one among the many Taj properties across India. At the end of their training, the participants would receive a joint certification, which would help them gain quick employment.[107] The Taj also stepped in to collaborate with Central and state government projects. For example, during the 2010 Delhi Commonwealth Games, at the call of the then Delhi chief minister Mrs Sheila Dixit, the '*Hunar Se Rozgar Tak*' (expertise to employment) project was started to train local, unemployed youth in hospitality skills such that they could earn a living when guests for the games thronged the national capital. A six to eight week intensive training module in diverse areas, including accommodation, food and transportation, was provided to enable the youth to get mainstream jobs. Subsequent to its success, the ministry of tourism initiated a nationwide replication of the project model.

Yet another project was initiated under the Integrated Child Development Services (ICDS), a national programme for the health and nutrition needs of children in the Nadurbar district of Maharashtra. It was chosen as a pilot location due to the high incidence of malnutrition in its migratory tribal population. The chefs of the Gateway Hotel Nashik accepted the challenge of making a difference to the quality and taste of meals prepared for the target group—children less than six years of age, lactating mothers and pregnant women. The nutritious recipes were to be made using locally available ingredients, and at the same time ensuring an intake of 300 calories and 8 grams of protein per day. Led by Ratnakar Prabhu, a Maharashtrian specialities chef at the Gateway Nashik, forty recipes for breakfast and lunch were developed within the ICDS budget of Rs 1.98 per child per day.[108] As a result, over 1.5 lakh children had six different types of food every week.[109]

No project is without its challenges. The Taj's livelihood initiative was no different. Vasant shared with me four major challenges that the team faced while executing the project. First was the attraction of the daily wage schemes. The draw of instant money on a daily basis for doing casual work created a strong deterrence for working in a skilled job with a monthly salary. The former required no discipline, the latter demanded a lot of professionalism. The second challenge was lack of proficiency in spoken English. In the hospitality industry, with international guests forming the majority, English is a very important component of success. While rural schools taught English, it was limited to the slate and blackboard variety. The language never graduated from the head to the lips. This made them diffident and created a glass ceiling they could rarely cross. The three-month training provided by the Taj was helpful but inadequate to help them master the language. The third challenge was the lack of ambition. No one talked of careers in villages. Even the sarpanch (village head) had no clue of opportunities beyond government jobs. The last and most important challenge was the lack of importance given to the girl child. The moment the father got an opportunity to marry her off, he would do so simply to avoid social pressure. This problem was predominant in north India. The girls who found the courage to step out of their homes to join the programmes faced not only social ridicule but also demeaning comments from within the family. The Taj team was not in a position to handle this deep-rooted social problem. Sustained efforts at the national level were the only solution. The '*Beti Bachao-Beti Badhao*' programme[110] of the Narendra Modi-led government was an important step in creating awareness about the role of girls' education and empowerment.

Every cloud has a silver lining. For scores unable to handle the aforementioned challenges, there were dozens who faced them and emerged victorious. Vasant shared the example of Mangala, the first girl to join the skills programme in Aurangabad in 2009. Till then, no girl had ever left the village she hailed from. She was the first one, and faced resistance when she did. She joined the course because she didn't have money and her parents were in debt. Post training, she began working with the Taj. When she first joined, her monthly salary was Rs 4500. She emerged as a hardworking person and was quickly confirmed in her job and went on to receive a monthly salary of Rs 10,000. With her savings, she was able to pay back all her parents' loans and eventually became the pride of her village. The other story is of Kishore from a remote village near Kolhapur. He couldn't speak a word of English, but soon realized the opportunities if he picked up the language. Through sheer hard work, he learnt the language and finally landed himself a job in the Taj in Goa. With this success, his hopes soared higher. His hard work was rewarded and in a short time he became a supervisor. From the initial Rs 10,000, his salary doubled. From the average monthly household income of Rs 2000, Kishore had managed to earn ten times that amount within a couple of years. Without the skills training, he would have remained in the village doing odd jobs. Now his destiny was in his own hands and the sky was the limit. Hundreds of Mangalas and Kishores have their own unique story to share. They represent a young, resurgent and aspirational India. All they need is a helping hand. Companies such as the Taj had taken the first step in the right direction.

There is another example of a different genre that we need to look at: a category of human beings whose lives become hell because of circumstances and the vicious desires of a handful. They lead a spiteful and undignified existence in a 'profession' called prostitution. In 2006, in Goa, the tourist hotspot of India, a renowned NGO, Anyay Rahit Zindagi (Arz), started Swift Wash (SW), a laundry aimed at being a non-shelter alternative economic programme for rehabilitated female sex workers from Baina beach, Goa's notorious red-light area that was partially demolished in 2004.[111] Aware of the Tata Group's social focus, Arz approached Taj Hotels in Goa to provide training and support for operationalizing SW. The Taj CS team visited and assessed its potential. The initiative was not without challenges. They had inefficient infrastructure and zero capacity to deliver quality output at scale. Though laundry services for room linen, staff uniforms, spa dresses and others form a major requirement for any hotel, the question was whether SW could match Taj standards. So even without considering it as a service provider, the Taj team planned an integrated training programme for technical and soft skills. For ten months, Taj volunteers worked with the Arz team to build capacity among women. Finally, in 2007, they gave the first order for 25 per cent of Taj's spa linen. Unfortunately, the output was not up to standards. However, Foram Nagori, now corporate director of CSR at IHCL, and the Taj staff, did not lose hope. They continued to provide mentoring. Usually the Taj is not soft with vendors on quality issues. However, in this case, they considered it as a commitment to the community. Eventually, through hard work and a zeal to emerge victorious, SW was able to win orders for 100 per cent of the Taj's spa linen. The quality and quantity of work had made the relationship financially sustainable.[112] Remarkably, the Taj did not take the charity route to support Arz's social focus. It paid SW the market rate for its laundry services. Of course, through its year-long training and mentoring efforts, it had compensated many times more by building a competitive capacity in the beneficiaries who, in their own words, were now able to earn a living with respect. Their kids knew them as working mothers, with jobs in a company. The women now looked forward to a dignified life with their children and grandchildren. In 2016, when SW completed a decade, Arz released 'Beautiful Women—Despair to Dignity', a compilation of life-transforming experiences of its women.[113] The other jubilant feature of the decennial celebrations was their expanded network of clients that included dozens of companies, hospitals and educational establishments. And yes, Taj Hotels continued to be one among them.

Encouraging India's Rich Crafts and Historic Arts

Weavers in India have been patronized by rulers for over twenty centuries. Unfortunately, in the last couple of decades, power looms substantially substituted a hereditary craft form that was traditionally passed down from generation to generation, thereby endangering livelihood. What typically takes a couple of months to design by traditional craftsmen can be completed in a couple of hours by power looms. This drove the weavers to extreme steps for survival. One fine evening, Ratna Krishna Kumar, the wife of then vice chairman of the Taj, was shocked at a news item presented on television that showcased a thirty-year-old weaver from Varanasi who lost his life while selling blood to support his family.[114] She reflected upon how the Taj could make a difference in their lives, not through charity, but by supporting their craft. Through subsequent discussions, the Taj decided to have the front-office staff across its luxury and palace hotels wear authentic Banarasi silk sarees.[115] For this purpose, Sarai Mohana, a village of 5000 residents, 5 kilometres away from Varanasi, was selected. The weavers, some of whom had sold their looms or even used them as firewood, were given new looms. Dyed silk yarn from Bengaluru was provided to them for weaving, along with solar lamps to prevent disruption of work due to frequent power cuts. Fashion designer Jay Ramrakhiani was taken on board to create motifs for the sarees. All these efforts aimed at reducing the weavers' personal investment in the production of these sarees. They only needed to contribute their skill and make quality products. Each of them produced about three sarees every month, and collectively supplied over 1000 in two years.[116] The Taj paid them Rs 3500 for every saree and Rs 550 for every blouse. This was ten times the amount they received from middlemen who exploited them due to lack of access to markets. Over 550 women in a dozen Taj luxury and palace hotels became brand ambassadors of this craft. Custom-made sarees were also sold to tourists at the Taj Khazana stores across India.

To complement weavers' economic empowerment, the Taj also embarked on a comprehensive social welfare programme focusing on child nutrition, medical assistance through camps, providing spectacles for weavers with weak eyesight, and supporting surgeries for cataract and glaucoma patients. Water pumps were installed to make lives easier for women. In addition, training programmes were also funded to ensure that the skill was passed down to the next generation and the craft continued. To expose tourists to the weavers' work, staff from the Taj and Gateway Hotels in Varanasi accompanied guests on a tour to Sarai Mohana. The village that had almost collapsed into destitution had now become an integral part of the tourist circuit, and was also featured in July 2015 in the *New York Times*! (Appendix IV.A elaborates many interesting efforts by IHCL to encourage India's rich cultural traditions.)[117]

The Tata Approach to Dealing with Dilemmas

'No success or achievement in material terms is worthwhile unless it serves the needs or interests of the country and its people and is achieved by fair and honest means'[118]

—J.R.D. Tata

Let's go back two decades to one of the Taj properties in Kerala.[119] One Sunday morning, a food inspector arrived at the hotel and approached the deputy general manager (DGM) with his intention to inspect the premises. He was promptly invited into the kitchens for his checks. However, he was hesitant. Instead, he said, 'If you insist I'll check. But I'm a reasonable person and don't like to create trouble.' The DGM knew where he was heading and so he said,

'You're most welcome to join us for lunch.' The inspector declined the offer saying that he didn't have time and had to leave at the earliest. After a lot of back and forth he said, 'You give me Rs 6000 rupees and I'll leave.' The DGM flatly refused. He said, 'I will not, I cannot.' The inspector threatened him with serious repercussions and said that he could put the hotel in trouble. Concerned with his attitude, the DGM shared the matter with the GM. But the answer remained the same—the inspector was welcome to do whatever assessment he wanted and satisfy himself.

Finally, he entered the kitchen and went straight to the yogurt section to check the quality. The chef was very happy, because the practice at the Taj was that after buying milk, milk powder was added to it to ensure that the curd set very well. So there was no question of any problem. Yet, surprisingly, the inspector's report indicated that the fat percentage in the curd was lower by 2.4 per cent. Now, the Prevention of Food Adulteration Act, 1954, is a non-bailable offence. A GM could go to jail if his hotel was found guilty, and nobody except the chief minister of the state had the authority to save him. So the inspector slapped those charges against the Taj hotel. With a villainous smile he said, 'All I was asking for was Rs 6000. I told you, I'm a reasonable man. But you didn't want to listen.' Now the hotel had to approach lawyers to defend the case. In those days, a lawyer charged Rs 10,000 as appearance fees. On the first appearance, the inspector intentionally didn't turn up at the court. The second time he came without his file and apologized. The third time he came, but made some other excuse. Now this had cost the hotel over Rs 30,000 simply in legal charges. Finally, the GM decided to go and personally meet the chief minister of Kerala in Thiruvananthapuram. In those days, the Taj did not have a property in Thiruvananthapuram. And so the GM and DGM had to stay in another hotel for two days. That amounted to Rs 8000 per day plus meals and travel costs. Finally, when the GM met the chief minister, he was surprised at a case filed against the Taj. 'What is this case? How can there be a food adulteration case against the Taj! I myself eat at the Taj Hotels,' he said. Realizing the ridiculousness of the case, he instantly squashed the inspector's order.

In hindsight, instead of Rs 6000 that the food inspector was asking for as a bribe, the Taj ended up spending Rs 50,000 to defend themselves, including precious man hours spent on the visit to the chief minister. Yet, what was the outcome? This former DGM of the hotel, who narrated this entire episode to me, said that after that day, that inspector never came back to any of the Taj Hotels in Kerala, because he knew it was a waste of his time. He knew that every time he would come and level wrong charges against the Taj, he would get called to the court, and his 'earning time' would get wasted in legal hassles. Thereafter, he would always tell his peers, *'Tata ka hotel hai—chhodo.'* (It's Tata's hotel, leave it.) He knew that he wouldn't get any money out of them. A permanent behavioural change was made possible. That was the real output of the Rs 50,000 investment by the Tatas.

The Tata Way of Leadership, for the next 100 Years . . .

'To be a leader, you have got to lead human beings with affection'[120]
—J.R.D. Tata

Each of the senior leaders at IHCL that I interacted with personally had a unique story to share about their years with the company. Deepa recalled the day when she got the job at the Taj. Back in those days, women working for hotels was not seen in good light. So her parents retorted, 'Isn't there any other job you can take up? Are you crazy that you're joining a hotel?' She turned around and said, 'You know, it's owned by the Tatas. I'm going to work for a Tata company.' That pacified them completely and they encouraged her to go ahead. Deepa believed the reason for this was the celebrated century-old Tata culture. 'It's really a culture which is not self-serving but rather focused on nation building.' At international events, most people would tell her that the Taj was doing so much in the CSR sphere. When she shared the same with Ratan Tata, he would always say that the company was not doing enough. So the levels of expectation of the top leadership in terms of contributing to society and the community were way above normal. 'There is so much about that trust factor and that halo of what the Tata brand stands for. To nurture and build on it as equity for ourselves would be the way going forward,' she concluded.

As GM of the Taj Mumbai, Karambir had the opportunity of watching Ratan Tata from close quarters. He would come often to the Sea Lounge for his traditional breakfast of Akuri and toast. What really impressed him were the times when Tata would come driving himself in his Honda City, or sometimes in a Tata Indigo. He would go and park the car himself and quietly settle down for breakfast. In contrast were industrialists who would come with police escorts and big, flashy cars. A memorable meeting was when he had gone to pay a courtesy visit to Ratan Tata in his office after being appointed as the GM. The meeting was delayed by five minutes, and so he waited outside. The first thing Tata said on coming out was, 'I'm so sorry to keep you waiting.' He apologized not once but twice. After a twenty-minute conversation, when he was leaving, he saw Ratan Tata following him. So he said, 'Mr Tata, I know the way out.' The reply was, 'This is the first time you've come to my office. I will see you right down the steps of Bombay House.' He was amazed at the heights of humility and professionalism practised by the chairman of India's largest conglomerate. In his sales and marketing days, he had visited dozens of CEOs of big companies. Many of them had made him wait for over two hours. At the end of that, there wasn't a single word of apology for the delay.

Tata's warmth didn't end at the level of the general manager. He knew almost the entire staff at the Taj Mahal Palace Hotel Mumbai and would often inquire about their families. Due to his fondness for dogs, he would talk to the staff about their dogs! Of course, it didn't end with exchanging pleasantries alone. It also involved a great eye for detail. For example, when Taj Lands End was acquired, Ratan Tata, along with the then managing director, Krishna Kumar, toured the property. One of Tata's first comments was that the look and feel of the hotel needed to be toned down. He wanted it to look classy rather than gaudy. At the Taj Mahal Palace Hotel, there was just one reception at the Tower. So post the terror attack, when renovation was almost done, Tata recommended that the hotel should have an additional reception in the Palace and Heritage Wing so that when people walk in, there was more recognition and warmth. That was the kind of hands-on involvement he had.

When I asked him if he had ever had the opportunity to meet J.R.D. Tata, there was a twinkle in his eye. 'I was too junior then. Once J.R.D. had come to the Taj Palace Delhi. I walked up to him and said, 'Mr Tata, my name is Karambir Kang, and I work for you.' J.R.D.'s reaction surprised me. Instantaneously, J.R.D. hugged me and patted my back while politely inquiring about my work and background.' In response, he shared that he had completed his MBA and that his father served the Indian army. 'I mean, he genuinely chatted with me. I was just a junior sales executive. Yet, that warmth, that Taj-ness, was very visible in him. It just felt fantastic, you know. I still vividly remember that moment even after twenty-five years,' he recalled with a smile that stretched from ear to ear.

The Taj was the only company Karambir had worked with since he started his career. I asked him his understanding of the leadership philosophy of the group through his silver jubilee years. 'You should never forget that any business or any organization is actually made up of people in flesh and blood. Any decision that we take, we should keep in mind that an organization has a life and soul too. So when dealing with any organization or people, if you're not genuine and authentic, you'll never be able to make that impact,' he emphasized. He believed that when history is written, Ratan Tata and J.R.D. Tata would be remembered more for their genuineness, authenticity and humility than their remarkable corporate achievements, because that is the core of the Tata leadership. With such a leadership approach, he was convinced that people who work for the company would give their very best. 'They will do anything for you. Even give their lives for you.'

While Deepa and Karambir belonged to the group of lifers at the Taj, Raymond Bickson was a stark outsider, and the first expatriate to lead a Tata company. In his four-decade long experience spanning four continents, he had lived, on average, for three years in fourteen cities and eight countries. To get an appointment with him was quite a challenge. So many times our meeting was confirmed and then cancelled at the last minute due to some urgent developments at his end. Finally, when we met, it was a full year since I had first requested a meeting. It was scheduled at 5.30 p.m. When I reached his office on the first floor of the Taj Mahal Tower in Colaba, Chrisa D'Souza, his secretary, apologized on his behalf that he would be delayed and that our meeting would be at 6 p.m. I was just hoping that our interaction time wouldn't get reduced. At 6 p.m., he himself came to where I was sitting and with a broad smile ushered me into his office. With a great deal of familiarity he said, 'I know we haven't been able to meet for a year.' After exchanging pleasantries he said that he wanted to show me a video. Especially for our meeting, he had identified a video on the theme of hospitality. We both watched it for nearly thirty minutes while having watermelon juice. It was nearly 7 p.m. The scheduled appointment time was over. My concern was that he would conclude the conversation even before I could start with my long list of questions. To my surprise, after the video was over, he said, 'Yes, now tell me what do you want to know about the Taj?' I was relieved. After an hour, and only halfway through our conversation, my relief was converted into satisfaction. At the end of our chat, satisfaction was transformed into delight. Way past his office hours, he spoke to me for nearly two hours, sharing his decade-long experiences at a company that just concluded its 113th annual general meeting. No doubt, he was the senior-most representative of the culture of Taj-ness and the philosophy that 'employees are ambassadors of customers'. The customer in me was superlatively delighted!

'What have been your key learnings while at the Taj?' I asked. 'Each place has its own flavour, its own food, culture and music. The experience of being in India at a time when this emerging country is coming of age on the global map has been very interesting,' he said. He had been at the Taj at a time when the Tata Group transitioned from a predominantly India-focused group of companies to a multinational conglomerate with 65 per cent of revenues from overseas operations. He was fascinated by the changing mindset of the group and modernizing its policies and ways of doing business to meet international benchmarks. In a single decade, he had personally witnessed the launch of the Nano, the world's most value-for-money car, the acquisition of Jaguar, one of the world's most prestigious car brands, and the international success of TCS. In 2010, while at the Tata Suite of the Taj Mahal Palace Hotel, when President Barack Obama and First Lady Michelle Obama met Ratan Tata, Michelle expressed her desire to see the 'wonder car'—Tata Nano. The very next morning, a glistening Nano was parked on the porch of the hotel. When the first couple of America stepped out that morning, they had a good look at the car. Michelle even sat in the car for a first-hand experience.[121] Bickson was an eyewitness. The Tata Group had emerged on the world stage in substantial measure. Through all this, there was one thing that remained constant in the group. 'A big thing I learnt while at the Taj was the code of ethics that the company stood for. To live that code of ethics has been fascinating. It's been an unbelievable experience to be a part of it,' he admitted.

Bickson's decade at the helm of affairs was full of crisis management of sorts. A tsunami that hit eleven of the Taj Hotels across the Indian Ocean rim, the chikungunya epidemic and a terrorist attack on the company's flagship property in Mumbai that resulted in thirty-one deaths and property loss worth crores. Through these difficult situations, he realized that such events can be faced well when each member of the larger team perfectly plays their role. The final outcome is always a team effort. That's what the Taj did, and did so well, that its efforts and approach were nationally and internationally acknowledged by corporations and academia alike. The Harvard Business School published a case study documenting the people practices and code of ethics at the Taj Group of Hotels that distinguish it as a unique institution.

Referring to the importance of the Taj, the Tata Group's oldest company, a dream of the founder Jamsetji Tata, Bickson said, 'I think people forget that you are a custodian of a jewel of a heritage which represents an institution built over a long period of time.' This desire to ensure that the jewel continued to shine in its firmament would not let him sleep at night. His resolve, and indeed the company's resolve, was to ensure that in spite of dozens of international brands thronging the Indian hospitality industry, this 100-year-old institution should continue to remain a brand, a company, a force to be reckoned with. 'We have been here for the long run, and we are here for the long run. One hundred years from now, the decisions we make during our time at the Taj should enhance the business and make it nationally and globally competitive.'

Figure 4.12: Win-Win Learnings from the Taj Group of Hotels

LESSONS FROM
THE TAJ GROUP
OF HOTELS

1. BRAND POWER

A strong brand nurtured with
care can survive many
generations

2. MOMENTS OF TRUTH

Delight customers during every
interaction to win customers for
life

3. AMBASSADORS OF CUSTOMERS

Employees should represent
customers' interests in the
organization

4. PURPOSE-ORIENTED PEOPLE PRACTICES

Hiring and training employees
for values than just for skills can
create a committed talent pool

5. SUSTAINABLE SUCCESS

Innovation and measurement are
powerful tools for impact-
oriented environmental practices

6. RESPONSIBILITY BEYOND PHILANTHROPY

Businesses can creatively enable
social and economic
empowerment beyond pure
charity

V.

Hindustan Unilever

Doing Well by Doing Good

'I believe that nothing can be greater than a business, however
small it may be, that is governed by conscience; and that
nothing can be meaner or pettier than a business, however large,
governed without honesty and without brotherhood'
             —William Hesketh Lever, founder, Lever Brothers

It was 8.55 a.m. on Monday. I rushed up the elevator to the sixth floor
of the historic Lever House Building, headquarters of Hindustan
Unilever Ltd (HUL), the market leader of the Indian packaged
consumer goods (also known as FMCG—fast moving consumer
goods) sector. My interactions with the senior management
at HUL were to begin with D. Sundaram, then vice chairman
and chief financial officer (CFO) of HUL.[1] This was the first of
several insightful interviews that I was to have with HUL's senior
management from 2008 to 2010, which became the basis of my
understanding of the company's approach to multi-stakeholder
management. Our meeting was scheduled to start at 9 a.m. in
his chamber on the senior executive floor of the building. I was
there on time. As soon as I entered his office, his secretary, Raju
Kamakodi said, 'Sir has already come, fifteen minutes ago. He
is waiting for you.' I was quite surprised. A young researcher, I
slowly entered the office of the vice chairman of India's largest
FMCG company. Very cordial and unlike 'serious-looking'
CFOs, Sundaram warmly asked about my journey to Mumbai.

He wanted to know more about the research I was doing and the executives I would be interacting with. During the hour-long conversation, he didn't overwhelm me with financials of the FMCG market leader, whose products are used by nine out of ten households across India. Instead, he focused on HUL's basics, a company he believed had grown with India. Based on his thirty-four years of experience, he encapsulated the century-long journey it had traversed from the times when the first consignment of Sunlight Soap landed on the shores of Calcutta, the then capital of British India.

Introducing Hindustan Unilever

'Our vision is to grow our business while reducing our environmental footprint and increasing our positive social impact'
—Unilever

Hindustan Unilever Ltd is a subsidiary of Unilever, an Anglo-Dutch multinational company headquartered in Rotterdam in the Netherlands and London in the United Kingdom. It is one of the world's leading suppliers of fast moving consumer goods, with annual sales of €53.3 billion (Rs 4,00,000 crore) in 2015. Its products are available in 190 countries across continents. By 2016, emerging markets accounted for nearly 60 per cent of its business. The Unilever Group has about 400 brands spanning various categories of home care, personal care and food and refreshments. Of these, thirteen brands generate annual sales of more than €1 billion (Rs 7461 crore). These include brands like Axe/Lynx, Dove, Omo, Becel/Flora, Wall's ice creams, Hellmann's, Knorr, Lipton, Lux, Magnum, Rama, Rexona, Sunsilk and Surf. The group takes pride in its claim that on any given day, nearly 200 crore of the 700 crore people in the world use Unilever products.

To cater to this volume and geographic reach, it employs more than 1,68,000 people worldwide with 45 per cent of its managers as women.

In 2016, Unilever had 67.2 per cent shareholding in HUL. Though incorporated in 1933, HUL products have been sold in India since 1888. With annual sales of Rs 31,987 crore in 2015–16, it operates through four categories: home care, personal care, food and refreshments. Nine out of ten households in India use one among the thirty-five brands from twenty distinct business segments in home and personal care products and food and beverages manufactured by HUL. This reach and scale is possible through 2000 HUL dealers. An employee base of 18,000 runs the company across India.

Figure 5.1: HUL Factsheet

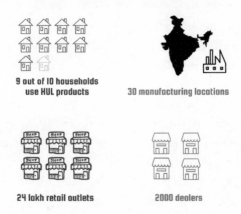

Headquartered in Mumbai, HUL has a national sales network with five branch offices and more than thirty manufacturing locations across India. Along with geographic diversity in production locations,

HUL has an impressive sustainability track record that is visible through some key statistics reported in the public domain. During the annual investor meet in June 2015, HUL CEO and managing director Sanjiv Mehta highlighted that over thirty HUL production sites had 100 per cent zero non-hazardous waste to landfill, besides more than 92 per cent reduction in total waste per tonne of production, 48 per cent reduction in water use per tonne of production, and 42 per cent reduction in carbon dioxide per tonne of production (all compared to a 2008 baseline). Inspired by the Unilever Sustainable Living Plan (popularly called USLP), by 2030, the parent company and all its subsidiaries, including HUL, aimed at halving the environmental footprint of the making and use of its products, besides sourcing 100 per cent of its agricultural raw materials sustainably and enhancing the livelihoods of millions of people across the value chain.

The Eight-decade Odyssey

The Pre-Independence Colonial Era (1888–1947)

The first consignment of Sunlight Soaps manufactured in England by the Lever Brothers landed on the shores of east India at the Calcutta harbour in 1888. In 1924, the Lever Brothers started manufacturing a new soap called Taj. It started manufacturing in India in 1932 by establishing a factory just outside Bombay to make Vanaspati (vegetable ghee). In 1934, it constructed another modern soap factory, also in Bombay.[2] Between 1931 and 1937, Unilever established its three subsidiary companies in India: Hindustan Vanaspati Manufacturing Company (1931), Lever Brothers India Limited (1933) and United Traders Limited (1935). The Indian population, then in the thick of the freedom struggle from colonial British rule, had become familiar with brands such as Lifebuoy, Pears, Lux and Vim, which had been imported since 1895.

The Post-Independence Era (1948–91)

The Unilever Subsidiaries formed between 1931 and 1937 were merged to form Hindustan Lever Limited (HLL) in November 1956. It was the first international company to offer 10 per cent of its equity to the Indian public.[3] By 1965, the Indian shareholding increased to 14 per cent. Unilever realized the importance of having Indian managers lead HLL. So, after a series of non-Indian chairmen at HLL,[4] in 1961, Prakash Tandon was appointed as the first Indian chairman of Hindustan Lever. Tandon's appointment was among the very first in India when an Indian became the chairman of a large, foreign-owned company. His appointment created an Indian identity for HLL and worked to its advantage in an era of growing nationalism. By 1966, HLL's 360 managers included only six expatriates.[5] By 1967, with a turnover of Rs 93.28 crore, HLL was among the top five private sector companies in India in terms of sales. By then, it had six factories and an employee base of 7000.[6]

In 1959, when HLL introduced Surf washing powder in India, it also affected a huge transition in the way Indians washed clothes. The act of washing gradually changed from beating the clothes against a stone or a club (while washing) to rinsing them inside a bucket. The establishment of Hind Lever Chemicals, a subsidiary for chemicals, marked the beginning of its backward integration strategy. Between 1971 and 1978, HLL launched a number of personal care products that have since become iconic brand names. These include Clinic shampoo, Liril soap, Close-up toothpaste and Fair & Lovely skin cream.[7]

In 1972, Unilever acquired Lipton, the world-renowned tea brand that had belonged to Brooke Bond,[8] whose presence in India dated back to 1900. By 1982, Unilever had largely divested from HLL and held only 51 per cent stake in the company. In 1984, Unilever acquired Brooke Bond, with its ownership of the well-known Red Label brand. Pond's (India) Limited,[9] which had been present in India since 1947, joined HLL in 1986 when Unilever acquired Chesebrough Pond's USA.

Figure 5.2: HUL's Eight-decade Odyssey

HUL: The Eight-decade Odyssey

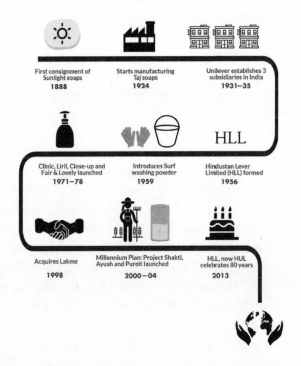

The Post-Liberalization Era (1991 onwards)

The landmark year 1991–92 saw the end of the Licence Raj[10] in Indian industry. After forty-five years, Indian industry had opened up to international players. With multiple players in the FMCG industry, this period saw greater consolidation, mergers and acquisitions between companies in the Indian market. The first one happened in 1993 when the erstwhile Tata Oil Mills Company

(TOMCO), a leader in the Indian FMCG industry and a part of the Tata Group,[11] merged with HLL. HLL also acquired the Kissan[12] business from the UB Group[13] and the Dollops Ice cream[14] business from Cadbury India,[15] expanding its base in the food category.

In 1996, HLL and yet another Tata Company, Lakme Ltd,[16] formed a 50:50 joint venture—Lakme Lever Ltd, to distribute Lakme's market-leading cosmetics and also other products of both companies. In 1998, Lakme Ltd sold its brands to HLL and divested its 50 per cent stake in the joint venture. In 2000, the Government of India sold 74 per cent of the equity in Modern Foods to HLL. The company's entry into bread was a strategic extension of its wheat business. In 2002, HLL acquired the government's remaining stake in Modern Foods.

The 1980s and 1990s proved to be outstanding years for HLL in terms of top line (sales) and bottom line (profits) growth. It beat its international competitors like Procter & Gamble and Indian competitors like the Tatas and Godrej, and became a market leader under many categories in the FMCG sector. However, by 1999, its top line growth had stagnated. Analysts suggested three major reasons for this: HLL's high margin structure, large overheads compared to local competitors and lack of sufficient innovation. To give momentum to the company's growth story in the new millennium, a task force of middle managers from within the company was selected. The team was charged with finding new ideas and models.

Nitin Paranjpe, who eventually went on to become the managing director of HUL eight years later, was part of this team.[17] In April 2000, at the annual general meeting, Keki Dadiseth, then chairman of HLL, launched the Millennium Plan, a strategic blueprint for the company prepared in consultation with external experts. These ventures were selected based on the changing business environment in India, HLL's then existing resources and its ability to build capabilities over a period of time.[18] Nearly 150 new business ideas were proposed before the list was narrowed down to nine. These included a foray into drinking water, a plan for network marketing, entering into herbal therapy products and targeting rural consumers through a novel distribution system.[19]

Accordingly, in 2001, HLL started Project Shakti (meaning feminine energy), a rural initiative that targeted the bottom of the pyramid customers from small villages (with a population less than 5000 individuals). This award-winning initiative focused on rural affluence and women's empowerment with business benefits.[20] In 2001, it also launched 'Sangam' (meaning confluence), its direct-to-consumer retail venture. Over 3500 grocery and household products, mainly from HLL's portfolio, and some other brands like Garnier and Godrej were available on the portal.[21] In 2002, HLL ventured into the Ayurvedic beauty products category. It started the Ayush Therapy Centres, a chain of Ayurvedic clinics. To beat competition from a number of network marketing FMCG companies such as Amway India[22] and Modicare,[23] HUL started its own direct-to-home distribution network called the Hindustan Lever Network in 2003.[24] In 2004, the company forayed into water purifiers through its Pureit range, which provided water as safe as boiled water at a highly subsidized price of Rs 1500, especially for consumers in the lower rungs of society.

In 2007, the Hindustan Lever Ltd (HLL) name was changed to Hindustan Unilever Ltd (HUL). In the same year, it also launched a new logo, which comprised twenty-five different icons representing the company and its prominent brands. By January 2010, HUL shifted its headquarters from the landmark Lever House office in south Mumbai to a new and large site in Andheri, a northwestern suburb of Mumbai. When HUL celebrated its eighty years in India in October 2013, the 'soap and soup' company had established itself as a market leader in the FMCG sector. It was recognized as the number one brand in laundry, soaps, hair care, home care and skin care; and number two in oral care and tea. [25]

Figure 5.3 A and B: Net Income and Return on Equity of Leading Indian FMCG Companies

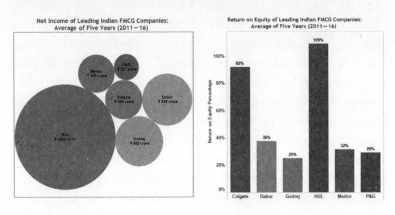

Net Income of Leading Indian FMCG Companies: Average of Five Years (2011–16)

Return on Equity of Leading Indian FMCG Companies: Average of Five Years (2011–16)

Delighting Crores of Indian Consumers, Every Day

'Our purpose is to make sustainable living commonplace. We work to create a better future every day, with brands and services that help people feel good, look good, and get more out of life'

— Unilever

Consumer understanding is at the heart of the HUL business. It helps its brands to constantly evolve and retain consumer preference, and is the key reason why brands such as Lux and Lifebuoy have remained most preferred and trusted brands in their categories, over several generations. HUL believes that this has helped it to grow the markets through innovations—from introducing affordable sachets to driving penetration in shampoos and fabric wash segments to introducing top-end skin care products catering to emerging consumer needs such as anti-ageing. The company's endeavour to serve the many 'Indias' embedded in the one India has enabled HUL to build an enviable portfolio of products. From premium brands to the affluent, from value-for-money brands to middle-income consumers, and from affordably priced brands to the low-income consumers.[26]

According to an AC Nielsen study, sixty-two of the top 100 brands in the Indian FMCG sector were owned by MNCs, and the balance were owned by Indian companies. Fifteen companies owned these sixty-two brands, and twenty-seven of these sixty-two were owned by HUL. The personal care category had the largest number of brands, with HUL accounting for eleven of the twenty-one brands in this category. In 2016, six of its brands were valued at Rs 2000 crore each. These included Surf Excel, Brooke Bond, Wheel, Rin, Lifebuoy and Fair & Lovely. That is the power of HUL brands!

Given such an elaborate set of consumers covering the entire spectrum from the affluent to the rural, how does HUL define what a typical customer needs? I asked this very question to Sanjiv Kakkar, then executive director of customer development at HUL and now executive vice president at Unilever NAMET—North Africa, the Middle East and Turkey. He said that a 'customer value proposition', in simple terms what a company uniquely offers to a consumer, is the function of:

Consumption need (product) + Quality + Price + Psychological need associated with the brand

Firstly, every consumer expects that the product which she is buying is a good product and provides value for money, i.e. it should satisfy the consumer's value equation. She should perceive the value addition to her when paying the price for a particular product. Secondly, the consumer expects that since she has chosen the product, it is a better quality product as compared to others. Most importantly, the consumer has certain expectations from the brand of the product as well. A good brand satisfies certain psychological needs of the consumer.

For example, Knorr Soup. The product proposition is: Soup (basic product) + Knorr Soup (brand). The advertising of the soup helps the consumer family supposedly relate to its values of a 'wholesome family soup product' while consuming it. So, a brand satisfies a basic consumption need and a higher order psychological need. Both are equally important because otherwise a company could just be selling commodities; why would it sell brands? It can just sell the product as soup powder in the market without any label, isn't it? The reason why a product is branded is because it helps the company to differentiate its products from competitors and also satisfy certain psychological needs of the consumer.

While the formula looks rather easy to achieve, there are challenges. The major challenge is finding the right balance between corporate profitability, product quality and pricing. From the consumers' point of view, they would be thrilled if they get a better quality product at a lower price. However, this would be disastrous for the company in terms of profitability. So it's a challenge to find the right price from the consumers' viewpoint. The company may find that though it considers its price to be the best price, it is not able to make enough money. So the other thing would be to bring down the quality to make the profitability right. But, if the company does this, it would be upsetting the value equation of the consumer, and the consumer may not want to buy the product at that price for that quality.

Summarizing this whole balancing act, Sanjiv said, 'According to me, managing that trinity is the greatest challenge. The value (quality) that the consumer seeks from you, the price at which you sell, and the profitability which the shareholder is demanding from you by virtue of having invested in your business. Trying to manage these is always a key challenge as far as the consumers are concerned.'

The 'Holy Trinity': Needs, Challenges and Solutions

Discussions with HUL leaders and following its performance, I observed that in order to achieve the trinity of needs and overcome the trinity of challenges, HUL has used a trinity of solutions that have made it the preferred FMCG brand for crores of Indian consumers. I have attempted to capture each of these along with an anecdote that represents actual implementation.

Constant, Integrated Innovation

A systematic innovation programme at HUL converts consumers' needs into products, mixes and advertising. Over the years many innovations that have now become part of our regular usage have been contributed by the Hindustan Unilever Research Centre that was set up way back in the year 1967 in Bombay. Some of these, now available as products in the market, include structured bar soap, fairness cream, zero alcohol soap, intelligent deodorant, poly-coated scouring bars for dishwashing, fortified salt, instant tea, healthy ice creams and a water purifier that works without electricity and running water. HUL continues to plan for the next round of innovations based on the evolving needs of its existing and prospective consumers. The company has a pipeline of future research programmes. Some of these include: making a soap bar more economical by lasting longer; enhancing the tea drinking experience through high aroma and taste as well as through additional health and nutrition benefits; and reducing water usage and making washing detergent/bars more tolerant to the quality of water in which washing is done. Interestingly, the pace of innovations at HUL intensified since 2010.[27]

Among its innovations that have now been successfully commercialized, I got really interested in the one that also achieved a social objective and benefitted India and Indians at large. The Pureit Water Purifier is a remarkable example of an integrated innovation by HUL. The product, its pricing, promotion and distribution have all been devised keeping the stakeholders' interests in mind.

Pureit Water Purifier: First in the World, for India

As part of the Millennium Plan, HUL embarked on a number of new opportunities outside their core products and markets. One of them was to create a water purification and storage system meant for consumer use at the point of water usage. In 2008, water purifier usage in India was just 8 per cent.[28] A vast majority of the Indian population either boiled water, used ceramic filters or did nothing. The counter-top water purifiers were cheaper than the UV (ultraviolet) and RO (reverse-osmosis) technology products and hence, more popular. They also did not need electricity, which was another limitation in many parts of India. Their limitation was that they did not provide protection from select viruses, bacteria and parasites. Boiling water was the privilege of a minority in India because of the time and expenses involved. The working couples had almost given up boiling water and were looking for easier and safer options.

HUL wanted to achieve the international standards of the United States Environment Protection Agency (USEPA) through a counter-top water purifier at a price that was about 20 per cent of the UV/RO water purifiers that met that standard. For achieving this, the company followed a new approach to product innovation. It formed an inter-functional innovation team that collaborated with many international experts, including the London School of Hygiene and Tropical Medicine. The HUL team had mandated for itself that the proposed product should meet the USEPA without the need for electricity and running water. Given that the target audience belonged to the lower strata of society, with limited levels of literacy, the HUL team wanted the device to be 'fail-safe', i.e.

the device should have an indicator signalling the need for a change in the filter, and also an auto-shut mechanism that would stop the flow of water when the germ-killing capacity of the filter was over. Besides, to meet the typical Indian psyche, the purified water had to also 'look good' and 'taste good'! Surprisingly, at the time of product development, even the high-end UV/RO filters did not have these features. Unilever's market research team also realized that there was no such product anywhere in the world. To achieve the envisaged product, the HUL team went through 200 design changes over the years of product development. In each of these iterations, it ensured that it met the dual requirements of international quality with super-local prices. The journey overshot the estimated one-year time frame for product development by over two years. Yet, the team did not yield to internal time deadlines till they were ready with the near 'miraculous' solution to the drinking water problem in India. Finally, the team used the novel biocide-cum-filter-based approach that achieved the USEPA standards. The traditional pricing approach in such cases is cost-based, i.e. selling price = cost + profit margin. However, to make this product affordable to low-income families, HUL priced it at a level at which the prospective consumers could afford the product. According to a 2010 *Business Today* estimate, over 600,000 villages, 120,000 government-licenced hospitals, 100,000 schools and 65,000 restaurants needed clean water supply.[29] This was HUL's target audience.

Sharing his experience of what motivated the Pureit project team, Yuri Jain, then vice president (water) at HUL,[30] said, 'What gives this team its sharp edge is the belief that in protecting people's lives, we make a really big social difference. Working in a corporate environment, the two "C"s of cash and career are important for people. But what we want to do is add the third big "C" of cause. When people are driven by their own cause-inspired commitment, there is little doubt that they fulfil their full, innate potential and perform accordingly.'[31]

The 2008 launch of the Classic model of Pureit was the first of HUL's foray outside its core FMCG business into the consumer durables sector. The idea-to-execution period had taken nearly a decade. The Classic model attempted to provide clean drinking water of international standards to consumers at the base of the pyramid. HUL innovated even with the distribution model. To educate prospective consumers and book orders for its water purifiers, HUL used the direct-to-home (DTH) network, which proved to be successful. In October 2009, the company launched the Auto-Fill model of Pureit. Instead of manual filling, this model had the additional feature of connecting the filter with the direct source of water. For a large population in India that had an erratic and uncertain water supply schedule, this was a great advantage. In January 2010, just before the launch of Tata Swach, a competing product with similar benefits and an extremely low price, HUL crashed the timelines of its product innovation programme and brought forward the Pureit Compact model. By releasing the Pureit Marvella model targeted at high-end customers, HUL completed the spectrum of its water purifying line in June 2010.

Figure 5.4: Pureit Classic Model

Pureit was thus not just a product innovation, but innovation in all the four 'P' s of traditional marketing: product, price, promotion and place (distribution). The interesting aspect of Pureit was that it was a stakeholder-centred innovation. It was designed keeping in mind the needs of the final consumer, at a price that she can afford and at a place where she can buy. My mother is one such satisfied customer of Pureit for the last eight years! By 2015, Pureit provided 7000-crore litres of safe drinking water pan-India. The product was also taken to other emerging economies, including Bangladesh and Indonesia.[32] Underscoring the uniqueness of this innovative product, Unilever's chief marketing and communications officer Keith Weed said, 'When I visit countries around the world, I see sales numbers flashed on the walls. When I see the Pureit team, I see the number of lives protected.'[33]

Redefining the Cost–Quality Paradigm

For a behemoth like HUL, using its skills, whether against competition, for optimizing an opportunity or for making a technological or process change, are critical for consumer success. Its immense scale (in terms of depth, breadth, brands and products) and ability to use them at critical junctures is commendable. Quoting the example of Nirma, one of its fiercest rivals in the 1970s and the 1980s, Dhaval Buch, then executive director of supply chain at HUL and now chief procurement officer at Unilever, told me, 'This goes back to the times when Nirma came into the markets in India and created, by virtue of its pricing, a huge low-end market for detergents. Till then, everyone thought that detergent powders can be sold only at Rs 21 or 22. But Nirma came with its detergents at Rs 8 per kilo.'

Wheel Detergent: Low on Cost, High on Quality[34]

In 1969, Karsanbhai Patel, a chemist with the Gujarat Minerals Development Corporation in Ahmedabad, decided to do

HDFC Bank: Board members 2015–16.

HDFC Bank: Aditya Puri receives the CNBC-TV18 Outstanding Business Leader of the Year Award 2015–16 from Finance Minister Arun Jaitley.

Larsen & Toubro: Baha'i Temple of Worship, New Delhi.

Larsen & Toubro: Hitec City, Hyderabad.

Larsen & Toubro: Kempegowda International Airport, Bengaluru.

Larsen & Toubro: Chennai Metro Rail.

Larsen & Toubro: The Sri Sathya Sai Institute
of Higher Medical Sciences, Bengaluru.

The Taj Group of Hotels: President Barack Obama with Ratan Tata
and his senior team at the Taj Mahal Palace Hotel Mumbai, 2010.

The Taj Group of Hotels: The Taj staff as
ambassadors for the Banarasi saree weavers.

The Taj Group of Hotels: The Taj Umaid Bhavan Palace, Jodhpur.

Hindustan Unilever: Dream girl Hema Malini as brand ambassador of Lux.

Hindustan Unilever: The evergreen Lalitaji endorsing washing powder Surf.

Bharat Petroleum Corporation: Gas discovery in Mozambique.

Bharat Petroleum Corporation: Forays into shale gas in Australia.

Bharat Petroleum Corporation: Prime Minister Manmohan Singh and Chief
Minister Shivraj Chauhan at the inauguration of the BPCL Bina Refinery, 2011.

TVS Motor Company: Senior leadership
at the Deming Prize ceremony, Japan, 2002.

TVS Motor Company: Venu Srinivasan receives the Padma Shri, 2010.

something new to earn an additional income. His existing monthly salary of Rs 400 was insufficient to run the family. During a series of kitchen experiments using his knowledge of chemicals, he was able to prepare an effective and inexpensive detergent powder. The prudent Gujarati entrepreneur began selling this powder to his neighbours for a small profit. This yellow-coloured powder was named Nirma (after his one-year old daughter, Nirupama). The powder came as a boon to housewives struggling to manage their monthly budgets. So, Karsanbhai's home-based industry continued. He used to manufacture the product in a bucket, without using any electricity. He used soda ash as the main ingredient in Nirma washing powder. Unlike its high-priced competitors, Nirma contained no 'active detergent', whitener, perfume or softener. Every morning, he rode his bicycle marketing Nirma door-to-door, and sold an average of 200 kilograms every day. Through word of mouth, the product became very popular across Gujarat, and distributors started lining up at his doorstep to place orders. To meet this increasing demand, he started a company called Nirma Chemical Works and established two more production facilities in the next couple of years.

A sensible Gujarati businessman, Karsanbhai believed in the power of scale and made his money not through margins per unit, but through volume. He also outsourced all administrative functions by contracting out accounting, sales and distribution. The Nirma ingredients were mixed by hand, requiring no mechanized production process. The company was thus granted a number of exemptions for saving on electricity, and was also exempted from paying excise duties that were levied on MNCs. As a cottage industry, Nirma was not required to pay minimum wages to its workers. The contract workers hired in the production plants were paid Rs 85 per tonne. The company was not required to pay worker benefits as most of its employees were hired on a temporary basis. Thus, he saved lakhs of rupees on operating costs and was able to negotiate costs during lean sales periods.

A believer in the time-tested Coca-Cola maxim that a product should be available within an arm's length of desire, Karsanbhai concentrated on widening his distribution network. Without the need for establishing a sales network, Karsanbhai used wholesale distributors to make Nirma available across India. With a minuscule advertising budget of 2 per cent of revenue, and with its catchy jingle, *Nirma detergent tikiya ke jhaag ne jaadu kar diya'* (The Nirma soap cake has worked wonders), Nirma reached lakhs of households across India. By 1977, it became the number two brand (after Surf) in the detergent category with 11.90 per cent of the market share, compared to Surf's 30.60 per cent.

HUL's first reaction to the now visible competition was to launch two successful Unilever brands—Ala and Rin—that were 35 per cent less than the price of Surf. However, this attempt failed to attract consumers. HUL's second attempt was to revive an old and popular brand—Sunlight. Popular as a soap bar, it was launched as a washing powder to compete with Nirma. HUL made exceptions in the packaging of Sunlight by using plastic vis-à-vis the traditional cardboard packaging. HUL experienced success with Sunlight in western and northern India. However, this was temporary. Many small brands like Ghadi and Fena that followed the low-cost price strategy of Nirma ate into Sunlight's market share. These solutions emerged as temporary.[35]

HUL continued to believe its market research that the low-priced products were not very effective in washing clothes (research showed that they even harmed the quality of clothes), and that their soda ash-based solutions were harmful to the skin of its users. So in the long run, consumers would reject them. But they were in for a surprise. By 1985, Nirma became the number one detergent brand in India with 58.1 per cent market share. Surf, the once unbeatable detergent brand, was reduced to 8.4 per cent market share. The top management of HUL was concerned. To add to their sense of dismay, Nirma started developing a competing product for Rin, HUL's market leader detergent soap. The Nirma soap cake was being given free along with two bags of Nirma powder. The soap reached lakhs of Indian households and was well received. At one-third the price of Rin, it captured 40 per cent of the market share by 1989.

HUL realized that Nirma and its ilk were here to stay. More importantly, it recognized a huge untapped market that it wasn't reaching out to in spite of its scale and spread. All along it believed that the Indian urban middle and upper classes were its target consumers, and that its high operating and overhead costs would inhibit it from producing a low-cost detergent targeted at low-income and rural consumers. This belief was held even though India had the largest rural market in the world. In the early 1980s, nearly 50 crore Indians lived in rural India. This was 12 per cent of world population, twice the population of USA, and almost equal to the population of continental Europe. It was time for HUL to redefine its strategy.

It is popularly believed that the company launched Project STING: Strategy to Inhibit Nirma Growth. The discussions were led by HUL chairman Dr Ashok Ganguly and were attended by senior managers. The objective was not just launching a new product, but a change in the business model. Once again, HUL was focusing on a new stakeholder with unique requirements. The HUL team had to come up with an alternative that had the following characteristics:[36]

- High quality
- Lack of toxicity with minimum pollution
- Sufficient durability for rough transportation
- Tolerant of heat and dust with a long shelf life

- High value for money
- Low unit price and high functionality
- Self-visibility and display
- Packaging and contents that are disposable and dispensable
- Availability in small packages
- Strong but cost-efficient marketing campaign
- Wide distribution throughout rural India

While the company was pushed to rethink its detergent market strategy, the approach was not just focused on responding to competition or capturing a new market. The HUL R&D team was given a mandate to produce a low-cost product that gave better performance in terms of whiteness, but without the side effects of wear and tear and itching caused by Nirma's high soda ash content. While product affordability was the prime concern, consumers' safety was equally important. After a successful test market in 1987, HUL finally launched Wheel detergent in 1988, priced slightly higher than its direct competitor, Nirma.

The journey, however, did not end with R&D and developing a new product that was a match to existing competition. HUL used its scale and expertise as an FMCG behemoth to redefine its business model from all angles—pricing, production, promotion and distribution. It decided to learn from the experience of small manufacturing plants in India. In order to provide the product at an affordable price for the price-sensitive customer, and making this introduction sustainable, it decided to reduce the cost of production by using third-party production and locating the plants closer to the areas where raw material was available. The semi-automated production units replicated the small-scale manufacturing model and benefitted from low costs. HUL also modified its distribution strategy for Wheel. Traditionally, HUL products were given to carrying and forwarding (C&F) agents, who in turn supplied the products to stockists, and finally sold them through retailers. In the case of Wheel, HUL bypassed C&Fs and sent the product directly to stockists. Eventually, HUL started Stepan Chemicals, a subsidiary company in Punjab, and entirely outsourced to it the production and distribution of Wheel.

In fact, in creating Wheel, HUL also kept in mind that rural consumers would wash their clothes in rivers and other water bodies commonly used by village folk. So it ended up substantially reducing the amount of oil that Wheel contained, thereby making it as environmentally benign as possible. By 1989, Wheel became the second largest brand in India. By 1990, Wheel was larger than any other HUL brand in India. Being pushed by competition and a changed business model led to this success—not only in scale and reach, but also in revenues. It registered a 25 per cent growth in profits between 1995 and 2000. Its market capitalization grew to US$ 12 billion, an annual growth of 40 per cent. By 2002, HUL and Nirma had equal market shares of 38 per cent each. HUL had risen from its 7 per cent market share in 1987, and Nirma had fallen from its 61 per cent market share during the same period. By 2010–11, Nirma's market share had fallen to 10 per cent.

Summarizing the HUL approach of using its scale to its advantage and providing a benefit to a new category of consumers through a revised strategy, Dhaval said, 'This is an example of how we bring our strengths into focus and gain a competitive advantage. Initially, the feeling was that low-end detergents was not a market which could grow. We [HUL] already cover such a large market in the detergent area with Surf. So why go into that small low-end market? In this case, scale was working towards our disadvantage because it was building in us what can be called 'intellectual arrogance'. Later, when HUL was able to choose its scale, its technology and the speed in order to introduce Wheel as an alternative to Nirma in the low-end market, and the resources that we were able to focus for this purpose, led to the result that we have a much larger market than Nirma. This exemplifies, in a way, how our scale can be a disadvantage as well as a huge advantage.'

The story doesn't end there. By the time HUL was able to cater to the lower end of the detergent market, it faced another challenge in the early 1990s. This was from Procter & Gamble's premium product Ariel that was eating into Surf's market share. This competition was at the higher end of the market. Unlike in the case of Nirma, HUL swiftly responded with a super-premium product 'Surf Ultra' that was based on advanced enzyme technology, just like Ariel. While HUL researchers had developed this technology much earlier, their market research showed that India was not ready for a super-premium product. However, with the launch of Ariel, HUL was quick to gauge that the growing middle class in India was ready for aspirational products. Compressing conventional methods of new product development and using the might of its scale to carry out each stage of the development process in parallel, HUL reduced the lead time from two years to four months. Surf Ultra was launched in February 1992 and was received very well by target consumers. (Appendix V.A elaborates HUL's initiatives after its experience with Nirma and Ariel.)

Creative and Customer-centric Communication

The last of the trinity for HUL's success with consumers is its communication strategy. In the early 1970s, HUL was a prominent advertiser on radio, print media and billboards across India. Since those days, almost 10 per cent of its revenue is spent on advertising and media.[37] In the 1980s, when television became the most powerful medium of advertisement and promotion, HUL used characters that instantly clicked with the masses. Most people remember the 'Liril Girl' promoting Liril freshness, Lalitaji promoting the value-for-money Surf detergent, and well-known Bollywood film stars sharing their beauty secret—Lux!

Figure 5.5: Leela Chitnis Endorses Lux Soap

What is the reason for this sustained emphasis on communication over forty-five years? The answer is that in a retail, consumer-focused business, even if a company has a great product, if it's not able to make the consumer aware of it through the right choice of media mix,[38] or it's not able to reach the consumer because of lack of appropriate distribution channels, the company's product will fail. During our conversation, Dhaval emphasized HUL's expertise in activating this mix in the market through the right choice of media, through large, national mass media as well as local activities. The Surf and Wheel campaigns clearly revealed how the right message to the target audience made all the difference.

Surf Excel

In India, laundry consumes nearly 20 per cent of household water. HUL's proprietary technology that reduced water consumption and the time taken for rinsing by 40 per cent was of great benefit to most parts of India facing water scarcity. Using the example of Surf Excel, where product quality and the right media mix made all the difference, Prasad Pradhan, now head of sustainable business and communications at HUL, said, 'Usually detergents need a lot of water. But Surf Excel required less water to do as good a job. We communicated this specific benefit to the final consumers effectively. As a result, both advertising and the product were a great success. We received an excellent response from consumers.'

Wheel Detergent

After the launch of Wheel, HUL had to promote two detergents—Surf and Wheel. It clearly emphasized the difference between the two products so that the distinction between the two customer segments was clearly maintained. It did not want cannibalization[39] of either brands. While Surf was aimed at a quality conscious urban housewife, Wheel was aimed at a cost-conscious 'rurban' housewife. In the case of Surf, it emphasized its superior quality through the famous television and radio commercial featuring the legendary Lalitaji, a value-conscious and sensible Indian housewife who wanted to give the very best to her family. Tag lines such as *'Sasti cheez aur achhi cheez mein fark hota hai'* (There's a difference between a cheap product and a good product) and *'Surf ki kharidari mein hi samajhdari hai'* (Purchasing Surf is an intelligent decision) attempted to impress upon consumers, especially housewives, that by trying to save a little on the price of the product, they were losing out on quality; and that half a kilo of Surf was as effective as a kilo of a cheaper product (indicating Nirma).

In promoting Wheel, which was a direct competition to Nirma, HUL indirectly highlighted the negatives of using cheaper products that have harmful effects on the hands of the housewife using them. This time, the TV commercial showed a depressed-looking housewife staring at the washing powder and saying the famous tagline, *'Maine mangi safai aur tune di haathon ki jalan!'* (I asked for whiteness but you gave me hand burns.) The TV commercial distinguished Wheel detergent from its competitor (a white powder resembling Nirma) and stressed that Wheel gave whiteness and cleanliness while maintaining the softness of the hands of a housewife.

Rural Communication

Besides the advertisement for the urban and cost-conscious housewife, HUL went for rural-focused advertising for promoting Wheel. They created short video ads that were shown via cinema vans throughout India. Whereas the typical TV commercials lasted for maximum sixty seconds, these rural promotions were anywhere between two to seventeen minutes long. They were not mere advertisements, they were entertainment for the rural masses. The innovative approach clicked.[40] For the first time in the history of advertising in India, special stickers promoting Wheel were placed on hand pumps, the walls of wells were lined with advertising tiles, and tin plates were put on trees surrounding village ponds. The main objective of this promotional campaign was to advertise not only at the point of purchase, but also at the time of consumption.

Figure 5.6: Innovative Rural Promotion for Lux Soap

Yet another innovative rural campaign launched by HUL in October 2013 was the '*Kan Khajura Tesan*' (KKT) (The Earworm Channel). Aimed at promoting its brands among price-sensitive consumers, the campaign was focused on the media dark regions of Uttar Pradesh and Bihar. To benefit from this free entertainment facility, people from these areas could give a missed call on the advertised number and in turn receive a call from KKT that provided eighteen minutes of free entertainment, along with brief promotional messages on HUL products. 'Give a missed call and get free entertainment' was the tagline. By June 2014, it had attracted over 1.1 crore subscribers. In a matter of six months, this first-of-its-kind rural promotional campaign had engaged with its consumers for 18 crore minutes. The ads were heard over 10 crore times. It led to an instant increase in awareness for all three brands promoted through it: Wheel by 20 per cent, Pond's White Beauty by 56 per cent and Close-Up by 39 per cent. All this at a cost of just Rs 3 per contact![41] Consequently, HUL stopped radio advertising in these regions and planned to extend KKT to other parts of north and central India. This powerful and impacting ad campaign not only brought numbers to HUL, but also three Gold Lions Awards at the Cannes International Festival of Creativity 2014.[42] (Appendix V.B elaborates HUL's commitment to the Clean India Mission.)

Over the last fifty years, HUL has successfully used a wide gamut of communication campaigns targeted at different segments of consumers. As a commercial entity, increasing awareness about its products has been an important objective of these efforts. Through its communication strategy, HUL has creatively captured the changing societal scenarios, and through an eclectic mix of advertisements that have become legendary, it has attempted to make behavioural and attitudinal changes in the lives of its consumers for the better. The intricate connection between personal and home care products on one hand, and their impact on personal and community health and hygiene on the other, has been subtly brought forth through each of these campaigns.

Figure 5.7: HUL's Three-pronged Consumer Strategy for Achieving Three Win-Win Priorities

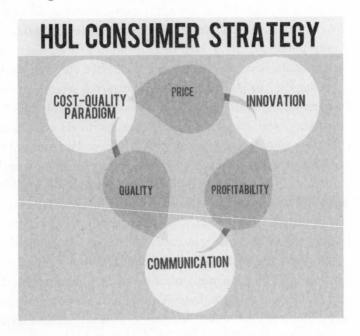

Starting a Supply Chain, from Scratch

In HUL's journey of catering to crores of consumers, who have been its collaborators? Was it easy to get quality inputs on time for their manufacturing plants to run as per their schedules? Eight decades ago, when HUL started manufacturing in India, there were no suppliers to provide inputs for the kind of products FMCG companies like HUL wanted to make. So, in most cases, HUL helped in building the supplier base for most of its inputs from scratch. Dhaval shared the evolution of HUL's supply chain in India: 'We have been in this country for over eighty years and a large part of this business in this country was built from scratch. We have built a branded business of products such as tea and detergents in India. As we did that, we created the supplier bases in this country.' For example, HUL played a major role in building the flexible plastic packaging industry because there was no plastic packaging happening in India before the company came in the 1930s. Laminated tube packaging was introduced by HUL in India. Dhaval mentioned Essel Packaging, the first company in India that brought in the required machines based on HUL's commitment that it will buy from them. 'In the chemical industry, we have created suppliers because we wanted those inputs for manufacturing our products. A large number of suppliers will tell you that it is HUL that is the reason for them to exist. Not that these suppliers are only our suppliers; they supply to other companies as well now. But they have a very unique relationship with our company,' Dhaval said.

By 2016, HUL had over 2000 suppliers and associates providing inputs for manufacturing products under their thirty-five brands. 'What's the secret to making such a large set of suppliers across your different businesses happy?' I asked Dhaval. As if in reflex action, he said, 'Professionalism. The suppliers' selection, their continuing with us and their commercial terms are done without any underhanded dealings or anything else except professionalism, transparency and efficiency. It's not that our suppliers have not left us, or we don't recruit new suppliers. It's just that we do all this on the basis of efficiency and transparency.'

He further added that in India, people know that when they deal with HUL, the FMCG major will go for a hard bargain. Yet, in the end, HUL will honour all its commitments—whether regarding picking up things, making payments within a stipulated time period, or even taking care of facilities that suppliers have set-up because of their instructions. 'Sometimes, even when business goes up and down a little bit, we have stood by our commitments,' he said. 'Does that mean that in order to keep them happy, you go soft with them?' I quipped. Dhaval smiled, 'We are businessmen. There is no need to be soft when you are ethical.'

'Good for India Is Good for HUL'

Scholars and practitioners increasingly accept business' role in nation building. It is a powerful means of giving gainful employment to individuals who, through their knowledge and skills, can add value to a company and through that, to the country. The HUL story has evolved alongside that of India as a country. At each stage, it attempted to contribute towards issues of national importance connected with the FMCG sector. In this context, Leena Nair, now Unilever's chief HR officer, said, 'Business is about creating value for each group of people who have a stake in the business. I believe it adds to the economic prosperity of the nation, it adds to employment generation for the nation. It is about helping people lead a more meaningful life.' HUL has consistently believed that what is good for India is good for HUL. Prasad shared a couple of examples at HUL that portrayed this core belief.

Negotiation and Appreciation from the Government

In 1974, after the enactment of the Foreign Exchange Regulation Act (FERA) in India, all companies in the non-core or non-technology industries were required to bring their shareholding down to 40 per cent. Many companies, including the likes of Coca-Cola and IBM, preferred to leave India rather than reduce management control.[43] Given its vast presence in India, Unilever decided to negotiate with the Government of India rather than leaving the country. It wanted to retain its 74 per cent shareholding that was permitted for high technology or core industry companies. After long and complex negotiations, HUL reached an agreement under which a foreign company was permitted to hold 51 per cent equity provided that it had 60 per cent of its turnover in the high technology and core sectors, besides 10 per cent of its production being used as exports. In order to fulfil this criteria, HUL became one of the five recognized export houses in India and ensured the minimum 10 per cent of mandatory exports from the small sector. Besides its own products, HUL also exported carpets, shoes, garments and marine products. By the early 1980s, HUL had become the second largest private sector exporter in India. In order to justify its identity as a high-technology company, HUL emphasized on the indigenous technology developed at its research centre that used non-edible oil in manufacturing soaps.

The team at the Hindustan Lever Research Centre in Bombay developed a technology to use non-conventional forest seeds oil for soap making. It was successfully able to manufacture soap using non-edible oils like castor oil and rice bran oil instead of imported oil.[44] As a result, the Government of India could use the foreign exchange allotted for the import of oil for importing the much-needed fertilizers to support India's agrarian economy. HUL proactively used R&D and substituted imported materials with locally available materials, thereby making a small contribution to India's economic situation.

Unilever's bargaining position with government agencies was facilitated by the goodwill it enjoyed in official circles. Its research and development initiatives were seen as enhancing its reputation with the government and professionals. Besides, its desire to invest in products beyond pure consumer goods, which were its forte, was appreciated.[45]

Support to Balanced Regional Development

In spite of seven decades of political independence, many parts of India continue to remain underdeveloped. As recently as 2016, Prime Minister Modi highlighted the need to raise the levels of development in the eastern parts of India to those achieved in its western states. Over the decades, the Government of India has attempted the dispersal of industries across different geographic areas in the country to develop rural areas and provide employment to people there. Many state governments have attempted to give tax and land-related benefits to attract companies to set up plants in their states. This is because the setting up of an industry in any place leads to many benefits to the local population such as improvement of infrastructure, creation of jobs and development of smaller entrepreneurial firms that act as suppliers of specific inputs required by these industries. Besides, through the route of corporate social responsibility (CSR), most companies undertake social welfare activities in areas surrounding the factories. Recalling HUL's role in promoting balanced regional development, Prasad said, 'Over the last many decades, HUL has taken a conscious decision that it will set up its factories in the backward areas of the country. If you see, the factories that have come up in the last thirty years are all in such areas—right from Haldia [West Bengal] in the east, to Silvassa [Union territory] in the west, to Pondicherry [Union territory] in the south, to Baddi [Himachal Pradesh] and Haridwar [Uttarakhand] in the north.'

One of the largest sets of its manufacturing units are in the northeastern state of Assam. Investment in Assam, which often suffered from a VUCA (volatile, uncertain, complex and ambiguous) environment, ensured the grant of industrial licence and provided tax benefits from the government. In spite of this, among all its competitors in the FMCG sector, including Colgate Palmolive, Procter & Gamble, Nestle and Cadbury, HUL was the only major company to invest in Assam. This was in alignment with HUL's policy, followed since 1977, of investing in designated industrially disadvantaged areas to catalyse employment creation leading to economic and social empowerment in the region. Prasad said, 'In a place like Assam, where it is not easy to operate because of local problems, we have one of our biggest factories manufacturing personal care products. We have provided employment to all local people, and the units are doing very well. We have been successfully able to share the benefits of industrialization with local people.'

The CEO Factory of India

'People are at the heart of our business. Our deep commitment to people and our ability to offer them exciting opportunities enables us to attract the best talent that gives us a competitive edge. We can hire and retain the best talent because of the value systems we uphold; it is the foundation on which we have built this business'[46]
—Harish Manwani, non-executive chairman, HUL

Leena Nair joined Hindustan Lever as Leena Menon (maiden name) for a summer internship in 1992. A gold medalist from the Xavier's Labour Relations Institute (XLRI, now known as the Xavier School of Management), she became the first woman board member and executive director of HR at HUL in 2007.[47] As I was waiting in her office for a conversation, Sumitra, her secretary, informed me that she was travelling from one of the HUL offices outside Mumbai and would be delayed. She had left early in the morning but was caught in traffic. I opted to come another day thinking she may be tired after a long journey. Sumitra reassured me that this was a regular feature for her and that Leena would see me in an hour's time.

An hour later, Leena arrived at the office. Within five minutes, she called me inside her room. After apologizing for the delay, she started our conversation by capturing the essence of the HUL employee story. 'The biggest strength of HUL is that we have been known as a "leadership machine"—over 400 CEOs in different companies of India today or those who sit on global boards are from HUL. People don't see us as just an FMCG company. They see us as a company that creates leaders for the country. This could be attributed to the training, culture, meritocracy and professionalism in the organization,' observed Leena.

HUL has the largest employee base in the Indian FMCG sector. By 2016, it had more than 18,000 employees. Marico Industries and Colgate Palmolive (India), HUL's close competitors, had about 2400 and 1800 employees respectively. Along with the large employee strength and the tag of being a leadership machine and the CEO factory of India, HUL has many legends associated with its employees.

Every Employee Matters

There is a saying within HUL: 'Normally you need not work for Hindustan Unilever as a company, but if there is a medical emergency, you should be working for Hindustan Unilever.' Workers' health welfare is ensured as all medical expenses are covered through an insurance scheme in case a worker falls sick. An incident, which occurred during the earthquake in Bhuj in Gujarat in 2001,[48] is notable. One HUL employee was missing in spite of all attempts made at tracing him. HUL personnel helicoptered down to Bhuj to locate that one employee. Finally, he was found, alive. In our conversation Dhaval recollected, 'We sent an entire team to find the one missing employee because we wanted to let him and his family know what was happening. In crisis, the company comes together and can go to any extreme.'

While HUL provides welfare and benefit packages to its workers, it also takes care of the welfare of employees' families after their passing away. Leena narrated her experience as the executive director of HR: 'I get a lot of thank you notes from widows of managers who have passed away in service and whose children's education has been fully supported by HUL for a period of twenty to twenty-five years. The children may have been just a year old when their father passed away, but the subsequent period of their education has been taken care of by the organization. In their letters they say that this care and concern of HUL for their employees and their families is commendable.' The deaths of some of these employees were not even on service, but due to a personal accident, a heart attack or other ailment.

Real Folklore

In 1991, an event, which has now become a part of the company's folklore, happened at one of HUL's factories in Doom Dooma, a tea town in the Tinsukia district of Assam. A demand was raised by militants from the United Liberation Front of Assam (ULFA)[49] for money. They threatened to kill or kidnap all HUL managers and their families associated with the plant if they were not paid. Leena shared the details: 'We were being threatened in Assam by some anti-social elements to give in to their demands and give a huge ransom. In response, we shut the factory. In plane loads we shifted our employees, managers, workers and their families overnight from Doom Dooma and Guwahati. That's the commitment of the organization to its people. Later, we did restart the Assam factory when the government stepped in. It was a big thing as everybody reassured us and that scared the anti-social elements too because the industry closing down is not good news for them either. They just wanted to bully us into submission. That just didn't happen. Even today, people remember that this company will care for us no matter what.'

In September 2003, HUL faced a similar problem at the Doom Dooma factory when the Residential Officers Colony was attacked following an extortion demand from insurgents. It was common for tea plantations in Assam to regularly pay insurgents to ensure peaceful operation of their business. However, as part of the HUL Code of Business Principles (CoBP), the company decided not to give in to pressure from anti-social elements and continued with the factory operations.

Gurdeep Singh, former director (HR, technology and corporate affairs), recollects, 'The company demonstrated courage and determination against threats and extortionist demands from militants of the United Liberation Front of Assam (ULFA) who targeted employees of our tea plantations and personal products factory in Assam. For the safety of all our employees, the company made massive and comprehensive security arrangements. We ended up spending much more than the sum demanded by ULFA, but we did not compromise our values and principles.'[50]

The Downturn

However, this CEO factory of India did face a downturn. Between 2003 and 2005, HUL faced increasingly intense competition and price wars, resulting in low, single-digit revenue growth. The organization was considered to be 'arrogant and conservative'. Some of the company's star performers left for other MNCs. These included D. Shivakumar for Philips India,[51] Uday Khanna for Lafarge,[52] Anand Kripalu for Cadbury India[53] and V.S. Sitaram for Dabur India.[54] Morale was at its lowest and HUL's reputation as talent's dream destination had started eroding. It was felt that its leadership culture needed to be re-energized at the earliest.[55] In 2007, HUL fell to the 14th position in the dream employer list among graduating business school students, after being the leader for almost two decades. Factors like job prospects and content, degree of independence, market standing of the company and salary package influenced the students' choice. 'They didn't see us as a global player and assumed that one got global assignments only after reaching the CEO level,' observed Leena.[56]

Why did this happen? Where did things go wrong? Was this a problem typical to HUL? It was a problem of the manufacturing sector competing with the fast-growing service sector employment opportunities. This changed the entire employment value proposition, especially for businesses that were traditionally operated in the Indian manufacturing sector. For example, employees did not want to get posted to far-off places. Nobody wanted to run a factory, for example in Haldia, for five years, with their family living in onsite accommodation. Employees wanted a better lifestyle, which meant urbanization. Service sector opportunities in IT companies and financial institutions were mainly located in fashionable metropolitan cities with the latest amenities and state-of-the-art infrastructure. People wanted their children to have the best education in the cities and wanted their families to have great medical care. This was not possible in a rural or small-town posting. The concept of what employees needed was becoming so different from the traditional employment model that matching the two was a challenge. The traditional formula in the manufacturing industry category, especially the FMCG sector, was that employees were first posted in a factory in a small town in the hinterland. This was typically followed by a sales assignment in a bigger town or city. Head office postings in Mumbai were always at a later stage in one's career as one rose up the career ladder. The traditional employment and job model was challenged by the work-life balance that new employees expected. Younger cohorts of premier business school graduates were not willing to wait that long. They wanted to work for five years and make it big in their life and career. Unlike the earlier generations, new recruits were questioning established fundamentals and existing social structures. There were clashes with established norms about age and hierarchy, even at the workers' level.

To rethink this changing employee equation, HUL put to task some of its seventy top leaders to do some serious 'intra-organizational introspection'. Around this time in June 2007, Leena had just taken over as executive director of HR. With fifteen years of experience up the corporate ladder at HUL, she analysed and identified the changing expectations of the new generation that had altered the employment equation in the Indian FMCG sector.

Decoding an Employee

Leena and her team identified some of the core needs of a newer generation of employees. The new recruits from premier B-schools were looking for many unique employment propositions.

First, they were looking for an exciting job that was meaningful. They were interested to know how their work would make a big difference to the ultimate stakeholder. Some of them even expected the organization to provide opportunities through which they could contribute to society and the environment.

Second, they wanted to have a career path, and had a desire to grow personally and professionally within the organization. They were also concerned about the future of the company to which they were contributing their time, talent and effort.

Third, they wanted the organization to be sensitive to their needs and welfare and have a responsible and caring work culture.

Fourth, the employees expected rewards and recognition for exceptional performance and special achievements. These played an important role in boosting their morale and encouraging them to give their best. The competitive working environment and increasing pressures of daily work and life made work-life balance another important factor for employees. 'This was not as important five years ago. However, today it is very important. People want a break, they want to work six months a year. The concept of employment is changing at a rate faster than what the HR heads can cope with!' shared Leena.[57]

During our conversation, she captured the employee equation in three core values. The first is 'economic value or financial value': am I getting paid commensurate to what I'm doing? Nobody expects to be paid the moon. Yet, everyone expects that if this is my job, I should be getting paid fairly for what I'm doing. The next is 'learning value': am I learning in this company? Is this going to look good on my resume? Are these skills going to be useful to me? Is this something that the industry will value? Is my boss teaching me something new that I did not know? Am I really learning on the job? Am I getting trained? The third is 'emotional value': whether the employee really likes the place, gets along well with her boss, etc.

Figure 5.8: The Employee Equation at HUL

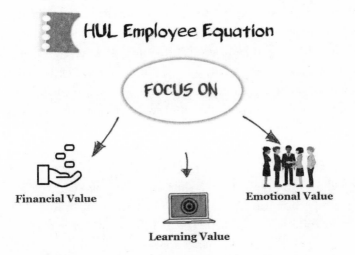

The Turnaround

The next five years saw a turnaround in the employment proposition at HUL. The initiatives started by her predecessor were further developed and continued by Leena and her team. An early priority was flattening the organization structure. As a result, employees could assume significant roles in their first five years in the company. People could move in their career at a much faster rate. In 2001, it typically took 16–18 years of experience to get to a senior management position. By 2011, this had been cut to fourteen years. HUL also started pushing expatriates in a big way because people wanted a global experience early on in their career. This was more out of a desire for exposure. It was observed that the company was more likely to lose the employee if it didn't do an early internationalization. So, HUL changed a lot of career paths. During the initial training period, the trainees were sent abroad for a brief period. Senior managers were seconded to Unilever.

In 2011, over 200 managers of HUL served Unilever globally. This was about 13 per cent of the HUL managerial strength. The number of managers expatriated had steadily increased over the years.[58] By 2016, Harish Manwani became the first chief operating officer in the new organization structure at Unilever; Dhaval became the chief procurement officer; Nitin Paranjpe became the president of home care; and Leena became the first woman chief HR officer with a responsibility of 168,000 Unilever employees across 190 countries.

In 2004, it was Gurdeep Singh, then management committee member and executive director (HR) at HUL, who was chief among those who pushed for a shift in the organization culture. 'The introspection was hard but we knew it was time to formalize a shift in culture,' he recalled. It was in the same year that the 360-degree process of performance appraisal was institutionalized. Nitin Paranjpe, the youngest-ever CEO of HUL, recollected, 'It was a huge cultural transformation. Some were big enough to deal with it, others struggled enormously.' Thereafter, mid-year reviews were made mandatory. 'Your self-image gets shattered pretty fast with 360 degree reviews,'[59] said Sanjiv Kakkar. 'You get the message about your performance gaps loud and clear.' By 2010–11, there was greater emphasis on real delivery and performance accountability, and the company had moved to a far more aggressive performance-based rewards system.

Inspiration, Not Compensation Alone

Leena observed that compensation was a lower priority for employees. HUL was at about 75 per cent of the market when it came to salaries. There was a good balance of variable, fixed and stock options.[60] The company benchmarked its compensation with select companies in the FMCG, telecom and banking sectors and made an annual revision to ensure fair salaries reflecting market trends. Differentiation in salary was made on the basis of performance.

Between 2008 and 2009, HUL increased the variable component of the salary, thus putting a great emphasis on performance and performance-based rewards. There was a marked improvement as compared to its previous and predominantly fixed salary structure. Rewards were based on the overall performance of the company, performance of the team the employee was associated with, and individual employee performance. Even for its shop floor workers, the compensation was better than competitors and beyond the amount stipulated by law for the workers. In the view of the top management, there were other aspects of the value proposition at HUL that attracted young talent. As a management trainee of fifteen months, fresh recruits were given responsibility for a market of a few crore rupees. The size and scale of this responsibility at an early age created the attractive proposition. The other part was the unique leadership training, which was the unique selling proposition of HUL's HR brand.[61]

However, the fact remains that HUL is among the best paymasters in the sector. In 2015, it reported 169 executives who drew eight-digit salaries. This was six times more than its closest rival ITC's twenty-three 'crorepati' employees. Interestingly, half of these 169 were less than forty years of age. Collectively, they receive a combined salary of Rs 310 crore. The HUL number was 50 per cent higher than IT major Infosys' 123 and more than double of Wipro's seventy eight-digit salary earners.[62]

Transforming Office Space to Personify the HUL Brand

Change of place has a big impact on human psyche. In 2010, HUL relocated to a new headquarters on a 12.6-acre site in Andheri, a suburb of Mumbai. Unlike the Lever House (HUL headquarters in Backbay Reclamation in south Mumbai for over seven decades), which resembled the traditional and hierarchical British structure, this was to be a new generation office. I recollect my visit to the senior executive floor of the Lever House office, when I had gone there to do the first round of interviews. It had a distinct feel of seniority—wall-to-wall white carpets, glass cabins and a very 'posh' appeal. As I stepped out and descended the floors, I perceived a distinct change in the interior—simple, colourful and frugal, with a very youthful feeling. However, in the new Andheri campus, the senior executive floor is scarcely different from other floors. Employees literally cut across all levels as they traverse the facility's length and breadth. Douge Baille, the CEO of HUL when this new facility was envisaged, was deeply involved in the space plan. He wanted that all employees park their cars in the basement and walk into the reception and the main atrium every day, rather than having separate routes to their floors from the basement, which could minimize interaction. The facility has been constructed keeping this vision in mind. The 'street concept', inspired from the British Airways headquarters in London, aims at binding people and spaces, knitting together the intangible and the tangible. Intangible values such as collaboration, openness, work-life balance and well-being are actively promoted by tangible architectural elements, employee amenities and technology.

The five-storeyed, 72,000 square feet atrium, the 87,000 square feet training centre, a recreation centre with multiple sports, a gym, an occupational health and safety centre with full-time doctors and nurses, and a day-care centre run by a day-care specialist are some of the interesting physical features. DEGW, London-based specialist space planners, were engaged to devise an open-plan environment that was comfortable, noise-free and adaptable to changes in team size and configuration. So the workstations used light, portable desks and low-height partitions and storage units, rather than bulky panel systems. The architects observed that there were hardly any other Indian corporate establishments that had focused on public spaces and interactive environments like HUL had done in its new premises. Leena drew a parallel between the new space and the brand identity that HUL wanted to espouse: 'An office which is iconic, futuristic, connected, modern—exactly the sort of brand values that I would like HUL to be associated with.'[63]

Within a decade, HUL went from not growing to growing, from criticism of its working style to being named India's best employer by Aon Hewitt, and from nurturing local leaders to inspiring global leaders. In 2015, for the fourth year in a row, HUL was recognized as the 'No. 1 Employer of Choice' in the Nielsen campus track B-school survey, retained the 'Dream Employer' status for the sixth consecutive year, and continued to be the top company considered for application by B-school students. HUL had started to listen more and was willing to learn from the new generation. It had discovered the win-win approach to employee excellence.

Figure 5.9: The HUL Standards of Leadership

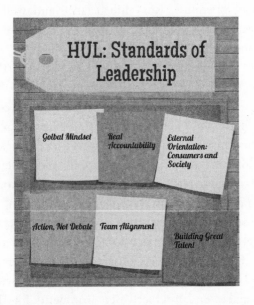

Doing Well by Doing Good

Among my interactions with senior management at HUL, a memorable one was with Ashok Gupta, then executive director of legal affairs and company secretary of HUL. An HUL veteran, he joined as legal manager in Lipton India, and rose up the ladder to the top legal position. 'Can you share your thoughts about how HUL has been focused on stakeholders' welfare while maintaining the letter and spirit of the law?' I asked. I thought he would talk about how HUL had appointed a retired high court judge as the ombudsman for consumer disputes redressal. I had read about it in the papers that it was the first time that an FMCG company in India had adopted an independent and expert mediation procedure for the benefit of the consumers. It had also set up a consumer care helpline 'Levercare' to help consumers. Instead, he went back in time, more than two decades, and elaborately narrated a series of events that in his opinion characterized what HUL stands for.[64]

He concluded by observing, 'Unilever's chairman often talks about "doing well by doing good". In my opinion, this sums up the core purpose of business, because you are taking into consideration many things while you're doing well. You are not harming anybody in the process, and that's a success for us. If I say that I want to get the highest returns as compared with the industry, for my shareholders and other stakeholders, and I do not care what kind of products I am selling, what my customers' needs are, whether my suppliers are happy or not—I am not doing anything great. I am only squeezing them and getting my profits out. That's not sustainable.'

Roadmap for the next Century

HUL's eight-decade odyssey has been momentous to say the least. Through its products and services, the company has created a very strong emotional bond with the Indian consumers—both urban and rural. Its products have been household names, and generations of Indians have grown using them as part and parcel of their daily lives. To be a market leader consistently for eighty years in the fiercely competitive FMCG industry category, where brand switching and shifting consumer loyalties is commonplace, is an achievement of its kind.

At the conclusion of our conversation that Monday morning, Sundaram shared with me a 'secret formula' that in his opinion successful companies follow. He said, 'The basic purpose of business is being relevant to society and in the process, creating value for the stakeholders. For the process of value creation, the shareholders are very important. But it is important that at the end of it, you integrate all stakeholders' interests. In this regard, there is a tripod in my mind: "Delight the consumer, reward the investor and govern responsibly."'

Figure 5.10: The Win-Win Strategy at HUL

He believed that governing responsibly was possible through internal mechanisms and guiding principles within which a company operates. To a very large extent, some of these things needed to be embedded in an organization and become an integral part of its culture. 'At the end of the day, culture is when people have collectively internalized their behaviour in every decision-making process and every business transaction which they really do,' he said.

Around 100 years ago, William Lever started this business by just manufacturing a bar of Sunlight Soap. The vision he talked about was, 'To make cleanliness commonplace, to lessen work for women, to foster health and contribute to personal attractiveness; that life can be more enjoyable and rewarding for the people who use our products.' All this—just from a bar of soap. This speaks volumes about the vision of the founder. It also provides a roadmap for the next 100 years, for India's largest FMCG company.

Figure 5.11: Win-Win Learnings from Hindustan Unilever

LESSONS FROM
HINDUSTAN UNILEVER

1. UNDERSTANDING THE CUSTOMER

Consumer understanding is the
core of a successful business
and the basis of iconic brands

2. DIVERSE PRODUCT PORTFOLIO

Multiple products and their availability
across income categories and
geographies is crucial for FMCG
market leadership

3. CONSTANT INTEGRATED INNOVATION

Innovation not just for products,
but also for pricing, promotion
and distribution; often combining
commercial and social objectives

4. DOING WELL BY DOING GOOD

Purpose beyond profit;
engagement beyond product

5. LEADERSHIP MACHINE

People are the heart of any
business; developing their
leadership potential is vital for
success

6. BE AWARE, BE ALERT

Never underestimate local and
regional competition

VI.

Bharat Petroleum Corporation

A Real Ratna . . . Redefining Public Sector Performance

Bharat Petroleum Corporation Limited (BPCL) is India's second largest oil marketing company (OMC) by volumes. With a consumer base of over 16 crore, it is among India's largest companies. In 2001 itself, its sales volume was as large as the oil consumption of an entire country of Pakistan's size.[1] By 2015, it enjoyed a domestic market share of 21 per cent with a nationwide network of thirteen installations, 114 depots, fifty LPG bottling plants, and thirty-five aviation fuelling stations. In the last decade, its pan-India retail outlets (popularly called petrol pumps) nearly doubled to 13,019, and so did its LPG distributors to 4294.[2] It ranked 358th among the Global Fortune 500 Companies in 2016.[3] With a gross revenue of Rs 2,53,254 crore and net profits of Rs 5085 crore in 2015, BPCL is considered one of the finest 'Navratnas'[4] among Indian public sector enterprises (PSEs).[5] Between 2010 and 2015, it witnessed a three-fold expansion in its market capitalization to Rs 58,600 crore. The Government of India holds the majority shareholding in BPCL, of nearly 55 per cent. However, compared to its peers, its return on investment to shareholders has been phenomenal. Suppose a shareholder invested Rs 1 lakh in BPCL stock in July 1996, her investment would have increased to Rs 26.85 lakh by July

2016. In comparison, Rs 1 lakh invested in the Sensex portfolio would have grown to just Rs 7.6 lakh during the same period. Thus, while the Sensex grew seven times, the BPCL stock grew twenty-six times in twenty years.[6] Not surprisingly, the company is often referred to as 'an MNC in the garb of a public sector undertaking (PSU)'.

Figure 6.1: Return on Investments in Maharatna Companies vs BPCL

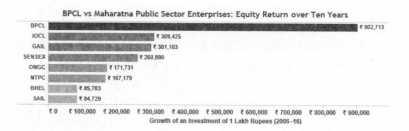

BPCL vs Maharatna Public Sector Enterprises: Equity Return over Ten Years

BPCL	₹ 902,713
IOCL	₹ 309,425
GAIL	₹ 301,103
SENSEX	₹ 260,890
ONGC	₹ 171,731
NTPC	₹ 167,179
BHEL	₹ 85,783
SAIL	₹ 84,729

₹ 0   ₹ 100,000   ₹ 200,000   ₹ 300,000   ₹ 400,000   ₹ 500,000   ₹ 600,000   ₹ 700,000   ₹ 800,000   ₹ 900,000

Growth of an Investment of 1 Lakh Rupees (2006–16)

While I have literally bombarded you with awesome statistics about BPCL, the company's evolution to its present form has been equally fascinating. The company has existed in India in some form or another for over a century. Its story began with the consolidation of Asiatic Petroleum in India in 1907 under the name Shell. It was a collaborative endeavour of Royal Dutch,[7] Shell and Rothschild companies against the rival company Standard Oil formed by John D. Rockefeller and his business associates.[8] In 1928, Shell joined hands with Burmah Oil Company[9] to form the Burmah-Shell Oil Storage and Distributing Company of India Limited (BSM). Its objective was to carry on the business of distributing and marketing petroleum products in India. For this purpose, it had established places of business in Bombay and other parts of India. At the time of Independence, Burmah-Shell had a dominant presence in India with a 67 per cent market share. In 1950, the government decided to do a one-on-one negotiated deal. Shell came to build a refinery in Mahul in Bombay, and formed the Burmah-Shell Refineries (BSR) in November 1952.

In the industrial policy of 1956, the Government of India announced that all future petroleum projects would be under the public sector. To further this mandate, on the eve of the tenth anniversary of Indian independence, the Oil and Natural Gas Commission[10] was established with the objective of hydrocarbon exploration and production (E&P). In 1959, the Government of India established Oil India Limited[11] with headquarters in Duliajan in Assam, with a focus on exploring oil in the northeastern states.

The northeast has been historically connected with India's oil story. The world's first oil well was drilled in 1859 in Titusville, Pennsylvania (USA). Seven years later, Asia's first oil well was drilled in Nahorpung in Assam (then British India). In 1886, the McKillop Stewart Company struck oil near Jeypore in upper Assam. Finally, the Assam Railway and Trading Company (ASTC) struck the first commercial oil in Digboi in 1889, marking the beginning of oil production in India. This was nearly two decades before oil was first discovered in the Middle East in Masjid-i-Sulaiman, the mountainous region of Persia (now Iran) in May 1908.[12] It is believed that the Canadian engineer at ASTC shouted at his men, 'Dig boy, dig', when they saw elephants with oil stains on their feet emerging from the dense jungles. That is considered to be one of the stories around the name 'Digboi', the place that eventually grew into Asia's first petroleum refinery.[13]

The Beginning of Nationalization

Figure 6.2: J.R.D. Tata with the Leopard Moth (He flew in 1962 to mark his historic first airmail flight from Karachi to Mumbai in October 1932—Burmah-Shell did the fuelling)

In 1959, the Government of India established Indian Refineries Limited (later amalgamated as Indian Oil Corporation Limited (IOCL),[14] the first PSE oil marketing company focused on the downstream activities of refining and marketing. (Appendix VI.A explains the upstream, mid-stream and downstream processes of the oil and gas industry.) In the 1960s, IOCL established three public sector refineries (at Noonmati with Rumanian collaboration, and in Barauni and Koyali, with Soviet collaboration).[15] With rising indigenous production by ONGC (especially from oil fields in Gujarat), and a parallel decline in the rate of growth of domestic consumption, the monopoly positions of international oil companies like Burmah-Shell, Esso[16] and Caltex[17] started declining in India from 100 per cent in 1960 to 60 per cent in 1968, and 42 per cent in 1973. With increasing independence in the sourcing of crude, the Government of India realized that international oil companies had been consistently charging them surplus margins and heavily profiteering. To counter this, these companies were asked to reduce their prices or process crude imported by the government for a fee. The oil companies consistently refused to refine crude for a fee as that was against their international policy and business model. Their business strategy focused on providing oil sourced from their own oil wells and fields, primarily because the largest margins were in the upstream business. They also benefitted immensely from international transfer pricing.[18] Undertaking refining activities for India would lead to similar demands from other host countries and would upset their business model. Moreover, their Indian operations formed a minuscule portion of their international operations. Hence, yielding to the government's requests did not seem to be a wise choice for them.

Figure 6.3: Burmah-Shell Aviation Service Office at Santacruz, Mumbai, circa 1960s

For nearly twenty years after Independence, the Government of India did not seem to have any plans of nationalizing the Indian oil industry. However, the devaluation of the rupee in 1966 was a turning point. Interestingly, the government also entered into bilateral agreements with many oil-producing countries in order to secure crude on credit or mutual cooperation terms.[19] Many of these countries belonged to the Soviet bloc, which the Western oil companies were not keen on working with. They increasingly saw a bleak future for themselves in socialist India. The other major reason for them to consider exiting the country was an increasing requirement for capital to explore newly found sites such as the North Sea and forms of crude such as shale[20] in other parts of the world. Most of the oil majors were not keen on taking a loan for this purpose and considered liquidation of existing assets as a more reliable means of funds.

It is believed that under these circumstances the MNC oil companies started selling their assets within India at throwaway prices. IOCL, being the only downstream company at that time, gladly purchased them and increased its asset base.[21] In this context, the willing acceptance of nationalization by the international oil companies appears logical. In 1974, the Government of India acquired 74 per cent share in Esso, and the remaining 26 per cent in 1976. In the same year, 100 per cent share was acquired in Caltex. Esso and Caltex were merged to form Hindustan Petroleum Corporation Limited (HPCL).[22] Pursuant to an agreement dated 23 December 1975, the government acquired 100 per cent equity shareholding of BSR on 24 January 1976, for a consideration of Rs 9.25 crore.[23] The name of BSR was changed to Bharat Refineries Limited (BRL) and subsequently on 1 August 1977, it was changed to Bharat Petroleum Corporation Limited.

Figure 6.4: Prime Minister Morarji Desai Received by Burmah-Shell Officials in Bombay

Due to the massive sale of assets by MNC oil companies (primarily purchased by IOCL), the market share of BPCL reduced from 60 per cent (of the erstwhile Burmah-Shell), to a meagre 15 per cent. IOCL, its largest PSE competitor, enjoyed a 60 per cent market share. From its presence in ninety airports across India, BPCL was reduced to two. From forty LPG plants, the company now had only two. The morale within the erstwhile multinational and now with the garb of a PSE was at its lowest ebb. There was mass exodus with over 500–600 people leaving the company in anticipation of no career for themselves in a PSE set-up with dismal market share. Consequently, the company faced a long period of stagnation and uncertainty.

However, the core team decided to make the most of its MNC roots and focus on a path of rapid growth. Large-scale recruitment

and training became critically important to meet the demands of
expansion. With a private sector mindset, it focused on profit share
rather than market share, and chose the path to recovery through a
large retail presence and a massive dealership network consisting of
entrepreneurial distributors. These were its strengths even during its
Burmah-Shell days. Given the former differences in ownership, the
fierce competition between BPCL, HPCL and IOCL continued
even after becoming PSEs.[24] To develop a niche identity even
within the public sector set-up, BPCL chose a focused growth path.

**Figure 6.5: Financial Performance of Public Sector Oil
Marketing Companies**

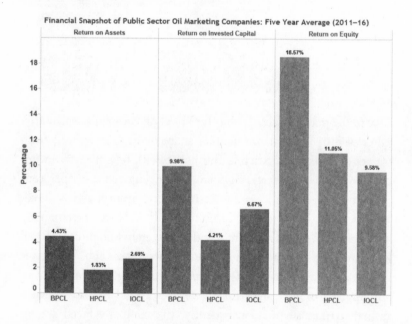

The Journey to Change Begins

For four years and four decades India followed the socialistic
approach to economic development inspired by the Soviet model,

with tight rules governing private enterprises in favour of public enterprises that faced little competition. Legislations such as the MRTP (Monopolistic and Restrictive Trade Practices) Act[25] played a crucial role in curtailing the role of private companies in the economy. The lack of competition and continued government backing led to a sharp decline in the quality and performance of PSEs during this period and also led to dismal contributions to India's growth. The notorious Licence Raj played an enormous role in limiting India's annual growth at 3 per cent. The West called it the 'Hindu rate of growth', acknowledging the country with the largest Hindu population in the world. Finally, the year 1991 came as an inflexion point in the economic history of independent India. The country began a new journey by unshackling private and public sector enterprises. The controlled and licensing-based approach to the economy finally gave way to liberalization, privatization and globalization of the economy.[26]

An important recommendation of the economic policy of 1991 was selling 20 per cent of public sector enterprises in the country. Ashok Sinha, then executive director of corporate affairs at BPCL observed, 'No one had a clue about how they were going to do it, because nobody really understood the public sector. You will not find BPCL or any other PSEs in the *Economic Times* or any business paper pre-1991. We were not in the economic scenario at all.'[27] Oil and gas products hadn't yet started fuelling the engines of India's economic growth. The first concrete steps were taken in November 1994 by a committee of oil industry officials headed by then chairman and managing director (CMD) of BPCL, U. Sundararajan. The committee studied the oil industry exhaustively and recommended a reform path. The report titled 'Hydrocarbon Perspective: 2010—Meeting the Challenges' was submitted in February 1995. It recommended measures to be adopted by the government for restructuring the upstream and downstream oil and gas sectors, and ensuring free and fair competition in order to protect consumers' interest in the deregulated scenario.[28] It primarily suggested the dismantling of the administered pricing mechanism (APM)[29] that guided the destinies of the Indian oil and gas sector companies.[30]

In anticipation of the changing scenario, oil and gas companies began to relook at themselves in the likelihood of increasing competition from private companies should the APM be dismantled.[31] The uncertainty of existence, probable reduction in size and volumes, and the prospect of acquisition by private or MNC companies created a sense of anxiety. The scenario was either change or perish.

Sundararajan realized the inability of his company to compete with MNCs (post deregulation) with existing structures and ways of doing work. He embarked on an intra-organizational restructuring process to equip BPCL to face challenges. Around the same time, in 1996, Dr Vijay Kelkar, then petroleum secretary, decided that each of the oil companies should take on a consultant to guide them in this transformation process. He suggested internationally renowned experts based on the needs of each company. IOCL selected McKinsey, HPCL took Andersen, and BPCL chose Arthur D. Little (ADL).[32] In his presentation to the BPCL board, Arun Maira, then head of ADL, explained the consulting company's role as that of providing necessary inputs to build capacity within BPCL to enable the company to design and implement a new structure, rather than suggesting what it should do. This was very different from what the company was always used to doing—taking instructions, mostly from the government, and implementing them. For the first time, this process provided the company and its many thousand employees a chance to think and chart its own roadmap for the future.

To facilitate this entire process, Project CUSECS (Customer Service and Customer Satisfaction) was launched. International evidence indicated that new entrants entering formerly regulated markets usually capitalized on the local companies' lack of customer orientation. Hence, the main objective of Project CUSECS was to communicate within the company that the customer is central to its survival. A core group of 25–30 members, with varied educational qualifications and experiences, was formed to champion the change process. Sundararajan wanted to provide opportunity to average employees within BPCL in an empowered environment. He recalled, 'I did not nominate the best managers in BPCL because I have observed many times in my career, if people are given the right environment and opportunities, they would rise up to it. And my faith was not misplaced. The youngsters did a wonderful job.'[33]

Sinha shared with me that CUSECS primarily focused on internal transformation. One of the first objectives of this change management exercise was to understand the current issues facing BPCL. This was done through 'reality workshops' championed by the core team of CUSECS. Syamal Bhattacharya (executive director of corporate affairs at BPCL), then a member of the core team, shared how the whole organization was 'allowed' to debate all issues during these workshops. The discussions took place in BPCL offices across India, at different levels, as he described—'chhota-chhota' levels—and feedback was sought. The debates brought to the fore the ills and problems and the deficiencies and difficulties that had become a part of the company's working style. For the first time, in a typical PSE, people started talking openly. They were given the licence to talk, and even criticize the intra-organizational processes and systems. All of this was compiled in the 'Current Reality Document'. The four major issues that emerged were: collective dissatisfaction with the status quo, low customer focus and customer orientation, a huge gap between vision and the capabilities to achieve it, and opportunities for quick improvement.

The other part of this discussion was solutions to overcome these challenges. The same people who were given the freedom of expression to criticize the system were also asked to define their long-term vision for the company. Right from the officers' level to the senior managers' level, all shared their vision for BPCL. A number of meetings also took place with unions and dealers. Their vision was understood and incorporated in the larger reformation plan. All of this was compiled in the 'Vision Document'. There were ten elements identified in the final vision document with over 200 initiatives as part of the change plan. The core elements included:[34]

- Be the best
- Make the workplace exciting
- Improve boundary management
- Fulfil social responsibilities; be ethical
- Apply the best technology
- Make systems strong and dynamic
- Establish first-class brands and corporate image
- Excellent customer care and service
- Go for excellent performance and operational efficiency
- Make people a source of improvement

So, on one side, BPCL had an understanding of the current reality, and on the other side it had the vision it wanted to reach. It was like the 'from address' and the 'to address' on a letter that was ready to be posted! Sinha shared with me that Project CUSECS marked the beginning of BPCL as a learning organization. 'We understood when we were transitioning in 1991 that we are going to be working and thinking in the same functional mode unless we become a learning organization. The transformation CUSECS brought in was enabling us to understand how we can learn from others and continuously upgrade ourselves.' The company linked learning with change. You change because you learn new things; and when you change, you become more relevant to the customer, markets and competition. The other imperative was to be prepared before MNCs like Shell, Total or Exxon hit the market. Many of these MNCs operated in hundreds of countries across the globe, and would bring along with them their knowledge and international expertise. 'So you learn from them, and then beat them at their own game,' he quipped.

Customer Focus, Even in Oil and Gas

One of the primary outcomes of CUSECS was the change in organization structure. Till then, BPCL was based on a divisional structure. Every geographic division looked after all products. There were about twenty divisions and each state was looked after by one division. For example, the Bombay division was looking after huge parts of Maharashtra, and the Madras division was overseeing huge parts of Tamil Nadu. The biggest problem of this structure was a lack of customer focus and communication. 'We were not able to reach, hear or give service to the customer,' observed Syamal. Earlier, a sales officer typically serviced customers from thirty retail outlets, twelve LPG distributors, six kerosene dealers and ten bulk customers. Although depots reported to the divisional manager, there was little coordination at the field level among the sales and operational officers. The divisional structure made it difficult for senior managers to devise strategies for specific businesses like lubricants or LPG, because they had to deal with a wide spectrum of products.[35] The company collectively saw a big reason to be restructured so that it could become customer-focused. This meant breaking up the structure into smaller sizes and going closer to the customer. The twenty divisions were broken down into 60–80 territories. A lot of decision-making power was decentralized at the territory level. Until then, the authority used to be in the hands of the central office or the regional office. They were considered very powerful. The typical dialogue in most Bollywood movies of those days used to be, *'Head office se message aaya hai'* (There's a message from the head office). As if it was writing on stone! In those years, every proposal would go to the central office and only after their approval would it get implemented. This took lots of time and provided no opportunity of innovation or leadership for employees at lower levels. Furthermore, the customer featured nowhere in this process.

The new structure aimed at greater delegation of authority at junior levels. These officers and managers were now close to the final consumers and in touch with ground realities. Earlier, only general managers had the right to decide on discounts offered to customers. Under the new structure, even sales officers could take these decisions. The empowerment made the jobs attractive and the company saw a rise in the number of recruits at junior levels. The number of customers and dealers they were overseeing also went up substantially. The experience gained in such decision-making groomed them to become potential managers. It was a win-win situation for BPCL. In these junior employees the company had its 'eyes and ears' on the ground to get the right customer feedback, and in turn provide the right service and communication. On the other hand, the employees felt more empowered as an important part of this process, rather than just a cog in the wheel.

Figure 6.6: BPCL Brand of Lubricants

Under the new structure, the company was divided into six strategic business units (SBUs). Five of these were customer-centric: retail, industrial, LPG, aviation, lubricants, and one was asset-based: refinery. There were territories under each of the SBUs. Each territory dealt with specific customers and was able to optimize its focus on specific issues and provide solutions to that particular customer category. Under the new structure, a sales officer serviced customers only belonging to her SBU. This brought in a lot more focus. Sinha shared that everything short of the chairman's powers was given to business units. This was a fundamental change, something no PSE had ever contemplated—to the extent that the powers left with the directors were very limited and mainly focused on issues and documentation that had to go to the board. The majority of powers were devolved to business unit heads. Also, until then, finance, human resources and marketing were central functions, reporting directly to the CMD. The new structure involved embedding these into business decision-making and clubbing them with SBUs. So, individual units could directly benefit from the expertise of finance, HR and marketing executives, rather than routing every initiative through the top management. After this change, the functional executives started working closely with the business. They became a solid team taking their own decisions and keeping in mind consumers' interests. To ensure balanced decision-making, the authority was given to the team and not to a single person. At the territory level, everything was required to be cleared by a committee of four to five people. This was often referred to as 'fan structure' decision-making. Just as a fan has four blades, the committee had four members. Hence, the fan structure.

However, the transition was not as simple as it appears. Imagine an organization like a PSE used to working in a particular way for two decades. Each of the divisional heads had developed their own fiefdoms and networks. They weren't willing to change. There were many aspects of the new structure that everyone did not agree on. Finally, three years after Project CUSECS was set in motion, on 1 July 1998, the Transition Committee, headed by Sinha, put up a transfer list of 3000 people across territories in the new structure. 'It was utterly chaotic. How do you break up into six different structures, all self-contained? We picked the SBU leaders and told them to sort it out among themselves, pick their teams and do the asset reallocation. I got a lot of flak during that period, but we pushed it down somehow. Ultimately everybody took their share of the responsibility,' he reminisced.[36]

In order to smoothen this process, BPCL organized two management programmes for its people at the company's training centre in Mumbai. Over 600 managers underwent the Visionary Leadership Programme[37] and over 5000 management and non-management staff went through foundations of learning.[38] ADL played an important role in facilitating this entire process. It worked with the core team of Project CUSECS, and provided templates and metrics to design the roadmap for BPCL's transformational journey.[39] The uniqueness of the entire exercise was that all through this change process, the company was functional. The routine had to continue, and in parallel the employees adjusted to a new way of working. Those associated with the change remembered the days as being quite a difficult transition. Arun Maira described it as 'redesigning the aircraft while it's flying.' It could have crashed. Yet instead, it rose higher and faster. The dawn after a dark night is very pleasing and energizing. That's what happened once Project CUSECS was implemented.[40]

Inspiring Innovations, Even in the Public Sector

Through a company-wide consultative process, BPCL came up with three core values that its brand must stand for: caring, reliable and innovative (INCARE). 'The last triggered a lot of debate: Why "innovative", were we going to do R&D? How could a brand be innovative? But I felt that was the core of the brand, and without it we weren't going to get anywhere,'[41] recalled Sinha. Usually 'innovation' and 'public sector' are considered antonyms. However, BPCL was a trailblazer in this journey. It introduced not one or two but dozens of innovative products, processes and campaigns that redefined the way oil and gas companies worked in India thereafter. Explaining the logic for its innovation journey, Sinha told me, 'As a customer, petrol and diesel are products you never see, you never smell, you never touch. It's a tertiary benefit that you're able to travel through the use of these products. So to positively impact customers, one has to focus on services.' BPCL consistently worked towards building a strong corporate brand in India that was customer-centric and comparable to that of any global oil company. It introduced the maximum number of new customer-oriented schemes. (Appendix VI.B lists the major brands and services that BPCL introduced as part of this innovation journey.) Even HPCL and IOCL were focusing on this change. However, stock markets reacted differently to each of them. BPCL's stock was the only one that quoted above its net worth. The primary reason was the success and effectiveness of its retail strategy and better location of its retail outlets in areas with higher traffic density. Compared to IOCL's 28 per cent and HPCL's 45 per cent, BPCL had 60 per cent of its retail outlets under its own control. This provided a competitive edge.[42]

BPCL's efforts in improving customer services at its retail outlets started as early as 1992. A market survey revealed the requirement for good and accurate air gauge, facility to pay by credit cards and availability of soft drinks at these outlets. In response, the company tied up with Apollo Tyres and installed tyre gauges at most of its outlets. It also entered into an agreement with Pepsi to make its products available at most BPCL outlets.[43] The company then started modernizing and upgrading its outlets and launched the 'Bazaar' range of stores modelled on the lines of Shell's convenience stores.[44] By 1999, thirty-five retail outlets pan-India had the Bazaar stores. In 2000, it experimented with the establishment of McDonald's fast food outlet on the Delhi–Agra highway targeting tourists headed to the Taj Mahal. Based on extensive customer feedback and an analysis of the Bazaar stores' performance, the company further evolved an 'errand mall' concept which incorporated several initiatives including the launch of the 'In & Out' brand of stores. The underlying concept of an errand mall was that when a customer stepped out for errands, fuelling was positioned as one of the items on the list. The company aimed at providing a bouquet of services that included fuelling, thereby uniquely positioning these as destination stops rather than petrol pumps.[45] The 'In & Out' brand of stores were started at forty locations pan-India with operational hours from 4 a.m. to midnight. Compared with the Bazaar stores, these focused on popular products, especially impulse purchase items.[46] Around the same time, IOCL started its 'Convenio' range of stores providing similar services. Petrol pumps were no longer the poorly lit and grease-lined venues of the previous decades. They now had smartly-dressed customer service representatives and facilities including ATMs, Internet kiosks, car wash, food court and convenience stores. The innovation journey of the twenty-first century Indian OMCs had begun to work towards customer delight.

Buy Products, Win Rewards

In August 1995, BPCL signed an agreement with the Bank of Baroda to issue the first co-branded credit card in the Indian oil industry. The card was launched in select cities and enabled customers to purchase fuel and other products on credit from BPCL outlets in those cities. The cards could even be used by companies as a facility to its executives for reimbursement of their fuel costs. The vehicle owners could also authorize their drivers to purchase fuel using this card. By September 1999, BPCL launched its own 'Petro Card' (a smart card with a microprocessor chip embedded in it) for developing its band of loyal customers. It was a pioneering initiative with no other parallel except the airline industry's frequent flyer programmes. The chip used by BPCL was so powerful that it could hold as much as eighty times more data than a magnetic strip used in a normal credit card. The launch was even more striking because in the same year, in a presentation made by the Mastercard and Visa companies to the Reserve Bank of India, it was observed that India was not going to be ready for smart cards till the year 2008.

Sinha smiled and told me, 'Today, whatever Paytm and other wallet companies are doing, we did it in 1999. We broke the then prevalent hypothesis about customers' willingness to pay in advance against future purchases.' The card was primarily launched targeting urban markets and to complement its retail initiatives. A nominal membership fee of Rs 250 was charged. Cardholders could have a minimum of Rs 500 with multiples of Rs 100 loaded on their cards. The customers also earned loyalty points called 'Petromiles' for purchase of fuel and non-fuel products at BPCL outlets and In & Out stores. The success of this initiative can be judged from the fact that within the first eighteen months of launch, BPCL had 3.5 lakh card holders in twenty major cities, with 20,000 daily transactions at the company's retail outlets. The Petro Card emerged as one of the largest loyalty programmes in India.

Sounds exciting? But even this initiative wasn't without challenges. Sinha recalled how the company dealers in Mumbai were against the loyalty card. This was mainly because the dealers were sitting on advances from customers. With the launch of this card facility, the liquid cash would now move on to the card, meaning loss of liquidity for their businesses. So they were very diffident to accept this initiative. To avoid any friction, BPCL avoided launching Petro Cards in Mumbai. They were first launched in Hyderabad and then in Chennai. Once they succeeded, they were extended to eighteen other major cities. Mumbai was one of the last places where it was introduced. For this, the company had to work on changing the mentality of dealers before introducing the card. The philosophy behind the innovation and the long-terms benefits had to be explained. The dealers were counselled that their old approach of squeezing the customer was not going to work in the days ahead. That's not what the company stood for. It took time, but ultimately they saw the logic of the initiative and embraced it. Consequently, BPCL won a huge band of loyal customers for life.

Making Travel Comfortable for Truck Drivers

In February 2001, the company extended the Petro Card initiative to the owners of car fleets and transport companies. The biggest problem faced by transporters was the risk of its drivers carrying huge amounts of cash for refuelling purposes. The SmartFleet card met this very requirement and emerged as a big hit. The transport companies could make the payments centrally, and the drivers could carry these cards and use them for refuelling. They no longer had to carry cash. The card also allowed the truck owners to keep track of their vehicles. Whenever a driver used the SmartFleet card at a BPCL outlet, his company office would immediately get a message about where the card was used and at what time.[47] Using this facility, and at a time when cell phones were not yet ubiquitous, the company could even send messages to the drivers as and when required. The other benefit for transport companies was that reward points from bulk purchases could be centrally accumulated and redeemed, thereby creating financial benefits. It was a real win-win in commercial and convenience terms and created a big differentiator in the oil industry. In the first six months, BPCL enrolled 15,000 vehicles under the scheme and increased it to 80,000 vehicles in the next eighteen months. It gave immense leverage to the company compared to its competitors. IOCL and HPCL were quick to emulate their example. They launched the Indian Oil XtraPower Fleet cards and HPCL Drive Track Fleet cards respectively that provided similar benefits to the trucking community.[48] By 2015, there were 12.5 lakh vehicles under the SmartFleet programme, and over Rs 20,000 crore of annual business was transacted through the SmartFleet and Petro Cards.

Figure 6.7: The BPCL SmartFleet Campaign

BPCL's initiatives were not just intended to benefit the transport companies. The drivers, who were the actual front-end customers, were also the target. To make their lives simpler, the company started the One Stop Truck Shop (OSTS) Initiative as part of its 'highway strategy'. An internal study revealed the hardships and inconvenience typically faced by these drivers. First, they had to refill their vehicle every 400 to 500 kilometres. Secondly, they had nowhere to park their vehicles with precious cargo at times when they wanted to take rest or take a break for personal reasons. Thirdly, they had to stop at multiple locations for using toilets, having their meals or even making personal purchases. BPCL used OSTS, also called 'GHAR', as the central location catering to all their personal requirements. While highways (state and national) constituted just 6 per cent of the national network, they accounted for 40 per cent of national cargo. To increase its footprint, BPCL bought land along the major arterial national highways and put up large size OSTS outlets that provided all facilities, including secure parking, fuelling, minor and emergency truck care, affordable eating, washrooms, convenience stores and also places to rest. Certain outlets had small theatres for entertainment purposes. The SmartFleet card was central to accessing all these services. Typically 50–100 employees worked at these OSTS round-the-clock. The expenses of establishing and managing these multipurpose GHARs were divided between the company and the dealers. While all capital investments (ranging from Rs 2 to 4 crore per OSTS) were made by BPCL, the dealers typically met employees' salary expenses and non-fuel working capital. Between 1998 and 2003, over fifty OSTS were set up across India. The tangible benefits of this initiative were seen in the rise of average fuel sales to 8 lakh litres per month at each OSTS as against the earlier average of 1.5 lakh litres per month.[49]

Imagine driving a truck with tonnes of cargo and unendingly journeying through circuitous roads across the length and breadth of India as a lifetime career. The drivers hardly met their families as they used to travel long distances far away from their homes. A common problem that emerged from this was connected with HIV/AIDS. To cater to this, BPCL associated with various agencies working in this field for expanding the awareness of HIV/AIDS. Rajasekhar, then manager at the BPCL corporate office, shared with me, 'The truckers' community is largely affected by this problem. They are our major customers. So we have provided small clinics in our retail outlets where a doctor sits for a short period of time. We also provide free literature for their reading.'

Pure for Sure, Not Just a Slogan

In order to better understand customer perceptions about the company, its products and services, BPCL commissioned a nationwide survey in collaboration with ORG-MARG, a leading market research firm. Opinions of more than 70,000 people were captured. The major issue that emerged was customers' suspicion about the quality and quantity of fuel sold through retail outlets.[50] This was an issue that most oil companies had not been able to successfully address—the primary reason being that an oil company delivered the products to its dealers and the main touch point for the customers was the dealer. It was a big challenge for BPCL to deliver that promise of the right quality and quantity to the customer. That is when the 'Pure for Sure' (PFS) programme and campaign was launched. When the name was suggested by one of the consultants, the entire senior team fell for its powerful message. The implementation of purity and surety was a unique journey by itself.

In the PFS programme, the purity was about product quality and surety was about product quantity. While the fuel is being dispensed into a vehicle, nobody can see it going in. Hence, the suspicion about the quantity—whether 5 litres actually meant 5 litres? In spite of the opportunity of customers verifying the quantity through physical measurement, and the quality through simple tests such as the blotting paper test or the density test, it remained theoretical. Customers didn't have the time to get into all these processes. Customers usually followed their perception about a particular dealer being good or bad. Thus, the product was getting commoditized.[51] BPCL wanted to shift this towards a brand-based solution, where the brand communicated the genuineness of the product and assured its delivery as promised.

This process had to be initiated by sealing the probable prospects available to compromise product quality from the time the fuel left the company premises to the time when it was actually dispensed into customers' vehicles. A lot of 'mischief' was possible en route. The driver carrying the fuel to the dealers' depots could tamper with the seal, remove the good product and adulterate it. The dealer could also remove the good product and mix the remaining with kerosene. The high levels of differences in the prices of kerosene, diesel and petrol,[52] and kerosene's availability at subsidized rates through the public distribution system, provided a huge incentive for such malpractices.

BPCL hired a Germany-based company, TUV Suddeutschland[53] to monitor this entire process. One of the first recommendations was to instal a tamper-proof lock in every lorry carrying fuel. The Abloy lock, a Swiss product, was used for this purpose. The manufacturers guaranteed that nobody could tamper with the lock. According to the new process, one key was to be at the location where the product was filled into the lorry and one key was to be with the dealer at the delivery site. All the lorries, whether those belonging to the company or those rented from independent vehicle owners, were fitted with Abloy locks. If required, the fabrication was changed at company costs in such a way that the Abloy locks could be fitted on all lorries. Having sealed likely compromises on the way, TUV was given the responsibility of ensuring high levels of process orientation at the dealers' end: whether the dealer was adulterating the product when it reached her storage tank; and whether the dealer was manipulating the quantity by fiddling with the dispensing unit. At the time of receiving the fuel from the company, the dealer was expected to check the density of the fuel received and record the findings in an invoice. TUV undertook independent checks at the pumps to ensure that the highest standards as envisaged for PFS were maintained.

Figure 6.8: An Abloy Lock

At every PFS fuel station, BPCL wanted to ensure 100 per cent quality and quantity to the consumers' fuel tank. Besides other external aspects such as a clean and welcoming atmosphere for customers, a healthy environment for the forecourt service personnel and personalized and efficient service to consumers were also mandatory. All pumps were expected to have digital units. Those that had mechanical units were asked to replace them. A large number of dispensing units were bought at company cost and given to franchises. BPCL also spent money on repainting trucks with PFS artwork and colour combinations to ensure greater standardization. The company also worked on changing visual identity at retail outlets. It designed the huge monolith that displayed petrol and diesel prices. Earlier they used to display only the company emblem there. This was replaced with the monolith at all PFS outlets, such that it was visible from 5 kilometres, especially on highways. An enormous amount of work went into all these finer details. For this, a PFS group was formed inside the retail SBU, whose job was only to monitor the progress and solve problems.

After the infrastructure and processes were in place, TUV would perform an audit to ensure that everything was as per PFS standards. Only after this was certified could the PFS mnemonic be displayed at the petrol pump. Syamal recalled how this certification process used to be like a festival. The dealer and his entire team used to celebrate after being declared a PFS outlet. However, it didn't end there. TUV was engaged for continuous audit. There were mystery audits and special audits all through the year. BPCL encouraged panels of customers unknown to outlet owners to give feedback to the company on service quality levels at the outlets. They could use special apparatus available at petrol pumps to check whether the density of petrol sold to them was the same as that displayed in the concerned outlets. There were also surprise follow-up checks by company mobile vans, which collected samples and sent them for clinical and octane rating tests. The company officers and TUV were given the authority to close the outlet if it did not meet PFS standards during any such audit or inspection. The PFS logo would be removed and the outlet would lose its special status. Consequently, the customer would come to know that the outlet had lost its special identity and the dealer would further lose their customer base. Besides fuel, outlets were also judged on parameters such as efficiency of service and behaviour towards customers during these surprise inspection events, almost every fortnight. Launched on the occasion of Indian Independence Day on 15 August 2001, the PFS services were available at ninety-eight outlets in four metros. More significantly, in the very first year since the campaign began, BPCL recorded a 20 per cent increase in the sale of fuel, both petrol and diesel. This reflected the success of the effort.[54]

Any major behavioural change is not without resistance. In this case, even before the dealers could make noise, there was a lot of resistance within the company. One group of old-school thinking who had worked as divisional heads and used to control dealers, believed that by creating such a differentiator among dealers, BPCL was perpetuating a kind of 'caste system' among dealers! However, Sundararajan intervened and insisted that customer interests were paramount, and that the company must unfailingly deliver on parameters of quality and quantity. The initial reaction among dealers was also one of extreme resistance. Given that the quantum of commission they received from the company was less, they considered the hanky-panky as their route to earn some extra money.

To ensure that committed dealers participated in the PFS programme, BPCL took on board proactive dealers who were willing to improve their standards. The company chose good outlets in decent localities that had high potential to make a difference. When those dealers came forward and were certified as PFS outlets, other dealers started seeing their rise in sales because customers started going to PFS outlets as opposed to the generic ones. The differentiator was visible, and as a result, HPCL and IOCL outlets started losing sales. Even BPCL outlets without PFS, started losing customers. To further support the PFS-certified dealers, BPCL increased the commission to a higher slab. Yet, that wasn't a very big incentive. The real incentive was improved prestige in locality and the ability to attract new customers. PFS was also an opportunity for dealers indulging in hanky-panky to improve themselves or get left out. It became a prestige issue for many dealers and an irritating issue for others. However, the company stuck to its guns. Sinha asserted, 'Pure for Sure was to keep the black market at bay.[55] It was a fight against adulteration.'

After the success of PFS, BPCL moved on further to the path of automation. The company started linking retail outlets with the head office through IT. The dispensing unit, the storage unit, everything was monitored on a real-time basis through computerized systems. Sitting at the head office, the executives knew the stock levels at different outlets. For this, a lot of automation infrastructure was put into place at retail outlets. It was called 'Nano'—no automation, no product. The IT was then extended to vehicles through fleet tracking systems. All lorries were tracked through the GPS system to ensure zero deviation from the route to the dealers' depot. All this automation aimed at continuously and consistently delivering the brand promise to final consumers. By 2015, the number of PFS outlets increased to 5700. To move forward with changing times, the company introduced 'Pure for Sure Platinum' that aimed at providing round-the-clock service in a technology-enabled environment. It was promoted with the tagline *'Vaada Nahi, Daava'* (Not just an assurance, but a commitment).[56]

Figure 6.9: The 'Pure for Sure Platinum' Campaign

More Miles, per Drop

While the retail initiatives at the BPCL outlets provided convenience, the Pure for Sure programme aimed at ensuring product quality and quantity. Both of these contributed to increasing volumes and market share but did not provide any opportunity of charging more. So, the company aimed at supplying a differentiated product with premium pricing. Consumer research indicated that vehicle owners were not averse to paying more for fuel that enhanced their driving experience. Across the world, premium fuels were a popular genre of products targeted at high-end customers. This product was for customers who were busy yet active, and sought fuel that protected their vehicle, ensured its best performance and gave a trouble-free driving experience. With a rising affluent class, the Indian automobile industry had matured to making and marketing premium and luxury vehicles. The premium fuels were best suited to this category of vehicles.

BPCL sought partners who could supply the necessary additives for making premium fuels. The final product was tested at the Automobile Research Association of India (ARAI) laboratory in Pune. Then the company collaborated with Mercedes and other high-end car manufacturers to test this product and study its impact on efficiency and mileage. The results were positive, and the decks were cleared for launching Speed 93, BPCL's premium fuel. It was a blend of petrol with 93 Octane and other multifunctional additives.[57] Before the launch, BPCL dealers had to work towards providing additional storage at the petrol pump, create newer bays for vehicles using premium fuels, and separate dispensing units for Speed 93 (petrol) and High Speed (diesel).

The launch was well received and gradually premium fuels became very popular. With a marginal difference of a few rupees per litre, the Indian motorist was willing to pay for a premium fuel beneficial to the vehicle. So how did this positively impact the vehicle? In conventional fuels, total combustion doesn't take place, and there are leftover hydrocarbons that lead to the formation of tar. This chokes the piston and consequently additional heat gets generated and the engine efficiency drops. With premium fuels, there was near-total burning that led to lesser formation of tar (soot), lesser heat, increased engine efficiency and hence, better mileage. It also led to reduced emissions making it a popular product among environmental enthusiasts. I recollect my father conscientiously going for premium fuels at the

BPCL outlet in Churchgate (Mumbai) soon after it was launched. He preferred them for their positive impact on the car's engine life and also lesser pollution. At the company's annual general meeting in September 2002, Sarthak Behuria, the new CMD, reported that within a quarter of its launch, Speed constituted 35–40 per cent of BPCL's petrol sales.[58] IOCL and HPCL followed suit and launched 'Xtramile' and 'Power' brands of premium fuels to claim their share in the premium customers' wallet.[59] However, BPCL's product was such a success that Speed became a generic name for premium fuels. For quite some time, motorists would go into any petrol pump and ask for Speed irrespective of whether it was IOCL, HPCL or BPCL![60]

Figure 6.10: Multilevel Innovation at BPCL

Towards Newer Horizons on the High Seas

In August 2005, Ashok Sinha took charge as CMD of BPCL. The company was already making great strides on the retail front. The low-hanging fruit identified during Project CUSECS had been secured. He wanted the company to collectively revisit its strategy and prepare long-term plans for the next five years. Right from the senior leadership, this exercise involved over 1000 BPCL employees. They jointly explored the core strengths based on the four 'Ds' of discover, dream, design and deliver. Christened as 'Project Destiny', the company-wide exercise aimed at doubling sales volumes and quadrupling profits by March 2011.

The growth plan was two-fold. The first one aimed at increasing refining capacity to meet rising fuel demands. With refineries in Mumbai, Kochi and Numaligarh, the west, south and northeast regions were sufficiently covered. BPCL now focused its efforts on the establishment of the grass-root refinery in Bina in the Sagar district of Madhya Pradesh that was first conceived as the Central India Refinery in the 1990s. Spearheaded under Project Destiny with a revised estimated expense of Rs 12,200 crore, the Bina Refinery was the biggest ever project undertaken by BPCL and was scheduled for completion by 2010–11.[61] On completion, the refinery was to have a daily capacity of 1,20,000 barrels and an annual capacity of 6 MTPA (million metric tonnes per annum). In spite of inordinate delays due to environmental clearances, the liquidity crisis of 2008–09 and scepticism even from within government circles, BPCL remained committed to the project. On completion, the company not only gained a handsome premium on the sale of additional equity, but also enlarged its existing capacity to cater to increasing fuel demand in significant regions of north and central India.[62]

The second part of BPCL's strategy under Project Destiny was to take concrete steps into exploration and production

(E&P), an area that the PSE OMCs had not ventured into for multiple reasons such as the enormous investments required, lack of technical expertise necessary for E&P, and the need for international collaboration at global exploration sites. BPCL's tryst with E&P had begun as early as 1997, when its Articles of Association[63] were first modified to add E&P as an additional activity. Half a decade later, a special projects team was established to explore opportunities in E&P. Given the spiralling prices of crude, the company wanted to explore alternative sources of supply, besides benefitting from large margins through E&P that would positively impact its earnings. It also wanted to venture into gas exploration, which was a cheaper and cleaner fuel, and would complement its predominantly oil-focused product portfolio. BPCL got the first break when the government allotted twenty blocks to multiple oil and gas PSEs within India. The company won a block each in the Krishna–Godavari and Mahanadi basins.[64] Given its consistent commitment to increase its footprint in E&P, the special project team was converted into a wholly-owned subsidiary company called Bharat PetroResources Ltd (BPRL) in May 2006. The working arrangement involved operational decisions to be taken by BPRL and funding approvals given by BPCL. The main objective of the upstream strategy was to de-risk the existing business.[65]

Being an OMC, BPCL's existing expertise was primarily in the areas of refining and marketing. Sinha realized the need for differentiated skill sets in E&P. To bridge this vital gap, BPRL employed geophysicists and other technical experts from outside and began building the necessary expertise to gain a stronghold in this area. The company's focus was on gaining international opportunities in E&P. 'It was high risk because we had never done it before. But we realized that subsidies that were a cap on our profits were going to be there for a long time. We decided that our route to globalization was through exploration and production,' Sinha explained, highlighting BPCL's logic for its international upstream strategy. Till then, the company's margins came primarily from two sources: refining and marketing. While it had captured nearly 20 per cent of the retail markets through its innovative marketing efforts, there was a cap on the refining margin it could earn given the finite refining capacity it had across four refineries. Moreover, both these margins were minuscule as compared to margins possible from E&P. However, the risks were huge, and investments phenomenal. Drilling a single well in deep waters could cost as much as Rs 700 crore, with no guarantee of success in finding oil or gas. There was a lot of scepticism even within the company as to why it was venturing into an area that was beyond its expertise and existential mandate. Sinha and his senior team knew that if they succeeded, it would be a phenomenal win-win. Not only would they have access to an additional supply of crude, they would also gain greater market share and could cater to a larger customer base. Financially, it would positively impact its earnings and also reflect well in its stock prices. Being a finance man, Sinha had calculated the trade-offs well enough. With a plan to invest up to Rs 7500 crore in international E&P opportunities, the company started scouting for prospective partners. In parallel, BPRL started focusing on learning exploration terminology and gaining market intelligence from industry experts and external consultants.

The first breakthrough came when BPRL, in collaboration with Videocon Hydrocarbon Holdings,[66] acquired ten blocks owned by Encana Corporation (Canada) in the deep waters of Brazil. Petrobras,[67] Brazil's integrated national oil company, was operating nine of them and Andarko Petroleum[68] from USA was operating the tenth one. Despite the healthy diplomatic relations between India and Brazil, the deal was stuck in Brazilian bureaucracy for months. Sinha finally approached the Indian prime minister's office for help. The Indian ambassador followed up with the Brazilian government and in September 2008, the BPRL–Videocon stake was finally approved for US$ 283 million (Rs 1275 crore), just before the deadline. BPCL had to make the payment within four days to seal the deal. That was exactly the week in which Lehman Brothers declared bankruptcy. The international financial markets were in a tizzy. As if unaware of all these developments, BPCL ventured into the global markets for a huge loan. Its scale and reputation as a Fortune 500 company enabled BPCL to secure an international loan of US$ 100 million (Rs 450 crore) within forty-eight hours at the peak of the sub-prime crisis, and that too, at the best rates possible.[69] All this was well worth the efforts because within a month of the deal, the consortium first struck oil at Wahoo, an oil field operated by Anadarko Petroleum. The estimated reserves were 35 crore barrels. A year later, additional oil was discovered in the Campos Basin off the Brazilian coast.[70] The company couldn't have asked for more!

After the successful collaboration in Brazil, Andarko Petroleum invited BPCL to join a consortium for deep-water exploration off the coast of Mozambique in east Africa. It wanted to offload 20 per cent of its stake. So BPCL and Videocon picked up 10 per cent each. This also saved them the efforts of going through a tendering process. Moreover, the expression of interest by a US-based petroleum company to collaborate with a PSE like BPCL was indicative of the success of the company's efforts in the international E&P market. Within a year, the consortium struck a major natural gas find (estimated at 4–5 trillion[71] cubic feet) at the Windjammer exploration well (off the coast of Mozambique). At that time, it was rated as the first among the top ten oil and gas discoveries in the world.[72] By 2013, it was estimated that the Rovuma Basin, off the coast of Mozambique, may hold as much as 70 trillion cubic feet of gas resources, a phenomenal find for the consortium that BPCL was part of.[73] By 2015, BPRL had expanded its presence and had participating interests in seventeen blocks across six countries, including East Timor, Australia and Indonesia. BPCL was considered the only Indian OMC with a successful foray into the upstream business.[74] Two successful back-to-back finds in the first two years itself were a rarity for a new entrant like BPCL. Its risk-laden upstream strategy had shown signs of success and sceptics within and outside the company turned around. They started appreciating its visionary decision to diversify across the oil and gas value chain. Moreover, its gas finds in Mozambique played a major role in diversifying into that form of energy, especially at a time when gas was contributing to nearly 20 per cent of the energy mix in India. Going forward, the quantity of gas usage was likely to increase and that of oil likely to reduce—the primary reason being that natural gas is more carbon neutral and a cleaner source of energy, both during refining and usage. In the years ahead, this increasing investment in gas would be beneficial for the company commercially and in terms of market share. Additionally, it would reduce its environmental footprint.[75]

'I Have Navratna Powers'

The manner in which BPCL executed its expansion and diversification initiatives is very interesting. The usual belief is that PSEs take every major decision only based on government instructions and approvals. However, a lot depends on the leadership style and approach of each PSE. Furthermore, through the Navratna status, a lot of freedom has been given to high-performing PSEs. The onus is on them to utilize it. Sinha did just that. He did everything within the framework provided by the government to PSEs and inside the purview of the powers given to the board of directors, which also included nominees of the Government of India. The senior management presented a very compelling case before the board detailing the strategic and long-term commercial logic for venturing into E&P, which was approved.

Initially, the Government of India had only permitted ONGC Videsh Limited (OVL)[76] to venture into international E&P.

Later, IOCL and GAIL[77] requested permission for the same. They too were given approval to invest up to Rs 300 crore. While writing the note of approval, the ministry also permitted BPCL and HPCL, with the caveat that the government should be kept informed about their initiatives. However, Sinha never went with a formal request to the ministry. 'Why do I need to go and take special permission? As a Navaratna, my board was empowered for a per project international investment of Rs 1000 crore. So I kept it within those limits and operated only at the board level,' he shared with me. Sinha did not believe in seeking separate government approval for each project and investment. He took decisions within the board's permitted limits and the company's risk-taking abilities.

In this context, he shared a very interesting conversation. Some time in 2009–10, during a flight to New Delhi, he was sitting and reading a newspaper on board. To his surprise, on the seat next to his was T.K.A. Nair, principal secretary to the prime minister of India. By then, BPCL's name had become popular as the largest public sector investor from India in Brazil. Sinha had already visited Brazil twice as part of the Government of India delegation, once led by Prime Minister Manmohan Singh himself. During the course of the conversation, Nair asked Sinha, 'How come BPCL's papers don't come to me for any approvals? I find requests from IOCL, GAIL and ONGC. But your papers never come. And then you land up in the delegation to Brazil!' Sinha smiled and said, 'I have Navratna powers.' 'They have Navratna powers, too!' Nair said. So Sinha joked, 'I don't know why they're coming to you—please ask them!' Both laughed.

'Was Nair upset that you didn't seek written approvals from the government?' I asked. 'He was very appreciative,' Sinha replied. Those were the years when BRICS was getting formed. BPCL would always make sure the local ambassadors were kept informed. Sinha also kept the secretary of the ministry of petroleum and

natural gas (PNG) in the communication loop. He recalled how
M.S. Srinivasan, secretary in the ministry of PNG, encouraged him
for BPCL's E&P initiatives. In reciprocation, Sinha always kept
him informed. For example, when BPCL first hit oil in Brazil, he
had to inform the secretary even before the news reached the press.
Murli Deora, the then minister of PNG, would be answerable
to the prime minister about the details of the initiative. It would
have been embarrassing to get this vital information from the press
instead of being informed by the company, which was a government
undertaking. 'I needed to handle that boundary without offending
them. But I used to stop my communication at the level of the
secretary,' Sinha told me. Empowerment was not an order that the
government would sign on. It had put in place enabling provisions
in PSE operations that provided sufficient autonomy for successful
PSEs. Based on his three-decade experience at BPCL, Sinha
asserted, 'Empowerment comes for PSEs when they utilize that
which is available in the framework.'

The public sector set-up, whether banking, oil and gas,
or heavy industries, has regimented processes to ensure
transparency. Many times, more than doing business, PSEs and
their leaders have to constantly prove their innocence and non-
involvement in illegal or unethical practices. The principles of
fairness and equity are their watchwords. Unfortunately, these
are not easily provable. 'Almost every part of the government
thinks that we are existing for their purpose. So there may
be demands and pressures, but we have to keep in mind that
the stakeholders' needs have to be met.' Sinha shared with me
his experience of how a PSE leader has to report to multiple
agencies overseeing the working of the company. This included
communication to the petroleum secretary (ministry of PNG),
reporting to the Department of Public Enterprises (ministry of
heavy industries and public enterprises), presentations before the
Planning Commission, and providing responses to the various

parliamentary committees for questions raised during sessions in both houses of the Indian Parliament. Each of these has its own agendas and priorities. A PSE leader has to plan and implement company strategy while balancing these diverse interests; sometimes, even outright interferences. Moreover, many secretaries and members of bureaucracy hold positions for a year or two. They have short-term agendas, and their communication to policymakers and parliamentarians may not reflect the true grass-root level picture.[78] Furthermore, the government of the day may also have a populist mandate that they need to meet. All of these need to be balanced with the long-term strategy of the company. That's the job of the leader in a PSE. 'We called it "boundary management", and ensured that the top leadership of the company would manage that as a part of their job. We would minimize any interference from passing through us into the organization,' he told me.

Transparency, Quality or Both?

Then there are areas where government procedures have to be tactfully handled. For example, the tendering process. Tendering is a process by which the government and PSEs invite bids from suppliers for major projects. These applications have to be submitted within a finite deadline. The tendering process usually begins with an RFT (request for tender) or RFP (request for proposal) by the government agency/PSE that is accompanied by a tender paper with details on the project. This enables prospective vendors to understand the competencies required to apply for the tender and complete the project within timelines. Due to imperatives of transparency and fairness as demanded by the democratic system, PSEs that have a majority government-ownership are required to mostly select all major vendors through the tendering process. This also ensures that there is no collusion or bias towards certain private sector businesses for vested interests of PSE employees or leadership. Furthermore, the unsaid rule is that the vendor proposal offering the service at the lowest price is mostly selected. This is to ensure that public money is well-utilized. However, at such times, due to constant focus on costs, issues of quality and timely completion take a back seat. This can also be problematic at times when an innovative product/service is launched that has no precedent. 'How could I have created a Petro Card through the tendering process? I cannot give out my strategy as a tender paper to the whole world!' Sinha confessed.

At other times, the 'lowest cost' requirement had to be manoeuvred through. 'Many stakeholders may think that we have to do good to society. But doing only that may be fundamentally detrimental to the existence of the organization.' Sinha recollected the times when BPCL was inviting tenders for an operating system. At that time there were only two options: Windows[79] or Lotus.[80] Windows was on its way up, and Lotus on its way out. If the company would have opened both the bids, Lotus would have to be selected due to the lower price. That's what happened with a competing PSE. Due to the lowest price criterion, they went for Lotus. Four years later, they had to scrap the system and get on to Windows. Instead, BPCL ensured that at the level of the technical bid,[81] Lotus was rejected, so that issues of price did not influence decision-making. 'So there are areas where you need to balance it. If it's a technical issue, such decisions are valid. I'm using public money and the viability of my projects is at stake,' Sinha emphasized.

A balanced approach to the tendering process would be a key to efficient and effective outcomes. Issues of transparency cannot be taken to such extremes where lower investment leads to poor quality output. Effectively, the government systems would end up spending much more to maintain and redo such projects. Sinha believed that societal interests must be integrated into the purpose of a PSE. It should not be a separate activity that the company is attempting to do along with its business—primarily because a PSE has two categories of owners: individual and institutional shareholders, who are in minority but have invested money in the company; and the government that holds majority ownership through the investment of public money. Both of these investments need to be utilized in such a way that transparency and quality are equally emphasized. That was a win-win that BPCL attempted.

Sinha observed that the best way of problem-solving was to go back to the concerned parties within the government establishment and talk to them. 'It's not that they are not convincible. But there are differences in approaches. After all, business and bureaucracy have different styles of operation.' He believed that a PSE leader must be clear that what the PSE is doing is not only as per the government's mandate, but also that it is the right thing to do. 'If you think that what they are saying is not right, you should go back and discuss the matter with them,' he said.

Twenty years ago, the oil industry was not so much in focus because the products were serving a limited mandate. With the utility of oil increasing, things changed. Oil is no longer a commercial product, it's a political product. If an OMC needs crude, the ministry has to work for it. Healthy diplomatic relations with countries like Iran and Saudi Arabia play a major role in gaining access to sufficient quantities of crude to meet the ever-increasing demand in India. Hence, the government's priorities can't be wished away. It is not only the largest shareholder, but also a vital source of raw material supply for the OMCs. Thus, prudence lies not in confrontation but collaboration, through healthy engagement, dialogue and win-win decision-making where the interests of business and bureaucracy are balanced.

Explaining the larger role of companies, Sinha opined that business organizations exist because of society, and hence the prime objective should be that of meeting societal needs, as a trustee of public resources. This is truer in case of PSEs as they are in charge of public money, and hence, have a very strong responsibility towards the public. Sinha succinctly explained, 'The cycle would be to use the resources provided by society for the ultimate benefit of society through the medium of business. While doing that, generate sufficient profits that facilitate this process and also take care of all organizational stakeholders who facilitate this process.'

Figure 6.11: Four Dynamic Decades: The BPCL Journey (1976–2016)

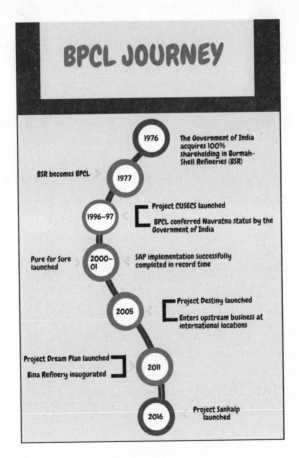

The Journey Continues

R.K. Singh took over as CMD from Sinha in 2010. Project Dream Plan, that was envisioned in the last year of Sinha's tenure, was put into motion with 2016 as the target year. The primary objective was to consolidate what was achieved until then and move forward.[82] The six strategic elements included: furthering BPCL's footprint in the upstream category and becoming an operator; expanding refinery capacity in Bina and Kochi; investing in gas; aggressive and profitable growth in marketing SBUs and making refineries world-class in the face of greater competition; enabling a high performing organization; and creating options in new businesses which can be scaled up if found profitable.[83] The project had many focused objectives. The first was to double sales volume from 28 MTPA to 55 MTPA. The oil ministry's petroleum planning and analysis cell estimated a 20 per cent rise (186 MTPA) by 2017.[84] BPCL aimed at claiming a share of this larger market. The second was to increase refining capacity from 0.5 million barrels per day (bpd) to 0.8 million bpd, (30MTPA to 45MTPA).[85] The company estimated a capital expenditure of Rs 57,000 crore for upgradation and increase in refining capacity across the four refineries and venturing into newer areas such as manufacture of niche petrochemicals to produce new import substitute products, besides continuing its investments in upstream projects. Through these and other initiatives, BPCL aimed at doubling its profits by 2016.

By the time S. Varadarajan, the next CMD, took charge in 2014, Project Dream Plan was halfway through. In the initial months, he continued the company's tradition of grass-roots interaction across the country. Through video conferencing, he interacted with over 1800 management staff and 2000 field staff and understood their aspirations. During these interactions, BPCL employees continued to focus on creating leadership for BPCL in the energy space, upstream opportunities, refining capacity, renewable energy and retail.[86] The times were also favourable for the OMCs as the Government of India finally deregulated diesel prices. The prices would now be linked to the international market prices, and under-recoveries would not be a burden on the balance sheets of the OMCs. (Appendix VI.C elaborates on the process of deregulation between 2002 and 2016.)

The OMCs also realized that their earlier expectations of privatization of PSE oil companies were not going to materialize. The government wasn't going to give up control of oil companies for multiple reasons. Hence, the approach to success was not in dreaming about the benefits of privatization, but in reorienting strategies to meet the current situation. The ideal approach was to balance social responsibility on one side, and the responsibility of becoming efficient on the other. The OMCs realized that customers would reward them with ample business if they became efficiently-operated companies. The path to long-term survival was through customer-centricity. On its side, the government increasingly realized the benefits of efficiency.

In an important change in approach, it started reducing the duplication of assets. Earlier, all PSE companies were mindlessly duplicating assets. Under the APM system, returns were connected to making investments. So each OMC had the same assets while none of them had 100 per cent capacity utilization. Realizing this wasteful expense, the government introduced the concept of 'Common User Facility'. Accordingly, one company could invest in a particular asset, say an LPG plant, and others could also utilize the facility. This resulted in reduced costs and the customer received the same product at a lower price. Going forward, this would get extended to the utilization of pipelines and for many other logistical purposes, thereby leading to optimal utilization of assets.

As 2015 was nearing its end, in typical BPCL tradition, Project Sankalp was launched by the company with an expansion plan of Rs 1 lakh-crore between 2016 (when Project Dream Plan would conclude) and 2021. Of these, Rs 40,000 crore were aimed at increasing refining capacity to 50 MTPA (1 million bpd) by 2021 through brownfield projects at existing refineries. Another Rs 25,000 crore would be invested in expanding the upstream business in Brazil and Mozambique and for acquiring new assets globally.[87] Rs 6000 crore was aimed at developing petrochemicals expertise at the Kochi Refinery. The remaining amount aimed at ramping up its non-fuel retail venture under the 'In & Out' brand. Sharing his vision at the annual general meeting, CMD Varadarajan said, 'Project Sankalp will see us going global not only with our upstream investments, but also with our expertise in the marketing of petroleum products. We are looking at setting up marketing infrastructure in the neighbouring countries as well as in the Far East, Africa and Latin America.'[88]

The time was ripe. The Indian OMCs had surplus refining capacity. While the domestic requirement was around 170 MTPA, the refining capacity was nearly 260 MTPA. India was getting ready to become an export hub. Most private companies like Reliance and Essar focused only on exports. The PSE OMCs were ready to follow suit. BPCL, the multinational in the garb of a PSE, was gradually unleashing itself. The structural and infrastructural investments of time, thought and resources collectively made by the BPCL team during Project CUSECS and Project Destiny had provided a strong basis to scale up. The economic, social and political environment was now conducive. The company was ready to grow profitably by consistently and creatively meeting the ever-increasing demands of the world's fastest growing economy.

Figure 6.12: Win-Win Learnings from Bharat Petroleum Corporation

LESSONS FROM
BHARAT PETROLEUM CORPORATION

1. ENTERPRISING LEADERSHIP

Visionary leadership and top management
commitment are critical success factors
even in a PSE

2. EMPLOYEES: THE REAL CHANGE-MAKERS

Employee involvement in organizational
transformation processes is essential
for long-term success

3. BRAND POWER

Focused brand building can transform
commodities into bestselling products

4. CONSTANT INTEGRATED INNOVATION

The innovation spectrum can span from
products to the service experience and also
include delivery processes

5. COLLABORATION, NOT CONFRONTATION

Proactive engagement and collaboration between
business and bureaucracy is the basis of a
mutually rewarding relationship in a PSE

6. PURPOSE WITH PROFITS

Balancing social responsibility with operational
efficiency and profitability is the secret sauce
to sustainable growth for every PSE

VII.

TVS Motor Company

Quintessential Quest for Quality . . . For Industry,
India and Ideals

'The essence of TVS culture lies in the name "TVS", where "T" stands for Trust, "V" for Values, and "S" for Service. The name epitomizes the culture'

—Dr Venu Srinivasan, chairman and managing director, TVS Motor Company Ltd

One day, when he was five-years-old, Venu Srinivasan woke up early and walked out of his house. To the guard standing outside the house, he asked what time it was. The guard didn't have a watch but said that the first TVS bus had not yet gone past, and so it wasn't yet 5.15 a.m.[1] Such was the reputation of punctuality that the TVS bus services enjoyed across south India. With 400 buses covering forty stops a day—a total of 16,000 stops—with zero breakdowns and zero late arrivals. Among their regular customers was a young boy who used to take the TVS bus to go to school every day. On one particular day, the bus was surprisingly late by five minutes. Upon inquiry, it was revealed that the conductor had overslept causing the delay. Enraged at this lazy attitude, one of the passengers slapped the conductor. When fellow passengers chided the angry person for having spanked the conductor, they were in for a surprise. The conductor himself intervened and said that he deserved the whack he got because he had brought disrepute to the

TVS name. Fifty years later, that young boy became the chairman of Cochin Refineries. The incident still fresh in his mind, he shared it with Venu while travelling together on a flight.[2]

These are the kinds of legends associated with one of the oldest business groups in south India—TVS. Founded by Thirukkurangudi Vengaramaswamy Sundaram Iyengar, who hailed from the Tirunelveli district of present day Tamil Nadu, he was the first to start bus service in the Madurai district in 1912. In 1923, he established T.V. Sundaram Iyengar and Sons Limited. In 1929, he launched Madras Auto Service Limited, a dealership of General Motors,[3] which eventually became the largest distributor of GM and was rated by the company as its best dealership.[4] In 1933, at the age of fifty-five, T.V. Sundaram Iyengar retired from the business he had built with sheer hard work and commitment to the highest value systems of his times and tradition. He distributed responsibilities among his five sons— Rajam, Doraiswamy, Krishna, Santhanam and Srinivasan. The illustrious second generation expanded into the logistics business in the 1940s, finance and insurance businesses in the 1950s, the manufacture of auto components in the 1960s, mopeds and motorcycles in the 1970s, and electronics in the 1990s. Sundaram Fasteners, Sundaram-Clayton, Sundaram Brake Linings and Sundaram Finance are among the prominent companies of the TVS Group.

A century later, T.V. Sundaram Iyengar and Sons Limited continues to be the holding company of the TVS Group, which is now a conglomerate with over ninety companies under its umbrella. It operates in areas as diverse as the manufacturing of two-wheelers, three-wheelers, auto components and computer peripherals, distribution of heavy commercial vehicles, passenger cars, finance and insurance, logistics and providing enterprise resource management solutions to varied industries. The TVS Group is India's largest automotive component manufacturer. The first four companies in India to have won the coveted Deming Prize are from the TVS Group. By 2016, the group had revenues of over Rs 50,000 crore and an employee base of over 40,000 working across the globe.

TVS Motor Company: A Journey of Many Firsts

'If it is not excellence, it is not TVS. At TVS, the system is even more sacred than the owners. The organization is sacred, and its values are sacred'

—Dr Venu Srinivasan

To this illustrious pedigree belongs TVS Motor Company Limited (TVSM), India's third-largest two-wheeler manufacturer, and the flagship company of the TVS Group. T.S. Srinivasan, T.V. Sundaram Iyengar's youngest son and Venu's father, envisioned a product which could comfortably carry two people at a low cost in the hills of Tirupati, the abode of Lord Venkateswara, in the state of Andhra Pradesh. This led to the launch of mopeds that were lightweight and affordable. Sundaram-Clayton (SCL)[5] started a Mopeds division in 1979 that manufactured TVS mopeds. In 1980, TVS 50, a two-seater, 50cc[6] moped was launched. These mopeds were designed in-house and were made with indigenous components sourced from various TVS Group companies. His vision created a new market and led to a paradigm shift in personal mobility in the Indian hinterland. The company hasn't looked back since then and has been on a continuous journey of innovation, indigenous design and manufacturing over the last three decades.

In 1982, Ind-Suzuki Motorcycles Limited (ISML) was started as a joint venture between Suzuki Motor Company, Japan, and SCL. Founded in 1909, Suzuki is a multinational automobile manufacturing company headquartered in Hamamatsu in Japan. It is ranked among the world's top ten automakers with production facilities in twenty countries and dealerships in over 190 countries. Representation on the ISML board was equal for both companies, but management control was with the Indian partner. With this collaboration, ISML became the first Indian company to introduce 100cc Indo-Japanese motorcycles in India kick-starting the motorcycle revolution in the country. For greater synergies, the Moped Division of SCL was acquired by ISML in 1986. The combined entity was renamed TVS-Suzuki Limited.

Figure 7.1: An Advertisement of TVS 50XL Moped (1986)

Unfortunately, the success was short-lived. TVS motorcycles faced aggressive competition from Hero Honda (a joint venture between Honda Motor Company from Japan and the Hero Group of India), Kawasaki Bajaj (a joint venture between Kawasaki Heavy Industries from Japan and Bajaj Auto of India), and Escorts Yamaha (a joint venture between Yamaha Corporation from Japan and Escorts Group of India). The company went through tough times during this period, culminating in closure of its factory in 1990. This chain of events provided an opportunity for introspection, and under Venu's leadership, the company put in place a turnaround strategy. It decided to be product-led and focused its efforts on product quality, R&D and production engineering. It also embarked on cost-cutting, reduced manpower and controlled inventory. The efforts paid off as TVS launched five new products in 1992–93, including Samurai, Shogun, Max 100 and Max 100R. In 1994, it launched the TVS Scooty, a light scooter. It also introduced the Super Champs model in mopeds. At a time when moped sales in India were shrinking, those of TVS were rising. In a matter of five years, the company became one of the strongest players in the Indian two-wheeler industry. By 1994, its market share in the 100cc segment had risen from 12 to 20 per cent. By 1995, TVS-Suzuki's turnover increased to Rs 620 crore and it became India's second-largest two-wheeler company.

Venu always maintained that TVS was not interested in competing with anyone head-on. It wanted to create a niche for its products. So, that's what it did in the case of TVS Scooty. It wasn't a replica of any of its competing products. Interestingly, the making of TVS Scooty is an excellent case in point for cost-effective design and the advantages of home-grown technologies. Its design cost the company a mere Rs 3 crore,[7] when the typical investment for new product development at that time was anywhere between Rs 50 and 100 crore. The product was so well-received that between 1994 and 1998, its monthly sales went up many times.[8] By 1996, TVS XL and Champ became the largest selling vehicles in India. In the same year, it launched India's first catalytic converter-enabled motorcycle—TVS Shogun; and India's first five-speed motorcycle—TVS Shaolin. In 1998, TVS established its second manufacturing unit in Mysore in Karnataka. The turn of the century witnessed the launch of TVS Fiero, India's first 150cc, four-stroke motorcycle. TVS decided to work on four-stroke technology by itself, in order to be independent of Suzuki. Thus, Fiero was developed specially for the Indian market.[9]

In September 2001, Sundaram-Clayton and Suzuki Motor Corporation, partners in the joint venture TVS-Suzuki, announced their decision to break up. The new entity was named 'TVS Motor Company Limited' (TVSM), and Venu Srinivasan took over as chairman and managing director of the new entity. The year 2002 was a milestone for the company for several reasons. Firstly, TVSM went international and opened its first subsidiary in Karawang in Indonesia. The factory was the first of its initiatives to go global, besides increasing its global footprint through exports to over fifty countries. Secondly and most stunningly, it achieved a feat which no other two-wheeler company in the world had—it bagged the super-prestigious Deming Prize.

The 'Demingod': Understanding the TVS Way to Total Quality Management

'Total quality management (TQM) is a methodical, structured, concrete, and a measurable approach suited to the engineering mindset'

—Dr Venu Srinivasan

Dr William Edwards Deming (1900–93) from Iowa (USA) is hailed as the father of statistical quality control (SQC). In July 1950, he was invited by the Union of Japanese Scientists and Engineers (JUSE) to help post-World War II Japan with his ideas on total quality control (TQC). Through his lectures and SQC tools, he inspired Japanese corporations and leaders to raise their product and process quality to the highest international levels. The transcripts of his courses were so popular that they were distributed across Japan for a price. Very humbly, Dr Deming donated his royalties to JUSE to support the cause of quality in Japan. In appreciation of his contribution, to commemorate the friendship in a lasting way and to promote the continued development of quality control in Japan, the donated amount was used to establish the Deming Prize.[10] Over the last half century, the Deming Prize is considered as the final word in the world of quality.

Historically, quality awards were set up to encourage corporations that maintained high levels of product quality and customer satisfaction. Winning these indicated a company's efforts and commitment to quality, the outcomes being attracting and maintaining long-lasting relationships with multiple stakeholders, including suppliers, distributors, transporters and retailers, and thereby expanding customer base.[11] While the Deming Prize is the oldest such honour in the world, the USA-based Malcolm Baldrige National Quality Award,[12] and the European Quality Model Award[13] are two other globally-renowned quality honours. However, compared to the Deming Prize, experts have highlighted their limitations. While the former is said to be without the zealous obsession with SQC, the latter is said to be lacking the depth of the Deming Prize's analyses. It is believed that no transaction, no speck of dust on the floor, no tightening of a nut, no disaffected worker escapes the scrutiny of the Deming Prize examination team.[14]

In 2002, TVSM became the first two-wheeler automobile company in the world to win the Deming Prize and was acknowledged for achieving distinctive performance improvement through the application of TQM.[15] At that time, Venu Srinivasan was the only corporate chief in the world to sport three prestigious quality medals awarded by JUSE. In 1998, SCL, was the first Indian company ever to win the Deming Medal. In 2002, it won the Japan Quality Medal (now rechristened the Deming Grand Prize) regarded as a class higher than the Deming Award. By 2003, a total of five TVS Group companies had won Deming Awards, including Sundaram Brake Linings Limited (2001), Brakes India Limited (2002) and Lucas TVS Limited (2003).[16] In appreciation for making India proud on the world stage, *Business Week* chose Venu Srinivasan as the 'Star of Asia' 2003, describing the turnaround at TVS as a 'saga of persistence'. The All-India Management Association conferred on him the prestigious J.R.D. Tata Corporate Leadership Award in 2004.

It is interesting to know how TQM became the path of the TVSM turnaround story. Venu's search for quality had begun in the mid 1980s. On his first visit to Japan, he saw the functioning of the Suzuki and Honda companies, the quality of service in Japanese hotels, and the punctuality of the Japanese transportation system. He felt that Japanese factories were running the TVS way. There was respect for humanity, cleanlines, and discipline like the old TVS working style. That's when he resolved to revive the TVS culture pioneered by his grandfather, through the TQM system.[17] The usual belief with respect to TQM is its connection with product quality. Actually, TQM is about the quality of all business processes. In this journey, Venu took upon the role of the owner–CEO. He looked after stakeholders' interests, long-term vision and medium-term plans. The other functions were delegated to the president and the CEO. Through the involvement of multi-functional teams, he was able to reinstate the TVS culture of excellence through TQM.[18] This was absolutely necessary for the awards as well, because the award examination team studied not only the results achieved and the processes used, but also the effectiveness expected in the future. 'From the moment you step into the plant, everything must be right: the grass must be cut properly, the canteen floor must be cleaned properly. It is an all-round excellence effort,' shared

Venu.[19] In TVSM's TQM journey, professors Kurohara, Yasutoshi Washio and Yoshikazu Tsuda from JUSE were accepted as gurus rather than coaches or consultants. This approach sprang forth from Venu's personal thirst for fundamental knowledge rather than quick-fix solutions. The TVSM top management implicitly implemented what was recommended to them by these professors, and went back only for clarification when things didn't work as per expectations. This working relationship emerged as a major recipe for success.

According to the Deming Prize Committee, quality is a system of activities that produces products and services as per the customers' expectations of quality and delivers them economically. Its model puts employees at the base of the pyramid, daily work management[20] on top of it, and erects five pillars resting on them: total employee involvement,[21] policy deployment, standardization, kaizen (continuous improvement) and training. Thus, quality is not limited to a department. Everyone, everywhere in the company, is a custodian of quality. JUSE also examined whether the medal challenger, as the applicant is referred to, established 'challenging customer-oriented business objectives and strategies under clear leadership' and precisely how TQM was implemented to achieve them, besides an assessment of the company's business objectives and strategies after implementing TQM. The overall process of planning and preparing for the award typically enables a company to do soul-searching and exposes its strengths and weaknesses.[22]

TVSM's quality journey that began in the early 1990s was no different. Awareness, promotion and implementation were three distinct phases in its decade-long journey to the Deming Prize. Developing the right organizational and employee attitudes was the first task. With a core team spearheading the TQM journey across levels, focused improvements in design, production and distribution were initiated. This was followed by dealer development programmes in 1993, supplier training programmes in 1996, and human resource development in 1998.

By 2000, lean manufacturing[23] and TQM were in place across TVSM plants. The new product development process that began through indigenous innovations in the early 1990s culminated in the launch of TVS Victor[24] in 2001.[25] Interestingly, the TVS Group companies adapted the TQM concepts and assimilated them in their own 'TVS way', to the extent that the JUSE auditors commended their practices as 'TVS TQM'.[26] Venu acknowledged the tremendous amount of commitment that he inherited from his grandfather and uncles, who had a single-minded vision of quality that TVS stood for. It was this approach that drove the company to achieve the feat.[27] Top management commitment and a pan-organization culture of employee involvement were real success factors at TVSM.[28]

By applying TQM principles, TVSM launched several new products that resulted in higher volumes, profits and turnover. In the first three years between 2002 (when it got the award) and 2005, its sales turnover doubled and exports increased by 176 per cent to thirty countries in Asia, Africa, Europe, Latin America and North America. Besides, the internal rejection rate on engines reduced from 50,000 ppm (parts per million) to 100 ppm in the five years leading to the award, as also the lead time for new product development, which nearly halved from the initial thirty months. JUSE praised TVSM as a learning organization and complimented the top leadership for developing new organizational competence. It identified the need for an integrated strategy for strengthening its brand recognition and recall and new tools to enhance technological capability.[29] Venu underscored that the award by itself did not improve profits. The processes implemented in the course of applying for the award contributed to profitability, capability, market share and volumes. That was the real objective. He equated the award to the starter in a car. It is needed to start the car, but not once the engine is running. Similarly, the Deming Prize was a starter mechanism, the ignition for the jet plane.[30] In the subsequent decade, TVSM's revenue increased six times as it continued to build on the momentum created by the Deming Prize.

Figure 7.2: Impact of TQM on the Resurgence of TVSM

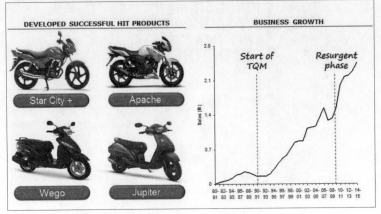

Building on the Deming Momentum

In 2006, TVSM inaugurated its first plant in north India in Nalagarh in Himachal Pradesh. TVS Apache, launched in the same year, won six awards in a row. Within the next decade, more than a million Apaches were zooming on Indian roads. In 2008, for the very first time, it entered the three-wheeler category and launched TVS King. TVS Jive, launched in 2009, became India's first clutch-free motorbike which aimed at a stress-free rider experience. The unisex scooter—TVS Wego—launched in 2010, was targeted at urban couples featuring body balance technology for easier handling. The launch of TVS Phoenix marked TVSM's entry into the 125cc premium segment in 2012. In 2013, it entered the 'male scooter segment' with TVS Jupiter. A sale of 5 lakh units within eighteen months since launch created history in the Indian scooter market. It was adjudged the scooter of the year in 2014.[31]

Figure 7.3: Bollywood Star Amitabh Bachchan Promotes TVS Jupiter

In 2013, BMW Motorrad from Germany and TVSM entered into a joint technical cooperation and manufacturing agreement to build and sell bikes below 500cc. The agreement complemented the expertise of both partners. Founded in 1923, BMW Motorrad was known for technology, quality, reliability and engineering perfection. By 2011, it had manufactured 20 lakh bikes up to the 1600cc range. TVSM's strengths included Indian brand equity, diversified product portfolio, high order of employee involvement, indigenous and low-cost manufacturing and a robust supply chain. The bikes were to be manufactured by TVSM under TVS and BMW badges, and both partners would sell them in India and overseas through their respective distribution networks.[32] While TVSM primarily catered to the low- and middle-income category products, this collaboration would facilitate an entry into the high-income segment.

In 2014, the fourth generation of the TVS family took charge of the company in substantial measure. Sudarshan Venu, son of the chairman, was appointment joint managing director at TVSM.[33] After gaining extensive engineering and management education from the University of Pennsylvania, USA, and the University of Warwick, UK, he worked closely with his father in shaping the collaboration with BMW Motorrad.[34] In the same year, his elder sister Dr Lakshmi Venu also joined the TVSM Board.[35] With the next generation in action, it could be said that the jet engine that was lit by the father with the Deming Prize, was all set to fly high!

Figure 7.4: Equity Returns of Leading Indian Two-wheeler Companies (2008–16)

Eight Year Equity Returns of Leading Indian Two-wheeler Companies

Investment
- TVS Motor Company ₹ 1,781,000
- Bajaj Auto ₹ 1,081,000
- Hero MotoCorp ₹ 478,000
- Sensex ₹ 155,000

₹ 0   ₹ 300,000   ₹ 600,000   ₹ 900,000   ₹ 1,200,000   ₹ 1,500,000   ₹ 1,800,000

Growth of an Investment of 1 Lakh Rupees (2008–16)

Customer, Competition, Complexity: Synonyms in the Indian Two-wheeler Industry

'Customer is not king. He is God. We have to treat him as such'
—Dr Venu Srinivasan

TVSM's product evolution can be distinctly divided into four phases. It started with the moped revolution in 1979, when their product became ubiquitous in south India. The collaboration with Suzuki in 1982 marked the introduction of Japanese motorcycles in India. The TQM journey that began in the 1990s marked the third phase that primarily focused on indigenous product design and production. It culminated with the Deming Prize in 2002 and the split with Suzuki. The fourth phase has seen a super-diversification of its product portfolio across the economy, executive and premium segments, culminating in the collaboration with BMW Motorrad for the super-premium category. At each of these stages, the underlying TVSM value proposition was innovative, high quality and environment-friendly products, backed by reliable customer service.

Figure 7.5: The TVSM Journey

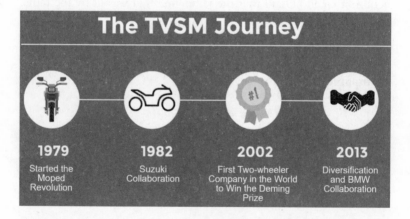

The company's strength lay in its diversified product portfolio of two-wheelers that constituted 77 per cent of its total revenues in 2015. It catered to the varied interests of a wide spectrum of customers. By 2016, TVSM increased its annual production capacity to 38 lakh two-wheelers and 1.2 lakh three-wheelers. With a revenue of Rs 11,290 crore, it sold nearly 27 lakh units (including an export of 3.5 lakh units), thereby commanding nearly 15 per cent market share in the domestic two-wheeler industry. Sales included more than 10 lakh motorcycles (with a market share of over 13 per cent), including premium brands such as the Apache RTR series; executive brands such as Flame, Jive, Phoenix 125, Sports and Star City; rural brands such as MAX 4R; over 8 lakh scooters (with a market share of over 15 per cent), including popular brands like Jupiter, Wego and Scooty (Pep+, Streak and Teenz); and 7.38 lakh mopeds under the TVS XL Super and TVS XL Heavy Duty brands. TVSM enjoyed complete monopoly in the Indian moped market.[36] The three-wheeler TVS King accounted for over 1.1 lakh unit sales, of which more than 90,000 units were exported, thereby accounting for more than 20 per cent of the three-wheeler export market share.[37]

Figure 7.6: The TVSM Product Portfolio

While the brand names sound cool and trendy, each of them attempts to cater to the precise needs of customers across India and international locations. Added to this was the intense competition in the Indian two-wheeler industry that manufactured over 1.68 crore vehicles of 2.15 crore manufactured across all categories of automobiles[38] in 2014. Over a dozen players continue to vie with each other for market share. These include foreign players such as Honda, Suzuki, Yamaha and Royal Enfield, and domestic players such as Bajaj Auto and Hero MotoCorp. Adding to further competition is the Government of India's approval for foreign equity ownership of up to 100 per cent in entities manufacturing vehicles and components in India. In such a highly competitive industry, the primary challenge is to understand prospective customers and remain the top-of-the-mind choice. But, in this maze of competition and complexities, how does one differentiate oneself? In our conversation, Venu identified four critical success factors for the two-wheeler automobile industry.[39]

First is quality, the primary factor for long-term success. Many a time, products come and disappear as they may not have met customer requirements. However, some products have a long life in spite of change in fashions. This could be because of their high quality, winning customers' trust. Basic product functions of durability, reliability and fuel efficiency, coupled with consistent performance, form the core of a quality product.

Second comes life-cycle cost. This includes initial cost plus usage cost.

Third comes fashion. Customers want trendy and fashionable products. 'Whatever be the product or service that a company offers to the consumer, it should actually appeal to her senses,' Venu observed. For example, someone may say, 'I wouldn't want to be seen on a TVS Star, I would rather be seen on a TVS Victor'. This could be because Victor is considered to be an executive product while Star is not. Though the parts and technical specifications are the same, the name and style are different. So there is a status attributable to a particular product. Venu believed that style is core to customers' aspirations and personality.

Finally, the brand is vital. It represents the values and benefits provided by a particular product. To maintain brand integrity, this benefit must endure over the lifetime of the product and win the customers' confidence and trust.

Figure 7.7: Essentials for Product Success

Product Success ⇨ Quality ✚ Life-cycle Cost ✚ Fashion ✚ Brand

Furthermore, there should be no difference between the product promised by the company and the one actually delivered. Here, the role of dealers is critical because they represent the company before the customers. There were times when companies introduced a new product once in two years. However, the new generation expects regular introduction of newer products with the latest technologies. Consequently, product development cycles have been drastically shortened with the introduction of many products every year. Then, there are requirements which aren't expressed much by customers but are still vital. These include product safety and environmental sensitivity. Vinay Harne, now president of new product innovation at TVSM, shared, 'It is the father who would be worried about the safety of young girls riding scooters. Hence, it is the duty of the company to provide safe goods and take care of such concerns.' Devarajan, now senior vice president of production engineering at TVSM, effectively summed up customer requirements. He observed that the key to product success and customer delight is the joy a customer experiences while riding. She should have the pride of ownership of a TVS vehicle.

The triad of cost, quality and fuel efficiency captures the primary challenge of the Indian two-wheeler industry. Getting the right balance between the cost of the product and its quality and reliability is important. However, as always, the customer is demanding. She wants low-cost products and expects high product quality and durability. The other Holy Grail is getting high fuel efficiency at prices a customer is willing to pay. While technology can improve fuel efficiency, an increase in cost is not what a typical customer is willing to pay. She wants both—high fuel efficiency at an affordable price. It is noteworthy that the joy of riding a two-wheeler through high power and acceleration consumes a high amount of fuel. There begins a compromise between power and fuel efficiency, and acceleration and fuel efficiency.

Venu believed that a mastery over the field of consumer-led engineering, a deep understanding of consumer psychology and aspirations and converting those to hard engineering and style formed the basis of new product development.[40] True to his observation, in 2013, when TVS Jupiter and Star City were launched after four years of focused quality improvement efforts, the market response was extraordinary and sales were stellar. To balance quick launching of products with its deep commitment to quality remains a prime challenge before TVSM in a highly competitive scenario.

Delighting Customers through Quality, Innovation and Trust

'Customer Relationship Management is an important part of maintaining the value system of the company. Sales and marketing managers have to be appraised not only on their performance but also on the manner in which they have maintained trust with customers'

—Dr Venu Srinivasan

'When do innovations happen?' asked K.N. Radhakrishnan (K.N.R.), CEO and president of TVSM.[41] 'When you are forced into a corner to think, people come up with brilliant ideas,' he answered it himself. During our conversation, he gave the example of the now-popular cone ice cream, which solved the dual problems of wastage and shortage. The big problem with the cup ice cream was wastage. The solution of the cone ice cream is more conducive to waste management. Conventional thinking may not give answers. Problems have to be addressed with fresh perspectives.

That's what TVSM did to address the challenge of balancing power and fuel efficiency. It developed a new technology wherein each vehicle had good power and also offered very high fuel efficiency. Through a lot of experimentation and design work it was learnt that it was possible to split the two. In the mid 2000s, TVSM offered this through power and economy modes. If the customer was riding in power mode, all parameters for power were optimized; and similarly in the case of economy mode. This patented technology developed in-house was called the 'Dual Mode Ignition System'. It was first offered with TVS Victor in 2001 and was extended to all products. As technology evolved, the bike communicated the mode of riding. The green and amber colours communicated economy and speed. In the TVS Flame Model launched in 2008, the mileage achieved at a particular speed was electronically communicated to the rider. The rider realized that with an increase in speed, the mileage reduced. This influenced the style of riding. With this innovation, TVSM was able to break the compromise that with good power the rider was also able to get good economy.

Emphasizing on the importance of connecting directly with customers to understand their requirements first-hand, K.N.R. shared, 'You have to be in touch with the markets. If I sit here and don't know what's happening in the rural areas and keep preaching, things won't work.' To achieve its vision of 'championing progress through mobility', TVSM identified four critical customer segments for which it develops products, access, networks and enablers. It predominantly focused at the bottom of the pyramid and at entry-level customers whose income levels were ordinary.

The company used the concept of a customer focus team to find the exact needs of customers through actual interaction and then deliver the same through its products. This cross-functional team consisted of members from the marketing, product development, R&D and purchasing departments. These undertook road trips twice a year, and while interacting with customers either through personal interviews or ethnographic research, attempted to identify the stated and unstated needs. Based on collated findings across different geographies, the team provided focused solutions. These were related to products, accessories and financing. The company's experience was that a lot of product and buying behaviour-specific information was generated through these personal and direct customer interactions. These inputs proved useful for the new product development process.[42]

A good example of this was when TVSM launched its first product in Indonesia. Before venturing into the new market, with a different culture and demography, the TVSM styling team visited Indonesia and studied its culture and people. This exploration into the native culture, people's preferences and buying behaviour proved to be a learning experience for the team, which had primarily operated in India. The learnings gained from the market research were well-adapted on to the product and were translated into many features that proved useful to the customers. TVSM decided to manufacture models exclusively for the Indonesian market rather than replicate its Indian versions. The Neo 110 was TVSM's first offering in Indonesia. Nearly a decade later, the advanced versions of Neo X3 continued to be popular in Indonesia and were also available in India.

TVSM's study of customer requirements led to a lot of innovative products that blended the best of engineering, style, utility and value for money. Devarajan shared four examples of TVSM products that offered features not provided by competitors till then. The first and all-time hit product was the TVS moped. Until the moped was launched by TVSM in the early 1980s, there wasn't a similar product at that price point which could comfortably carry two people. 'Now the moped carries the entire family along,' he quipped. The introduction of the TVS Scooty series was a success with young female customers as it met most of their requirements. The TVS Victor model used to literally 'talk' to the rider through its power or fuel-efficiency mode, and TVS Fierro was loaded with many digital features. These innovations served twin purposes—they proved TVSM's technological prowess by offering something before the competition, and they delighted customers by meeting latent needs. It was a win–win approach.

Leading the Way with Techno Dynamism

TVSM used the term 'techno dynamism' for its approach of bringing new and relevant technology and staying ahead of the curve in meeting customer expectations. Through techno dynamism, focus was given to superior handling and experience while keeping in mind the style and other aspects that would make a vehicle feature rich. Sharing his mandate on new product innovation, Harne said, 'We are making products which closely fit customer requirements and not 'one size fits all' type products. We understand the requirements of our customers very specifically and then make products for customers in that segment.' TVSM's close contacts with its customers and consistent customer-focus helped the company understand changing requirements and thereby modify existing products to keep pace with latest trends. Being an OEM,[43] TVSM made its own fixtures which gave it the flexibility to meet varying consumer demand while keeping investment low.

During our conversation, M.N. Varadarajan, now senior vice president of materials at TVSM, shared the challenges associated with new product development in a fluid market with intense competition. The process involved a series of steps, including understanding customer requirements, translating them into engineering inputs, designing the products, adding and deleting features, and many more. Many times a competitive product may emerge earlier and make the company product outdated. So a lot of flexibility and speed was required to push the product faster into the market. For this, the lead time to take the product to market had to be cut short. TVSM achieved this through extensive use of computer-aided design (CAD) and other IT tools in engineering applications, thereby reducing lead time for new product development from twenty-seven to eighteen months.

TVS Scooty was an example of the company's techno dynamism. It was a distinctive product built by TVSM through its own R&D and based on extensive customer feedback and an in-depth understanding of customer needs. The TVS Scooty brand was first introduced in 1994 as a new generation scooterette targeting both genders.[44] However, during the first two years, the sales figures indicated a greater preference for the product by females than males. So in 1996, the company embarked on a rebranding strategy and introduced Scooty ES targeting young girls and working women looking for a simple and elegant mode of transport with friendly features and convenience.[45] Since then, many new versions with added features, technical modifications and added utilities to satisfy the evolving customer segment have been launched. Scooty Pep in 2003, Pep+ in 2005, Teenz in 2007, Teenz Electric in 2008, Streak in 2009 and Zest in 2014 have been the evolutionary journey of Scooty over a decade. TVS Zest became the first 110cc scooter to reach Khardung La (in the Ladakh region of Jammu and Kashmir), the world's highest motorable road. Two decades since its introduction, the Scooty brand has become a generic name for its category.

Figure 7.8: Bollywood Star Anushka Sharma—Brand Ambassador of TVS Scooty Zest

Integrating Sales Growth with Women's Empowerment

Interestingly, TVS Scooty didn't end with just being a new and successful product category. TVSM promoted it as a symbol of women's empowerment. At the time of its launch, studies indicated that 97 per cent of women in India did not use any form of personal transport, but depended either on public transport or men in the household. Furthermore, bike riding was not encouraged in small towns or semi-urban areas as the need for a lady's mobility wasn't perceived to be as important. To tap this niche segment required thinking on gender and demographic parameters, undertaking which TVSM informally started the 'Women on Wheels' project in 1996. Through this, TVSM dealers approached women's schools and colleges to offer training in driving two-wheelers. Residential areas and beauty salons were also targeted.[46] By 2006, it was formalized and centralized as the TVS Scooty Institute. Combining theory and practice, the six-day training programme costing Rs 350 to Rs 700 offered lessons on traffic signals, bike parts and handling traffic. Students learnt straight on Scootys and classes were usually held in college campuses or traffic parks, ultimately escalated to city streets as the training drew near conclusion. The course was available for girls aged sixteen years and above, and the institute procured learner's licences before the commencement of training sessions. The success of the initiative could be judged from the fact that in the first two years since launch, over 4 lakh women were contacted and more than 55,000 were trained.[47] Dealers who participated in this project saw, on average, a 24 per cent increase in their sales over those dealerships which didn't.

The 'train and sell' strategy was devised based on a TVS–IMRB research study, which found that any girl who learnt to ride on a certain brand of bike would invariably like to buy the same brand, the training being a big influence on purchase decision. Towns where it was offered saw a 9 per cent increase in sales over others. Women undergoing training were of 18–25 years who didn't want to depend on family members or public transport systems for commuting. About half the users were students and working women, the other half comprised housewives. With the success of the initiative, the institute's presence expanded to 175 towns, especially Tier 2 cities pan-India with a team of 350 trainers.[48] These towns were targeted primarily due to the lack of sufficient public transport systems. The women's empowerment positioning was acknowledged at the MAA award function in 2009, which recognized the best of marketing programmes from around the globe.[49] It was undoubtedly a win-win strategy which served dual objectives of empowering women and increasing sales.

Forging Customer Relationships

K.N.R. emphasized the importance of talking to people at the grass-roots. He gave the example of kings of yore who used to visit incognito different parts of their kingdom and interact with subjects to find out their problems. Similarly, it was essential for top leadership to interact with employees and customers as equals to understand their expectations and provide solutions. He shared his experience: 'I get an opportunity to visit the market two days a week. When I go there, I make it a point to talk to twenty or thirty of our customers without telling them that I belong to TVS.' This approach gave him a tremendous amount of valuable and frank feedback.

To gain consistent feedback from customers, TVSM engaged with internationally renowned third-party research organizations like J.D. Power.[50] R. Anandakrishnan, now group head of HR at TVSM, shared that the feedback was primarily focused on levels of customer satisfaction at the product level and dealer level, and satisfaction regarding product performance, dealership experience and service experience.

K.N.R. shared with me his personal experience during incognito visits. On one such visit to a TVSM dealership, he observed that one of the prospective customers was interested in buying a TVS Scooty. She approached a salesgirl working at the dealership and communicated her interest. However, the condition was that she could accept the delivery only on a Sunday between 11 a.m. and noon. This was quite normal in India for the purchase of any asset, especially vehicles. In north India, delivery is usually taken based on a good *choghadiya* (time of the day) as per the *panchangam* (almanac), and in south India, delivery is taken outside *rahu kalam* and the *yama gandam* (inauspicious hours of the day) time. Now, irrespective of auspicious hours, Sundays are holidays! Fascinatingly, this young salesgirl, without consulting anyone, promised delivery to the customer. Not surprisingly, on the confirmed Sunday, the TVS Scooty was delivered. Not only delivered, it was done with all the associated rituals as is the practice. 'I know about this incident because when I went to that dealership, the lady who had purchased the TVS Scooty was waiting there, and said to me, "I am proud of TVS,'" shared K.N.R.. Getting this kind of commitment from company staff would please any CEO. Yet, when it is displayed by one of the junior-most employees at a company dealership, it is a matter of immense satisfaction as it indicates that a profound sense of ownership and high levels of commitment had percolated to the lowest levels of the hierarchy.

K.N.R. recalled the earlier decades of the TVS Group when TVS was also a car distributor: 'I believe that then, if a parcel service lorry driver would see a car broken down on the road, he would stop the lorry, check with the car driver about the problem, and if it was a TVS vehicle, he would try and call the nearest service station and get a replacement car. This was in the 1950s. Even then, this was the kind of service orientation. It exists today, too. Many other companies also have this. But it has been the TVS culture since more than half a century.'[51]

Sharing his vision for the future, K.N.R. gave examples of automobile giants like Honda and Toyota that considered customers their best salesmen. 'You need to improve customer loyalty; the same customer coming back to you again and again. That loyalty can be gained only by giving the customer a best-in-class sales experience, and much more than that is service experience.' He narrated the after-sales service example of leading automobile companies. They kind of 'owned the car' much more than the customer owned it. This was exhibited through consistent follow-up with customers for regular servicing. Sales representatives would remind customers with phone calls, 'Next week is your due date for service. When are you coming?' If the customer forgets even after three or four reminders, the company representatives would visit the customer to understand their problem and be of help. K.N.R. believed that such an approach impressed upon customers the company's commitment to their welfare and optimal fulfilment of their mobility needs. 'Automatically, you feel that the next time you buy a car; you would go back to them only. There should be a set of such loyal customers that keeps growing and growing,' he shared.

K.N.R.'s vision was essentially a reflection of the age-old TVS culture of customer service. In pre-Independence India, some time in the 1940s, there was a practice at TVS that every customer of cars sold through a TVS dealership received a postcard with a pre-paid reply form attached within thirty days of the sale. The main objective was to understand customer's satisfaction with the working of the car. If a car did not come for service within the scheduled time, a TVS salesman was sent to the customer to pick up the car. Not only that, if the customer did not get the serviced car back in time, he was given a spare car to use till the service was completed. One legendary incident is about an international customer who had a problem with a car purchased from TVS. In response, the company sent its representatives to the customer's doorstep and serviced the car. To receive such quality service from an Indian company in the 1940s was overwhelming. The underlying value for delivering this was the founder's belief that the 'customer is God'.[52] It's this healthy environment of trust and commitment that TVSM strives to maintain.

Employees as Extended Family

'People come first in the company; actually even more than the customer. It is our people who serve customers by creating products and providing services. Therefore, attracting, developing and retaining people are some of the most important processes in a successful company'

—Dr Venu Srinivasan

Historically, the TVS Group companies' approach towards their workers has been paternalistic and labour relations have been remarkable. Soon after Indian Independence, the then undivided Communist Party called a nationwide strike for shutting down production for three days. Instead of participating in the strike, TVS employees in Madurai chose to lock themselves inside the premises and continued to work.[53] This unique labour–management relationship has been fostered by the founders' conviction that employees are not just workers but members of its extended family. True to this belief, the TVS Group pioneered many labour-related benefits much before they became mandatory through regulations.

Understanding the Challenges of Manufacturing-sector Employees

TVSM employees belong to two major categories—managerial and operational. Both have distinct requirements. The expectations of the operational workforce or factory workers are more functional. They include ease of operations, a fatigue-free work environment, ergonomic plant infrastructure, neat and clean factory premises and availability of machines and equipment that improve work effectiveness. Sharing his understanding of the operators' psyche, Devarajan said, 'When the operator enters the plant, he should feel, "This is my plant." He should have a sense of ownership and feel fully involved.' He shared the efforts made by the company to enable operators to work with best-in-line equipment such as automatic robotic welding and painting systems, assembly with automatic testing of all machines, a very good press shop and an excellent gear plant. All of these eased their work load and also improved their efficiency and productivity—a win-win for the company.

The expectations of managerial staff are aspirational in nature. These include rewards and recognition, role clarity, challenging assignments, value addition through knowledge and skill development and healthy relationships with peers. Dr Kovaichelvan, now senior vice president of human resources at TVSM, observed that empowerment and delegation of authority and responsibility are important needs of executives. In a work–need–interest study undertaken by the company with its junior employees, autonomy emerged as the first requirement for the younger generation of employees. Kovaichelvan, who has been with TVSM for nearly thirty years, surmised that employee needs are based on their age and stage in their career: 'Based on the level of the employee, whether entry, middle or senior levels, an employee needs change. Once people progress for about four to five years, they look at career growth and opportunities. If you look at shop-floor workers, they have more basic needs as indicated in Maslow's Need Hierarchy Theory.'[54]

A high degree of trust and integrity in business transactions have always been a priority for TVSM. Venu highlighted that most of the 'Built-to-Last' companies[55] adopted these values successfully. However, making employees committed to company values has been a challenging task for companies of all genres. In this context, Kovaichelvan raised pertinent questions: 'When people have no choice, they comply with what is available. When people have more choices, how do we make people comply with process disciplines? If we say that TQM is our core philosophy, it will call for some amount of process disciplines. It requires a certain amount of rigour. Will putting pressure on the employees to comply in the light of other opportunities be sustainable?'

K.N.R. shared that for any company, whether in the auto industry or elsewhere, the availability of the right people is a critical success factor for growth. Since the turn of the millennium, a booming service sector in India made attracting and retaining talent in the manufacturing sector a difficult proposition. Though employees in manufacturing companies aspired for all benefits given to IT company employees, they may not be as qualified to get empowered. Engineering education in many parts of India lacks quality. Though there has been a fifty-fold increase in the availability of seats in engineering education, the quality itself has not been up to the mark. 'Over 50 per cent of engineers take up IT jobs, where their engineering skills aren't used sufficiently. We are consuming a small fraction of the 20 per cent that come to our industry and our ability to influence the education field is itself limited,' observed Kovaichelvan. Interestingly, the company has been entering into collaboration with regional institutions to devise industry-focused syllabi, financial support to meritorious students and internship opportunities during the course, so that they can be directly deployed soon after completing studies within any of the TVS companies.

Kovaichelvan noted that the inability to deliver desired results due to an apparent dearth of commercial sense and leadership traits is another limitation in engineering graduates. Coupled with this was the challenge of talent retention. A constant comparison of pay packages and autonomy by employees in the manufacturing sector with their IT peers was inevitable. To understand this better, let us briefly compare a typical employee in the manufacturing sector with the IT sector. A manufacturing sector employee works six days a week, wears a uniform to work, has fixed working hours and has to take permission for leaving the premises—all as part of industry norms. On the other hand, an IT company employee mostly works five days a week due to international clientele, wears cool and trendy outfits to work, has flexi-timing options, can even work out of home, gets opportunities to travel out of office and even out of the country for work-related assignments, among many other privileges. Thus, the work content and business processes of service and manufacturing sector companies cannot be compared. These evident differences lead to a constant feeling of lack of empowerment among employees and make them prime targets for poaching.

Employees: The Strongest Pillar of TQM

The TQM culture at TVSM is pervasive. The most striking feature of TVS TQM is its emphasis on total employee involvement (TEI), which is executed through suggestion schemes, quality circles, cross-functional teams, supervisory improvement teams and task forces. Complementing this was employee creativity, enthusiasm and involvement. Both led to mutually rewarding outputs. A noteworthy example was the suggestion scheme started in 1990. Initially, every employee who gave suggestions was rewarded. This led to a lot of eagerness among employees and increased their involvement in the quality enhancement process. A decade later, the company modified the format. Accordingly, the suggestion giver was made accountable to implement the suggestion. They could either implement it on their own or work with agencies that could help in implementation. What started as a reward scheme for every successful suggestion was modified into awards from the chairman for more than 100 suggestions in a quarter. So it progressed from the basic need of cash to the need for recognition. Photos of award winners were also printed in the company magazine. Awards from the chairman also indicated the commitment of the highest leadership to TQM practices. Such functions also provided an opportunity for direct communication between employees and the employer, and increased a sense of belongingness to the company.[56]

In 1990, TVSM also introduced quality circles (QC) in the factory. A QC is a group of employees (doing similar work) that regularly meet to identify, analyse and solve work-related problems. Within a decade, the suggestion scheme and QCs had 100 per cent participation of the labour force. By the late 2000s, more than 1 lakh suggestions were annually implemented. This meant an average of a suggestion implemented by each employee every single week. This was phenomenal compared to the 1994–95 figures when the number of suggestions implemented per employee every year was a mere 0.7. The number of improvement projects implemented by QCs also rose from forty-two in 1991–92 to 1500 projects by 2004–05. This change was indicative of immense innovation and ideation on the shop floor and also contributed to the new product development process. To encourage the innovation and creativity of these teams, every year, at least two top teams from the company participated in international conventions outside India. The next three teams were sent for national conventions. This kind of recognition and exposure motivated employees to enthusiastically contribute their ideas.

The TQM philosophy of kaizen[57] (literally meaning 'change for better') aimed at continuous improvement at the workplace and in participants' personal efficiencies. A study of the impact of kaizen at the TVS Mysore plant indicated that it helped in building an environment of trust, leading to positive organizational change and conducive organizational culture for a progressive human resource development in the company.[58] Kovaichelvan observed that since its implementation at TVSM, many employees carried the kaizen approach to their homes and shared ideas with their spouses. To encourage this improvement in their personal lives, the company showcased 'home kaizens' during Founder's Day celebrations on campus. On such occasions, a home kaizen stall displayed innovations and improvements made by employees' families in their personal lives. The family members manned the stall and explained enhancements at home that were effected through the kaizen approach. This idea sharing triggered the implementation of personal best practices by other employees. The employees' family members received a lot of exposure and satisfaction as they could share ideas with 15,000 people who participated in the Founder's Day celebrations in memory of the late T.V. Sundaram Iyengar.

TQM implementation requires employees to have skills enhancement, besides domain knowledge. For this, TVSM provides continuous learning through skill enhancement programmes for skills upgradation. Kovaichelvan explained how the maintenance role was also added for the workmen when total preventive maintenance (TPM) was first introduced on the shop floor. TPM is a holistic approach to equipment maintenance that strives to achieve perfect production and safe working environments. This approach called for a lot more skills in the workmen. Maintenance wasn't just repairing the equipment. It also involved understanding the machine, identifying abnormalities in the machine and proactively correcting them before a breakdown could lead to quality problems. He shared with me the company's objectives: 'We wanted to move to a higher level of maintenance where we could train the sensory organs and perceptions of the workmen that would enable them to find the difference between the sharpness of tools by their sound, or the coolant by its smell. Self-detection of these problems increased the levels of employee fulfilment. Towards this end we developed a lot of training for workers.' This learning led to continuous upgradation and higher levels of output.

Figure 7.9: Employee Commitment to TQM

TQM initiatives had a tremendous impact on employee psyche. Kovaichelvan shared the visible change in employees and their families. Earlier, employees used to request TVSM employment for their children. This changed over the years. Now they wanted their children to become engineers. This was backed by increasing opportunities in higher education and placements in India. So these employees were able to send their children for higher studies. Subsequent to this, TVSM provided them with year-long training that improved their employability. As a result they got good jobs. With immense satisfaction writ large on his face, Kovaichelvan said, 'All our employees now have their own homes and two-wheelers. About 90 per cent send their children to English-medium schools.' To contribute to a better quality of life for the employees' children, every summer TVSM conducts personality development and career guidance camps. This helps them improve understanding of their skills, thereby helping them be prepared for the right job opportunities.

Venu believed that by using TQM, the employees would internalize the implicit TVS value systems. Consequently, even when the generation changes, the legacy would be passed on to the new managers. The standard training and procedures would help in carrying it forward.[59] Not surprisingly, TQM proved to be a win-win approach for TVSM. While cooperative employees facilitated the introduction of modern manufacturing practices that helped the company compete better, the practices in turn improved employees' work-related performance and also changed their personal lives for the better. It even helped the next generation in their families. The employees increasingly believed that they were working in a socially and environmentally progressive company.

The top management profiles at TVSM indicated that all of them were internally grown, including the CEO, presidents and most vice presidents. Accentuating the importance of intra-organizational leadership development, Venu told me that the role of leadership was to build an organization capable of producing its own future leadership pipeline. The leader should revel in grooming and nurturing successors who could achieve greater heights than him. The leader should not be like a banyan tree under which nothing grows. Instead, he should know when to fade away into the background.

Values Congruence and Consequence Management

'Any company which does not have values will not live long or make a mark in history. Companies without values are like footprints in the sand—they get washed away with the next wave. One of the reasons why we succeeded is that we are a values-driven company'[60]

—Dr Venu Srinivasan

Values have been the central pillar of TVS. Venu believes that one cannot compromise on values and still attain long-term success. Integrity, lifetime customer service and time management were organizational values practiced by TVS in pre-Independence India, and much before most management thinkers in the West spoke about them. Preserving those values was sacrosanct for the founder.

To ensure that employees were appreciated for their commitment and adherence to company values, performance management at TVSM aimed at rewarding the right people. The company gave prime importance to values congruence (alignment of personal value systems with company value systems) during potential appraisals for responsible positions. Venu told me, 'I have realized one thing, that during a potential appraisal, if a person does not have values congruence, he should not be given positions of high authority even though he may have high performance. Such high performance is not sustainable in the long-term because at some point in time he will come in conflict with organizational values and therefore leave the company.' He emphasized that the assessment process should focus not only on employee performance but also on their commitment to company values. And if there was a lack of values congruence in certain employees, they must be encouraged to look for opportunities elsewhere. He believed that HR had a pivotal role in appraising employees' values congruence. The family sports day, Founders' Day, the medical centre and the involvement of the personnel manager were are all critical elements of TVSM values congruence process.

K.N.R. identified performance management and consequence management as the balancing elements of the values congruence process. He underlined that performance management included a strong emphasis on people who visibly demonstrated the company's values to move up the ladder. Venu suggested that feedback and encouragement were highly essential to retain this culture. He gave the example of the 2002 Asian Games held in Busan, South Korea.[61] The organizers knew that teams from forty-four different countries would not have supporters from their respective nations to cheer them on. In order to ensure equity in motivation, they created cheering squads for every participating country. This demonstrated a deep understanding of human needs—a fundamental requirement for encouragement.

For those who were 'value destroyers', K.N.R. recommended consequence management. He shared that whenever a malfunction or misappropriation was noticed within TVSM, after brief deliberation and on the very same day, the concerned person was asked to leave, irrespective of the level of management hierarchy he belonged to. He gave the common example of modification in bills submitted after international travel. 'If we find out that someone has put in claims for a car when he has actually used a bus; or many times I have observed that after an employee has returned from a company assignment overseas, he makes minor corrections in the reimbursement bills for US$ 100 or 200. The person may be a high potential candidate for the company with excellent performance, but there have been cases where we have asked them to leave on the same day.' He quoted another example of consequence management that happened in the 1990s. Every year, the company gives socks and shoes to all employees. On one such occasion, an employee intentionally took two sets of shoes and socks, thinking he would successfully evade notice. That day, to his ill luck, he was caught in the security line at the factory gate. Instantly he was relieved from work. While most labour unions invariably protest if the management takes punitive action against errant employees, TVS unions are said to be supportive.

While TVSM considers its employees as extended family, it takes very strict action with wrongdoers. K.N.R. emphasized that more than the dos, the don'ts have to be told to employees. This was demonstrated through strong consequence management. At the same time, employees who consistently practise company values should be publicly appreciated. This balance aims at convincing employees of the premium the company places on ethical behaviour at the workplace. Most often, in spite of top management commitment, the lack of organizational procedures leads to oversight of trivial malpractices in daily work life. These eventually snowball into major legal and ethical blunders that affect the company image and tarnish the goodwill accumulated over many decades. The TVSM approach to consequence management constantly keeps employees on guard to balance the means and ends throughout their growth trajectories.

Nurturing the Culture of Equality

An outstanding feature of TVSM organization culture is equality. It pervades the entire organization, irrespective of hierarchical differences. In our conversation, K.N.R. elaborated, 'In this company, we don't differentiate between employees. The material of the uniform I wear, the shop-floor worker also wears. The food that I eat is the same food they partake. The doctor who treats me, treats them also. So there is absolutely no differentiation between people.' Indeed, in my numerous visits to the TVSM campus in Hosur, I have seen this in action. The white and blue colour of the TVS uniform is omnipresent. Right from the shop-floor workers to the president and the CEO, all wore the uniform to work. I have visited the massive two-floored dining hall on the Hosur factory premises where breakfast, lunch and evening snacks are served to all employees. All workers and managerial staff eat the same meals sitting side by side. At the exit, there are extra snack packets of savouries such as murukku or chivda available for employees to take home. I was told that most often children would have returned from school by the time the workers reached home. They looked forward to the tasty snack from daddy's workplace! The focus on food and its quality is true of all TVS Group companies who ensure that their employees consume healthy food at the workplace. The choice of cooking oil, the quality of rice and the quantity of spices used in office canteens are all monitored closely.[62] On one occasion, I had the opportunity of joining Chairman Venu Srinivasan for a lunch session at the Hosur factory. He, too, sat at the same dining table and consumed the same food as was prepared for the entire staff. The culture of equality was palpable.

Leadership Values of Venu Srinivasan

'The basic purpose of business is to create wealth for all stakeholders. It has been the fundamental philosophy of TVS to maintain trust with all stakeholders. It goes back to the roots of the organization to the founder's values'

—Dr Venu Srinivasan

Though he inherited the TVS legacy, Venu started working on the shop floor in one of the group companies during his high school days. While he was pursuing his masters at Purdue University (USA), he worked as a door-to-door Bible salesman and gained the experience of 'slogging eighty hours a week, facing rejection when people slam doors on your face and set the dog on you'. Though born with a silver spoon, his journey has been one of self-effort and hard work. The TVS family believed in the idea of running the organization as if the management are not owners but only trustees. 'The family was also a great supporter of the Indian Independence movement. So we've always had an affinity to the Gandhian approach to society. [63] My grandfather was also a very simple man, much simpler than the businessmen of his times. He was the reason for this approach of trusteeship in our family that has passed on from generation to generation,' Venu told me. (Appendix VII.A elaborates on Venu's CSR vision, its manifestation and impact.)

Venu believes that a leader should lead by personal example, not words. He quoted the famous American poet Ralph Waldo Emerson who said, 'Your actions speak so loudly that I cannot hear what you say.' The first demand on the leader is to act as he says. Venu also mentioned that it is important for a leader to share company lore to inspire employees. The only person who could tell stories was the top leader, especially in a family-owned corporation because he would have been a part of the company's history. In long-lived organizations, storytelling and reinforcing organizational values and culture were recipes for success. In my many interactions with him, he consistently shared his focus on balancing business excellence with social well-being. With great humility, he's always eager to communicate to the younger generation the power of practising the right values in one's personal and professional lives.

Venu identified three critical success factors for companies desirous of successfully implementing stakeholder strategies in business.

The first was 'people focus'. He said that people-related costs were significant investments in business rather than expenses. 'Developing and maintaining a strong sense of loyalty to the company, its goals and its values is of utmost importance in retaining our valuable investment in our people. This can only be achieved by an organization which treats its employees as critical stakeholders and partners in business.' He emphasized that loyalty is a two-way journey. And salary doesn't beget loyalty because everybody pays a salary. It is the feeling of loyalty given by the company to the employee that echoes obligation beyond the call of duty. Hence, it is very important for a leader to demonstrate humility, trust, patience and loyalty to the people.[64] He often quoted his father, the late T.S. Srinivasan, who would tell him, 'You take care of your workers, and your workers will take care of you.' He believed in relieving those employees who were low on values though high on skills. Those high on values, even though low on skills, were to be retained and nurtured with compassion.

The second was a clear emphasis on safety, health and environment. He shared that socially responsible companies always understood that these aspects were crucial to the long-term survival of organizations. The irresponsible extraction of natural resources, pollution of the environment and providing unsafe products and services appeared profitable in the short-term. However, there were innumerable examples of how such companies ultimately suffered because of their myopic view and irresponsible behaviour. 'A good name is far more important than fleeting fame. This is why good saints and kings leave their enduring footprints on the sands of time,' he observed.

Lastly, a high degree of trust, integrity and transparency were required to run businesses successfully. For this, a great deal of intra-organizational transparency was a pre-requisite. Transparency in organizational practices and top leadership behaviour was vital to develop trust in multiple stakeholders.

Figure 7.10: Stakeholder Success Factors in the Indian Two-wheeler Industry

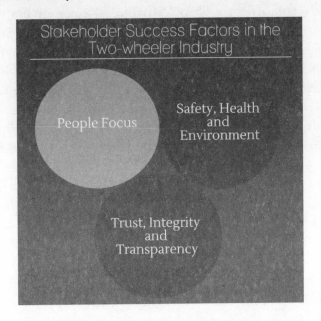

Given his strong adherence to value systems, I was intrigued about how he approached various business-related decisions and handled dilemmas. He shared his approach to problem-solving: 'Meeting the law in letter and spirit is always a dilemma. Sometimes you can meet the law in its letter but not in its spirit. These dilemmas always exist.' He emphasized that ethical dilemmas presented themselves before leaders who wanted to practise ethics. The others would usually do what was expedient. 'From my personal experience, let me tell you that these are very difficult decisions to make. That's why, in a leadership position, you have so much stress and fatigue because you have to constantly face dilemmas.' He quoted Harry Truman, former American president who once said, 'If you can't stand the heat, get out of the kitchen'. Anyone who aspired to lead a business would have to accept dealing with dilemmas as a part of the job. That's what leaders are paid for.

He opined that a dharmic (righteous) company has to go through various difficulties and pains before getting justice. Speaking about decisions to be taken when there is an ethical dilemma, he said, 'It all comes back to bearing pain. One has to understand that this kind of dilemma exists in all businesses. It is very difficult to give an exact answer when we deal with such a situation. It is because every situation is unique and dharma (righteous conduct) has to be applied to every case uniquely. A good example is the *Yaksha Prashna*[65] in the Mahabharata.' He shared the solution his guru, Sathya Sai Baba,[66] gave to address ethical dilemmas: 'Even though there are two alternatives, and both appear to be bad, through prayer, God shows you that one of them is not actually as bad as it appears to be.'[67] With a firm belief in the power of spirituality, he observed, 'If one does not have spiritual strength, however strong one may be, one will break. A man with spiritual strength bends outwardly, but is tough inside. I always believe that the grace of God is fundamental, and in our thinking and tradition, one obtains it through one's guru.'[68] Mahatma Gandhi and Ratan Tata are two personalities he admires.[69] He often acknowledged the role played by Ramnath Goenka, founder of the Indian Express Group, as a mentor in his life. He recalled the first lesson he learnt from him that in any battle, whether competition or otherwise, one must have the high moral ground. 'You must come with sound morals, principles and ethics before you start the battle, otherwise you have lost it even before you start it.' He resonated with the late J.R.D. Tata, chairman of the Tata Group of Companies, when he summed up the TVSM story: 'Although we might not have grown as fast as some others, we will never leave the relatively straight and narrow path of adhering to our values.'[70]

And the Story Continues . . .

The story of TVS Motor Company can be called the story of its chairman and managing director, Dr Venu Srinivasan. The company embodies the values that he has inherited, espoused and attempted to practise over a career spanning three and a half decades. The company learnt to manoeuvre through the complex maze of the two-wheeler industry, as he learnt to practise the personal and professional values he received from the earlier generations. It faltered in its initial years, when he admits he made mistakes in the choice of the right people to lead it. However, it rose from the ashes, as he was determined to prove that hard work, commitment to quality and practise of human values are sure to bring success. It achieved international recognition as none else in the industry did, because he aspired to implement nothing but the best. It gradually grew through indigenous efforts, benefitting from the learning curve and its strong foundation, working towards a bright future in the Indian two-wheeler industry, as he expanded the horizon of his commitment from individual success, to industrial growth, to Indian glory. As chairman of the Confederation of Indian Industry, as recipient of the Padma Shri, and the honourable consul general of the Republic of Korea, he remained modest and dedicated to industry, India and ideals. And so does TVS Motor Company need to remain steadfast in its quintessential quest for quality.

Figure 7.11: Win-Win Learnings from TVS Motor Company

LESSONS FROM
TVS MOTOR COMPANY

1. TOP MANAGEMENT COMMITMENT

The journey to world-class
quality and efficiency starts at
the top

2. TOTAL QUALITY MANAGEMENT

Total quality is a journey and not
just a destination

3. PURPOSE-ORIENTED INNOVATION

Create product categories that
fulfil societal needs

4. CULTURE OF PERFECTION

The goal of culture is perfection
in process, product and service

5. VALUES CONGRUENCE

Relieve employees low on values
even though high on skills;
groom employees high on values
with enhanced skills

6. PATERNALISTIC LEADERSHIP

Treat employees as extended
family through a culture of
trust, equality and loyalty

VIII.

Reflections

How to Become a Win–Win Corporation?

Reading the stimulating stories of these six win-win corporations means understanding Indian businesses from a cumulative time period of 400 years. It is truly insightful as to how each of these companies, belonging to diverse backgrounds, ownership structures, ideologies and industry categories, have, in their own unique way, designed and implemented mutually beneficial solutions and strategies that have created value for the company as well as its multiple stakeholders. One of the major criticisms that a section of management scholars have levelled against organizations working towards integrating multiple stakeholders' interests into long-term corporate strategy is the lack of feasibility to accomplish this with commercial success. The examples of these six companies dispel this 'myth' that catering to stakeholders' interests is at the cost of shareholders' wealth creation or the company's profitability. In fact, these companies have exhibited that it is imperative to do this if organizations want long-term success and wish to be distinctive among their peers.

However, the journey of WWC is not an easy one. The allegory of a merchant that I had heard about as a child portrays the difficult situations that stakeholders-focused companies have to often face: Once 'Wealth' and 'Poverty' approached a merchant and introduced themselves as goddesses. The merchant offered his salutations to both of them and said, 'May I know what brings you to my humble tenement?' The Goddess of Wealth said, 'We want you to judge and tell us who is more beautiful between the two of us?' The merchant was in a fix. He knew he was between the devil and the deep sea. If he were to declare wealth as more beautiful than poverty, poverty would curse him. If he were to declare poverty as more beautiful then wealth would forsake him. Regaining his composure he said, 'I have great respect for both of you. Would you please act according to my instructions? Only then I can judge you properly.' The goddesses agreed. He then said, 'Mother Wealth, would you please go to the entrance (gates) and walk into my house? Mother Poverty, would you please walk from here towards the gates? I can then have a good look at you both, from near and far.' The two goddesses walked as the merchant had wished them to. After seeing them walk, the merchant happily declared, 'Mother Wealth! You appear very beautiful when you enter my house. Mother Poverty! You look very beautiful when you leave the house!' The merchant had brilliantly handled the situation. In doing so, he did not hurt the goddesses' sentiments. In fact, the goddesses immensely appreciated his wit and wisdom. While the Goddess of Wealth happily stayed in his house, the Goddess of Poverty cheerfully walked away. This figurative tale indicates how WWC have to deftly handle conflicting interests of diverse stakeholders and yet ensure that most of them are happy. It is this approach to business and its management that helps them to stand apart and succeed.

Having personally held discussions with the top management of each of these companies, visited some of their manufacturing locations, and interacted with their employees and many other stakeholders, I was convinced that it wasn't enough to just write their success stories. It was equally important to present the key takeaways that their action-oriented strategies place before us. These tried and tested stakeholder management strategies are relevant not only for the spectrum of small to big corporations, but also for all those budding ventures that young entrepreneurs of my generation have embarked upon. These would also be useful for practitioners, consultants and enthusiastic executives willing to explore and experiment with novel ways of managing business and its diverse stakeholders. To make their job easy, I have provided a set of implementation tools in the Appendix that provide stakeholder-specific deliverables, developed based on my decade-long, multi-layered research.

While there are scores of guidelines by management scholars of the East and West, I can say with a sufficient degree of satisfaction that these takeaways represent the Indian way of shaping successful stakeholder strategies, grounded in real business practices. These learnings are also useful hypotheses for young business students, management researchers and proficient professors to further analyse and build upon. In the process of synthesizing them, I have actually ended up identifying thirty characteristics that personify a Win-Win Corporation, with respect to seven major business stakeholders.[1]

I. Customers

1. Win-Win Corporations (WWC) believe customer-centricity and satisfaction is the means to long-term success.
'At HDFC Bank, the idea was that you don't always look at complexity. What is the business purpose? If it is going to be something of value to the customer, whereby he perceives value in this relationship, the bank should do it, no matter how complicated it is,' observed C.N. Ram during our conversation. This typifies the core of a WWC, where the customer and her satisfaction is the basis on which the company builds its long-term success. The example of Karambir Kang and his team at the Taj Mahal Palace Hotel Mumbai reaching out to their competitor, the Oberoi–Trident for their premises in order to host their customers' reception

programme is the length to which WWC can go in order to satisfy their customers and fulfil their promise. Completing the Tirumala Water Supply Project in just seventy-seven days epitomizes this customer-centricity in action at L&T even for public welfare projects.

2. WWC raise the bar for providing excellent customer service.

WWC consistently aim at pushing the limits on delivering excellent customer service. The example of the Taj Group of Hotels mapping the number of times their employees interact with customers and calling them forty-one 'moments of truth' is reflective of their attempt to deliver this priority in action. Aditya Puri reflected a similar primacy when he told me, 'The winners in the banking industry will be those who establish relationships with customers through actual points of contact and service—what you call as moments of truth.'

The second part to this is raising the levels of customer service. This may require redefining the way a customer is served. For example, through the implementation of core banking solutions, HDFC Bank branches became sales and service outlets, with the front-end staff primarily focusing on customer service. This could also be achieved through the development of new infrastructure or the acquisition of new properties that would give customers a surreal experience like the Taj Hotels did, by becoming the only hospitality company in the world to have fourteen authentic small and big 'real palaces'. The ways of delivering this may be industry-specific, but the objective remains the same—to constantly raise the standards of excellence of customer service.

3. Gaining customer loyalty through customer delight is a consistent attribute of WWC.

'Most of the innovations HDFC Bank introduced were kind of latent needs. It was never a question of whether the customer wants it. It was like the "Steve Jobs" approach. The customer wants it, but doesn't know that such a thing is possible,' explained C.N. Ram. WWC exemplify this approach of going beyond customers' expectations and imaginations and delighting them as the route to gaining customer loyalty. To achieve this, most WWC do what is never done before in their industry. An interesting example is of TVSM introducing the ninety-nine colour scheme. No manufacturer had given that option until they introduced it. Another instance is the launch of the 'Petro Card' by BPCL. It had no other parallel except the airline industry's frequent flyer programmes.

4. Quality . . . Quality . . . Quality . . . A non-negotiable commitment of all WWC.
The fact that TVSM became the first two-wheeler automobile company in the world to win the Deming Prize symbolizes the level of quality commitment at WWC. However, they not only learn from international best practices and benchmarks, but also dovetail them to suit their own culture and priorities. That's why JUSE auditors commended TVSM's TQM efforts by referring to it as 'TVS TQM'. BPCL surprised the country by introducing the 'Pure for Sure' initiative and campaign, something considered impossible in a PSE set-up. This was yet another example of a WWC's commitment to quality, irrespective of perceived implementation difficulties.

5. WWC nurture the culture of innovation through strategic investments in research and development.
WWC focus on innovation. However, it isn't the popular 'Jugaad' innovation that India is known for. Instead, a strategic and financial commitment to research and development, especially for providing solutions to problems faced by emerging economies like India, is the means to cultivate this organization-wide innovation culture.

The Hindustan Unilever Lever Research Centre (established in 1967), L&T's Engineering Design and Consultancy Department (established in 1995) and TVSM's R&D facility (with 600 engineers) are examples of dedicated R&D infrastructure and highly qualified technical staff manning it, with the sole focus of consistent innovation in product and process quality.

HUL's Pureit is a classic example of rigorous R&D-based product innovation that focused on solving a basic problem of clean drinking water in rural areas. Not surprisingly, Keith Weed, the chief marketing and communications officer at Unilever, observed, 'When I visit countries around the world, I see sales numbers flashed on the walls. When I see the Pureit team, I see the number of lives protected.'

II. Employees

1. WWC foster a culture of trust and transparency through formalized systems and processes.

A common thread across WWC is the development of official channels and procedures to ensure open communication between senior management and employees. At HUL, Nitin Paranjpe, then CEO and MD, had lunch with 10–15 new managers every fortnight, where they could speak their mind and share their views, positive or otherwise, about the company. At L&T, the functional heads had one-on-one interactions with employees during the company's residential training programmes at Lonavala. The senior team shared with them customer expectations from the company, and also gained feedback from them about issues and challenges at different project sites. The form and format was different in each of the six companies, but the objective was identical.

2. WWC encourage high performance among employees through formalized rewards and recognition systems.

WWC use well-designed rewards systems to cultivate a high performance ethos within the company. In some cases, like HUL, it was a financial reward where the variable component of salary was increased to emphasize performance. In other cases, like L&T, it was global exposure, where high-performing employees were sent to international business schools for developing advanced leadership capacities. At the Taj Hotels, it was public recognition, where the STARS Awards winners were acknowledged during the TABE ceremony. Once again, the means were different but the end objective the same.

3. WWC empower leaders by giving adequate authority to deliver their responsibilities.
WWC change their people policies with a change in generational expectations. Employee empowerment is an underlying theme of most organizational transformation initiatives. At BPCL, the new organization structure focused on SBUs and aimed at transferring substantial decision-making to the junior levels, with the senior management focusing mainly on board-related decision-making. At HUL, the new organization structure was flattened such that employees could assume significant roles within their first five years in the company. As a result, a fresh recruit would have the responsibility of managing a market size of many crore rupees.

4. WWC genuinely invest in employees' well-being and development.
'If you think only of squeezing employees and not looking after their career development and their needs, and giving them a clean and professional environment to work in, you will not be left with the best employees in today's competitive world,' Aditya Puri told me. This is an underlying priority in all WWC, where employee well-being is a hygiene factor, not a motivation factor. At HUL, this emphasis on employee development was through fantastic succession planning and talent tracking, such that employees could take senior

management positions within fourteen years. The SPEED+ and Emerging Leaders programmes at the Taj Hotels aimed at meeting employee career aspirations at all levels. At the peak of a crisis situation, post the terror attacks, the company did not retrench a single employee. Naik's personal assurance of sending the company aircraft to enable an employee to see his ailing mother characterized the importance L&T gave to employees' personal needs.

5. Organizational pride among all employees is a visible feature of WWC.

While WWC make all efforts towards ensuring high levels of employee satisfaction, the sense of pride and belongingness that employees feel while working in a WWC is a distinguishing feature. This manifests in one form as top employer rankings, like those received by L&T, HUL and HDFC Bank from rating agencies, based on large grass-roots surveys. It also manifests in exceptional levels of employee commitment, like the labour unions at TVSM that are very supportive of the company's efforts in maintaining high levels of values congruence and accepts its consequence management practices. This sense of belongingness is taken to another level when employees go way beyond the call of duty, like L&T's temporary workers who vowed to stay off liquor, smoking and non-vegetarian food for the entire duration of work on the Tirumala Hills, to exhibit their commitment to the company. The highest level was displayed by employees at the Taj Mahal Palace Hotel Mumbai when they came in between the guests and the terrorists and willingly accepted the bullets on their chests. These are all varying manifestations of the immense pride and sense of belongingness and ownership that employees feel for their companies. This is one uncommon characteristic of WWC that is dependent not on what the company does for its employees, but what the employees feel and do for the company. It is perhaps a function of all that a company has done for them.

III. Shareholders

1. WWC achieve long-term wealth creation by avoiding temptations of quick gains.

During our conversation Ashok Sinha emphasized, 'Many stakeholders may think that as a PSE we have to do good for society. But doing only that may be fundamentally detrimental to the existence of the organization.' The major misconception about WWC lies in the area of shareholder wealth creation. It's usually believed that they do not create enough value for shareholders given their ample attention to all stakeholders. In practice, WWC focus on long-term return on investment for all shareholders. BPCL and TVSM gave returns many times over their industry leaders and Sensex stocks over a ten-year period. L&T's market capitalization grew over forty times within fifteen years. In twenty years since its inception, HDFC Bank is the most expensive banking stock in the world! That's the power of long-term focus.

2. WWC prefer profitable growth over market share.

WWC may or may not be the largest company in their industry category in terms of size or market share. Yet, they prioritize profitability over mindless expansion. In spite of a gigantic PSE competitor like IOCL, BPCL succeeded commercially due to its focus on profit share rather than market share. It chose the growth path through a large retail presence and a massive dealership network consisting of entrepreneurial distributors. The same is the case with HDFC Bank. Its market share is not the highest in the Indian banking industry. Yet, its market capitalization is larger than twenty of India's state-run banks put together!

3. WWC proactively explore organic and inorganic growth opportunities for greater wealth creation.

Organic and inorganic growth at WWC is primarily aimed at greater wealth creation and benefits for all stakeholders. This was characteristic of BPCL's international upstream strategy and collaboration with global oil companies. This was evident in HDFC Bank's acquisition of Times Bank and the Centurion Bank of Punjab. This was visible in TVSM's collaboration with BMW Motorrad.

4. WWC have structured approaches and practices for prudent risk management.

WWC prioritize prudent risk management while catering to the interests of all stakeholders. At HDFC Bank, customer service was never at the cost of the institution's interest. Managing risk was considered the paramount responsibility. Unsurprisingly, at 0.25 per cent, its net NPAs were the lowest among all banks. When the Taj Hotels' international expansion plans didn't yield the expected results due to the subsequent global financial crisis, it recalibrated its strategy. While charting the company's future growth plan, Rakesh Sarna, the new MD, observed, 'Our strategy will not be asset-light or asset-heavy, but asset-right. The aim is to be globally reputable, not globally present.'

IV. Society and Local Community

1. WWC identify themselves as institutions committed to the long-term development of society and the local community.

CSR is not a standalone activity in WWC. Rather, they consider the development of society and the local community as an integral part of their businesses. HDFC Bank's sustainable livelihood initiative, HUL's conscious decision that it will set up its factories in the backward areas of India and the Taj Hotels' decision of setting up capacity building centres in rural and tribal areas for easier accessibility to the local youth are all examples of the genuine commitment to societal and community welfare demonstrated by WWC.

2. WWC proactively respond to local community needs.
WWC function ahead of the curve in identifying and satisfying the unique needs of the communities in which they operate. Realizing the difficulties faced by family members of the terror attack victims outside the Taj, Ratan Tata decided that the Taj would provide financial help to all, whether security forces, police, fire service, hotel employees, guests of the Taj or the general public—killed or wounded. TVSM's CSR-arm, the Srinivasan Services Trust, recognized that village communities needed guidance and mentorship more than just financial help. Their integrated rural development programme was thus designed to meet multi-sector needs of rural communities in over 4000 villages across five states of India. HDFC Bank facilitated the opening of zero balance accounts for thousands of dairy farmers along with access to Rupay debit cards, cheque and pass books. This gave the underprivileged segment not only access to the bank's products, but also brought them into the banking mainstream. These demonstrate the varied and innovative ways in which WWC respond to the specific needs of their local and target communities.

3. WWC leverage their expertise for corporate social responsibility initiatives.
The CSR projects of WWC are not abstract, but closely connected with their core competence and where employees' skills can be effectively utilized through social volunteering initiatives. As a personal care company, HUL capitalized its expertise in hygiene through the Lifebuoy Swasthya Chetana Programme and the latest '*Hath-Munh-Bum*' campaign to improve personal hygiene habits, especially in rural areas. L&T optimized its expertise in construction by setting up the CSTI that provided vocational training and skill building for the under-educated rural youth. Similarly, the Taj Hotels

and HDFC Bank actively engaged its employees in training programmes connected with hospitality and financial literacy respectively.

4. WWC consistently explore opportunities to economically empower society and the local community.

Philanthropy is not the priority of WWC. They actively look for ways in which the community can become independent and self-sufficient through economic empowerment. HUL's Project Shakti is an internationally acknowledged example in this context. It evolved from the fact that it solves business needs as well as societal needs, and effectively integrates both. While HUL empowers communities through rural distribution, L&T and BPCL support local sourcing for greater employment opportunities in small and medium enterprises. HDFC Bank's support to SAI SEVA and other rural BPOs denotes its commitment to rural economic empowerment. The Taj Hotels contribute by organizing shows and presentations of rural artists and dance troupes at their luxury properties.

5. WWC collaborate with external experts to jointly solve social problems.

In the process of contributing to society and the local community, WWC collaborate with and use their convening power in bringing together the experience of NGOs and civil society experts. In its endeavours to support over forty vocational training centres, the Taj Hotels train the trainers and provide a curriculum and relevant resource material in areas such as housekeeping, food and beverage, bakery services and more to partner NGOs. HUL engages with over 300 NGOs to implement its Shakti Vani Programme. TVSM's SST partners with expert agencies such as NABARD, the Indian Institute of Handloom Technology and the Tribal Cooperative Marketing Development Federation of India for specialized advice and guidance to over 4 lakh rural women associated with various SHGs.

V. Supply Chain Partners

1. WWC foster long-term relations with high-performing supply chain partners.
WWC aren't opportunistic on price-related parameters. Instead, they encourage high performance by suppliers through long-term relations. Companies such as L&T, TVSM and HUL have helped small-time suppliers and dealers to grow substantially by hand-holding, training and mentorship initiatives.

2. WWC are committed to transparency in pricing and payment policies.
The size of WWC is not used as a singular advantage on price and payment procedures. While they go for hard bargains, they also honour their commitments in a time-bound manner. To reduce human bias, L&T and BPCL used information technology in a big way with their supply chain partners. L&T's Enterprise Information Portal and BPCL's SAP-ERP were the primary platforms through which tendering, auctions, payments and delivery were monitored.

3. WWC contribute to supply chain partners' progress through insightful and independent feedback.
Given that most consumers deal with a company's dealers and not with the company directly, it is judicious to ensure that dealers are living up to company standards. In case they aren't, the right kind of feedback can be instrumental in improving the quality of service. This is what WWC constantly attempt to do. In companies like TVSM, BPCL and HUL, the final consumers deal with distributors. So, TVSM used the JD Power

Research Group whereas BPCL used the German company TUV Suddeutschland to monitor dealers' performance.

4. WWC adopt a non-compromising stance on the ethical code of conduct with all supply chain partners.

An important objective of the annual suppliers' meet initiated at L&T by A. Ramakrishna, was to provide a common platform to openly communicate to all suppliers that they should pay nothing beyond what is official to any of the company employees. The top management wanted to prevent the prospect of any kick backs to unscrupulous employees, which is a common occurrence in the construction industry. Companies like HUL, TVSM, L&T, the Taj Hotels and BPCL, that deal with multiple supply chain partners, follow established rules while dealing with them. WWC tend to ensure that their selection, continuation and commercial terms are done with professionalism, transparency and efficiency.

VI. Natural Environment

1. WWC are committed to integrating long-term sustainability priorities with corporate growth.

WWC do not grow at the cost of the natural environment. A WWC integrates sustainability imperatives in its long-term growth strategy and as relevant to its industry category. For instance, TVSM ensures that its products' spare parts are obtainable even beyond the stipulated time of seven years so that its vehicles need not be scrapped for non-availability of spare parts. L&T Construction pioneered the use of alternative materials in construction to reduce the dependence on and excessive use of natural resources such as sand and timber. The Unilever Sustainable Living Plan is the guiding document for HUL's growth, production and sourcing initiatives.

2. WWC are committed to learn from national and international benchmarks and best practices.

The field of sustainable business practices is rather nascent and evolving, especially in an emerging economy like India. Hence, WWC make the most of international best practices and peg their performance against established benchmarks. L&T featured in the Carbon Disclosure Leadership Index and was the only company from India to feature in the capital goods segment of the Dow Jones Sustainability (Emerging Market) Index. The Taj Group of Hotels collaborated with EarthCheck, the world's largest environmental certification company, and became the world's first hospitality group with over fifty of its properties receiving the highest level of environmental certification.

3. WWC encourage employee participation in innovating for sustainable development.

WWC make the most of employee ingenuity and involve them in the process of ideation and implementation of sustainability practices. The success of the Taj Group of Hotels, HUL and L&T's environmental programmes is due to employee participation in substantial measure. In TVSM's journey to the Deming Prize, total employee involvement was a crucial pillar. Employees contributed immensely by providing suggestions for waste reduction and the efficient use of resources.

4. WWC proactively invest in R&D for green products and processes.
An essential element of R&D endeavours at WWC is devising green products and processes. At TVSM's R&D facility, over 600 engineers contributed to innovations in the development and upgradation of technologies that reduced emissions, improved fuel efficiency and enhanced customer value in terms of comfort and safety. Interestingly, all TVS vehicles are said to be 85 per cent recyclable. While creating the product Wheel, HUL kept in mind

that rural consumers would wash their clothes in rivers and other water bodies commonly used by village folk. So it used its advanced technical expertise to substantively reduce the amount of oil that Wheel contained, thereby making it as environmentally benign as possible. L&T has consistently increased its green building portfolio (now at 20 per cent) and successfully implemented the concept at gigantic construction projects like the Kempegowda International Airport in Bengaluru.

5. Leadership at WWC is impact-focused on their environmental performance.

Any success in the sustainability realm is not possible without top management vision, commitment and proactive participation. Leadership at WWC prioritize the impact assessment of its sustainability practices so as to consistently build upon them. Furthermore, environmental performance measurement and impact assessment are documented in great detail and made available in the public domain. L&T was the first engineering and construction company in India to publish a corporate sustainability report. HUL has been consistently measuring and reporting its performance against planned targets as part of the Unilever Sustainable Living Plan that aims at halving the environmental footprint in the making and use of its products by 2020. BPCL and the Taj Group of Hotels publish elaborate 'annual sustainability reports' that make insightful reading for practitioners and academics and also exhibit their strong commitment to the natural environment.

VII. Government

1. WWC are visionary companies that align their organizational aspirations with national priorities.

In September 2014, when Mangalyaan settled into the orbit around Mars, L&T employees and the senior team were jubilant as they were one of the vendors for the spacecraft's parts. This was archetypal of L&T's breadth of expertise from submarines to constructing the world's tallest statue. In spite of the long gestation periods involved in each of these projects, L&T is committed to them for national glory. As A.M. Naik often says, 'In whatever we do, our theme is to build a powerful India.'

In 1977, when many multinational companies like Coca-Cola and IBM preferred to leave India rather than reduce management control, HUL decided to negotiate with the government rather than leaving the country as it wanted to be a part of India's growth story. Since that year, it continues to invest in designated industrially disadvantaged areas to catalyse employment creation leading to economic and social empowerment in those regions. In spite of uncertainties in northeastern states like Assam, HUL is a major and among the only FMCG investor in that state. While launching the Sustainable Livelihood Initiative, Aditya Puri observed, 'If every company would aim at making 1 crore families self-sufficient, there would be no poverty. I think that's a major goal of this organization.'

In this manner, WWC look at distinctive ways to integrate their growth journey with national priorities.

2. WWC complement government schemes through their organizational core competence, infrastructural facilities and employee skill sets.

In my research of over 100 corporations across multiple industries, there isn't another example of an industry-specific skill building institution like the National Academy of Construction that was envisaged through collaboration among industry peers and government agencies, such that the benefits accrue to the industry and the economy. This is a major contribution of L&T to the government's consistent focus on Skill India. The Taj Group of Hotels contributed to the Hunar Se Rozgar Tak project of the Delhi government to train local, unemployed youth in hospitality skills such that they could earn a living when guests thronged the national capital for the Commonwealth Games. They effectively used their employees' skills and organizational core competence in the hospitality sector. HUL's contribution to the Swachh Bharat Abhiyan, the Taj Hotels' participation in the Incredible India campaign, HDFC Bank's support to Startup India (through engagement with young fin-tech entrepreneurs) are all examples of WWC commitment to synergistically supplement government initiatives for social welfare and nation building.

These thirty characteristics constitute a distinct win-win way of doing business. I believe these will act as benchmarks for organizations desirous of becoming Win-Win Corporations.

Parting Thoughts

As I conclude, I'm sure readers will have a few questions. I wish to briefly address them:

- Are these characteristics of WWC exhaustive? My answer is, 'No,' they are indicative. As Indian corporations further evolve and expand, there will emerge many more novel ways of achieving win-win outcomes with diverse stakeholders.
- Are these six the only WWC? Again my answer is, 'No.' These six companies are part of an increasingly growing set of business organizations that believe in succeeding by making others successful. The attributes of WWC clearly demonstrate that it is possible for businesses to play a transformative role in society and in nation building while being commercially successful.
- Will these companies remain win-win forever? Well, that depends on the continued commitment of the top management and the sustenance of an organizational culture that makes them WWC. The greatest advantage of WWC is that an organization can always recalibrate its goals and strategies

such that it creates win-win solutions for multiple stakeholder groups.

India's celebration of the silver jubilee of liberalization of the economy and initiation of market-based reforms is not without reason. The reforms have substantially eased India's balance of payments constraint. Our reserves today exceed US$ 350 billion, compared to less than US$ 6 billion in March 1991.[2] In 1991, India's GDP stood at Rs 5,86,212 crore. By 2016, this increased twenty-three times to Rs 1,35,76,086 crore.[3] The country has now reached a stage in its economic and corporate evolution when it can start devising its own unique approach to business and its management. While developed economies definitely provide valuable insights to Indian companies, the sheer scale of geographic distance and dispersion, customer and employee diversity, resource constraints, limited infrastructure and evolving government mechanisms place Indian businesses in a unique position. In the multiple complexities of Rubik's Cube-like situations, Win-Win Corporations manage to get the right set of colour combinations on all sides. That they have emerged as profitable and mutually value-adding, despite the challenges they continue to face, qualify them to provide lessons in business and its management to other developing economies of the world in Asia, Africa and Latin America. The prime objective of this book is to begin a journey in this direction, where the Indian way of doing business can be studied and shared.

India is also at an inflection point on multiple fronts. On the economic front, it has embarked on another major transformation in its structure with the implementation of the much-awaited goods and services tax (GST). This will provide immense impetus to businesses and benefits to consumers, thereby making India the largest economy with a uniform tax system. On the demographic front, the nation is getting ready to become the most populous country in the world by 2022, with nearly 60 per cent of its population above the age of twenty-five years, up from the current 40 per cent.[4] The interesting advantage of this scenario will be that by 2035, nearly 100 crore Indians will belong to the middle class and emerging middle-class income categories with a lot of aspirations. The per capita income is also estimated to increase three to five times from the current US$ 1500 per year by 2035.[5] This would have a multiplier effect on individual disposable incomes and spending capacity, thereby positively influencing demand in most industry categories. Hence, the Indian economy will have an amazing combination of ambition, size and capacity to purchase. This is the best scenario that Indian corporations can ever hope for, providing them a canvas on which they can grow in size and scale to find themselves among the world's top companies. At such a juncture, to grow the responsible and sustainable way would be the right, royal road for India Inc. The ideal of Win-Win Corporations provides this very pathway to a growth story that is truly inclusive, one that balances commercial success for the company and the economic and social well-being of all its stakeholders.

Implementation Toolkit

What Is This Toolkit for?

- If you want to do what WWC do, here is a list of suggested best practices.
- You may wish to explore where your organization stands on each of them and develop your own roadmap for becoming a WWC.
- Since WWC symbolize an approach to business, this toolkit attempts to make this approach tangible.

Elements of the Toolkit

- Potential impact: Prioritize initiatives (provided under this tool) that have high impact for your organization—financial impact or operational metrics/key performance indicators (KPIs) or goodwill/branding. *(Why should I do?)*
- Implementation owner: The person implementing it or the person accountable for it. *(Who will do?)*
- Ease of implementation: Efforts required by the implementation owner. *(How should I do?)*
- Resource requirements: Could be in terms of peoples' time, financial allocation, physical resources and infrastructure. *(What do I need?)*

As a valuable extension of this book, an implementation toolkit with the aforementioned elements has been provided for each of the seven key stakeholders: customers, employees, shareholders, society and local community, supply chain partners, natural environment and government and regulatory authorities. They suggest eighty-four actionable ways in which you can initiate the process of becoming a Win-Win Corporation.

For ease of access and use by business leaders, managers, entrepreneurs and their multifunctional teams, the toolkit can be downloaded from my website: http://www.shashankshah.com.

Appendix I

Overview of the Research Process

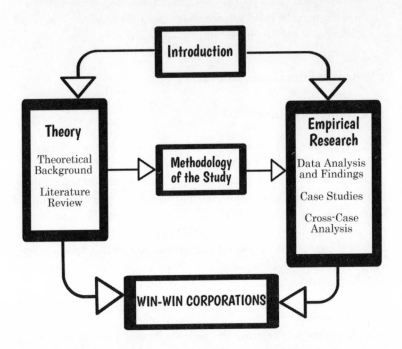

This study is based on the Phenomenological Research Philosophy[1] with an Inductive Approach[2]. The study of contemporary practices of stakeholder well-being and value creation is a blend of the Exploratory, Descriptive (Explanatory) and Causal Research Designs. The study followed a mixed-method approach of qualitative and quantitative methods as follows:

- The perceptions of corporate executives and managers relating to various aspects of stakeholder management and its implementation in their respective organizations have been gained through survey administration. (quantitative study)

- The understanding of organizations' and top managements' approach towards stakeholder management has been gained through personal interviews with industry captains, company heads and functional heads from diverse organizations and industries in corporate India. (qualitative study)
- The compilation of case studies is a mixed method approach wherein the quantitative inputs gained through the surveys and the qualitative inputs gained through personal interactions have been combined; supplemented by information available about the respective companies in the public domain. (mixed method approach)

Elements of the Research Process

A. Exploratory Survey

The first survey was an exploratory study for collecting information pertaining to various stakeholders' relative importance in corporate organizations and their influence on the organizations' decision-making process. The existence of stakeholders-related policies, practices, reporting mechanisms and models/frameworks was also explored. Since the survey was of an exploratory nature, no specific response scale was adopted for each of the questions. Some of the questions had dichotomous options, some had multiple choices, some had an 'importance scale' and some others had the Likert's scale. Some open-ended questions were also included. A total of 700 responses were received from 325 companies. Respondent details are as below:

- **Management Hierarchy:** The respondents were from all levels of the organizational hierarchy: topmost level (includes CXO levels) – 103 respondents; top level (reporting to the CEO) – 157 respondents; middle level (reporting 2–3 levels below the CEO) – 238 respondents; and junior level (includes entry level employees) – 190 respondents.
- **Functional Domain:** Executives from across functional areas responded. These include: general management (418 respondents), finance (76 respondents), sales and marketing (62 respondents), human resources (30 respondents), operations/production (58 respondents), systems (43 respondents) and others (13 respondents).

- **Industry and Sector:** Respondents were from across eighteen industry categories (both in the public and private sectors) and from eighteen metropolitan and Tier 2 cities of India.

B. Perception Survey

The second survey was a perception study of best practices identified for top eight stakeholders: shareholders, customers, employees, society and local community, suppliers and dealers, natural environment, government and competitors, selected on the basis of the findings of the exploratory survey. The best practices for each of the stakeholders were based on those identified in the available Indian and international stakeholder management literature, best practices by leading companies in corporate India, and doctoral research work undertaken in similar areas. A total of 124 variables across the eight stakeholders were identified and included in this survey. The study sought to gain perceptions of the respondents regarding the level of importance of the stated best practices for each of the identified stakeholders in their own organization. In addition, the responses provided information on the areas in which work was already being done by the organizations and also the areas where there was scope for improvement relating to each of the identified stakeholders. A total of 400 responses were received from 125 companies. Respondent details are as below:

- **Management Hierarchy:** The respondents were from all levels of the organizational hierarchy: topmost level (includes CEO levels) – 34 respondents; senior level (reporting to the CEO) – 127 respondents; middle level (reporting 2–3 levels below the CEO) – 151 respondents; and junior level (reporting 4–5 levels below the CEO) – 88 respondents.
- **Functional Domain:** Executives from across functional areas responded. These include: general management (71 respondents), finance (64 respondents), sales and marketing (83 respondents), human resources (46 respondents), operations/production (38 respondents), systems (42 respondents) and others (56 respondents).
- **Industry and Sector:** Respondents were from across eighteen industry categories (both in the public and private sectors) and from eighteen metropolitan and Tier 2 cities of India.

C. Interviews

The personal interviews aim at bridging the gaps not clarified through the survey responses. The process of conducting the interviews was as follows:

- Firstly, an appointment was taken with the respective executive for a mutually convenient date and time for an interaction and interview. Background material on the work done by me and the focus of the interview was sent through email to the respective executive prior to the interview. Two different sets of question schedules were used—one for the company heads and the other for functional heads.

- Each of the interviews lasted 30–90 minutes. With prior permission of the executives, the interviews were recorded.

- Later, the interviews were transcribed and a copy of the same was sent to the concerned executive for ensuring factual accuracy. Any corrections/alterations were appropriately incorporated.

- While most of the interviews were conducted personally, few of them were done through the telephone or over the Internet, as direct access was not possible due to the non-availability of a mutually convenient date and time.

The table below lists the interviewees I interacted with for compiling the case studies included in this book:

Name of the Interviewee	Current / Last Designation at the Company	Name of the Company
Aditya Puri	Managing Director	HDFC Bank Limited
Anumolu Ramakrishna	Deputy Managing Director	Larsen & Toubro Limited
Ashok Gupta	Executive Director (Legal) and Company Secretary	Hindustan Unilever Limited
Ashok Sinha	Chairman and Managing Director	Bharat Petroleum Corporation Limited

Name of the Interviewee	Current / Last Designation at the Company	Name of the Company
Ashoke Joshi	Chairman	Srinivasan Services Trust
B. Ramakrishnan	Director	Larsen & Toubro Oman
C.N. Ram	Chief Information Officer	HDFC Bank Limited
D. Sundaram	Vice Chairman and Chief Financial Officer	Hindustan Unilever Limited
Deepa Misra Harris	Senior Vice President – Global Sales and Marketing	Indian Hotels Company Limited
Dhaval Buch	Chief Procurement Officer	Unilever
G.D. Sharma	Vice President and Head – People and Organization Development	Larsen & Toubro Construction
H.N. Shrinivas	Senior Vice President – Human Resources	Indian Hotels Company Limited
H.S. Goindi	President of Marketing	TVS Motor Company Limited
K.N. Radhakrishnan	Chief Executive Officer and President	TVS Motor Company Limited
K.S. Krishnan	Field Director	Srinivasan Services Trust
K.V. Rangaswami	Director and President, Construction	Larsen & Toubro Limited
Karambir Kang	Area Director USA	Indian Hotels Company Limited

Name of the Interviewee	Current / Last Designation at the Company	Name of the Company
Kumar Vikram	Vice President – Bulk Materials Handling Unit	Larsen & Toubro Construction
Leena Nair	Chief HR Officer	Unilever
M.N. Varadarajan	Senior Vice President of Materials	TVS Motor Company Limited
M.P. Govindrajan	General Manager (Human Resources), Kochi Refinery	Bharat Petroleum Corporation Limited
Meeta Singh	Global Sustainable Business Director	Unilever
Narendra Dixit	Company Secretary	Bharat PetroResources Limited
Niranjan Gupta	Global Finance Director – Household Care	Unilever
Nusrat Pathan	Head, Corporate Social Responsibility	HDFC Bank Limited
Paresh Sukthankar	Deputy Managing Director	HDFC Bank Limited
Philip Mathew	Chief People Officer	HDFC Bank Limited
Prasad Pradhan	Head Sustainable Business and Communications	Hindustan Unilever Limited
R. Anandakrishnan	Group Head of HR	TVS Motor Company Limited
R. Gopalakrishnan	Director	Tata Sons Limited
Rajsekhar Saha	Manager	Bharat Petroleum Corporation Limited
Raymond Bickson	Managing Director and Chief Executive Officer	Indian Hotels Company Limited

Name of the Interviewee	Current / Last Designation at the Company	Name of the Company
Rohit Mull	Executive Vice President and Head – Marketing and Depository Services	HDFC Bank Limited
S. Devarajan	Senior Vice President of Production Engineering	TVS Motor Company Limited
S.G. Murali	Chief Financial Officer	TVS Motor Company Limited
Sameer Nagarajan	Director - Human Resources and Corporate Relations	Unilever Sri Lanka Limited
Samir Bhatia	Country Head, Corporate Banking	HDFC Bank Limited
Sanjay Dongre	Executive Vice President – Legal, and Company Secretary	HDFC Bank Limited
Sanjiv Kakkar	Executive Vice President – North Africa, Middle East, Turkey, Russia and Ukraine	Unilever
Shirin Batliwala	Vice President – Food and Beverage	Indian Hotels Company Limited
Syamal Bhattacharya	Executive Director (Corporate Affairs)	Bharat Petroleum Corporation Limited
T.S. Sundaresan	Vice President and Head – Materials Management and Vendor Development	Larsen & Toubro Construction
V. Kovaichelvan	Senior Vice President of Human Resources	TVS Motor Company Limited

Name of the Interviewee	Current / Last Designation at the Company	Name of the Company
V.S. Ramana	General Manager - CSR and Construction Skills Training	Larsen & Toubro Construction
Vasant Ayyappan	Associate Vice President – Corporate Sustainability	Indian Hotels Company Limited
Venu Srinivasan	Chairman and Managing Director	TVS Motor Company Limited
Vinay Chandrakant Harne	President of New Product Introduction	TVS Motor Company Limited

D. Case Studies

The extant literature reviewed enabled the identification of gaps that were studied through the exploratory survey, which facilitated the identification of the main stakeholders. These were studied through a second survey that was a perception study. Based on the data gathered through the second survey and the personal interviews with senior executives, coupled with information available in the public domain, these companies have been analysed.

A multiple case study design is attractive because it permits the detection of patterns across classes or clusters to understand complex phenomenon and its dynamics and produces compelling evidence in a robust manner.[3] Such a design also facilitates the examination of how a phenomenon performs in different settings and environments.[4] Each case in a multiple case study is seen as a distinct analytic unit and multiple cases are treated as discrete experiments that serve to replicate, contrast or extend the emerging theory. A multiple case study approach offers a powerful means to generate a descriptive and explanatory theory because it permits comparison across cases and facilitates replication, extension and contrast among individual cases.[5] Varied empirical evidence provided by different cases often surface complementary aspects of a phenomenon, and so, by piecing together the individual patterns, it is possible to generate a holistic understanding and a robust theory.[6]

The motivation to pursue a multiple case study approach for this research was twofold. First, since a macro level phenomenon like stakeholder management could only be understood by studying its micro-level instances, multiple cases needed to be examined so as to understand the terrain of the phenomenon and its focal aspects. Secondly, the identification of multi-stakeholder practices currently in vogue in leading corporate organizations was one of the key objectives of the study. This was possible through the multiple case study approach, such that the outputs of this research would be relevant to a broad cross-section of the phenomenon. Usually, four to ten cases are considered effective for deriving full benefit from a multiple case study research.[7]

One would assume that given the subject, most organizations would have been very cooperative in sharing their work and would have made copious material available. However, it was not so. Though an effort was made to cover the entire spectrum of industries in corporate India, many organizations declined to be a part of this study. Some others did not respond at all despite repeated requests.

Ethics of the Data Collection Process

All efforts were made to ensure that ethical issues such as informed consent, anonymity and interview-related ethics were followed in the process of data collection. The survey respondents were assured that their identity would be kept confidential and the results would be in a consolidated format so as not to reveal their individual opinions and perceptions. The same has been followed through the data collection and analysis process in this study. The interviewees' permission was sought to record their interviews and to subsequently include their excerpts for future publication.

Appendix II

HDFC Bank

A. Identifying Latent Needs: Supply Chain Financing

One day, about a year and a half after the bank started, Aditya called Samir to his office. He took a piece of paper, drew some arrows on it and told Samir, 'We have to launch this.' Totally confused with the 'model' and its arrows, Samir quipped, 'What is this?' 'It's called supply chain financing [SCF].' 'And what is that?' queried Samir. Aditya explained to him that as he reached out to all corporate clients, he should tell them that they have thousands of vendors and suppliers. HDFC Bank would give money to all the people who work with the company, thereby strengthening their entire support system. 'With this, I think we'll grow,' concluded Aditya. Subsequently, HDFC Bank launched this service and pioneered SCF in the BFSI. It grew into a massive business and brought the bank close to all its customers. Before other banks woke up, HDFC was already doing extensive amounts of SCF with all large business groups, a requirement very close to their heart.

Interestingly, the tech-savvy way in which Samir and his team made presentations to corporate clients really impressed them. What was tech-savvy about what they did? They used to make PowerPoint presentations using a projector! Today, it is child's play. However, going back to 1996, it was a big deal. The projector itself was huge in size, and it used to be carried around in a big box like an Indian *tijori* (heavy safe). Then, at the client's office, it was unpacked, set up and the interesting diagrams on the PowerPoint immensely impressed the corporate clients. Remembering those days, Samir chuckled, 'While making the pitch, we used to show the details through the projector. And the customers had the experience of seeing a movie! It was very funny when we used to do that, and they used to think that this practice indicated that the bank was tech-savvy—just the fact that we carried a big projector and made a presentation!'

The SCF business actually started off the SME (small and medium enterprise) financing focus at HDFC Bank. The experience dealing with supply chain partners of large corporates gave the bank a good understanding of small businesses, how they operate, and what they need. Soon the bank decided to run SME financing as a separate division with focused growth objectives. Thereafter, there was no looking back. Within a decade, the bank's greatest strength was its SME business. In 2008, after the Centurion Bank of Punjab merger, HDFC Bank's SME book size was Rs 37,000 crore, compared to Rs 16,000 crore of its closest competitor.[1] And all of that started with a few arrows on a piece of paper in Aditya's office!

Appendix III

Larsen & Toubro Construction

A. Visionary Steps for Skill Building

At the turn of the last millennium, India needed 3 crore skilled workers. That was the shortage created with the boom in infrastructure and construction industries and the opening up of the Indian economy. Realizing this much ahead of the curve, in 1995, L&T set up the Construction Skills Training Institute (CSTI) in Chennai to provide vocational training in the construction field. Permanent infrastructure and training facilities were established at the Chennai campus. Over the next two decades, CSTI expanded to six other locations pan-India. In these twenty years, it trained over 50,000 technicians, besides 125,000 workmen through tie-ups, 150,000 workmen of subcontractors and 200,000 workmen through e-learning modules.[1] Winner of the Best CSR Award from the Bombay Stock Exchange, CSTI had visible social and human resource benefits for the Indian construction industry and the rural economy.

Given its innovative approach, many other construction companies appreciated CSTI. Resultantly, they joined L&T's efforts and in 1998 formed the National Academy of Construction (NAC) in Hyderabad. It was the first of its kind institution for skill building through PPP (public-private partnership) mode. The Government of Andhra Pradesh provided land, and the chief minister served as the chairperson of NAC. Its funding was through contractors, who paid 2.5 per cent of the bill deducted at source to the Government of Andhra Pradesh (now of Telangana also). Stressing on the need for replicating this model, A.R. told me, 'If every state encourages this sort of activity, it would make a lot of impact.'

In a study conducted in the early 2000s it was observed that every crore invested on a construction project generated employment of 22,000 unskilled man-days, 23,000 skilled/semi-skilled man-days and 9000 managerial and technical man-days. Lamentably, only 3 per cent of total teaching in India addressed the direct needs of construction, engineering and management aspects required in the construction industry. Given this trend, the 14th Engineering Congress on Human Capital Development observed that unless remedial steps are taken in the near future, India may not have sufficient quality civil engineers even to undertake basic infrastructure work.[2] In this context, initiatives such as CSTI and NAC deserve the widest possible replication and government support if India is to indigenously achieve its infrastructure growth targets.

B. Beyond Business: Collaboration for Social Welfare

In March 2006, at the Fourth World Water Forum (WWF) in Mexico, Professor Anantaraman, an United Nations Industrial Development Organization (UNIDO) expert, presented a series of water projects from India that provided drinking water to 1.2 crore people (1 per cent of the Indian population) in the states of Andhra Pradesh, Telangana and Tamil Nadu, within a span of twelve years, at a cost of Rs 700 crore. Interestingly, these weren't executed by a single agency, but were a rare collaboration between state governments, a public charitable trust and L&T Construction. The WWF adjudged them as one of the ten best local action projects in the world that helped translate the principles and recommendations of the Millennium Task Force on water and sanitation into action. These were the 'Sathya Sai Water Supply Projects' jointly executed by the Government of Andhra Pradesh, L&T and the Sri Sathya Sai Central Trust.[3]

The Anantapur district in southwest Andhra Pradesh has a population of nearly 40 lakh people. It is considered to be the second most arid district in India after the Rajasthan desert. Successive droughts and heavy withdrawal of ground water for irrigation resulted in continuous lowering of ground water from 50 metres in the 1960s to 150 metres by 2010. Chronic water scarcity adversely affected food security and income-earning opportunities, particularly of the rural poor. Of the fourteen famines in India between 1900 and 1959, Anantapur was affected eleven times. For half a century since Independence, the Central or state government did not take any substantial steps. That's when a unique collaboration emerged in 1994. Sathya Sai Baba, born in that region nearly seventy years earlier, decided to commission a project to provide drinking water to 12,50,000 people in all the 731 villages of the Anantapur district. The trust requested R. Kondal Rao (then engineering chief in the Panchayat Raj division of the AP government) to assist and guide in project planning. The implementation was given to L&T–ECC, headed by A. Ramakrishna. The Sri Sathya Sai Central Trust provided the entire fund of Rs 300 crore to complete the project.

This mega project was unique for L&T for two reasons. Firstly, it was an unusual collaboration involving the government and a charitable organization, both working solely for social welfare. Secondly, this project initiated the company into a new niche of water supply and sanitation related developmental projects. Two decades later, water projects annually contributed Rs 2000 crore to L&T's bottom line.

The colossal scale of the project involved a pipeline of 2500 kilometres, construction of 268 overhead reservoirs (capacities ranging from 40,000 to 300,000 litres), 145 ground-level reservoirs (20,000 to 10,00,000 litres capacity), forty booster pumping stations, 280 deep bore-wells, and thirteen infiltration wells to meet the current and future demand factoring the population growth for the next thirty years. It provided 1700 stand posts and 1000 concrete cisterns for enabling 12,50,000 people to collect safe drinking water every single day. And all this was accomplished in a record time of sixteen months.

For focused implementation, the entire project was divided into sub-projects and water was provided for each sub-project in a period of four to six months. The technology, systems and practices were situation-specific and localized. The project staff took complete charge of project management, construction and commissioning, including design. They often worked long hours at a normal day rate. A.R. recalled: 'Everyone was inspired by the feeling that they were working for a project for the good of the people. Many of these workers were villagers who were beneficiaries of the project. When people are deeply associated and have the feeling that they are doing the right job, the output is phenomenal. He does not think that he is doing brick work, but works with the feeling, "I am working to give water to people like me." Because of this involvement of the beneficiary community, there was a sense of complete ownership and therefore, heightened cooperation and output.' Since all stakeholders were convinced of the necessity for quick execution, the materials required for the entire project were purchased from the market by the trust and L&T directly, without the cumbersome procedures of repeated tendering, right at the beginning of the project. This resulted in freezing of the project costs, ensuring ready material availability, total avoidance of stock-out and inconsistent quality. Furthermore, recognizing the project as a part of their CSR, L&T based their unit rate and the cost of supplies on the basis of the actual cost plus a fixed contribution to overheads. Therefore, the profit they denied themselves also became a source of funding for the project.[4]

In the estimate of the Human Settlement Management Institute of the Housing and Urban Development Corporation of the Government of India, which did an impact evaluation study of the project for the Asian Development Bank (ADB), the cost would have escalated by an additional Rs 300 crore, and project completion would have taken sixty months instead of sixteen months, but for the synergies that emerged from a common purpose shared by all stakeholders. This ADB study also indicated that the project demonstrated true partnership, transferability, replicability and sustainability.[5]

After the successful completion of the Anantapur water project, a similar collaborative approach was followed to provide water to 450 upland and tribal habitations in the East Godavari and West Godavari districts of coastal Andhra Pradesh, and to 320 villages in the Medak and Mahbubnagar districts, now in the state of Telangana.[6] The most notable of the projects in terms of beneficiary scale was the one that provided drinking water to 80 lakh people suffering from acute drinking water shortages in the bustling metropolis of Chennai. While the city required 75-crore litres of water per day, it had only 25-crore litres available. In 1968, four neighbouring states signed an agreement to release five TMC (thousand million cubic feet) of water annually from their share of a common river, Krishna, to Chennai, for augmenting its water supply. However, there was no change in the problem for four decades. Water that was released from the Krishna River in neighbouring Andhra Pradesh did not reach Chennai due to the poor state of the linking canal that suffered heavy seepage and erosion. Residents of Chennai resorted to ferrying water from distant places through communal sources at phenomenal costs. The loss of productive man-days due to poor health and time wasted in accessing drinking water was unimaginable.

Nonetheless, in the twenty-four months between October 2002 and November 2004, 4000 workers employed round-the-clock lined the bed and walls of large portions of the 150-kilometre long Kandaleru–Poondi

Canal with 100 mm of concrete.[7] In certain sections, geo-membranes made of HDPE (high density poly-ethylene) sheets were placed on the canal bed to prevent the seepage of water. By revetment of sections of the dam, the capacity of the Kandaleru Reservoir increased four times. The project not only ensured adequate water supply to Chennai, but also helped irrigate about 3 lakh acres of agricultural land in the Nellore and Chittoor districts of Andhra Pradesh, en route Chennai. Emphasizing on the victory of collaborative power in such public welfare projects, and the role that corporations like L&T can play in making them happen, A.R. said, 'These projects have demonstrated that this model is replicable.'[8]

Appendix IV

The Taj Group of Hotels

A. Ideas Galore for Supporting Rich, Indian Traditions

The Taj always looked for win-win solutions even in its sustainability focus. Many decades ago, when the Taj Mahal Hotel was built in the heart of Lutyen's Delhi, marble cutters and Pichhwai painters from Rajasthan,[1] carpet weavers from Panipat, mural artists from Pune and block-painters from Kolkata were engaged.[2] The opening of the Khazana store in the late 1970s at the Taj Mahal Hotel, New Delhi, saw a new style of store, offering exclusive handicrafts and textiles from all parts of India. Shirin recollected that Mrs Indira Gandhi was a frequent visitor, selecting both personal and state gifts from the store. On the one hand, these efforts improved beneficiaries' quality of life while on the other, they also created value for the hotels. Supporting craftsmen from Varanasi and Pochampally[3] (Telangana) was an example of this approach. The other was the expedition in Madhya Pradesh national parks. All Taj Safari properties were built around locally available, environment-friendly material, using local skills and handicrafts.[4] Moreover, 60 per cent of the staff who had been trained for hospitality roles were locals.[5] This ensured business for local traders, and employment for local youth, besides guaranteeing an authentic experience to the Taj guests. To encourage local artforms in dance and music, the Taj invited artists from the vicinity to their hotels for special performances during conferences and marriage programmes. This was a special feature at the Lake Palace Hotel in Udaipur that supported a few dozen such artists and helped them generate annual revenue of Rs 15 lakh. At the Taj Falaknuma in Hyderabad, the Qawalli music performance representing Sufi traditions was an attraction. The singers consisted of artists from the marginalized sections of society. Across Taj properties, the number of such artists and cultural troupes supported was over 1370. It served a dual purpose: the guests didn't have to go looking for these rare features of Indian culture, and the artists could earn a livelihood and remain committed to their artform nurtured over centuries.

Vasant elaborated on how Taj Hotels also sourced several products from local entrepreneurs. At the back end, items of daily requirements like peeled raw onion, garlic, pickles and staff cafeteria snacks, along with candles, jute bags, room amenities and stationery were sourced from income-generating NGOs.[6] On the front-end, a lot of innovation was attempted to facilitate local sourcing. For example, at Chennai's Fisherman's Cove Vivanta Hotel, guests were welcomed with locally sourced shell garlands. At Varanasi's Taj Nadesar Palace, garlands made from river-clay beads painted locally were used to welcome guests instead of traditional flowers.[7] Most Taj corporate gifts also consisted of local handicrafts. To make all this happen, the company faced the challenge of maintaining a regular supply of high-quality products worthy of regular use, sales, and gifts through the Taj. To facilitate this, a team from the corporate office coordinated competence and quality building efforts in local suppliers, NGOs and social entrepreneurs. These were complemented by decentralized volunteering efforts at the hotels. The Tata culture naturally encouraged junior staff to emulate the passion of their seniors during such social volunteering opportunities.[8] A third-party study of the emotional quotient of the Taj staff correlated with the Taj service philosophy drivers of passion, sensitivity and giving stood at 82 per cent.[9]

Support to indigenous arts and crafts plays a major role in local economic development, especially because the crafts sector employs the second largest number of rural people in India after agriculture. Official sources indicate that over 2 crore people are dependent on the crafts sector for livelihood. Unofficial figures indicate ten times the size. Thus, support from the hospitality industry can play a big role in their revival and growth, besides creating synergies of providing authentic regional experiences to tourists from across the globe. Notably, all Taj management trainees in India are provided an opportunity to live with rural communities as part of their internships. This enhances their stewardship commitment and helps develop programmes that enhance the hotels' ability to support villages and target communities.[10] Over the years, this rural exposure programme has seen 100 per cent participation of all trainees. The Taj model may serve as an example to the dozen players in the Indian hospitality industry.[11]

Appendix V

Hindustan Unilever

A. HUL Gains from Competitive Challenges

After these two experiences with Nirma and Ariel, HUL proactively studied various segments within the detergent market, identified the gaps and launched specific products to fill those gaps. The new methods of production and distribution learnt in the course of Project STING helped HUL replicate its success in many other cases. Extending the value proposition used in Wheel, S.M. Datta, chairman of HUL from 1990–96, endeavoured to make HUL the lowest cost and highest quality producer in a variety of products. Through this approach, HUL gradually repositioned itself at the frontier of emerging markets in India and gained substantial success in engaging with a new set of stakeholders. Even Unilever benefitted from HUL's Wheel success story. It replicated the low-cost, high-quality model followed by HUL in many other emerging economies, including Brazil, Indonesia, the Philippines and Congo. During the Asian Economic Crisis of the late 1990s, Unilever made its products available in smaller size packaging so as to encourage consumers to continue to buy their products. In 2008, on the occasion of HUL's 75th anniversary, Dr Ganguly, who had led Project STING, said, 'We often talk of the opportunities at the bottom of the pyramid these days. But the bottom of the pyramid was discovered way back by HUL. We discovered that wealth lies in rural India, and we reached out to the wider market base with the low-cost Wheel and the Re 1 sachet of shampoo. The creation of the whole Wheel brand on an entirely different business model is a great tribute to the marketing prowess of Hindustan Unilever. None of this would have been possible without powerful human resources development within the company.'[1]

B. HUL's Commitment to Clean India Mission

In 2006, HUL launched an ad campaign for Lifebuoy Soap focused on young schoolkids. In this 'now famous' ad, a school-going kid is shown as 'Little Gandhi', who takes the initiative of sweeping the dirty street in his neighbourhood to make a difference in his own little way. Seeing him, other boys in the lane join him in this act. The mothers of these children are shown encouraging their children to go and help. At the end of the cleanliness drive, the kids are shown bathing with Lifebuoy Soap. 'Koi darr nahin' (No fear) was the central thought and tagline for the campaign. The 'fear' was indicative of fear from germs and fear from social ills. For greater awareness, HUL conducted essay competitions and demonstrations on hygiene in 300 schools across thirty-one cities. Cleanliness drives were organized in thirty-one cities pan-India on World Health Day, in which people were encouraged to clean up a landmark in their respective cities. As a result of this campaign, not only did Lifebuoy get 20 lakh additional consumers but the sheer quantum of the awareness campaign was acknowledged by the Limca Book of World Records.[2] Reflecting on the success of the Lifebuoy communication campaign, Prasad Pradhan said, 'If the advertisement delivers such exalted messages, the product is also well appreciated by the consumers.'

This and many other ad campaigns at HUL have focused on social themes that resonate with the masses and inspire them to support a cause. For example, in 2015, HUL launched the 'Swachh Aadat, Swachh Bharat' programme to create large-scale 'Water, Sanitation and Hygiene' (WASH) behaviour change. The programme aimed at the adoption of three simple clean habits—washing hands with soap, using a toilet and keeping it clean, and adopting safe drinking water practices. Within a year of its launch, the 'Swachh Aadat' national mass media campaign of 'Haath Munh aur Bum, Bimari Hogi Kam' reached 7.5 crore people, wherein children as change agents promoted awareness on the three clean habits. Speaking about the campaign, Sanjiv Mehta said, 'We believe that companies like HUL have a key role in helping the country achieve the "Swachh Bharat Abhiyan". More than 90 per cent of households in India use HUL products. This gives us both an opportunity and the responsibility to make a meaningful difference. Our expertise in behaviour change programmes in the area of hand washing and sanitation, and our experience in developing and delivering innovative partnership models positions us uniquely in doing this.'[3] That appears to be the power of corporate-backed social campaigns!

Appendix VI

Bharat Petroleum Corporation

A. Understanding Upstream, Midstream and Downstream Processes of the Oil and Gas Industry

The oil and gas industry value chain starts with the exploration of crude[1] oil or gas discovered on the high seas, deserts, river basins and other geological structures in the form of oil fields or oil wells. This process of exploration and production of oil and gas is called upstream. This crude gets transported by dedicated pipelines to the refinery. The transportation and storage components are often called midstream processes. At the refinery, the crude is processed through geochemical processes such as distillation (also called cracking). Through this process, the crude gets segregated into three types of finished products: heavy distillate, middle distillate and light distillate. Light distillate consists of end products such as motor spirit (petrol/gasoline), naphtha and LPG (liquefied petroleum gas). Middle distillate includes products like HSD (high-speed diesel), SKO (superior kerosene oil) and aviation fuel. The heavy distillate consists of products such as furnace oil, bitumen and LDO (light diesel oil). In the Indian markets, the maximum consumption is of middle distillate products. They constitute 45 per cent of the fuel requirements. Light distillate constitutes 25 per cent, and heavy distillate constitutes 30 per cent. The choice of the end product processed during distillation depends on market requirements. For this purpose, different refineries have different configurations. Some are capable of producing more amounts of light distillates, which are commercially valuable products. Contrarily, heavy distillate products have to be sold sometimes even below the crude prices.

A company's aim is to optimize on the output. The larger the quantity of light distillate products it is able to crack, the higher will be the contribution to its earnings. The refining technology plays a vital role in this process. The better the technology, the more light distillates a company can crack. Besides, the sulphur content of the crude also determines the output. A

379

higher content of sulphur in the crude makes it cheaper. Nigerian crude is known for very high quantities of sulphur. On the other hand, Brent crude[2] is known for low sulphur content. With advanced technology, oil companies have increasingly developed capabilities of handling even high sulphur crude to get light distillate products. From the refinery, the finished oil products go to the company depot or terminal for storage. From the depot the finished products are transported to the retail outlet or pump through dedicated company vehicles or through a contract with authorized agencies. In the case of LPG, the product (LPG) is transported to the LPG filling plant. The processes of refining, marketing and distribution are called downstream.

Due to India's enormous energy requirements, nearly 70 per cent of crude is imported. The indigenous content is about 30 per cent. This is sourced from major exploration sites such as Bombay High[3] (near Mumbai), Khambhat (near Gujarat), Krishna–Godavari basins[4] (near Andhra Pradesh), among others. The major PSEs involved in the Indian oil and gas upstream business are ONGC, GAIL and OIL. The major PSEs involved in downstream business are the three OMCs—IOCL, BPCL and HPCL.

B. Major Brands and Services of BPCL

- Highway Network Assurance Programme (Ghar and Highway Star Outlets): This constitutes OSTS GHAR and Highway Star outlets and emphasizes on customer enablement and enhancement.
- E-commerce: B2B portal enabling customers to place and order online, track status of the order and view dispatch information.
- Pure for Sure: This ensures the quantity and quality of all products sold at the retail outlets of the company.
- SmartFleet: It provides a range of benefits for members like cashless transactions, MIS reports, credit options and a vehicle tracking system.
- Beyond LPG: A value-added service to reach the product at attractive offers to the customers' doorstep.
- Petro Card: A loyalty programme for customers.
- V–Care: Service stations for the maintenance of cars at their retail outlets.
- In & Out stores: Customer convenience stores at retail outlets, which include utility payments, courier services, ATMs, coffee shops, music counters, impulse stores, etc.

- Quick Service Retails Outlets: A tie-up with food chains like McDonald's, Pizza Hut, Nirula's, etc.
- Rural Marketing Vehicles: Spot LPG refuelling to reach out to village customers.
- E-charge: It provides the convenience of purchasing recharge cards from the cellular company and denomination of the customers' choice at any point of time.
- Customer Relations Centre: LPG consumers' forum for giving feedback and obtaining clarification.
- Carnet Card: This identification card allows the purchase of fuel at airports and ad hoc locations with convenience. It gives the operator the convenience of a nationwide accepted card, which is accepted at many non-BPCL locations as well.
- Reticulated LPG System: Supply of LPG through a pipeline network from a centralized cylinder bank or bulk installation to the customers' kitchen.

C. Deregulation of Fuel Products

In October 2014, the Government of India, under Prime Minister Narendra Modi, finally lifted the control on diesel pricing. This is often referred to as deregulation of fuel products and dismantling of the APM system. The retail price would now reflect the movement in global oil prices.[5] It was an opportune time to initiate this as the international crude prices were at an all-time low. This was the second time in two decades that diesel had been deregulated. The government, under Prime Minister Atal Bihari Vajpayee, had deregulated petrol and diesel for the very first time in April 2002. However, during the first term of Prime Minister Manmohan Singh, when global crude prices started increasing, the deregulation was reversed. In June 2010, petrol prices were once again deregulated. The process of deregulating diesel prices was reinitiated in 2013.

The importance of these developments directly reflects on the performance of the OMCs, whose commercial destinies are linked to the pricing mechanism of fuel products. Diesel, kerosene and LPG (the latter two being still under the subsidy mechanism) are vital products from economic, social and even political perspectives. They are fuel products used primarily by the masses for domestic consumption. A market-linked pricing would mean that a rise in international crude prices would reflect in domestic fuel prices rising. This would have a direct impact on the affordability of essential products thereby affecting the daily lives of crores of Indians. Hence, governments of the day have been cautious in decisions relating to these products.

The quantum of subsidies involved can be understood from the fact that during the two years of 2013 and 2014 alone, the under-recovery (revenue loss) on selling diesel, LPG and kerosene at prices lower than imported costs was around Rs 2,25,000 crore.[6] This revenue loss is usually met by a cash subsidy from the government to the OMCs. Part of the payment burden is also borne by upstream companies like ONGC. With the deregulation, the OMCs would have the freedom to fix the prices of fuel products according to global market rates, and the government would substantially be relieved from a diesel subsidy.

For plugging the loopholes in the kerosene and LPG subsidies, the direct benefit transfer (DBT) scheme was initiated in 2013 for LPG and in 2016 for kerosene. This system aimed at transferring the subsidy amount directly to the bank accounts of beneficiaries, thereby saving huge amounts of money typically lost due to corruption and ineffective public distribution systems. Between June 2014 and June 2016, as many as 3.34 crore duplicate/fake/ inactive domestic LPG connections were identified through an elaborate exercise undertaken by government agencies to identify actual users and link their bank accounts for transfers of the subsidy. During the same period, the DBT system facilitated savings of over Rs 21,000 crore.[7]

Appendix VII

TVS Motor Company

A. 'Corporate Social Responsibility is a Function of the CEO'

Venu firmly believed in this and drew inspiration from the Sanskrit adage, *'yatha raja, tatha praja'* (As is the king, so are the subjects). People take cues from what the leader does. Since the CSR benefits to a company are derived over the long-term, it is the CEO and his team that can understand potential benefits and make necessary investments in the CSR programmes of the company. He classified these into three categories: those that have an immediate and direct connection with the business objectives, those which have a relationship with the community surrounding the factories, and those which have a broader impact on industry leaders and the government and therefore, help with the emerging brand of the company. Venu shared that in his experience, in areas where TVSM had undertaken significant social development programmes, there was a clear impact on improved sales of its products as well. In areas surrounding TVSM factories, the goodwill of villagers had helped tackle many problems that normally arose in running a business with the local community, employees and local political forces. He felt that TVSM had benefitted from enormous goodwill with industry leaders and the government due to its CSR initiatives.

To give a concrete structure to his expansive social vision that was much beyond strategic CSR, in 1996, Venu Srinivasan established, in the memory of his late father, the Srinivasan Services Trust (SST) as the social arm of SCL and TVSM. Over the next two decades, SST expanded the holistic and sustainable development of rural communities from two villages in Tamil Nadu to 3449 villages in Maharashtra, Karnataka, Andhra Pradesh, Himachal Pradesh and Tamil Nadu. The rural development projects of SST attempted to achieve its aim by improving the socio-economic status of people through a multi-pillar approach of strengthening the education system, providing access to water, sanitation and irrigation facilities, improving health services, developing community infrastructure, and creating a clean and green environment.

Experience taught SST that development programmes could only be successful when people evolved from being passive recipients of welfare schemes to becoming champions of change in their own lives. SST believes that change can only begin with the empowerment of people, by providing them with livelihoods that can lift them out of poverty. This includes extending economic opportunities to the most needy and marginalized members of society, who have traditionally been women. Hence, SST's notable focus was women's empowerment through increase in agricultural production, better livestock management, micro-enterprises, thrift, savings and credit funds, revolving funds and other income generation programmes. This income helped rural families with food and financial security.

Led by SST Chairman Ashoke Joshi,[1] the field staff spent up to a year building trust among the local residents and village elders before setting up formalized programmes to improve local livelihood. SST adopted the model of Self Help Groups (SHGs) for rural development. These programmes first helped women and farmers form SHGs. Then, SST facilitated regular meetings to educate and monitor members' contribution to and the utilization of collective savings. After a SHG reached relative maturity as measured by its cumulative savings, record-keeping, and consistent loan repayment, SST helped villagers initiate and scale up income-generating projects (IGPs) using loans from local public sector banks. These IGPs enabled villagers to augment their daily farming income by participating in activities such as soap manufacturing, silk making, basket weaving, baking and producing banana chips.[2] With skills training, these women became successful managers of micro-enterprises. This gave them the confidence to accumulate savings, raise their living standards and find a voice in society. In doing so, they became flagbearers of change in their own communities. Once SST's services were familiar to villagers in an area, those from nearby villages often originated contacts directly and requested SST's assistance.[3]

By 2016, over 1 lakh families supported by SST initiatives earned more than Rs 10,000 per month. The villagers could reinvest these savings into new business prospects or education for their children. During my interactions with women SHG members at Padavedu, one of the SST sites in Tamil Nadu, most of the second-generation children had joined colleges in larger cities and were pursuing lucrative careers. A sense of accomplishment coupled with gratitude towards SST initiatives was visible on their faces. For their pioneering work in empowering 400,000 rural women to become self-reliant, SST received the prestigious *Times of India* Social Impact Award 2011. Half a decade later, TVSM was again chosen as the *Economic Times* Corporate Citizen of the Year 2016,[4] for applying principles of running a top-class business to improving the livelihoods of marginalized communities in terms of holistic development. The company's commitment to all-round improvement and its contribution towards creating thousands of micro-entrepreneurs was applauded.[5]

Venu's involvement has been complete through each of the SST milestones. He has personally visited many villages and participated in SST programmes, interacting and inspiring rural folk to lead more empowered and fulfilling lives. His approach has not been one of charity, but of being a catalyst in the process of the social and economic empowerment of rural India. With a nominal CSR budget of Rs 10 crore, SST achieved a standard of grass-roots impact, which companies with ten times that budget haven't. The secret to this is channelizing the rural enthusiasm in the right direction through advice and support, rather than mere money and resources. This is SST's win-win approach.

Acknowledgements

The completion of a book is an event, the joy of which is known only to the author. As I experience immense satisfaction on sharing with my readers some of the learnings from my decade-long research through this book, I deem it a responsibility to express my gratitude to a number of individuals and institutions for their invaluable role in making this happen.

I am appreciative of the J.N. Tata Trust for their munificent grant that facilitated my pursuit of advanced research. My research has taken the shape of this book during my years as a visiting scholar at Harvard Business School, USA. I am thankful to the Harvard ecosystem, especially the Baker Library, for being a researcher's delight and providing access to published data and knowledge resources that are essential elements in the making of this book.

The senior leadership in each of the six companies has been incredibly supportive. They gave time for personal interviews and also arranged interactions with other functional heads within their organizations. I wish to highlight the support of:

- Venu Srinivasan, chairman and managing director, TVS Motor Company Ltd
- Aditya Puri, managing director, HDFC Bank Ltd
- Ashok Sinha, former chairman and managing director, Bharat Petroleum Corporation Ltd
- Late A. Ramakrishna, former deputy managing director, Larsen & Toubro Ltd
- D. Sundaram, former vice chairman and chief financial officer, Hindustan Unilever Ltd
- Raymond Bickson, former managing director and CEO, Indian Hotels Company Ltd

I am grateful to each of them, their team of senior executives and their office staff, all who graciously gave their time for responding to surveys, sharing their experiences during our interactions, and providing rare photos and documents from their archives that have been included in the book.

My insights on *Win-Win Corporations* is based on their vision, actions and commitment to purpose. They are the real protagonists of this book.

Business research calls for a lot of primary data collection, including surveys and interactions with business leaders. A number of individuals have been very helpful to me in this process:

- Sarlaben Parekh, industrialist and philanthropist, who went out of her way to connect me with top executives and entrepreneurs in Mumbai.
- Arunkumar N.T., managing director, UBS India, and C.N. Ram, former CIO, HDFC Bank, who connected me with senior executives from the Indian IT and banking industry.
- P. Vijaya Bhaskar, former executive director, Reserve Bank of India, who introduced me to the Indian banking ecosystem.
- Satish Pradhan, executive vice president, Tata Sons, and Radhakrishnan Nair, former vice president (Talent Acquisition), Tata Services, who connected me with the senior leadership in various Tata companies.

The alumni and visiting faculty of the Sri Sathya Sai Institute of Higher Learning, Prasanthi Nilayam, also facilitated primary data collection through survey responses from and interactions with many senior executives in companies from diverse industries across India.

I am thankful to my teachers who introduced me to the fascinating world of management research. A special mention is due to Professor Peter Pruzan, Copenhagen Business School, Denmark, for being my mentor in the formative years of my doctoral research and inculcating methodological rigour in my approach to research and writing. Professor A. Sudhir Bhaskar, former dean, Sri Sathya Sai Institute of Higher Learning, and my doctoral advisor, introduced me to the fascinating field of social systems engineering. My long conversations with Professor V. Kasturi Rangan, co-chairman, Social Enterprise Initiative, Harvard Business School, and Professor Tarun Khanna, director, Harvard University South Asia Institute, opened up new vistas in my understanding of the interplay between the commercial and social dimensions of business in the developed and emerging economies of the world.

My brief yet memorable interactions with certain eminent individuals in the last decade have contributed to my understanding of values-centred leadership. These include: Dr A.P.J. Abdul Kalam, former president of India; Dr Duvvuri Subbarao, former governor, Reserve Bank of India; Professor

Moolchand Sharma, former vice chairman, University Grants Commission; and Ratan Tata, chairman Tata Sons.

A number of eminent international scholars and subject experts have deeply influenced my understanding of business and its management. I'm immensely grateful to Professor R. Edward Freeman, Darden Business School, University of Virginia, for his ideas and publications in the field of stakeholder theory for more than three decades. My interactions with him have been a cherished experience. I also acknowledge the time and insights received during personal interactions with a number of faculty from leading business schools in USA and Europe, including Harvard Business School, Harvard Kennedy School, MIT Sloan Business School, INSEAD, Copenhagen Business School, Boston University's School of Management, New York University's Stern School of Business, Bentley University, University of Virginia's Darden School of Business, University of Richmond's Robins School of Business, Boston College's Carroll School of Management and Baruch College's Zicklin School of Business.

With the explosion of information on the Internet, there has been a meteoric rise in the number of websites providing authentic and referenced information about diverse topics and individuals relating to multifarious fields of study. I have had the benefit of accessing these to cross verify a lot of details relating to various fact files, individuals, institutions and events. I wish to appreciate the efforts of those who contribute to these portals, and those who meticulously collate and maintain these high-quality storehouses of genuine information, thereby providing free access to world citizens.

Over the last dozen years of my association with academia, I have immensely benefitted from enriching discussions with my teachers and colleagues, and stimulating conversations with my students. They are too numerous to be listed here. Yet, I truly appreciate their time and love for me, and acknowledge their role in catalysing my thoughts and supporting my research endeavours. In particular, I wish to thank my friend Aman Jhaveri for our constructive debates during the initial stages of this book, and my friends Nikhil Kaushik and R. Viswanath for the many long discussions and insightful comments in the final stages of the book. My former student and now colleague Kundan Madireddy deserves special thanks and praise for assisting me in designing all the infographics and data charts presented in this book. His eye for detail and specificity are noteworthy. Ajith Sankar, faculty from the PSG Institute of Management, Coimbatore, collaborated with me in publishing early versions of select stakeholder studies on some of these companies as case studies. Professor Prabhakar Raya, dean, School of Management, Pondicherry University, and Professor Panduranga Vithal, Indian Institute of Plantation Management Bengaluru, provided valuable feedback in the early stages of my research.

Among a wonderful set of teachers that I have benefitted from, I wish to specially mention Professors Siva Sankara Sai, Vishwanath Pandit, Lakshminarasimham, Anil Kumar, U.S. Rao, V.E. Ramamoorthy, Kumar Bhaskar, Mohan Ajwani and Indu Shahani; Dr Srirangarajan and Dr N. Sivakumar; S.V. Giri and M. Nanjundaiah, who have all played a significant role.

Over two dozen corporate leaders and subject experts have been amazingly supportive. In spite of their exceedingly busy schedules, they read the manuscript of *Win-Win Corporations*, and provided an advance quote for the book. I wish to thank each one of them. Their words of appreciation and insightful comments make this book truly meaningful. In particular, I wish to thank Anjali Raina, executive director, Harvard Business School India Research Center, and her team for their support.

Penguin Random House, my publishers, deserve a distinct mention. Lohit Jagwani, my commissioning editor, redefined an editor's role in the making of a book. My year-long interactions with him at every stage of the book have been a source of immense value addition to its content. He provided very relevant feedback on the early drafts of each chapter and highlighted pertinent issues that I could consider. He went way beyond the call of duty to make this journey enjoyable, providing all possible elaborations on the nuances of the publishing world to a debut trade author. The success of *Win-Win Corporations* owes a lot to his time, enthusiasm and commitment. I also thank Dipti Anand, my copy editor, for her keen eye for detail and for accommodating many last minute corrections in making this book truly up to date. I acknowledge the entire team of Penguin Random House for their professionalism and the wonderful form and format in which the book has been released. They truly deserve being the top-notch publisher they are for delighting their authors through a collaborative journey from ideation to distribution.

Finally, I wish to express profound gratitude to my guru, Sri Sathya Sai, for exposing me to the fascinating world of Indian culture and spirituality during the formative years of my life. Our conversations, and his discourses on business and management based on Indian ethos and values compiled in the book *Man Management*, have been deeply impacting. His message and mission perennially inspire me. For over two decades, I have also been a beneficiary of the Sri Sathya Sai educational and service institutions in India and overseas, which provide an extraordinary ecosystem for self-discovery and nation building.

I am beholden to my mother, Shefali, for her loving care. Her warmth and affection are my greatest strengths. She remains my moral compass during all dilemmas of daily life. My father, Jagesh, has been a pillar of strength and encouragement through all my academic endeavours. I remain grateful for his sustained support and constructive criticism. Discussions with my late grandfather, Professor Chandrahas Shah, kindled the curiosity in a young schoolboy from Mumbai. Three decades later, they continue to motivate me in my research. My grandmothers Charulata and Jayavati have played important roles in the foundational years of my life. My late aunt Smita would have been delighted to see this book. I cherish her fondness for me. I am also indebted to the late Bhasvaryashashri Maharajsaheb for her elevating exchanges on the Indian way of life.

This book, the first in the series of many more, is for business managers and entrepreneurs, students and teachers, researchers and analysts, policymakers and government officials. I am sure each of them will find in it valuable insights that have been gathered from the collective experience of four centuries of these six companies, and my interactions with over 200 practitioners and academics with a cumulative experience of 4000 human years. I am thankful to all my readers for their time and hope they have enjoyed reading this book. I'd be delighted to receive your thoughts, comments and feedback on how you liked *Win-Win Corporations*. Do write to me at: shashankjshah@gmail.com.

Do also visit my website www.shashankshah.com. There, you'll find many more stories, interviews, podcasts and lots of other resources that will provide greater insights to help you take win-win decisions and become a Win-Win Corporation!

Notes

I: Introduction: A Millennial's Journey Begins . . .

1. Gandhi's concept of 'Sarvodaya' conceived of a non-exploitative, egalitarian society engaged in service and self-sacrifice for the 'good of all'.
2. Shah, Shashank and V.E. Ramamoorthy. *Soulful Corporations: A Values-Based Approach to Corporate Social Responsibility*. Springer India, 2013.
3. The era of Licence Raj, also known as the Permit Raj, refers to the elaborate licences, regulations and accompanying red tape that were required to set up and run businesses in India between 1947 and 1990. It was a result of India's decision to have a planned economy, where all aspects of the economy were controlled by the state and licences were given to a select few.
4. 1 trillion = 1 lakh-crore.
5. Founded in 1945 and headquartered in New York, it is the second largest exchange (after the New York Stock Exchange) in the world by market capitalization.
6. Gaither, Chris and Dawn C. Chmielewski. 'Fears of dot-com crash, version 2.0'. 10 July 2006. *Los Angeles Times*.
7. Manikutty, S. *Being Ethical: Ethical Foundation of Business*. IIM Ahmedabad Business Books. Random House India, 2011.
8. 1 billion = 100 crore.
9. Founded in 1913 and headquartered in Chicago, it was one of the 'Big Five' accounting firms in the world that provided audit, tax and consulting services to large corporations. The other four, now known as the 'Big Four', are PricewaterhouseCoopers (PwC), Deloitte Touche Tohmatsu, Ernst & Young (EY) and KPMG.
10. Shah, Shashank and Sudhir Bhaskar. *Corporate Stakeholder Management: Why What and How—A Dharmic Approach*. Unpublished Monograph. Sri Sathya Sai Institute of Higher Learning, India.
11. Hoffman W.M. and M. Rowe. 'The Ethics Officer as Agent of the Board: Leveraging Ethical Governance Capability in the Post-Enron Corporation'. 2007. *Business and Society Review*, Vol. 112.
12. Norris, Floyd. 'A corporate hero admits fraud'. 7 January 2009. *New York Times*.

13. Leahy, Joe. 'The $1bn black hole at heart of Satyam's finances'. *Financial Times*, 8 January 2009.

14. N. Kasturi. 'Questions Answered'. *Sathya Sai Speaks Volume 10*. 1970. Sri Sathya Sai Sadhana Trust – Publications Division, Prasanthi Nilayam.

15. The Institute of Company Secretaries of India defines 'corporate governance' as: 'It is the application of best management practices, compliance of law in true letter and spirit and adherence to ethical standards for effective management and distribution of wealth and discharge of social responsibility for sustainable development of all stakeholders.'

16. Narasimhan, C.R.L. 'Corporate governance at its nadir'. 19 January 2009. *The Hindu*.

17. The financial crisis of 2008 was considered by many experts as the worst since the Great Depression of 1929. The collapse of large financial and banking institutions was prevented through bail-out packages from national governments. Its impact was so severe that it eventually led to the sovereign debt crisis in Europe.

18. Stoney, C. and D. Winstanley. 'Stakeholding: Confusion or Utopia? Mapping the Conceptual Terrain'. 2001. *Journal of Management Studies*, 38:5–6.

19. Freeman, Edward. 'Divergent Stakeholder Theory'. 1999. *Academy of Management Review*, 24:2.

20. This definition was jointly developed by me and Professor Peter Pruzan, professor emeritus, Copenhagen Business School and visiting faculty, Sri Sathya Sai Institute of Higher Learning.

21. In his seminal work, Freeman (1984) states that the concept of 'stakeholder' has been put forward as one way to revise the conceptual maps of managers. Drawing on research in strategic planning, systems theory, corporate social responsibility and organization theory, the development of this concept can serve as an integrating force to pull together and interpret a broad base of research. The fact that an organization's environment can be interpreted in stakeholder terms implies that the concept can serve as an umbrella for the development of an approach to strategic management.

22. Some of the writings on stakeholder thinking which have focused on theory development include: strategies for managing stakeholders (Macmillan and Jones, 1986; Savage, Nix, Whitehead and Blair, 1991), approaches for viewing groups with which management must interact (Goodpaster, 1991), assessing corporate social performance (Clarkson, 1991, 1994; Lamb, 1994), operationalizing theory (Weber,

1992), understanding management morality (Halme and Nasi, 1992), understanding the business and society relationship (Carroll, 1993), examining the stakeholder expectations of the board of directors (Huse, 1994), studying organizational justice (Husted, 1994), evaluating new ventures (Mitchell, 1994), investing corporate governance and green values (Halme, Huse and Jystad, 1994), studying strategies in a conflict process (Nasi and Savage, 1994), and stakeholder theory having the potential of being an integrating theme for business and society disciplines (Donaldson and Preston, 1995; Jones, Wood and Jones, 1995).

23. In various Hindu traditions, Manu is a title accorded to the progenitor of mankind and also the very first king to rule this earth, who saved mankind from the universal flood. He was known to be absolutely honest, which is why he was initially known as 'Satyavrata' (one with the oath of truth).

24. He was an advisor and prime minister to the first Maurya emperor Chandragupta (c. 340–293 BCE), and was the chief architect of his rise to power. Also known as Chanakya, he has been considered as the pioneer of the field of economics and political science. In the Western world, he has been referred to as the Indian Machiavelli, although Chanakya's works predate Machiavelli's work by about 1800 years.

25. Shah, Shashank and Sudhir Bhaskar. 'Corporate Stakeholders Management: Western and Indian Perspectives—An Overview'. 2008. *Journal of Human Values*, 14:1.

26. (469–399 BC); he was a classical Greek philosopher; credited as one of the founders of Western philosophy.

27. (428/427–348/347 BC); he was a classical Greek philosopher, mathematician, writer of philosophical dialogues, and founder of the Academy in Athens—the first institution of higher learning in the Western world. Along with his mentor, Socrates, and his student, Aristotle, Plato helped to lay the foundations of Western philosophy and science.

28. (384–322 BC); he was a Greek philosopher, a student of Plato and teacher of Alexander the Great.

29. Gordon, Barry. *Economic Analysis before Adam Smith*. London: MacMillan Press, 1975.

30. Sivakumar, N. *Value Based Management—Historical Roots and Current Practices*. Unpublished PhD Thesis. Sri Sathya Sai Institute of Higher Learning, India, 1995.

31. This was a year-long MBA project of Giridharan Menon on the topic, 'Stakeholders Management: A Study of Scriptures from World Religions', which I guided.

32. (5 June 1723–17 July 1790); he was a Scottish moral philosopher and a pioneer of political economics, widely cited as the father of modern economics.

33. Andriof, J., Waddock, S., Husted, Brian and S. Rahman. *Unfolding Stakeholder Thinking Vol.1*. UK: Greenleaf Publishing, 2002.

34. There was a lack of any empirical study (based on primary data) on the perceptions of Indian managers on the existence and implementation of stakeholder management policies and practices in their companies. Occasional newspaper and magazine articles on these issues hardly constituted a corpus of systematic analysis. There was even a dearth of historical work taking a comprehensive look at stakeholder management in Indian organizations and a lack of comprehensive case studies highlighting stakeholders-related best practices of leading organizations in corporate India.

35. The Appendix on the research process provides details of surveys and interviews that formed the basis of this book.

36. A list of interviewees has been provided along with the overview of the research process.

37. Founded in 1941 by the Shroff family and headquartered in Mumbai, Excel Industries is considered to be one of India's first domestic chemicals manufacturer.

38. Shah, Shashank. 'The Needs of The Stakeholders are the Seeds of Growth for the Organization: Vignettes of Wisdom from G. Narayana'. 2011. *Journal of Values-Based Leadership*, IV: II.

39. Established in 1960, TAFE is a member of the Amalgamations Group. With an annual turnover of INR 93 billion (2014–15), it wields 25 per cent market share of the Indian tractor industry, and has annual sales of over 150,000 tractors (domestic and international).

40. Shah, Shashank. 'Integrating Stakeholders' Welfare and Corporate Success: In an Indian Family-Owned organization'. 2016. *Journal of Values-Based Leadership*, Vol. IX:I.

41. Founded in 1948, Cadbury India is a market leader in confectionary products, especially chocolates. In 2014, it changed its name to Mondelez India Foods Limited.

42. Shah, Shashank. 'No Business Is Complete Without Sensitivity to Society and Environment: A Candid Interaction with Cadbury's Chairman'. *Metamorphosis*, 9:2. Lucknow: Indian Institute of Management, 2010.

43. Mackey, John and Raj Sisodia. *Conscious Capitalism: Liberating the Heroic Spirit of Business*. USA: Harvard Business Review Press, 2013.

44. Founded in 1994, ICICI Bank is India's largest private sector bank.

45. This refers to a company's priority focus on increasing profitability on a quarterly basis.

46. A 2002 Economics Nobel Prize winner, Professor Kahneman is professor emeritus of psychology at Princeton University's Woodrow Wilson School.

47. Professor of psychology and behavioural economics at Duke University, North Carolina, USA.

48. Founded in 1987 as a joint venture between the Tata Group and Tamil Nadu Industrial Development Corporation, it the world's fifth largest wrist-watch manufacturer.

49. Including the Harvard Business School, Harvard Kennedy School, MIT Sloan Business School, Boston University, New York University's Stern School of Business, University of Virginia's Darden School of Business, and experts from the Federal Reserve Bank of New York and the United Nations.

50. In his landmark work of 1984, Professor Freeman identified four areas as being very crucial for future investigation. These include: development of the stakeholder concept as a stakeholder theory, linking it with disciplines of organization theory, economics and political science; empirical validity to measure the responsiveness of organizations to social issues; the role of values in the stakeholder management process; and the manager being a fiduciary to stakeholders i.e. the manager must act in the interest of the stakeholders. The objectives of my study strongly resemble the issues highlighted for future research by Freeman. In fact, during our conversation, he expressed his satisfaction that I had ventured to study Indian companies from the stakeholder lens, something that had not been attempted in the last two decades.

51. The other prominent companies that emerged include Infosys Ltd, Wipro Ltd, Reliance Industries Ltd, IBM India, Birla Group, HSBC Bank, ITC Ltd, ONGC, Standard Chartered Bank and Citibank.

52. There were no index ETFs (Exchange Traded Funds) in 1996. So the assumption is that an investor would invest 1 lakh rupees in the Sensex portfolio and rebalance as and when the Sensex constituents change, effectively tracking the Sensex itself. All stock market-related statistics in this book have been sourced from the FactSet Database.

53. Wherever share price/equity value increases are mentioned, either in a graph or in the main text, they have been calculated using the standard compounded annual growth formula (CAGR). The CAGR represents the growth rate of an initial investment assuming it is compounding by the period of time specified. The CAGR rate for a specific equity share

is taken from the FactSet database and includes the effect of stock splits, bonus shares and dividends as well.

54. Peters, Tom and Robert Waterman. *In Search of Excellence: Lessons from America's Best Run Companies.* New York: Harper Business Essentials, 1982.

55. Collins, James and Jerry Porras. *Built to Last: Successful Habits of Visionary Companies.* New York: Harper Collins, 1994.

56. James Collins. *Good to Great: Why Some Companies Make the Lead . . . And Others Don't.* New York: Harper Collins, 2001.

57. A six-year long research work at the Stanford Research Institute was based on the analyses of eighteen visionary companies which fulfilled varied criteria such as: being the industry leader, having multiple generations of chief executives, having been through multiple product life cycles and being founded before 1950. The companies included in their study are the likes of 3M, Boeing, Ford, GE, Procter & Gamble, Sony, Walt Disney and many more.

58. I am fully conscious of the limitations of this study, both in quantitative and qualitative terms. As a result, all the questions that exist in this area may not be answered. However, I hope that the deficiencies will themselves highlight what needs to be done and stimulate other like-minded researchers and management practitioners to take up the challenge and fill the gaps in this field of study.

59. A mixed economic system allows a level of private economic freedom in the use of capital, but also allows for governments to interfere in economic activities in order to achieve social aims.

60. Kumar, Nirmalya. *India's Global Powerhouses.* USA: Harvard Business Press, 2009.

61. Rao, Aprameya and Kishor Kadam, '25 years of liberalization: A glimpse of India's growth in 14 charts'. 7 July 2016. *Firstpost.com.*

62. An economic and political system in which a country's trade and industry are controlled by private owners for profit, rather than by the state.

63. An economic system in which private business operates in competition and is largely free of state control.

II: HDFC Bank: World-class Services . . . Indian Experience

1. Pandit, Vishwanath; Srirangarajan, G.S. and Shashank Shah (Eds.). *Ethics and the World of Finance.* November 2010. Sri Sathya Sai Institute of Higher Learning, Prasanthi Nilayam, p. 80.

2. Sheth, Hiral. 'Puri Magic'. 10 January 2010. *Business India*, pp. 54–64.

3. It is a financial measurement that explains the efficiency at which a company uses/employs its funds. A higher ROCE indicates more efficient use of funds and better generation of returns for shareholders.

4. Market capitalization is the market value of a publicly traded company's outstanding shares. The investment community usually refers to this figure to determine a company's size, as opposed to sales or total asset figures.

5. In India, it refers to a bank that is listed in the Second Schedule of the Reserve Bank of India Act, 1934. Scheduled banks are usually private, foreign and nationalized banks operating in India. They conduct normal banking business such as accepting deposits, giving out loans and providing other banking services.

6. Companies sell shares to the general public to raise long-term funds. People have to subscribe to these shares to buy them. Over-subscription is a situation where the demand for shares exceeds the total number available under the sale.

7. A bank which is a member of a clearing corporation such as the National Securities Clearing Corporation Ltd, and assists in settlement of amounts after buying and selling of securities (such as shares, bonds, etc.) in the securities market.

8. Capital markets are part of the overall financial system and facilitate raising long-term funds by dealing in shares, bonds and other investments.

9. Dividend is the share of profits paid by a company to its shareholders. A maiden dividend is the first ever dividend paid by a company.

10. Rodrigues, Ryan. 'An oasis of calm'. 2 November 2008. *Business India*, pp. 68–82.

11. Mohan, Raghu. 'Winner again, no surprises there'. 26 January–8 February 2016. *Business World*.

12. It is the cumulative image of a product or service in the minds of consumers, resulting from its frequent use.

13. Founded in 1792 and headquartered in Boston, State Street Corporation is a US-based worldwide financial services holding company, and the second oldest financial institution in USA.

14. Headquartered in Jakarta, Bank Mandiri is the largest bank in Indonesia in terms of assets, loans and deposits.

15. Adhikari, Anand. 'Digital banker'. 18 January 2015. *Business Today*.

16. Founded in 1933 and headquartered in central Hong Kong, it is part of the HSBC Group.

17. Mahanta, Vinod. 'How Aditya Puri has managed to pull off 30 per cent plus growth for HDFC Bank'. 29 June 2012. *Economic Times*.

18. These are loans that are granted to borrowers who do not have a good credit rating and have higher chances of defaulting. These loans have a higher interest rate due to the increased risk associated with such borrowers.

19. In finance, a derivative is a contract that derives its value from the performance of an underlying entity. This underlying entity can be a share, currency, physical asset, etc. A complex derivative is one whose pay-offs (returns) are more complicated to calculate when compared to simple derivative products.

20. Lorenzetti, Laura. 'This is the most valuable bank in the world'. 23 July 2015. *Fortune.*

21. Adhikari, Anand. 'Digital banker'. 18 January 2015. *Business Today.*

22. A new private sector bank promoted by Bennett, Coleman & Co. (Times Group) in the post-liberalization period.

23. Mandeep came with two decades of experience with leading companies across industries, including Eicher Tractors, ANZ Grindlays Bank, Arthur Anderson and Times Bank.

24. Rodrigues, Ryan. 'An oasis of calm'. 2 November 2008. *Business India*, pp. 68–82.

25. Formed out of the merger between the Centurion Bank and the Bank of Punjab in 2005, it was a private sector bank providing retail and corporate banking services.

26. Founded in 1994 in Panaji (Goa), it was a joint venture between 20th Century Finance Corporation and its associates, and the Keppel Group of Singapore. It was headquartered in Mumbai and led by Rana Talwar, an eminent banker, who lost his life during the unfortunate terrorist attacks on the Taj Mahal Hotel in Mumbai in November 2008.

27. Founded in 1994.

28. Founded in 1940, Lord Krishna Bank was a private sector bank in the Thrissur district in Kerala. In the 1960s, it acquired three commercial banks: Kerala Union Bank, Thiyya Bank and Josna Bank. In 1971, it became a scheduled commercial bank and merged with the Centurion Bank of Punjab in 2007.

29. Bala, Vaishnavi. 'A people's person'. 29 November 2009. *Business India*, pp. 130.

30. Sheth, Hiral. 'Puri magic'. 10 January 2010. *Business India*, pp. 54–64.

31. Bandyopadhyay, Tamal. *A Bank for the Buck*. Mumbai: Jaico Publishing House, 2013.

32. Rao, Rohit. 'The bank that sees tomorrow'. 30 October–12 November 2000. *Business India.*

33. Subsequent to leaving HDFC Bank in 2011, Rohit Mull was chief marketing officer at AIG. In 2016, Rohit Mull moved to Selective Insurance of America as senior vice president and chief marketing officer.

34. The various financial characteristics that banks/lenders evaluate when scrutinizing a prospective borrower. Credit criteria can include a borrower's assets and liabilities, income sources, expenses and credit history. Favourable criteria usually results in a loan getting approved.

35. Neeraj Swaroop joined HDFC in 1999, after an eight-year stint with Bank of America. In 2005, he took over as CEO of Standard Chartered Bank, India Region.

36. An ISO 9001:2000 certified organization, SAI SEVA is one of India's first exclusively rural BPOs established in 2005 in the pilgrim town of Puttaparthi (Andhra Pradesh). Started by the alumni of the Sri Sathya Sai Institute of Higher Learning (Deemed University) and inspired by their alma mater's mission of social welfare, SAI SEVA's vision is to improve the Indian economy by bringing about significant improvement in unemployment rates across rural India by effectively leveraging the resources in the villages to support the business requirements of companies.

37. Having a population between 5000 and 10,000.

38. Such a service has now become mandatory for all banks.

39. I-flex was the financial services software provider for HDFC Bank. Eventually, it was renamed Oracle Financial Services Software. Headquartered in Mumbai, it ranks among the top ten IT companies in India.

40. Sheth, Hiral. 'Puri magic'. 10 January 2010. *Business India*, pp. 54–64.

41. Rangan, Govardhana and Joel Rebello. 'Customer is your wife, and she changes every day'. 4 November 2015. *ET Exclusive*.

42. Law, Vivek. 'Prospects exceedingly bright in the next 5–10 years'. 22 November 2012. *Mint*.

43. Adhikari, Anand. 'Best in class'. 14 February 2016. *Business Today*.

44. Mukherjee, Shubham and Mayur Shetty. 'Worst over, we're seeing beginning of green shoots: Aditya Puri'. 12 May 2014. *Times of India*.

45. To know more about how HDFC Bank successfully used analytical marketing techniques, log on to my website: www.shashankshah.com.

46. In 1978, RBI mandated all banks to direct 33.33 per cent of net bank credit to priority sector areas. Later, this was expanded to 40 per cent for domestic banks and 32 per cent for foreign banks. The philosophy of mandatory PSL in India has been to ensure that banks'

profitability concerns should not deprive employment generating sectors such as agriculture, small-scale enterprises and even export-oriented units from getting sufficient funding as compared to medium and large enterprises.

47. Financial access involves providing access to different financial products and services. Financial inclusion or inclusive financing is the delivery of financial services (such as opening accounts, accepting deposits, money transfer, etc.) at affordable costs to disadvantaged and low-income segments of society.

48. Maxim Rodrigues, Ryan. 'Harvest time'. 14–27 October 2013. *Business India*, pp. 60–9.

49. Founded in 1987 and headquartered in Mumbai, CRISIL is a global analytical company providing ratings, research, and risk and policy advisory services.

50. 'Financial Inclusion in India: Moving Beyond Bank Accounts'. 18 September 2014. Knowledge@Wharton.

51. The Rangarajan Committee of 2014 proposed a per capita expense of Rs 32 per day in the rural areas as being above poverty line. This meant a monthly per capital expenditure of Rs 1000 in the rural areas. In 2012, according to the Government of India estimates, about 22 per cent of the Indian population (approximately 26 crore individuals) was below the poverty line.

52. Over 7000 employees (about 10 per cent of the bank's total employee strength) were working on this project. In 2013, the total size of the rural business was Rs 2250 crore. The bank aimed to reach Rs 10,000 crore by 2016. Though this was a small proportion of the bank's total book size, the positive social ramifications were immense.

53. Mohan, Raghu. 'Steady hand on the wheel'. 2 December 2013. *Business World*, pp. 52–53.

54. *Ibid.*

55. To know more about the interesting challenges that HDFC bank faced in its rural journey and the innovations that helped it overcome them successfully, visit my website: www.shashankshah.com.

56. Telephone density or tele-density is the number of telephone connections for every 100 individuals living within an area.

57. 'India's technology opportunity: Transforming work, empowering people'. December 2014. *McKinsey Global Institute Report*.

58. Adhikari, Anand. 'Digital banker'. 18 January 2015. *Business Today*.

59. Puri, Aditya. 'Digital banking in a digital India'. 28 March 2016. *Business Standard*.

60. Mohan, Raghu. 'Winner again, no surprises there'. 26 January–8 February 2016. *Business World*.
61. Adhikari, Anand. 'Digital banker'. 18 January 2015. *Business Today*.
62. Adhikari, Anand. 'Been there, done that'. 3 January 2016. *Business Today*.
63. Rao, Parag. 'HDFC Bank launches nationwide campaign to go digital'. 9 October 2015. *Economic Times*.
64. Adhikari, Anand. 'Been there, done that'. 3 January 2016. *Business Today*.
65. Lakshminarasimhan, Pranay. 'We are digitizing entire bank, simplifying the process: Nitin Chugh, HDFC Bank'. 9 March 2016. *Financial Express*.
66. See, http://summit.hdfcbank.com/.
67. Bhakta, Pratik. 'HDFC Bank gets start-ups on board to increase customer convenience'. 11 March 2016. *ET Tech Beta*.
68. In 2014–15 alone, 22,700,740 equity shares were allotted to the employees in respect of the equity stock options under the ESOPs.
69. Maxim Rodrigues, Ryan. 'Harvest time'. 14–27 October 2013. *Business India*, pp. 60–9.
70. After a dozen years at Citibank, Shailendra was a founding member at HDFC Bank. From 2004 to 2008, Shailendra was the MD and CEO of the Centurion Bank of Punjab. After CBoP merged with HDFC Bank, he briefly held the position of executive director at HDFC Bank. From 2009–14, he was the CEO of ING Vysya Bank.
71. In 2009, Samir Bhatia was nominated as CEO of Equifax Credit Information Services Pvt. Ltd. In 2012, he founded SMEcorner.com, an online platform that enables SMEs to access loans from banks and NBFCs.
72. After seventeen years at Hindustan Lever Ltd and Bank of America, Neeraj joined HDFC Bank in 1999. From 2005 onwards, he headed Standard Chartered India, South East Asia Region and Singapore.
73. Sheth, Hiral. 'Puri magic'. 10 January 2010. *Business India*, pp. 54–64.
74. Adhikari, Anand. 'A healthy balance'. 5 January 2014. *Business Today*.
75. Judged based on six parameters: leadership, strategy and innovation, performance, stature, social contribution and governance.

III: Larsen & Toubro Construction: Building India . . . Through Imagineering

1. Interview in the commemorative film by Zafar Hai, November 2014.

2. A French industrial company that was a world leader in building materials. In 2015, it merged with the Swiss Cement Company—Holcim—creating a new world leader in the building materials sector: LafargeHolcim.

3. Incorporated in 1997, it was a joint venture between the French company Lafarge and the Spanish company Cementos Molins. Lafarge Surma Cement Plant is the only fully integrated dry process cement plant in Bangladesh.

4. 'L&T wins Lafarge contract for conveyor belt'. 4 October 2002. *Economic Times*.

5. T.J. 'Cement ties'. 29 September 2014. *The Economist*.

6. Both figures in March 2015.

7. As per Census 2011, India had 640 districts.

8. Coal gasifier facilitates the process of coal gasification, which is the conversion of solid coal to synthetic natural gas or a gaseous mixture that can be burned as fuel.

9. A long, high bridge that carries a roadway or a railroad across a valley or other low ground.

10. Hydrocracker is a unit in a petroleum refinery. It facilitates the process of Hydrocracking, which is a catalytic chemical process used in petroleum refineries for converting high-boiling constituent hydrocarbons in petroleum crude oils into more valuable, lower-boiling products such as gasoline, kerosene, jet fuel and diesel oil.

11. Dalal, Sucheta. 'A.M. Naik—A rare interview to MoneyLIFE'. 15 September 2008. *Money Life*.

12. Sanskrit word for 'destroyer of the enemy'.

13. Only five other countries (all permanent members of the United Nations Security Council) have the capability to indigenously build a nuclear submarine.

14. It is the inner hull of a submarine that holds the difference between outside and inside pressure.

15. The largest construction and civil engineering company in USA, headquartered in San Francisco. It consistently ranks among the top three construction companies in the world.

16. Paul, Cuckoo. 'L&T: Armed but not commissioned'. 29 September 2014. *Forbes India*.

17. Larsen & Toubro Sustainability Report 2015.

18. Sardar Patel was responsible for unifying more than 500 princely states into a united India during his tenure as the first home minister of independent India (1947–50).

19. 'Statue of Unity to be built by Larsen & Toubro in nearly Rs 3000 crore contract'. 28 October 2014. *NDTV Profit.*
20. Survey conducted by *Engineering News Record Magazine*, 2014–15.
21. See, http://www.indianmirror.com/indian-industries/2012/construction-2012.html.
22. It also contributed 71 per cent of the Rs 232,700 crore order book and 55 per cent of the Rs 155,400 crore order inflow.
23. The terms ECC and L&T Construction have been interchangeably used. For over sixty years, L&T's construction business was known as L&T–ECC, and hence the term has historical value.
24. Muthiah, S. *Madras Miscellany*. Chennai: EastWest Publishers, 2011.
25. Founded in 1936, ACC is one of India's largest cement manufacturers.
26. Based on a personal narration to the author by Dr Anumolu Ramakrishna, former deputy MD of Larsen & Toubro.
27. Muthiah, S. *Madras Miscellany*. Chennai: EastWest Publishers, 2011.
28. By 1969, L&T's agency business was abolished.
29. Shah, Shashank. 'Stakeholders Management in the Indian Construction Industry: Insights into the Approach at Larsen & Toubro's Construction Division'. 2014. *Journal of Values-Based Leadership*, 7:1:6.
30. John, Satish. 'Succession at L&T: How India Inc.'s most mysterious succession plan might work out'. 26 February 2012. *Economic Times.*
31. Balse, Hemangi. 'Succession race begins at L&T'. 15 June 1998. *Business Standard.*
32. An acronym for Lean, Agile, Knowledge, Speed, Human, Yield Value, Action-oriented.
33. While Naik overhauled all divisions, the chapter continues to focus on the ECC.
34. Although not legal entities, the ICs were vertically-integrated business segments with their own internal boards. Each IC board included a number of independent directors and a representative from the parent company. This was done with the objective of providing greater independence in functioning and broader business perspectives to the IC management.
35. Larsen & Toubro Annual Report 2010–11.
36. Larsen & Toubro Investor Presentation, 6 February 2016.
37. *Ibid.*
38. It was proposed that he would be responsible for L&T's businesses and Naik would focus on completing the portfolio restructuring, institutionalizing the IC structure, and mentoring and developing the leadership team and future leaders to face global challenges.

39. Prasad, Rachita. 'L&T elevates S.N. Subrahmanyan as deputy MD and president'. 21 September 2015. *Economic Times.*

40. *ECC Concord*, January–March 2015.

41. Headquarters of L&T Construction in Chennai.

42. 'The engineer behind the giant'. 4 July 2007. *The Hindu Business Line.*

43. The very first contract was signed with the Government of Maharashtra in 2015 to provide CCTV-based surveillance in Mumbai—the largest of its kind in India—which involved design, development, implementation and maintenance of 6000 CCTV cameras, data centres, command and control centres, viewing centres and network connectivity across multiple locations of strategic importance.

44. The apex administrative body of the temple established under the TTD Act in 1932 by the Government of India.

45. India's largest manufacturer of pumps and valves, it is a part of the Kirloskar Group founded in 1888 and headquartered in Pune.

46. In Hindu-Vaishnavite temple precincts, these three practices are prohibited.

47. Most fact files in this narrative are based on a personal narrative in: Hariharan, K.G. 'Tirumala Water Supply Pipeline'. *Water: The Elixir of Life.* Corporate Communications Dept., L&T-ECC Division, Chennai.

48. A concept popularized by Peter Senge, faculty at MIT Sloan School of Management, in his 1990 bestseller, *The Fifth Discipline.* According to Senge, learning organizations are places where people continually expand their capacity to create the results they truly desire, where new and expansive patterns of thinking are nurtured, where collective aspiration is set free, and where people are continually learning how to learn together.

49. Jaykar, Roshni. 'The man behind the mask'. 10 October 1998. *Business Today.*

50. All business units and facilities are certified for ISO 9001. Competency cells for diverse areas including formwork, foundation engineering, quality management, concrete technology, special projects and construction methods have been developed to provide best-in-class to customers. For example, the L&T Construction Research and Testing Centre was the first major testing centre established by a construction company in India, and accredited by the National Accreditation Board for testing and calibration Laboratories (NABL) for testing wide varieties of construction materials like cement, fine and coarse aggregate, concrete blocks, bricks, plywood, water, chemical admixtures, geo textiles, soil, rock and asphalt. Besides, this ISO17025

certified centre also focused on applied research on innovation of new material, cost reduction and techniques of construction. 'Srishti', a first-of-its-kind 3D studio, was established for translating designs into virtual reality. Features like virtual-prototyping, walkthrough and analysis by controlling virtual models, including design reviews, gave the customer a feel of the actual project before execution. This was very useful during the construction of complex projects like airports, IT parks and even industrial plants.

51. Chatterjee, Pritha and Aniruddha Ghosal. 'Death by Breath: Construction destruction'. 6 April 2015. *Indian Express*.

52. Joshi, Mallica. 'Half of world's 20 most polluted cities in India, Delhi in 11th position'. 13 May 2016. *Hindustan Times*.

53. 'Govt. in dark on number of construction-related deaths'. 2 January 2012. *Times of India*.

54. These included crushed sand instead of river sand, recycling of aggregates and concrete, introduction of lightweight concrete, self-compacting concrete, use of aluminium H-Beams instead of timber, and Ground Granulated Blast Furnace Slag (GGBS).

55. A sustainable building or green building is the outcome of a design philosophy which focuses on increasing the efficiency of resource use— energy, water and materials—while reducing building impact on human health and the environment during the building's life cycle, through better siting, design, construction, operation, maintenance and removal.

56. Shah, Shashank and Sudhir Bhaskar. 'Natural Environment Management at Larsen & Toubro's ECC Division—A Case Study'. 2010. *Asia Pacific Journal of Management Research and Innovation*, VI:1, pp. 115–121.

57. In February 2016, it was India's first to receive a 'GreenCo Platinum Rating' by the Green Business Centre of Confederation of Indian Industry. The award was evaluated on criteria like implementation of water-saving projects, energy efficiency, utilization of renewable energy, GHG emission, waste management, optimizing the three R's of reduce, reuse and recycle, and a green supply chain.

58. A 2009 McKinsey technical study suggested that instead of the traditional L-1 basis of awarding contracts, where the lowest-price tender gets selected for executing government-funded infrastructure projects, technical consultants should be selected using a quality-cum-cost based approach (QCBA), similar to what other countries follow.

59. Bureau Veritas, headquartered in France, is a global leader in testing inspection and certification.

60. To avoid lax behaviour on the part of suppliers, L&T had a penalty system for late delivery of raw materials. This was deducted through the EIP. To be fair, these were not always charged. When suppliers approached the company requesting a waiver of penalty, the EIP checked the extent to which the delayed delivery affected progress of work. The penalty was levied only when the company heavily suffered or if the supplier had taken L&T for a ride, else it was waived. Given that it was a centralized, computerized process, there was almost no scope for any hanky-panky.

61. In 2014–15, more than 80 per cent of L&T's requirements were met by local suppliers.

62. Though very popular in Europe, leasing of heavy construction equipment started in India only during the last decade.

63. 'L&T bags Rs 5400cr Delhi airport contract'. 11 December 2006. *Times of India.*

64. Sharma, E. Kumar. 'Shaking up the workplace'. 13 March 2016. *Business Today.*

65. Parikh, Daksesh. 'The great gamble'. 22 February 2009. *Business India.*

66. C.R.R. joined the ECC in 1947 and retired as joint managing director of L&T in 1991. A.R. joined the ECC in 1962 and retired in 2004 as deputy managing director of L&T. Rangaswami joined the ECC in 1965 as a junior engineer and retired in 2011 as president of L&T Construction.

67. Dalal, Sucheta. 'A.M. Naik—A rare interview to MoneyLIFE'. 15 September 2008. *Money Life.*

68. This is usually called a 'hockey stick' mechanism, where good performers are paid disproportionately higher pay than others.

69. In his own estimate, Naik was the biggest victim of this change. Between 1965 and 1974, he had the fastest-ever growth in L&T. Yet, between 1974 and 1986, he was the slowest ever to be promoted. He spent six years as deputy general manager and seven years as joint general manager. And during that decade, resistance to change infested L&T culture.

70. *Voices on transformation: Insights from business leaders on creating lasting change.* McKinsey & Company, 2010.

71. Larsen & Toubro Sustainability Report 2009–10.

72. L&T Construction has an independent HR set-up for those verticals that are under its domain. It enjoys a fair level of decentralized decision-making in the HR domain. This chapter focuses on the HR practices of L&T Construction headquartered in Chennai, and not the parent company headquartered in Mumbai. However, there could be certain

overlapping initiatives with the parent organization that have been highlighted in the chapter.

73. Several schemes for induction of trainees included L&T Build India Scholarship Programme at the IITs, Post-Graduate Engineer Trainees, Graduate Engineer Trainees through Campus Recruitment, Diploma Engineer Trainees through Campus Recruitment and Graduate Trainees.

74. Mangaleswaran, Ramesh and Adil Zainulbhai. 'Reinvigorating a corporate giant: Interview with the chairman of India's largest infrastructure company'. March 2011. McKinsey & Company.

75. To know more about training initiatives at L&T, log on to my website: www.shashankshah.com.

76. Vasuki, S.N. (with bureau reports). 'The Ambanis: On the firing line'. 30 April 1990. *India Today*.

77. Chatterjee, Dev. '40 years ago . . . And now: L&T—the graveyard of corporate raiders'. 17 September 2014. *Business Standard*.

78. General Insurance Corporation, Unit Trust of India and Life Insurance Corporation.

79. Dalal, Sucheta. 'A.M. Naik—A rare interview to MoneyLIFE'. 15 September 2008. *Money Life*.

80. Surendar, T. 'L&T Faces Leadership Vacuum'. 24 February 2010. *Forbes India*.

81. An international management consulting firm founded in 1963 and headquartered in Boston, USA.

82. Besides the cement business, L&T was involved in a number of non-core businesses, including shoes, merchant exports, computer peripherals, shipbuilding, ready-mix concrete and many others.

83. Roy, Subir. *Made in India: A Study of Emerging Competitiveness*. New Delhi: Tata McGraw Hill Publishing, 2005.

84. Carvalho, Brian. 'The battle for L&T'. 22 December 2002. *Business Today*.

85. The group's combined installed capacity was augmented to 31 million tonne per annum (of which 17 million came from L&T Cements), making it the eighth-largest cement maker in the world. In October 2004, L&T Cement was renamed Ultra Tech Cement.

86. Dalal, Sucheta. 'A.M. Naik—A rare interview to MoneyLIFE'. 15 September 2008. *Money Life*.

87. 'Restructuring has been a way of life'. 10 August 2009. *Business World*.

88. *ECC Concord*, January–March 2015.

89. Singh, Pritam and Asha Bhandarker. *In Search of Change Maestros*. Sage Publications, 2011.

90. *Ibid.*
91. The government, financial institutions and insurance companies owned 29 per cent; FIIs and GDR owned 19 per cent; individuals owned 23 per cent; mutual funds and private companies owned 14 per cent; and 3 per cent was owned by others.
92. For details on L&T's initiative in integrating IT with HR, log on to my website: www.shashankshah.com.
93. This was based on the opinions of 6310 respondents across companies.
94. Global attrition was much lower at 11.20 per cent.
95. The Bureau of Labor Statistics, USA, reported the fatality rate at 3.3 per 100,000 workforce in 2014.
96. *ECC Concord*, January–March 2015.
97. *ECC Concord*, April–September 2009.
98. 'India's PM Modi visits L&T workers' residential complex in Riyadh'. 2 April 2016. *Eurasia Review.*
99. A.R. passed away in 2013. On Republic Day 2014, the Government of India conferred the Padma Bhushan on him posthumously.
100. Kozami, Azhar. *Business Policy and Strategic Management.* New Delhi: Tata McGraw Hill, 2002.
101. Prashant Gupta et al. *Building India: Accelerating Infrastructure Projects.* McKinsey Company India, August 2009.
102. An American MNC founded in 1892 and headquartered in Connecticut, USA. Considered among the top ten American companies, it had 305,000 employees worldwide and $117 billion in revenue in 2015.
103. Founded in 1847, Siemens is a German MNC headquartered in Berlin and Munich. Considered the largest engineering company in Europe, it had 348,000 employees worldwide and €75 billion in revenue in 2015.
104. A Japanese multinational engineering, electrical equipment and electronic company founded in 1934, and headquartered in Tokyo. In 2011, it had over 80,000 employees and revenue of $35 billion.
105. 'Restructuring has been a way of life'. 10 August 2009. *Business World.*
106. John, Satish. 'Succession at L&T: How India Inc.'s most mysterious succession plan might work out'. 26 February 2012. *Economic Times.*

IV: The Taj Group of Hotels: Atithi Devo Bhava . . . Ambassadors of Indian Hospitality

1.   In an interview to Lovat Fraser, editor of the *Times of India*, who subsequently became a director at IHCL.

2.   Lala, R.M. *For the Love of India: The Life and Times of Jamsetji Tata.*
     Penguin Books India, 2004.
3.   Lala, R.M. *The Creation of Wealth: The Tatas from the 19th to the 21st
     century.* Penguin Books India, 2004.
4.   *Ibid.*
5.   Other firsts by the Taj Mahal Hotel include American fans, German
     elevators, chandelier polishing machines, Turkish baths and English
     butlers. Eventually, it had Bombay's first-ever licensed bar—the Harbour
     Bar—India's first all-day dining restaurant, its first twenty-four-hour
     coffee shop and the first international discotheque.
6.   As per the Tata Group website, The Indian Hotels Company Limited
     (IHCL) and its domestic and international subsidiaries are collectively
     known as the Taj Group. Hence, the chapter has been titled as the Taj
     Group of Hotels and includes the broad range of products and services
     offered by IHCL under various brands, subsidiaries and joint ventures.
     IHCL has been primarily used to denote the company, whereas the
     Taj has been used mostly to focus on the brand, Taj Hotels Resorts and
     Palaces.
7.   Chughanee, Bhakti. 'The grand old lady'. 6–19 January 2003. *Business
     India.*
8.   The Merry Weather Road entrance of the Taj was closed for good.
     Finally, the front side of the hotel on Colaba Causeway became its
     rear side, and the rear side near the Gateway of India became its main
     entrance.
9.   Majumdar, Shyamal. 'The story of Taj'. 17 December 2011. *Business
     Standard.*
10. Allen, Charles and Sharda Dwivedi. *The Taj at Apollo Bunder.* Pictor
     Publishing, 2010.
11. When IHCL first entered Goa in the 1970s, it was still not a prominent
     place on India's tourist map, having just been liberated from Portuguese
     rule in 1961, after 450 years. In the next four decades, tourist growth
     was phenomenal. By 2010, it accounted for 20 lakh tourists every year,
     of which over 10 lakh were international tourists. Thus, it constituted
     about 15 per cent of the total inbound international tourists to India.
12. Law, Vivek. 'Crowning glory'. 24 February 2003. *India Today.*
13. In Kerkar's times, the Taj's remuneration was 15–30 per cent below
     market rates in India.
14. Accordingly, the hotels were classified into three new divisions: luxury,
     business and leisure hotels, and other (international hotels and air
     catering). Each of these divisions, also called strategic business units
     (SBUs), were under the umbrella of the 'Taj' brand. However, they

offered differentiated products and services at varied price points to compete with offerings of international brands in Indian markets.

15. By 2010, it was estimated that China had 30 lakh rooms and USA had 50 lakh rooms.

16. These are approximate figures based on World Bank Data on international tourism and number of arrivals, accessed in June 2016.

17. Many from developed countries tend to look at those with long-standing civilizations as backward and their people as requiring to catch up with the West. This opinion often extends to India, the oldest surviving civilization in the world.

18. This Taj-ness was communicated through two landmark ad campaigns between 1998 and 2005:

   i. The first one was around the theme 'She is the Taj'. It tried to give a human touch and feel to the nonagenarian first lady of Indian hospitality. The ad tag lines were: 'She greets presidents and kings. She also greets you. She treats you like a family. She works with tycoons and chairmen. She is the Taj.' Karambir shared with me that 'She is the Taj' did not refer to the two women walking in sarees throughout the ad. It meant something much deeper—that the Taj itself is alive, it's got a life, a persona and a soul. It was considered one of the most powerful ad campaigns and stuck to the consumers' mind. It was an innovation in that, when for the first time a hotel advertisement came on television, it had more to it than the decor and the food. Each of the landmark Taj properties, such as those in Goa, Kerala, Rajasthan and the Maldives, were showcased with the lady personifying the Taj, pervading each of the properties, thereby symbolizing that the Taj-ness was present in each of the Taj Hotels, whether in India or overseas.

   ii. The second campaign had the theme 'Quintessential Taj'. It focused on diverse aspects of its offerings and guests' expectations from the Taj. Each of the words listed were pre-fixed with the word 'quintessential', indicating that the best place to experience that aspect of life was the Taj, and each of the visuals representing these key words were of different Taj properties across the globe and the kind of experiences that each of them are known for. The words were: fairy tale, business and pleasure, wilderness and civilization, classic and contemporary, meeting, conference and convention, office hours and happy hours, art and culture, occupation and past-time, dream and awakening, sin and temptation, occupation and escape, 19th, 20th and 21st century, address and hotel.

19. 'A much-deserved Padma for Pallonji Mistry'. 26 January 2016. *Business Standard*.

20. Zachariah, Reeba. 'Taj brand is valued at Rs 4000 cr: Ratan Tata'. 18 August 2008. *Economic Times*.

21. This is an indirect example created to communicate the kind of feedback IHCL was receiving from diverse guests over many years.

22. Making a good or service easy to obtain by making it as uniform, plentiful and affordable as possible, and hence interchangeable with those provided by competitors. In simple words, the Taj would become synonymous with five-star luxury hotels, and the brand a common noun. Just like Xerox became synonymous with photocopying and Bisleri became synonymous with mineral water.

23. Gupta, Anjali. 'Outbound travel industry grows, but challenges remain'. 10 February 2016. *Economic Times*.

24. While business travel, holiday and visiting friends and relatives (VFR) trips dominated outbound volumes, people were also opting for niche products like sports tourism, luxury travels, meetings/conferences, honeymoon packages and cruises.

25. The e-tourist visa scheme for India, introduced in 2015 by the Modi government, available across 150 countries and at sixteen airports in India, would play a key role in attracting a much larger number of international tourists to India.

26. Khandari, Timmy and Sandeep Ladda. 'Hospitality Insights from the Indian CEO's desk'. February 2012. *PWC–CII Report*.

27. The study used the National Council of Applied Economic Research (NCAER) data, and defined real annual household disposable income as between Rs 2–10 lakh.

28. Jonathan Ablett et al. 'The "Bird of Gold": The Rise of India's Consumer Market'. May 2007. *McKinsey Global Institute Report*.

29. Like the Arabs in the 1970s, the Japanese in the 1980s, the Russians in the 1990s and the Chinese in the 2000s, Indians will reach an impressive scale by 2025.

30. Founded in 1941 and headquartered in San Francisco, it has been a pioneer in the research, design and consulting methods of the branding industry.

31. Where the core Taj brand was like the sun, the other brands were like planets revolving around the main brand. The distance of the other brands from the sun was indicative of the similarities or differences with the Taj brand.

32. The competition for this category was from luxury hotels belonging to the Oberoi, Leela, Peninsula, JW Marriott, Ritz-Carlton, St Regis, Fairmont, Grand Hyatt and Four Seasons.

33. The competition for this brand category would be from the Trident, Westin, Hilton, Le Méridien, Radisson Blu and Marriott.

34. To cater to the tech-savvy, on-the-move guests, Vivanta's mobile application was launched in 2015 across all OS platforms including Apple IOS, Windows, Blackberry 10 and Android.

35. The competition for this brand category would be from brands such as Lemon Tree, Double Tree by Hilton, Four Points by Sheraton, Hilton Garden Inn, Hyatt Place, Movenpick and Courtyard by Marriott.

36. *Our Essence, Our Evolution.* A Taj Group Publication.

37. The idea of the budget hotel was not a direct outcome of the rebranding exercise. It had started to take shape during the years of Krishna Kumar as MD, who proactively collaborated with Professor C.K. Prahalad (from the University of Michigan, USA) for ideation and implementation. The competition for this brand category would be from brands such as Hotel Formule1, Travelodge Hotel, Home Inn, Premier Inn and Super 8.

38. Dutta, Prosenjit (Ed.). 'The Ginger chain—smart business at work'. 2010. Innovation: Making Aspirations Count, *Businessworld.*

39. 'Ginger wins "Best Budget Hotel Chain" in India award at SATTE'. 30 April 2009. *Business Standard.*

40. To ensure uniformity in delivery, full training manuals were prepared for each of the brands, so that every time a new hotel is acquired or built, all employees are trained according to the brand standards. Each of these was benchmarked with the best in the world belonging to that category/star status. The initial challenge was convincing employees who were used to working only with the 'Taj' brand to now work with a 'Gateway'. Slowly, changes did percolate to the grassroots. The senior management within the properties were retained to a large extent to implement the transition to a new brand, and salaries of managers were kept at parity across all four brands. This ensured that the rebranding exercise did not affect the earning prospects of senior employees.

41. This multi-branding also enabled IHCL to have maximum wallet-share from corporate clients, as it could cater to the diverse requirements of every company. Furthermore, as customers grow in age or in standard of living, they could indulge in aspirational purchasing and go up the ladder from Ginger to Gateway to Vivanta to Taj.

42. Chacko, Philip. 'Jewel in the Chennai Crown'. January 2011. *Tata Review*.

43. The study surveyed over 10,000 consumers across sixteen cities and covered over 1400 brands from more than 100 categories.

44. Founded in 1923 and headquartered in New York, Y&R is an internationally renowned marketing and communications company.

45. Brands that have the potential to break away from the pack and successfully differentiate themselves from their peers are called 'breakaway brands'.

46. 'Taj Group of Hotels leads breakaway brand category in Y&R study'. 18 February 2014. *The Hindu Business Line*.

47. 'Taj ties up with Korean group'. 7 March 2006. *Business Standard*.

48. 'Taj inks marketing pact with Okura Hotels of Japan'. 5 September 2007. *Economic Times*.

49. In simple words, source markets are international geographies from where the Taj gets its major customers.

50. Padmanabhan, Anil. 'Tata buy in NYC'. 20 June 2005. *India Today*.

51. In spite of lower market share, IHCL had a revenue share of 20 per cent indicating that guests were willing to pay higher prices for the Taj offerings and brand.

52. With the number of hotel rooms in India tipped to expand to 500,000 rooms, IHCL aimed at expanding its base to 50,000 rooms in order to maintain its market share at 10–12 per cent. Bickson had recommended a de-risking strategy to Ratan Tata. He suggested that IHCL make the most of the synchronicity of international markets, especially when the hospitality industry was cyclical in nature and the slightest of perturbations in some part of the world due to natural or manmade calamities badly affected tourism, and hence the hospitality industry. For example Egypt, where 40 per cent of the economy was dependent on tourism. But the Arab Spring affected the number of incoming tourists, and the economy suffered.

53. Mithas, Sunil. *Making the Elephant Dance: The Tata Way to Innovate Transform and Globalize*. Penguin Books India, 2015.

54. Menon, Sangeeta. 'Transforming to meet the future'. January 2013. *Tata Review*.

55. The award recognizes Tata companies that achieve high scores in the Tata quality framework called the Tata Business Excellence Model (TBEM).

56. Layak, Suman. 'How the Indian Hotels Company Ltd is counting on a new strategy to put its house in order'. 5 August 2015. *Economic Times*.

57. During our conversation, Bickson had emphasized the multiplier effect of investments in the travel and tourism industry to the larger economy. If India increased its investments in this industry from the current 6–7 per cent to the global average of 10–12 per cent, the industry had the potential of creating 1.5 crore additional jobs and adding Rs 4500 crore to the economy every year.

58. India ranked third in the world in terms of anticipated growth in travel and tourism's total contribution to GDP, expected at an annual rate of 7.5 per cent between 2016 and 2026. The total contribution of travel and tourism to the Indian GDP in 2015 was 18.36 lakh-crore (7.2 per cent of GDP by 2026). For the same decade, the world average was 4 per cent and the Asia-Pacific was 5.6 per cent.

59. With this focus, in 2016, IHCL sold a 6 per cent stake in British luxury hospitality group Belmond Ltd (formerly Orient Express Hotels) for Rs 82 crore.

60. 'At Indian Hotels, CEO Sarna has a room with clear view'. 21 April 2015. *Economic Times*.

61. 'Tajness: Experience Indian tradition at its best'. 6 August 2016. *Indian Express*.

62. The hotel and room inventory statistics across the chapter are from the corporate presentation May 2016, accessed on the company website in June 2016.

63. An area comprising six states of northeastern USA, which were among the first to be inhabited by settlers from Europe.

64. During our conversation, Bickson gave the example of how a Taj loyalty card can be used to provide customized guest experiences when a regular customer arrives at the reception of any of its properties. Through such a data-centric approach, the hotel can arrange for all that he or she needs by the time the customer settles down in their room. For example, providing two foam pillows because the guest is allergic to feather pillows. Providing preferred newspapers in the morning when he or she wakes up; and a gluten-free diet instead of a regular menu. Technology would be the key to customizing client service.

65. Located in the centre of Lake Pichola, the Taj Lake Palace was formerly a pleasure palace called Jag Niwas built by Maharana Jagat Singh II in 1743. It was restored as the Taj Lake Palace Hotel in 1963.

66. The Rambagh Palace was home of the Jaipur royalty until 1957, when the royal family decided to convert it into a luxury hotel. It has gone

through many transitions since 1835 when it was a simple garden house. By early 1900s, it became the principle residence of Maharajah Sawai Man Singh II. In 2009, it was rated as the world's best hotel by *Conde Nast Traveller* magazine.

67. Home of the erstwhile Jodhpur royal family, it is currently the world's sixth-largest private residence. It was constructed between 1929 and 1943 by Maharaja Umaid Singh to provide employment to the famine-stricken populace of Jodhpur. Part of the palace continues to be the residence of the royal family. In January 2016, it bagged the award for world's best hotel at the Travellers' Choice Award organized by TripAdvisor.

68. Built between 1884 and 1893, the Falaknuma Palace (meaning the 'mirror of the sky') was the residence of the Nizam of Hyderabad until 1948.

69. For example, the Falaknuma Palace underwent renovation for nearly a decade under the guidance of Princess Esra Jah, first wife of the VIIIth Nizam of Hyderabad.

70. Harper, Andrew. 'Taj Falaknuma Palace: A new experience of palatial splendor'. 17 October 2012. *Forbes*.

71. IHCL's spa brand is available at thirty-three luxury hotels across the group.

72. The Taj rates were driven on differentiation and at a premium of about 20 per cent as compared to its competitors.

73. To know more about how IHCL gained commercial success through technology and innovation, log on to my website: www.shashankshah. com.

74. Refers to the 'Parable of the Good Samaritan', a story narrated by Jesus in the Christian Gospel of Luke that encourages people to help others that are in need and danger.

75. Companies like Tata Consultancy Services (TCS) had an employee base of over 3,50,000, and annually hired 15,000 fresh recruits. 'How do they take these fresh kids just out of college, and what do they put them through to work in a foreign country? What kind of language, skills, cultural and work ethics-related training can be provided such that they imbibe the cultural sensitivities?' Bickson observed. Thus, the opportunity for innovation at IHCL could be through fast-tracking of training facilities such that new people can be brought into its culture of service.

76. 'MiUniversity', IHCL's e-learning platform provided its employees with more than 300 courses ranging from operational to managerial

areas, from universities like Harvard and Cornell, along with the American Hotel & Lodging Educational Institute.

77. Noronha, Christabelle. 'People are our most important asset'. November 2015. *Tata Review.*

78. These are used for measuring psychological variables such as intelligence, aptitude and personality traits.

79. Deshpande, Rohit and Anjali Raina. 'The Ordinary Heroes of the Taj'. December 2011. *Harvard Business Review.*

80. Deshpande, Rohit and Anjali Raina. 'How Taj trains its ordinary heroes'. 27 November 2011. *Economic Times.*

81. Shirin provided a historical perspective to training at IHCL. In the early 1970s, the hotel did not have a formal training programme. Yet, on-the-job training was imparted. Great emphasis was paid to developing chefs. Those were the years of severe shortage of foreign exchange in India, and getting a foreign chef to India to impart training was next to impossible. In spite of this, two chefs from the Taj were sent every year to well-known hotels in Germany, France and England to work and train for a year each. The same was true of teams of GMs and food and beverage (F&B) managers, who were sent to the best hotels in the Far East to stay and study practices. The team would stay in different hotels in the city so as to get maximum exposure to their systems and practices. These were then compiled, analysed and implemented in the Taj.

The Taj's tie-up with InterContinental Hotels helped. When the Apollo Bar opened in 1974, the hotel got a German bar manager to train the barman and the staff. Often, food promotions were held with other InterContinental Hotels, where a team went to host Indian food. During this period, they got the opportunity to learn the cuisine of that particular country. These promotions were reciprocal, so the hotel in India also hosted international food promotions. The Taj also hosted world-renowned three-star Michelin chefs as early as 1975, starting with the great Paul Bocuse. Many more like Michel Roux and Anton Mossiman followed.

82. 'Taj Hotels: icon of hospitality'. 16 August 2010. *People Matters.*

83. Deshpande, Rohit and Anjali Raina. 'The Ordinary Heroes of the Taj'. December 2011. *Harvard Business Review.*

84. Robinson, Jennifer. 'How 24,000 Employees Worldwide Keep One Brand Promise'. 24 September, 2013. *Gallup Business Journal.*

85. To know more about IHCL's award-winning rewards systems and its unique approach to employee engagement and well-being, log on to my website: www.shashankshah.com.

86. Kamath, Gayatri. 'A century of service, style and substance'. October 2013. *Tata Review*.

87. The Taj is like how Levers is in marketing. Anybody from the Taj could possibly walk out and get a job with four times their current salary. And not just in the hospitality industry, but also at banks, call centres and many other service sector companies. In spite of that, many people continue to work at the company for long years. And this was despite the fact that the Taj used to pay salaries quite below market price. For example, when Karambir was the GM at Lands End, the hotel wage cost was 9 per cent of the turnover. The industry standard in India was 18–20 per cent, whereas in developed countries like USA, it was 40 per cent. That has changed over the years, and the Taj has raised its remuneration to almost industry standards. But even in those years, compared to the hospitality industry with attrition rates of about 30 per cent, IHCL's attrition rate was 18 per cent. In 2015, IHCL's turnover was 17.96 per cent, of which 70 per cent was in the age group between twenty-two and twenty-nine years.

88. Delong, Thomas and Vineeta Vijayaraghavan. 'Taj Hotel Group'. Boston: Harvard Business School Publishing, 9–403–004, October 2002.

89. 'Obama praises India's resilience, strength after attacks'. 6 November 2010. *Economic Times*.

90. Founded in 1987 by Hafiz Muhammad Saeed, LeT is one of the largest terrorist organizations in South Asia, headquartered in Muridke near Lahore in Pakistan. It is banned by USA, the UK, the European Union and many other developed countries of the world, and sanctioned by the United Nations since 2008.

91. Built to commemorate the arrival of King George V and Queen Mary at Apollo Bunder in 1911.

92. Levy, Adrian and Cathy Scott-Clark. *The Siege: 68 Hours inside the Taj Hotel*. Penguin Books India, 2013.

93. *Conde Nast Traveller*—UK Reader's Travel Awards 2008.

94. It was established in 1932 by Sir Dorab Tata, the elder son of Jamsetji Tata. It is among the oldest philanthropic organizations in India, started with the prime purpose of encouraging learning and research and of meeting the costs of relief during crises and calamities, besides carrying out worthwhile charitable activities.

95. It was established in 1918 following the death of Sir Ratan Tata, the younger son of Jamsetji Tata. It operates in accordance with his will and gives grants to institutions in the areas of rural livelihood and

communities, education, enhancing civil society and governance, health and arts and culture.

96.   'Indian Hotels forms the Taj Public Service Welfare Trust'. 15 December 2008. *Tata Group Media Release.*

97.   Since then, the trust has supported rehabilitation efforts during the 13/7 Mumbai bomb blasts, Bihar fire and cyclone, Ladakh cloud burst, Sunderbans flood, Uttarakhand cloud burst and the Jammu and Kashmir cloud burst.

98.   Mahanta, Vinod and Nandini Raghavendra. 'Rebuilding scarred lives, the Tata way'. 26 November 2009. *Economic Times.*

99.   Mahajan, Nupur. 'Taj ka raj'. 5 April 2009. *Business India.*

100. Bickson, Raymond. 'Our hotel was attacked'. 7 February 2009. *New York Times.*

101. Post 26/11, IHCL constituted a Crisis Management Advisory Team at the enterprise level and crisis management teams at the hotel level. All hotels are assessed by an external agency for security risks, and the crisis management teams deploy emergency preparedness/crisis management plans that are periodically tested and updated based on national and international security alerts.

102. Seth, Urvashi, Vibhute, Kranti and Vinod Kumar Menon. 'Mumbaikars celebrate with Obama'. 8 November 2012. *Mid-Day.*

103. The eight Millennium Development Goals (MDGs) ranging from halving extreme poverty rates to halting the spread of HIV/AIDS and providing universal primary education, all by the target date of 2015, formed a blueprint agreed to by 189 member countries and twenty-three leading international development institutions at the United Nations Millennium Summit in 2000.

104. This was a set of ten ideas that Prime Minister Manmohan Singh shared in his address at the annual general meeting of the Confederation of Indian Industry on 24 May 2007.

105. *Travel and Tourism Economic Impact 2016: India.* World Travel and Tourism Council Report.

106. Menon, Sangeeta. 'A hospitable future'. October 2013. *Tata Review.*

107. Since 2009, over 12,000 youth had received such training in hospitality-related fields, through forty-two skill development centres. Over 90 per cent got jobs, while the remaining pursued higher studies or started their own venture. The CS team observed that advertisements brought in only 30 per cent of candidates into the training centres. More than 70 per cent came through word of mouth. The large numbers were hence proof of the beneficiaries' positive experience. Among the

NGO partners were Pratham, Don Bosco and the Industrial Training Institutes (ITIs) of the Government of India.

108. John, Reji. 'Taj's Rs 2 meal feeds 1.5 lakh children'. February 2010. *Financial Chronicle*.

109. Interestingly, there was a 13 per cent rise in the number of children attending the Anganwadis as compared to the baseline. The Bhavishya Alliance, a facilitating agency for mother and child care, is formed by leading corporate houses including HUL, HDFC, ICICI and Tata Group. This programme trained 12,000 SHG workers and local women in cooking, cash management and hygienic practices to ensure that the project was sustainable.

110. Launched in January 2015 with an initial corpus of Rs 100 crore by Prime Minister Narendra Modi, this programme, literally meaning 'Save the girl child, educate the girl child', is a Government of India scheme aimed at generating awareness and improving the efficiency of women's welfare services.

111. Kohli, Namita. 'Washed clean and ironed out'. 13 April 2008. *Hindustan Times*.

112. Sharma, Garima and David Hyatt. 'Taj Hotels: Building Sustainable Livelihoods'. October 2013. Canada: Ivey Publishing, 9B13C032.

113. Sengupta, Anuradha. 'On a clean sheet'. 27 May 2016. *The Hindu Business Line*.

114. Vora, Shivani. 'For Indian weavers in Varanasi, help for an endangered craft'. 17 July 2015. *New York Times*.

115. Considered among the finest silk sarees in India, and a must for most brides during their wedding, they are known for their heavy, intricate designs and rich colours. Historically practiced since over 500 years, this craft currently provides employment to over 12 lakh weavers. In 2009, the weavers of six districts of Uttar Pradesh secured Geographic Indication Rights (a kind of Intellectual Property Right) for 'Banaras Brocades and Sarees'.

116. Rodrigues, Cynthia. 'A net spread wide'. October 2013. *Tata Review*.

117. To know more about IHCL's successful approach to integrating environmental concerns with its core hospitality focus, log on to the my website: www.shashankshah.com.

118. Nohria, Nitin, Mayo, Anthony and Mark Benson. 'J.R.D. Tata'. April 2014. Boston: HBS Publishing, 9–407–061.

119. While I have personally interviewed the senior executive who shared this experience first-hand, he did not wish to be identified, and hence the name hasn't been mentioned.

120. Witzel, Morgen. *Tata: The Evolution of a Corporate Brand.* Penguin Books India, 2010.

121. 'Tata's Nano catches world's most powerful man's eyes'. 7 November 2010. *Economic Times.*

V: Hindustan Unilever: Doing Well by Doing Good

1. D. Sundaram served as vice chairman and CFO of HUL from 1999 to 2009. Since July 2009, he serves as the vice chairman and managing director of TVS Capital Funds Ltd.

2. Fieldhouse, David. *Unilever Overseas.* London: Croom Helm Publishers, 1978.

3. By 2016, Unilever held about 67.25 per cent equity in the company. The rest of the shareholding was distributed among 329,534 individual shareholders and financial institutions in India.

4. W.G. Shaw (1944–47), C.S. Petitt (1947–53), A.J. Hoskyns-Abrahall (1953–57) and S.H. Turner (1957–61).

5. Jones, Geoffrey and Stephanie Decker. 'Unilever as a "Multi-Local Multinational", 1945–1979'. November 2010. Boston: Harvard Business School Publishing, 9808025.

6. Jones, Geoffrey. *Renewing Unilever: Transformation and Tradition.* New York: Oxford University Press, 2005.

7. Clinic-shampoo was launched in 1971, Liril soap and talc in 1974, Close-up toothpaste in 1975 and Fair & Lovely skin cream in 1978.

8. Brooke Bond was an independent manufacturer of tea, established in 1845 in Lancashire, England by Arthur Brooke.

9. An internationally renowned name in cosmetics, the 'T.T. Pond Company' was formed in the United States in 1846. The company merged with the Chesebrough Manufacturing Company in 1955.

10. The Government of India's policy requiring elaborate licences, regulations and the accompanying red tape to set up and run businesses in India between 1947 and 1990.

11. Tata Group is a century-old Indian multinational conglomerate company with ninety-six operating companies in seven major sectors and one of the largest conglomerates in India by market capitalization and revenue.

12. A leading brand of jams, ketchups and squashes.

13. An Indian conglomerate company with core businesses that include brewing, distilling, real estate, engineering, fertilizers, biotechnology, information technology and aviation.

14. A leading Indian ice cream brand.
15. The Indian subsidiary of the confectionary market leader, Cadbury, based out of London, and taken over by Kraft Foods in 2010.
16. A market leader in the Indian cosmetics industry.
17. Johnson, Mark. *Seizing the White Space: Business Model Innovation for Growth and Renewal.* Harvard Business Press, 2010.
18. Peng, Mike. *Global Business.* Ohio: South-Western Cengage Learning, 2011.
19. A 2007 *Economic Times* report mentioned that HUL had spent over Rs 20 crore to hire McKinsey to create the new ventures blueprint. Over 40–50 top-notch managers were handpicked for the new ventures unit. By February 2007, CEO Doug Baille shut down its new ventures division conceived in 2000 under the Millennium Plan and housed the five businesses (worth Rs 450 crore) within the mainline business. These included Project Shakti, Ayush Therapy Centres (chain of Ayurvedic clinics), Hindustan Lever Network (direct selling/network marketing venture), Sangam (e-tailing business) and Pureit Water Purifiers.
20. Project Shakti has been sufficiently documented through multipart, longitudinal studies and cases by leading international business schools including Harvard, MIT, Ross and IMD. Hence, it has not been discussed in detail in this chapter.
21. Although Project Sangam met many of its business milestones successfully, HUL did not consider it a part of its core strategy to be present in organized retail. Further, the manpower and transportation costs associated with the Sangam model affected margins and hence, the sustainability of the business. Thus, in April 2007, HUL sold its Sangam business to the Wadhawan Group.
22. Amway India, a subsidiary of the US-based, US$ 11.3-billion Amway Corporation, started operations in India in 1998. Amway India retails its products through 'Amway Business Owners' or ABOs, and has provided income-generating opportunities to over 15 lakh active, independent entrepreneurs. The company runs 149 offices and has sixty-five warehouses with a strong distribution network reaching out to over 10,000 PIN codes across 4000 cities/towns in the country. In 2012–13, it posted sales of Rs 2228 crore.
23. A part of the K.K. Modi Group, Modicare was started in 1996. By 2013, it had 1.5 lakh distributors and fifty centres across India that supplied its 200 products to over 2700 cities. In 2012–13, its sales were nearly Rs 100 crore.

24. In 2016, it had active partners across 500 towns and cities and was backed by thirty offices across India.

25. In the *Economic Times* 2014 'most trusted brands of India', sixteen of the 100 were HUL brands. These included (with ranks in parentheses): Lux (6), Surf Excel (7), Clinic Plus (8), Rin (13), Lifebuoy (15), Close-up (21), Pond's (22), Pepsodent (24), Fair & Lovely (29), Dove (30), Sunsilk (34), Vim (48), Wheel (67), Vaseline (70), Pears (78) and Lakme (91).

26. HUL Annual Report 2008–09.

27. *Equitymaster-Stockselect Report on Hindustan Unilever Ltd.* 5 April 2012. Equitymaster India.

28. Roy, Saumya. 'Pure water, dirty linen'. August 2009. *Forbes*.

29. Sharma, E. Kumar. 'Liquid riches'. 27 June 2010. *Business Today*.

30. In 2016, Yuri Jain was global vice president at Unilever, leading the company's global water purification business.

31. Rangan, V. Kasturi and Mona Sinha. 'Hindustan Unilever's "Pureit" Water Purifier'. April 2013. Boston: Harvard Business School Publishing, 9511067.

32. 'HUL to launch Pureit in Latin America and Africa'. 15 November 2010. *Economic Times*.

33. Anthony, Scott. 'How to prepare for the fourth era of innovation'. 30 August 2012. Co. Design.

34. This case has been compiled from multiple sources and documents available in the public domain. Prominent among them are two well-written case studies: Buttler, Charlotte and Sumantra Ghosal. 'Hindustan Unilever Limited: Levers for Change'. 2002. INSEAD Euro Asia Center, Fontainebleau, France, 3021991; and Werhane, Patricia, Ahmad, Pia Sabharwal and Jenny Mead. 'Hindustan Lever Limited and Project STING (A), (B), (C) and (D)'. April 2010. Darden Business Publishing, University of Virginia, UVA-E-0266, 0267, 0268, 0269.

35. London, Ted and Maulin Vakil. 'Hindustan Lever at the Base of the Pyramid'. November 2006. WDI Publishing, University of Michigan, W86C04.

36. Hart, Stuart L., Prahalad, C.K. and S. Ramachander. 'The Concept of Marketing Insight: Linking Innovation to Business Goals'. 1998. International Conference on Corporate Marketing Communication, University of Strathclyde.

37. The proportion has remained the same over four decades. In 2015, for net sales of Rs 30,171 crore, HUL's advertising and promotion expense was Rs 3875 crore.

38. Media mix refers to the various advertising channels through which a company communicates with its audience in order to fulfil a campaign as outlined in the media plan. Generally, a media mix includes radio, TV, print and online advertising endeavours.

39. In marketing strategy, cannibalization refers to a reduction in sales volume, sales revenue or market share of one product as a result of the introduction of a new product by the same producer.

40. A 2007 study published in the *MIT Sloan Review* highlighted similar innovative advertising campaigns that HUL undertook for building brand awareness in personal care products. In their article on 'Strategic Innovation at the Base of the Pyramid', co-authors Anderson and Markides noted that 'HUL made widespread use of street performers— magicians, singers, dancers and actors, adjusting their scripts and acts based on the clientele the company wants to reach. Following a series of street performances in northeast India, HUL saw public awareness of its low-priced shampoo soap 'Breeze 2-in-1' rise from 22 to 30 per cent.'

41. Warsia, Noor Fathima. 'Unilever's Kan Khajura Tesan redefines mobile innovation in India'. 16 June 2014. *Digital Market Asia Case Studies*.

42. Pinto, Viveat Susan. 'Rural radio plays HUL's new tune of invention'. 19 June 2014. *Business Standard*.

43. Encarnation, Dennis. *Dislodging Multinationals: India's Strategy in Comparative Perspectives*. New York: Cornell University Press, 1989.

44. HUL also developed new chemical processes for relying on Indian lemongrass oil for perfumes.

45. Behrman, Jack and William Fischer. *Overseas R&D Activities of Transnational Companies*. Cambridge, MA: Gunn & Hain, 1980.

46. HUL Annual Report 2011.

47. In 2012, Leena went on to head leadership and organization development as senior vice president at Unilever at the London headquarters. In March 2016, she was appointed as the first woman chief HR officer at Unilever.

48. The 2001 Gujarat earthquake struck the Kutch district of Gujarat on 26 January and measured 7.7 in the moment magnitude scale. Over 13,800 people were killed, 167,000 injured and 400,000 homes destroyed.

49. A separatist outfit operating in Assam since 1990.

50. Singh, Gurdeep. 'Values that Endure'. *Hamara, The Hindustan Unilever Employee Magazine*. (A special issue to mark the seventy-five years of HUL.)

51. In 2003, D. Shivakumar (head of HLL's Haircare Division) left the company to become senior vice president at Philips India. He later

became the managing director of Nokia India, and in 2013, the chairman and CEO for Pepsico India.

52. In 2005, Uday Chander Khanna (formerly director of Exports) left HLL to become the managing director and CEO of Lafarge India Pvt. Ltd. Subsequently, in 2011, he became the non-executive chairman of Bata India.

53. Anand Krupalu (former general sales manager of Detergents) left HLL to become the managing director of Cadbury India. Subsequently, he became the CEO and managing director of United Spirits Ltd.

54. V.S. Sitaram (marketing controller) left HLL in 2005 to become executive director at Dabur India. In 2010, he left Dabur India as the chief operating officer to start his own venture.

55. Menon Carroll, Arati. 'Hindustan Unilever: the CEO factory'. 12 September 2008. *Economic Times*.

56. Vijayraghavan, Kala. 'HUL is dream employer at campuses again'. 8 February 2010. *Economic Times*.

57. Shah, Shashank, Sankar, Ajith and David Sharp. 'Hindustan Unilever Ltd: Meeting Employee Expectations'. December 2013. Ivey Publishing, Canada, W13532.

58. Singh, Namrata. 'People leave bosses, not organizations'. 5 July 2011. *Times of India*.

59. Menon Carroll, Arati. 'Hindustan Unilever: The CEO factory'. 12 September 2008. *Economic Times*.

60. With effect from 2001, HUL has a unique Stock Grant Scheme (SGS) that is linked to the share performance of both HUL and the parent company, Unilever PLC. This scheme covers all current HUL directors, managers and management trainees. Fresh recruits in the management cadre too were entitled to it from their very first year with the company.

61. To know more about how HUL training aims at ingraining leadership, log on to my website: www.shashankshah.com.

62. Malviya, Sagar. 'The crorepati club: 169 executives of HUL, most below 40, drew 8-digit salaries last year'. 20 July 2015. *Economic Times*.

63. Raje, Aparna. 'Designed for Leverage'. 3 February 2010. *Live Mint*.

64. To know more about HUL's handling of the mercury leak at their Kodaikanal factory, log on to my website: www.shashankshah.com.

VI: Bharat Petroleum Corporation: A Real Ratna . . . Redefining Public Sector Performance

1. Modak, Shrikant. 'High-octane-heads-all'. October 29–November 11 2001. *Business India*.

2. There are three kinds of retail outlet dealership:
   i. COCO: Company-Owned Company-Operated Outlets; the officers running the COCO outlets are BPCL employees.
   ii. CC: Company-controlled outlets where the company owns immovable assets (land, building, etc.); the working capital is provided by the franchisee/dealer.
   iii. DC: Dealer-controlled outlets where the dealer owns immovable assets; the dispensing unit belongs to the company.

   BPCL has about 300 COCO outlets. Among the others, nearly 80 per cent are CC and 20 per cent are DC.

3. Dutt, Rimin. '7 Indian firms are on this year's "Fortune 500" list compared to over 100 from China'. 22 July 2016. *Huffington Post*.

4. In 1997, the Government of India identified nine Public Sector Enterprises (PSEs) and gave them the title 'Navratna', literally meaning 'nine gems'. As a result, these companies were given comparative advantages, which allowed them greater autonomy to compete in the global market. The Navratna companies could invest up to Rs 1000 crore without explicit government approval. By 2016, the number of PSEs having Navratna status increased to seventeen. These included: Bharat Electronics Limited, Bharat Petroleum Corporation Limited, Container Corporation of India Limited, Engineers India Limited, Hindustan Aeronautics Limited, Hindustan Petroleum Corporation Limited, Mahanagar Telephone Nigam Limited, National Aluminium Company Limited, National Buildings Construction Corporation Limited, NMDC Limited, Neyveli Lignite Corporation Limited, Oil India Limited, Power Finance Corporation Limited, Power Grid Corporation of India Limited, Rashtriya Ispat Nigam Limited, Rural Electrification Corporation Limited and Shipping Corporation of India Limited.

5. They are a class of institutions/companies established by the Government of India under its various ministries to undertake commercial activities in various industries on its behalf. The majority stake (51 per cent or more) in such organizations is held by the government. In many cases, the entity is 100 per cent owned by the Government of India. By 2015, the Government of India administered and controlled over 250 PSEs. Each of these was headquartered primarily in the capital city of a state or the Central capital. The important indicators to measure the performance of PSEs are their share in India's GDP, in gross domestic capital formation, total employment in PSEs and prices deflator for the sector. This share increased from 10 per cent in 1970s to 25 per cent by 1991. By 2011, PSEs accounted for one-fifth of the total GDP.

6. During the same twenty-year period, investments in its competitor HPCL's stocks provided a return of Rs 9.13 lakh. IOCL's stocks provided a return of Rs 7.21 lakh, which was even below the Sensex returns.

7. Royal Dutch Petroleum was a Netherlands-based company founded in 1890. It was merged with the UK-based Shell Transport and Trading Company (founded in 1897) in 1907 to form Royal Dutch Shell PLC with its registered office in London. It is one among the six largest oil and gas companies in the world.

8. A US-based company founded in 1870. It was the world's largest refinery for nearly four decades when in 1911, the US Supreme Court declared it an illegal monopoly. The company was then transformed into ESSO (now Exxon) and SO (now Chevron).

9. The Burmah Oil company was founded in 1886 and headquartered in Glasgow in Scotland. In the year 2000 it was acquired by British Petroleum (now BP).

10. The Oil and Natural Gas Corporation Ltd (ONGC) is India's largest oil and gas exploration and production company. It produces more than two-thirds of the country's oil and gas. Founded in 1956, it is headquartered in Dehradun, and is under the administrative control of the ministry of petroleum and natural gas, Government of India.

11. Oil India Ltd (OIL) is the second largest hydrocarbon exploration and production company in India. A Navratna company, OIL is under the administrative control of the ministry of petroleum and natural gas, Government of India.

12. Owen, Roger. 'One Hundred Years of Middle Eastern Oil'. January 2008. Crown Center for Middle East Studies, Brandeis University, USA, Middle East Brief No. 24.

13. Sanyal, Santanu. 'Digboi, 100, still alive and kicking'. 17 December 2001. *The Hindu Business Line*.

14. IOCL is the largest OMC in India with nearly 50 per cent market share in petroleum products, one-third share in refining capacity and nearly 60 per cent ownership of downstream pipelines. By 2016, it was the largest public corporation in India in terms of revenue (Rs 4.45 lakh-crore) and the world's 161st largest corporation as per the Fortune 500 list. It has been conferred the Maharatna status by the Government of India.

15. Chaudhury, Saumitra. 'Nationalization of oil companies'. 5 March 1977. *Economic and Political Weekly*, 12:10.

16. Founded in 1912, Esso is a trade name for ExxonMobil and related companies that were earlier called Standard Oil. ExxonMobil was

formed in 1999 out of the merger between Exxon (formerly Standard Oil Company of New Jersey) and Mobil (formerly Standard Oil Company of New York). Headquartered in Irving, Texas (USA), it is among the largest six global oil and gas companies.

17. The petroleum brand name of Chevron Corporation, a US-based multinational energy company. Founded in 1879 as the Pacific Coast Oil Company, Chevron Corporation (formed in 1984) is headquartered in San Ramon, California (USA). It is among the largest six global oil and gas companies.

18. The price at which subsidiaries or divisions of one MNC in different parts of the world sell goods and services to each other. Though not illegal in itself, it is often used by MNCs to artificially distort the prices of products and services to minimize overall tax liability.

19. Chaudhury, Saumitra. 'Nationalization of oil companies'. 5 March 1977. *Economic and Political Weekly*, 12:10.

20. An organic rock from which liquid hydrocarbons called shale oil can be produced.

21. Noel Machado et al. 'Bharat Petroleum's Upstream Strategy and Exploration Success'. February 2014. Canada: Ivey Publishing,W13574.

22. Among the top three OMCs in India and a fierce competitor of BPCL, HPCL is headquartered in Mumbai. Conferred the Navratna Status, it is a Forbes 2000 and Global Fortune 500 company.

23. Simultaneously, through the Burmah Shell Acquisition of Undertakings in India Act, 1976, the government also acquired the right, title and interest and liabilities of BSM in relation to its undertakings in India for a consideration of Rs 27.75 crore. By notification dated 24 January 1976, it vested the same in BSR without any specific consideration payable by BSR.

24. There were major differences in the culture and style of management among the three PSE OMCs. So integrating them into one organization was an extremely difficult proposition. Furthermore, in 1976 the Damle Commission, appointed by the Government of India, recommended that the entities be kept separate for strategic security. If one created a monolith, the country could be held to ransom. The Government of India, under Prime Minister Atal Bihari Vajpayee, had again explored the possibility of merging PSE oil companies. Once again in 2005, the Government of India set up a committee led by V. Krishnamurthy to explore the possibility of consolidating all PSE oil companies. But the committee recommended status quo under the given circumstances. In 2016, nearly forty years after nationalization, the Government of India,

under Prime Minister Narendra Modi, began consultations to explore a plan to merge thirteen PSE oil firms to create an integrated oil giant consisting of upstream, midstream and downstream activities. Such a company would dwarf the global oil majors and would emerge as India's largest corporation in terms of sales, profits and market capitalization. These would include ONGC, OIL, IOCL, BPCL and HPCL among others.

25. Instituted in 1969, it intended to curb monopolistic practices and the concentration of wealth in the hands of a few. It was repealed in 2009. The Competition Act, a modified version of the MRTP Act, was passed in 2000.

26. Shah, Shashank and V.E. Ramamoorthy. *Soulful Corporations: A Values-Based Perspective to Corporate Social Responsibility*. Springer India, 2013.

27. Ramachandran, J. and Vani Venkatesh. 'Shaping the Destiny of a Public Sector Enterprise: In conversation with Ashok Sinha'. December 2006. *IIMB Management Review*.

28. Diwan, Parag and Debesh Patra. *Where is Oil in National Reforms*. Excel Books India, 2008.

29. To understand the APM system better refer to the article: 'Administered price mechanism in oil sector: bane or boon? How does APM work in India?' by Pradeep Puri, published in *Business Standard*, 20 May 1997.

30. From the 1970s–2002, the APM system operated in the Indian oil and gas sector. Under this system, the sector was controlled at four stages: production, refining, distribution and marketing. The supply of raw materials to the refineries at the point of refining was done at a predetermined price called 'delivered cost of crude'. The finished products were also made available at predetermined prices called 'ex-refinery prices'. The overall regime was based on the principle of compensating normative costs and allowing a pre-determined return on investments to the oil companies.

31. In 1993, BPCL entered into a joint venture with Shell for lubricants. This helped the company to increase its margins substantially in spite of competition. It also led to lot of learning and knowledge transfer for BPCL that had been working in isolation as a PSE OMC for nearly two decades. It gave its new generation of employees a first-hand experience on how 'its former ancestor', Shell, operated.

32. An international management consulting firm originally founded in 1886 and headquartered in Boston, USA. Currently, it is a multinational management consulting company operated as a partnership, and is headquartered in Brussels in Belgium.

33. Jeyavelu, S. 'Bharat Corporation Ltd (A)'. 2006. IIM Kozhikode, IIMK/CS/17/OB&HR/ 2006/02.

34. Kazmi, Azhar. *Strategic Management and Business Policy.* Tata McGraw Hill Education, Third Edition.

35. Raju, Satya and R. Parthasarathy. *Management: Text and Cases.* PHI Learning, 2004.

36. Ramachandran, J. and Vani Venkatesh. 'Shaping the Destiny of a Public Sector Enterprise: In conversation with Ashok Sinha'. December 2006. *IIMB Management Review.*

37. The VLP programme was designed to help teams clarify and understand the reasons for their unique existence, co-create team aspirations, realistically assess current reality and formulate a strategy to bridge the gap.

38. The FOL programme was designed to create a common language of learning in organizations.

39. Once the structure was in place, a conceptual framework was required even at the process level, as both had to go hand in hand to ensure delivery. Over 900 processes across the company were mapped. Customer delivery remained the core of the entire exercise.

40. To know more about how BPCL successfully implemented SAP-ERP, a first by a PSE, log on to my website: www.shashankshah.com.

41. Ramachandran, J. and Vani Venkatesh. 'Shaping the Destiny of a Public Sector Enterprise: In conversation with Ashok Sinha'. December 2006. *IIMB Management Review.*

42. Modak, Shrikant. 'High-octane-heads-all'. October 29–November 11 2001. *Business India.*

43. 'BPCL's Petrol Pump Retail Revolution: The Pioneer'. 2001. ICMR India, MKTG016.

44. These stocked over 1000 different items including eatables, soft drinks, stationery, newspapers, magazines, frozen foods, light bulbs, audio cassettes and CDs.

45. Modak, Shrikant. 'High-octane-heads-all'. October 29–November 11 2001. *Business India.*

46. By 2015, the In & Out brand of stores operated at 169 outlets with an annual turnover of Rs 186 crore. Of these, fifty-one stores had monthly sales of Rs 10 lakh, and twenty-eight stores had monthly sales of Rs 20 lakh. Added to this were a 100 Quick Service restaurants belonging to leading national and international food chains such as McDonald's, KFC, Subway and Nirula's. These paid a fixed rent, besides a percentage of its sales to BPCL, for using the facility.

Syamal shared with me that these stores were not as successful as anticipated. The primary reasons being high operating costs and lower margins as compared to fuel products. Consequently, the dealers did not pay much attention to developing this as an important component of their business.

47. Kumar, Venkata Srinivas. 'Customer relationship management in the Indian context: A study of select organizations'. 2006. University of Hyderabad.

48. Badlani, Manish and Davendra Kumar Singhal. 'A Study on Value Added Service in Fuel Retailing: Impacting Consumer Buying Behaviour'. January 2016. *International Journal of Business and Management*, 4:1.

49. D'Rozario, Denver and Keshav Shenoy. 'Bharat Petroleum Company Limited's (BPCL), India One-Stop Truck Shop (OSTS) Retailing Format'. 2011. *Emerald Emerging Market Case Studies*, 1:3.

50. Mukherjee, Kaushik. *Customer Relationship Management: A Strategic Approach to Marketing*. PHI, 2007.

51. Commoditization refers to a process in which goods or services become relatively indistinguishable from competing offerings over time, with the only distinguishing feature being pricing.

52. In July 2016, the price per litre in Mumbai of petrol was Rs 70, of diesel was Rs 60 and of kerosene was Rs 15.

53. TÜV SÜD was founded in 1866 and is headquartered in Munich in Germany. With operations at 800 locations across the globe, the MNC focuses on testing, training and certification.

54. Narayanan, R.Y. '"Pure for Sure" fuels success for BPCL'. 26 March 2002. *The Hindu Business Line*.

55. He believed that any subsidy gave rise to black market. He explained this to me with the classic example of a supply and demand curve from the theory of economics, where the price is artificially pegged before the equilibrium point.

56. The cornerstones of PFS Platinum were hi-tech and environment-friendly offerings. PFS Platinum fuel stations promised a fresh and welcoming environment. The product and services such as restaurants, convenience stores and refreshment corners, and the add-on facilities such as windshield cleaning, additional toilets, water and air-points, CCTV monitoring, were focused on the needs of the motorist. The aspects factored in the design of PFS Platinum Fuel Stations were convenience, comfort and charm. By 2015, BPCL had 600 PFS Platinum outlets pan-India.

57. 'BPCL launches Speed-93 brand'. 23 October 2003. *The Hindu*.

58. '"Speed" forms 35–40 per cent of BPCL petrol sales'. 26 September 2002. *The Hindu Business Line.*

59. The premium fuels that started with as minimal a price difference as 60 paise in 2002, were targeted by the government for additional excise duty and consequent VAT from 2009. As a result, by 2012, premium diesel cost 43 per cent more than ordinary/non-branded diesel and premium petrol price witnessed an increase of 10 per cent. Consequently, product sales plummeted. By 2012, the three public sector oil majors almost stopped manufacturing branded fuels. As one BPCL executive confided, 'The government killed the product.'

60. To know more about how BPCL was a pioneer in retail aggregation, log on to my website: www.shashankshah.com.

61. The refinery was inaugurated in May 2011 by Prime Minister Manmohan Singh. Bharat Oman Refineries Ltd, a joint venture between the Oman Oil Company (26 per cent) and BPCL (74 per cent), owns and operates the refinery. It is a subsidiary of BPCL.

62. Gopalan, Murali. 'How BPCL drafted the Bina refinery script'. 20 May 2011. *The Hindu Business Line.*

63. A legal document prepared during a company's formation that defines the kinds of businesses it will undertake besides other details connected with directors and shareholders.

64. Lying in the states of Chhattisgarh and Odisha.

65. Noel Machado et al. 'Bharat Petroleum's Upstream Strategy and Exploration Success'. February 2014. Canada: Ivey Publishing, W13574.

66. A wholly-owned subsidiary of the Rs 30,000 crore diversified private sector conglomerate, Videocon Industries founded by the Dhoot family. At the time of its collaboration with BPRL, it had interests in the oil and gas sector and had invested in the upstream business by acquiring assets in the Krishna–Godavari basin.

67. Founded in 1953 and headquartered in Rio de Janeiro, Brazil, the company ranked among the top thirty companies in the 2015 Fortune Global 500 list.

68. A petroleum and natural gas exploration and production company founded in 1959 and headquartered in Woodlands in Texas, USA.

69. Paul, Cuckoo. 'The Adventures of BPCL'. 27 August 2010. *Forbes India.*

70. 'BPCL–Videocon strikes more oil in Brazil'. 25 November 2009. *Times of India.*

71. 1 trillion = 1 lakh-crore.

72. BPRL Annual Report 2010.

73. 'Videocon, BPCL strike natural gas in Mozambique block'. 22 April
    2013. *Economic Times.*
74. BPCL Investor Presentation, November 2015.
75. To know more about how BPCL grooms talent, log on to my website:
    www.shashankshah.com.
76. OVL is an international subsidiary of ONGC and has been awarded the
    Miniratna status by the Government of India. By 2016, it had thirty-
    seven oil and gas assets in seventeen countries.
77. Founded in 1984 and headquartered in New Delhi, the Gas Authority
    of India Ltd (GAIL) is the country's largest natural gas processing and
    distribution company. In 2013, it was awarded the Maharatna status by
    the Government of India.
78. Among all the petroleum secretaries that Sinha worked with, he
    commended the contribution of Dr Vijay Kelkar (1994–97), an eminent
    economist, in enabling the OMCs to rethink their growth strategies
    and recalibrate their long-term journey. At the acme of his career, the
    President of India appointed Dr Kelkar as the chairman of the 13th
    Finance Commission of the Government of India. In 2011, he was
    conferred the Padma Vibhushan.
79. Windows was among the first graphical operating systems introduced
    by Microsoft, a multinational tech company co-founded by Bill Gates in
    1975, and currently headquartered in Redmond in Washington, USA.
80. Provided by the Lotus Development Corporation, founded in 1982
    in Cambridge in Massachusetts, USA. Its Lotus 1-2-3 spreadsheet
    application was popular at a time when a graphical user interface had
    not become the order of the day. In 1995, the company was acquired by
    IBM. It is believed that one of the co-founders of Lotus, Mitch Kapor
    was inspired by the Yogic posture padmasana, and hence named the
    software as 'Lotus'.
81. In an open tender system, a double envelope system may be used.
    This separates the technical proposal from the commercial proposal.
    Accordingly, the technical proposal submitted through a sealed envelope
    is first evaluated even before opening the commercial proposal submitted
    through a separate sealed envelope. The technical part contains details
    from the bidder towards meeting the technical specifications as listed
    in the RFT/RFP. This ensures that the decision to approve or reject a
    proposal is made on its technical merits rather than a bias due to cost-
    related advantages. If the technical proposal is not considered sound
    enough, the vendor is rejected at that stage itself. This system ensures a
    fair evaluation of the proposal.

82. 'BPCL working on blueprint for "Dream Plan"'. 12 August 2010. *The Hindu Business Line*.

83. BPCL Sustainability Report 2009–10.

84. Chakraborty, Debjit. 'Bharat Petroleum plans $2.8 billion expansion for two refineries'. 22 January 2014. *Live Mint*.

85. The target for Mumbai Refinery was 12 MTPA, of Kochi Refinery was 15.5 MTPA (from the existing 9.5 MTPA), of Numaligarh Refinery was 9 MTPA (from the existing 3 MTPA), and of Bina Refinery was 8 MTPA (from the existing 6 MTPA).

86. Goplan, Murali. 'BPCL chief connects with staff to take Dream Plan forward'. 29 July 2014. *The Hindu Business Line*.

87. Mukherjee, Promit. 'BPCL to invest Rs 1 trillion for its next phase of growth'. 11 September 2015. *Live Mint*.

88. 'Bharat Petroleum to invest Rs 40,000 crore to up capacity to 50 MTPA by 2021'. 11 September 2015. *Economic Times*.

VII: TVS Motor Company: Quintessential Quest for Quality . . . For Industry, India and Ideals

1. Church, Peter. *Profiles in Enterprise: Inspiring Stories of Indian Business Leaders*. New Delhi: Roli Books, 2015.

2. R. Sridharan 'Excellence is a Moving Target'. 22 November 1998. *Business Today*.

3. Founded in 1908, General Motors, popularly known as GM, is an American multinational corporation headquartered in Detroit in Michigan, USA. By 2015, it operated in 396 locations across six continents with 216,000 employees.

4. 'TV Sundaram Iyengar dead'. 29 April 1955. *The Hindu*.

5. Sundaram-Clayton was founded in 1962 in collaboration with Clayton Dewandre Holdings, United Kingdom. It manufactured brakes, exhausts, compressors and aluminium and magnesium castings for the automotive industry. SCL was the flagship company of the TVS Group before being overtaken by its subsidiary—TVS Motor Company Ltd.

6. 'cc' stands for cylinder capacity or cubic centimetres. Bigger cylinders are considered more powerful because they can burn more fuel per stroke.

7. Das, Sanchita. 'Lone rider now'. 15–28 October 2001. *Business India*.

8. Ravindranath, Sushila. 'The making of Spectra'. 7–20 September 1998. *Business India*.

9. Sinha, Suveen. 'TVS-Suzuki: the third coming'. December 2000. *Business Today*.

10. See, http://www.juse.or.jp/deming_en/award.

11. Rajashekhariah, Jagadeesh. 'Quality Leaders: Learning from the Deming Prize Winners in India'. 2014. *International Journal for Quality Research*, 8: 3, pp. 431–46.

12. Founded in 1988, it is administered by the Baldrige Performance Excellence Programme and managed by the National Institute of Standards and Technology, an agency of the United States Department of Commerce. It is named in the memory of Malcolm Baldridge, United States Secretary of Commerce, who died in 1987.

13. Now known as the EFQM Excellence Award, it was instituted by the European Foundation for Quality Management headquartered in Belgium, and was first awarded in 1992.

14. Sridharan, R. 'Total Quality Ltd'. 22 November 1998. *Business Today*.

15. 'TVS Motor bags Deming Award for quality mgmt'. 3 November 2002. *Financial Express*.

16. 'TVS group: smitten by Deming'. 27 November 2004. Domain-b.com.

17. Pandit, Shrinivas. *Exemplary CEOs: Insights on Organisational Transformation*. Tata McGraw Hill Education, 2005.

18. Pandit, Shrinivas. *Quality Leader: Venu Srinivasan*. New Delhi: Tata McGraw Hill Publishing Co., 2007.

19. R. Sridharan 'Excellence is a moving target'. 22 November 1998. *Business Today*.

20. This consists of defining and monitoring key processes, ensuring that they meet set targets, detecting abnormalities and preventing their recurrence. TVSM encouraged continuous improvement in all aspects of work, using Cross Functional Teams (CFT), Supervisory Improvement Teams (SIT) Quality Control Circles (QCC) and suggestion schemes.

21. This ensures that responsibility for the company's performance is the shared responsibility of employees across levels. It provides all employees with the opportunity to be involved in breakthrough activities and other improvements, over and above their daily routine.

22. Junkins, J.R. 'Confessions of a Baldrige winner'. 1994. *Management Review*, 83:7.

23. A Japanese approach of continuous efforts in waste reduction that is useful in production, distribution and customer service-related processes.

24. With TVS Victor an early attempt to build the first complete four-stroke motorcycle by TVSM, issues with reliability and durability of the motorcycle cropped up. The declining sales, market share and

profitability in the three years after the launch led to low morale among employees and dealers. At such a time, the company used TQM to understand the root causes of the failures. It realized the need to learn the 'know-why' for improving durability and reliability. Inadequate understanding of the target customer requirements was another identified root cause. Based on the learnings, the company focused on a holistic approach towards quality covering design, service, manufacturing and supplier quality. Deep understanding of target customers became the base for developing new products.

25. Roy, Subir. *Made in India: A Study of Emerging Competitiveness*. New Delhi: Tata McGraw Hill Publishing, New Delhi, 2005.

26. 'TVS group: smitten by Deming'. 27 November 2004. Domain-b.com.

27. Sridharan, R. 'Excellence is a moving target'. 22 November 1998. *Business Today*.

28. Moballeghi, Mustafa. 'Total Quality Management (TQM) Implementation in Automotive Industry: A Case Study of Selected Firms in India'. PhD Thesis, University of Mysore, 2014.

29. 'Zipping in the fast lane'. 29 November 2004. Domain-b.com.

30. R. Sridharan 'Excellence is a moving target'. 22 November 1998. *Business Today*.

31. 'TVS sells 5 lakh Jupiter scooters in India'. 18 May 2015. *Overdrive*.

32. Madhavan, N. 'TVS Motor, BMW sign long term cooperation agreement'. 9 April 2013. *Business Today*.

33. Sudarshan joined TVSM as vice president in 2011. He was brought on board as a full-time director in 2013. He has also been a non-executive director of SCL since 2011.

34. Madhavan, N. 'Sudarshan Venu's fresh thoughts for TVS Motor'. 14 March 2016. *Forbes India*.

35. Lakshmi took charge as the joint managing director of Sundaram-Clayton in 2014.

36. Saraswathy, M. and Swaraj Baggonkar. 'TVS Motors lone warrior in shrinking moped market'. 23 September 2012. *Business Standard*.

37. Bajad, Kiran. 'Threewheeler market remains flat this fiscal'. 20 March 2016. *Autocar Professional*.

38. These include passenger vehicles (four-wheelers and more), commercial vehicles (four-wheelers and more), three-wheelers and two-wheelers.

39. Shah, Shashank and Sudhir Bhaskar. '"Corporate Social Responsibility is the function of the CEO"—Face to Face with Dr Venu Srinivasan'. 2010. *Journal of Values-Based Leadership*, 3:2, pp. 33–42.

40. Narasimhan, T.E. 'TVS steps up its two-wheeler challenge'. 31 July 2014. *Business Standard*.
41. K.N.R. was general manager of business planning at SCL. He served as vice president and executive vice president of business planning at TVSM till 31 March 2006. He was appointed as president of TVSM on 1 April 2006.
42. Shah, Shashank. 'Endeavouring Towards Customer Satisfaction: A Case Study of TVS Motor Company Ltd'. 2012. *Asia Pacific Marketing Review*, 1:1, pp. 113–19.
43. Original Equipment Manufacturer (OEM) is a company that makes a part or subsystem that is used in another company's end product.
44. 'TVS Scooty Pep launched'. 10 February 2003. *Times of India*.
45. Srinivasan, Sriram. 'Women on Wheels'. 17 October 2009. *Outlook Business*.
46. 'A campaign for mobility'. 17 September 2009. *The Hindu Business Line*.
47. Akhouri, Priyanka. 'TVS Scooty rides high on Women on Wheels notion'. 5 October 2009. *Financial Express*.
48. See, http://www.tvsscooty.com/women-on-wheels.aspx.
49. Mudra Max, TVSM's media partner, won the award for 'Best Activity Generating Brand Loyalty' category, besides awards from the Ad Club Bombay and many others.
50. J.D. Power and Associates is a global marketing information services firm that specializes in customer satisfaction research in the automobile industry. Headquartered in California, USA, it was founded in 1968 by James David Power.
51. To know more about TVSM's 'eco-dynamism', log on to my website: www.shashankshah.com.
52. Pandit, Shrinivas. *Exemplary CEOs: Insights on Organisational Transformation*. Tata McGraw Hill Education, 2005.
53. Madhavan, N. 'Nurturing the family'. 12 June 2011. *Business Today*.
54. In a 1943 paper, Abraham Maslow, a famous American psychologist, described human needs through a pyramid. From the base to the summit, these include—Physiological, Safety, Love/Belonging, Esteem and Self-actualization. He suggested that as one progresses in life, needs graduate from basic to evolved levels i.e. from physiological to self-actualization. In later years, he added a sixth factor—Self-transcendence, which involved focus on higher goals such as altruism and spirituality.
55. A set of eighteen visionary companies studied by Jim Collins and Jerry Porras in their eponymous best-selling book first published in 1994.
56. Rao, Sree Rama. 'An illustration of TQM at TVS Motor Company'. 19 February 2009. *Citeman Network*.

57. Masaaki Imai originally introduced kaizen in his book, *Kaizen: The Key to Japan's Competitive Success* in 1986. Kaizen is internationally recognized as a vital pillar of an organization's long-term competitive strategy.

58. Khadri and Khan. 'Kaizen Movement as Key for Organizational Change—A study at TVS Motors, Mysore'. 2013. *International Journal of Engineering and Management Research*, 3: 1.

59. Pandit, Shrinivas. *Exemplary CEOs: Insights on Organisational Transformation*. Tata McGraw Hill Education, 2005.

60. Sridharan, R. 'Excellence is a moving target'. 22 November 1998. *Business Today*.

61. Pandit, Shrinivas. *Exemplary CEOs: Insights on Organisational Transformation*. Tata McGraw Hill Education, 2005.

62. Madhavan, N. 'Nurturing the family'. 12 June 2011. *Business Today*.

63. Dr T.S. Soundaram, daughter of T.V. Sundaram Iyengar, was an active participant in the Quit India Movement and the founder of the Gandhigram Rural Institute, which eventually became Deemed University.

64. Pandit, Shrinivas. *Quality Leader: Venu Srinivasan*. New Delhi: Tata McGraw Hill Publishing Co., 2007.

65. Yaksha Prashna (in the Vana Parva of the Mahabharata) is a discussion between King Yudhisthira and Yaksha, a nature-spirit, about ethics, morals and righteousness.

66. Founder trustee, Sri Sathya Sai Central Trust, and revered founder chancellor, Sri Sathya Sai Institute of Higher Learning (Deemed University), Prasanthi Nilayam (Andhra Pradesh). Sri Sathya Sai Baba (1926–2011) is a highly revered spiritual leader, whose life, message and mission have inspired millions from all religions across the world, to lead more meaningful and moral lives. Sri Sathya Sai Seva Organization, a socio-spiritual organization founded in 1965, operates across 120 countries and have over 1 million volunteers, who serve all sections of society without distinctions of caste, creed, clime or colour.

67. Shah, Shashank and Sudhir Bhaskar, '"Corporate Social Responsibility is the function of the CEO"—Face to Face with Dr Venu Srinivasan'. 2010. *Journal of Values-Based Leadership*, 3:2, pp. 33–42.

68. Shrinivas, Pandit. *Exemplary CEOs: Insights on Organisational Transformation*. Tata McGraw Hill Education, 2005.

69. 'Q&A with Venu Srinivasan'. 9 August 2009. *Business Today*.

70. Church, Peter. *Profiles in Enterprise: Inspiring Stories of Indian Business Leaders*. New Delhi: Roli Books, 2015.

VIII: Reflections: How to Become a Win-Win Corporation?

1. The chronology of the seven stakeholders is based on the findings of the Exploratory Survey, where 700 respondents ranked the stakeholders in this order of importance.
2. Balakrishnan, Pulapre. 'The ease of living in India'. 18 June 2016. *The Hindu.*
3. Rao, Aprameya and Kishor Kadam. '25 years of liberalization: A glimpse of India's growth in 14 charts'. 7 July 2016. *Firstpost.com.*
4. *Future of Digital Content Consumption in India.* EY Publication, January 2016.
5. *Future of India: The Winning Leap.* PwC Publication, 2014.

Appendix I: Overview of the Research Process

1. Phenomenological approaches research from the perspective that human behaviour is not as easily measured as phenomena in the natural sciences. Human motivation is shaped by factors that are not always observable, e.g. inner thought processes, so that it can become hard to generalize on, e.g. motivation from observation of behaviour alone. Furthermore, people place their own meanings on events; meanings that do not always coincide with the way others have interpreted them. Phenomenological approaches are particularly concerned with understanding behaviour from the participants' own subjective frames of reference.
2. It is a reasoning process that begins with a case and draws from it a conclusion of wider and more general relevance. For e.g., a research process starting with empirical data and proceeding to draw generally applicable conclusions from it.
3. Stake, R.E. *The Art of Case Study Research.* Thousand Oaks, CA: Sage Publications, 1995. Yin, Robert K. *Case Study Research: Design and Methods.* Thousand Oaks, CA: Sage Publications, 2003, Third Edition.
4. Stake, R.E. *Multiple Case Study Analysis.* New York, USA: Guilford Press, 2006.
5. Pettigrew, A.M. 'Longitudinal Field Research on Change: Theory and Practice'. 1990. *Organisational Science.* 1:3, pp. 267–92.
6. Eisenhardt, K.M. and M.E. Graebner. 'Theory Building From Cases: Opportunities and Challenges'. 2007. *Academy of Management Journal,* 50:1, pp. 25–32.

7.   Eisenhardt, K. 'Building Theories from Case Study Research'. 1989.
     Academy of Management Review, 14:4, pp.532–50.

Appendix II: HDFC Bank

1.   Rodrigues, Ryan. 'An oasis of calm'. 2 November 2008. *Business India*,
     pp. 68–82.

Appendix III: Larsen & Toubro Construction

1.   See, http://www.lntecc.com/HOMEPAGE/multislug/demos/images/
     common/csti_english.pdf.
2.   Laskar, Arghadeep and C.V.R. Murthy. 'Challenges before Construction
     Industry in India'. 2004. Indian Institute of Technology Kanpur.
3.   Founded in September 1972 by Sathya Sai Baba, it is a public charitable
     trust headquartered in Puttaparthi in the Anantapur district, Andhra
     Pradesh. It oversees major projects in the field of education, healthcare,
     water supply and rural welfare schemes. Since 1991, the trust spent over
     Rs 700 crore on free healthcare services delivered through its two general
     and two super specialty hospitals located in Puttaparthi and Bangalore. By
     2015, the total value of the projects in the area of drinking water supply
     executed by the trust and transferred to the government and public was
     over Rs 750 crore. Since thirty years, education from under-graduation
     to postdoctoral research is provided gratis to over 1500 students studying
     annually in the four campuses of Sri Sathya Sai Institute of Higher
     Learning (Deemed University). Over 25,000 students have benefitted
     from its system of education that has a distinct values-orientation and
     social focus.
4.   Shah, Shashank and V.E. Ramamoorthy. *Soulful Corporations*. Springer
     India, 2013.
5.   An Impact Evaluation Study of Sri Sathya Sai Water Supply Project,
     Anantapur district, Andhra Pradesh, India, HUDCO Report to
     ADB.
6.   'Water projects: CM all praise for Satya Sai Trust'. 13 February 2004.
     The Hindu.
7.   'Chennai benefits from Sai Baba's initiative'. 1 December 2004. *The
     Hindu*.
8.   Chandrashekar, B. and K.M. Ganesh. 'Sri Sathya Sai Water Project:
     Partnering for MDG'. 2010. Institute of Water Policy, Lee Kuan Yew
     School of Public Policy, National University of Singapore.

Appendix IV: The Taj Group of Hotels

1. Marble and marble cutters from Makrana in Rajasthan are famous since many centuries. Among the landmark structures built using their work are the Taj Mahal in Agra and the Victoria Memorial in Kolkata. The Pichhwai, prepared by artists from the pilgrim town of Nathdwara in Rajasthan, are world-renowned for miniature paintings depicting instances from the life of Lord Krishna. The images of Shrinathji, the presiding deity of Nathdwara, and a form of child Krishna are also extensively painted.

2. Lala, R.M. *The Creation of Wealth: The Tatas from the 19th to the 21st century*. Penguin Books India, 2004.

3. Also known as Ikat sarees, they are popular for their geometric designs. Made in many villages of Andhra Pradesh (and now Telangana), they are known most often by the name of Pochampally village located in the Nalgonda district of Telangana, where over 5000 looms make this textile. It has also been included in the UNESCO's tentative list of world heritage sites as part of 'iconic saree-weaving clusters of India'.

4. Some of the arts supported by the Taj Group across include stone, wood and sandalwood carving, lacquered wood toy-making (popularly known as Channapatna toys in Karnataka), metal ornamentation work (famous as Bidri work in Karnataka), hand-block printing (famous as Bagru painting in Rajasthan), chikan work (hand embroidery famous in Lucknow, Uttar Pradesh), and filigree (jewellery metalwork, famous in Cuttack, Odisha).

5. Menon, Sangeeta. 'Training for Tomorrow'. December 2011. *Tata Review.*

6. For instance, the Cancer Patients Aid Association received annual business of Rs 1 crore from the Taj Hotels.

7. The Gateway Hotel (Ganges, Varanasi) has recently supported the Ganga Seva Nidhi, an NGO, for the maintenance of the Dashashwamedh Ghat and the performance of the Ganga Maha Aarti every evening at twilight. A part of the 'Incredible India' campaign, this daily event is a spectacle watched by thousands of tourists. I was an eyewitness in August 2014.

8. As per the IHCL Sustainability Reports, between 7000 and 11,000 employees participated in diverse service activities including mentoring and guiding youngsters, maintaining public gardens, activities in hygiene and sanitation, local education and promoting local art and culture, every year between 2012 and 2015.

9. Conducted by Leading Quality Assurance, a company specializing in providing benchmarking analysis, quality assurance audits and training services to the global luxury hospitality industry.
10. Kanani, Rahim. 'Taj Hotels Resorts and Palaces on fighting poverty and sustainability'. 4 May 2014. *Forbes*.
11. In recognition of its social empowerment efforts, IHCL won the *Condé Nast Traveller*'s World Savers Award 2013 for Poverty Relief.

Appendix V: Hindustan Unilever

1. Ganguly, A.S. 'From Challenges to Opportunities'. *Hamara, The Hindustan Unilever Employee Magazine.* (A Special Issue to mark the seventy-five years of HUL.)
2. Joshi, Devina. '"Gandhigiri" can work wonders for brands too'. 15 November 2006. Afaqs.com.
3. 'HUL launches "Swachh Aadat, Swachh Bharat" programme in India'. 4 December 2015. Company Press Release.

Appendix VI: Bharat Petroleum Corporation

1. It originates from ancient fossilized organic materials found in geological formations beneath the earth's surface.
2. A grade of crude that is light and has low sulphur content, it is primarily extracted from the North Sea. It is suitable for production of light and middle distillates. Brent crude serves as a benchmark for international purchase prices of oil.
3. Also called Mumbai High, it is an offshore oilfield 176 kilometres off the coast of Mumbai. The operations are led by ONGC. Discovered around 1965, the first well was sunk in 1974. By 2010, it contributed nearly half of India's domestic oil production.
4. Spread across more than 50,000 square kilometres in the Krishna and Godavari River basins in Andhra Pradesh, these have immense natural gas reserves.
5. Dutta, Sanjay. 'Diesel prices deregulated like petrol, down Rs 3.37 in Delhi'. 19 October 2014. *Times of India*.
6. 'Union Cabinet deregulates diesel price, approves new gas price formula'. 18 October 2014. *Times of India*.
7. 'Direct benefit transfer scheme saves Rs 21,000 crore in LPG subsidy: government'. 20 July 2016. *NDTV Profit*.

Appendix VII: TVS Motor Company

1. A former IAS officer, Ashoke Joshi retired as secretary to the ministry of road transport and highways, Government of India.
2. Rangan, V. Kasturi and Shashank Shah. 'An Overview of Corporate Social Responsibility in India (A)'. 15 May 2015. Boston, USA: Harvard Business School Publishing, N9-515-080.
3. Xue Shirley Li et al. 'Srinivasan Services Trust: Combating Poverty with Entrepreneurship'. 2011. *MIT Sloan Management.*
4. The other contenders were Godrej Consumer, Hindustan Unilever, Mahindra & Mahindra and Tata Chemicals.
5. 'ET Awards for corporate excellence: TVS Motor wins corporate citizen award'. 3 October 2016. *Economic Times.*